Twelve-Part Harmony

Pat and Jill Williams
with Beth Spring

Fleming H. Revell
Old Tappan, New Jersey

Library of Congress Cataloging-in-Publication Data

Williams, Pat
    Twelve-part harmony / Pat and Jill Williams with Beth Spring.
      p. cm.
    Includes bibliographical references.
    ISBN 0-8007-1640-X
    1. Williams, Pat. 2. Williams, Jill (Jill M. P.)
  I. Williams, Jill (Jill M. P.) II. Spring, Beth. III. Title.
  IV. Title: 12-part harmony.
  BR1700.2.W516   1990
  306.874—dc20   90-33620
                                          CIP

We lovingly dedicate this book
to homeless children around the
world with the fervent prayer
that they will soon be at home
with their "forever families."

For those who wait,

Pat and Jill Williams

Contents

Foreword

What a pleasure it is to share in the day-to-day lives of the Williams family! As I read how Pat and Jill deal with the challenges of parenting a large family, I was reminded of how it was when Harry and I adopted our eight 2-year-olds from Korea so many years ago. Like Pat and Jill, I learned that you must be thoroughly organized and priorities must be clearly in place.

While it is not easy to parent a large family, it is possible when you look to Him for daily guidance and support. Reading about the everyday lives of the Williamses provides a solid testimony to how God touches our lives in so many ways.

I hope this book will be an encouragement to those families who are considering adoption. I also pray for waiting children everywhere, that this book might help them to come home to their "forever family" through adoption.

Mrs. Bertha Holt, Founder
Holt International Children's Services

Twelve-Part Harmony

1
Eight Grafted Limbs

Sunday morning, 8:15 A.M. One by one, Jill Williams places banana-oat muffins, hot from the oven, on fourteen paper plates, alongside half a banana and a wedge of cantaloupe. The sweet fragrance fills the kitchen of their Winter Park, Florida, home, drawing her husband and twelve children to a quick breakfast. In they file. Each one picks up a plate and sits around a custom-built oak table long enough to haul grain down the Mississippi River.

Sarah, the 9-year-old adopted from Korea, is shrill with exasperation. "Mom, where are my shoes?" she demands.

Jill doesn't have a clue where her daughter's good shoes might be. The soccer shoes and sneakers are easy to find. They are lined up as evenly as birds on a telephone wire, just outside the front door: forty-eight of them—two pairs per child.

Keeping the shoes outdoors became a tradition in the Williams household the night Stephen and Thomas, twin boys from Korea, came to join the family at age 6. Before entering the house for the first time, they removed their shoes, silently and automatically, and lined them up by the side of the house.

The Sunday shoes are another story. Each child is responsible for keeping track of dress shoes, storing them in a closet, shining them, remembering to find them and wear them at the appropriate time. Shoes are a very big deal when there are twelve pairs of growing feet to tend. Affording them, storing them, finding them are matters of consequence.

Sarah's lapse this Sunday morning means she wears her sneakers to church. It means also that shoes, and other lost articles, are the focus of Pat Williams's "Question of the Day."

8:30 A.M. Seated around their sixteen-foot-long kitchen table, the family pauses to pray before breakfast. David, the eldest of four Filipino brothers adopted by Pat and Jill, says grace as everyone holds hands. Then Pat begins warming up. "Who went jogging this morning?" A chorus of "I did"s rings out. "Okay. Now here is the question of the day," he announces with all the fanfare of a game-show host. "Why is it important to put something that belongs to you back in its right place?"

Around the circle he goes, looking for answers. Sammy, the youngest Filipino brother, pipes up right away. "So Mom won't find it and t'ro it away." As usual, Pat has the last word. "This family operates on a tight time schedule, and we can't afford the luxury of fifteen minutes here and ten minutes there looking for lost items. And we put things away so we can learn self-discipline."

Pat Williams is a walking portrait of self-discipline. The general manager of professional basketball's Orlando Magic, he is a driven sports executive and a popular humorist and speaker. He jogs four miles a day, usually after his mile-and-a-half walk with Jill in the morning. And somehow he manages to remain fully engaged in the lives of all twelve of his children.

"I think Karyn needs to be involved in swimming after school on the days she's not in dance class," he tells Jill one day just before school starts. "She has some aptitude, and it's good exercise," he reasons. Pat schedules time to go to the kids' swim meets, with scorecard and timer in hand. "When the Filipino boys came in November 1988, none of them could swim," Pat explains. "By the end of their first summer here, one of them—Brian—won ribbons in three events."

Jill has a slightly different perspective on Karyn's after-school schedule. It's tough enough coordinating times to get the children to soccer practice, swim team, art classes for Andrea, and Little League. "Couldn't Karyn just come home and do her homework on the days she doesn't dance?" Jill wonders.

Describing Jill Williams as a "full-time mother" is akin to calling Disney World "just a playground." She manages her home and all her children, and has found time to study for her real estate license, take up oil painting, and take a weekly photography class. In a twenty-five-foot aviary, she raises and breeds more than a hundred birds, including parakeets, cockatiels, two miniature parrots, finches, and quail. Jill taught music at her kids' school one day per week, until she and Pat decided to begin a home school with eight of their children. Also Jill sings and speaks at churches and local civic groups.

Pat's lessons in self-discipline have not been lost on her. When people hear of her dozen children, they often take it for granted that she has domestic help. She doesn't, apart from some assistance with the laundry and a weekly housecleaning service. Those banana-oat muffins are her own, baked from scratch.

9:45 A.M. The service is about to begin at Orlando's First Baptist Church, and the Williams family occupies one entire, reserved pew near the front. Sarah's tattered sneakers clash with her fresh, white dress. She scuffles quietly with Brian over pencils in the pew. Andrea, who along with Sarah was abandoned on the doorstep of a police station in Seoul, Korea, draws a nighttime landscape complete with perfect five-point stars in the sky. Thomas, one of the Korean twins, snuggles next to Pat.

Sportswriters in Florida love to poke fun at Pat and his personal "expansion team." Once, before the Orlando Magic had come into being, a columnist mused about what the city could do with its brand-new arena if the basketball team never materialized. "Pat Williams and his wife, Jill, just adopted four more children, giving them an even dozen," wrote Bob Morris of the *Orlando Sentinel.* "Maybe they could use it for closet space."[1]

The thought of twelve children in one family is overwhelming—even, at times, for Pat and Jill. The children include four who were born to them ("homegrown," Pat says):

Jimmy, 16
Bobby, 13
Karyn, 11
Michael, 6

Then came two sisters adopted from Korea in 1983 when they were toddlers. Nothing is known of their birth parents, because they were left on the doorstep of a police station in Seoul:

Sarah, 10
Andrea, 9

Next, twin boys arrived from Korea in 1987. Their mother, who was single, had an affair with a married man and gave birth to the boys. For five years, she tried to raise them, relying on her extended family for help. When the twins proved to be too much of a handful for the woman they remember as their "old-old grandma," they were placed in an orphanage:

Thomas, 9
Stephen, 9

Late in 1988 came four Filipino brothers. Their mother relinquished her parental rights after being deserted by the boys' father:

David, 11
Peter, 10
Brian, 9
Sammy, 6

Why in the world would two busy parents decide to adopt, and adopt again, and then again? For Jill, it has been nothing less than a lifelong dream come true. For Pat, it is a way of reaffirming his love for Jill after their marriage ran aground because of poor communication and dashed expectations. Most of all, though, they see adoption as a way of meeting children's needs. There are plenty of children in need, the Williamses have discovered, and the window of time during which they can find permanent homes is fleeting.

Through their personal experiences with international adoption, the Williamses have become champions for adoption. Jill chairs The Adoption Centre, a Maitland, Florida, agency known for placing children with "special needs." Some of these children are born with AIDS or cocaine addiction. Some may be physically or mentally handicapped. Many are black or biracial. All of them desperately need families.

Jill doesn't view her commitment as a heavy burden. For her, the adoption process is a window on the world. Ask her a question, and she is likely to answer with a snatch of Spanish, French, or even Korean. She toured Guatemala to see if an Adoption Centre program could be started there; and a planned visit to India may eventually bring more abandoned children into the fold of American homes.

For Pat, what began as a campaign to save his marriage has evolved into a deep appreciation for the privileges of parenthood and the miracle of adoption. Each time an adopted child arrived at the airport, it was somehow different from picking up the little stranger he was expecting. "We've never seen them apart from a photograph, and they come from six thousand miles away. They walk into our lives, and there is an instant love for them. A parental love. That's an absolute miracle."

Jill, it seems, has an unquenchable capacity for receiving children into her home. Once, as she picked up Andrea from art class, she noticed a sign on a bulletin board. Exchange students from France needed homes in Orlando for one summer month, it said. Jill didn't think twice before calling the number. For the month of July that year, the Williams home accommodated 15-year-old Thomas Le Bec from France along with the usual twelve.

11:30 A.M. After church, the Williams kids tumble into their navy blue, fifteen-passenger Dodge Ram van. Pat rumbles up the highway with his vanity license plate, "12 KIDS," glinting in the sunlight. On the way, they stop at a Howard Johnson's for breakfast. It's an all-you-can-eat Sunday buffet at which the Williamses are regular customers.

As they wait to be seated, an elderly woman eyes the children curiously, her glance darting between kids and parents. "Which of these are your children?" she asks Jill. "All of them," Jill replies cheerfully. The woman frowns in disbelief. "No, I mean your REAL children," she says. Jill doesn't miss a beat. "They are all real," she points out. Three of the Filipino boys clamor for Jill's attention. "Mom, Mom," they say. The elderly woman's expression dissolves into sheer astonishment.

The family occupies one large corner booth and two side booths, and the kids beat a path to and from table and buffet. As Pat and Jill munch on salad and fruit, another diner cannot contain her curiosity. "Are these children adopted?" she asks Pat. His eyes twinkling, he playfully says, "No, we have a Korean milkman." Then he grimaces from the pain of a swift kick delivered by Jill under the table.

The check for brunch totals forty-two dollars.

Pat and Jill do not go looking for attention, but inevitably they attract it. Feeling comfortable in the limelight is important when adopted children do not look like their parents. It's one way to affirm the heritage of their homeland and, most important, to affirm them as individuals.

People often ask Jill, "Aren't you afraid they'll want to go back?" Jill harbors no uneasiness about that prospect whatsoever. In fact, she plans to take them all to Korea and the Philippines someday—somehow. Holt, the agency that facilitated all the Williams adoptions, offers "Motherland Tours" regularly.

Another comment Jill hears frequently goes like this: "Aren't you the most wonderful people in the world to take in these poor children!" Jill may groan inwardly when a well-meaning acquaintance tells her this, remembering how loudly she yelled at half-a-dozen kids that morning. Well-meaning or not, however, the "you're so wonderful" comment speaks volumes about society's misunderstandings of adoption.

People who put adoptive parents on a pedestal miss the point. It is not, after all, such an unnatural and unusual thing to do. Most adoptive parents will admit to a streak of selfishness, rather than saintliness. For one reason or another—often because they cannot conceive—they seek to build a family another way.

Adoption has been around for a long time—remember Moses being discovered among the reeds of the Nile and raised by Pharaoh's daughter?—but the myths die hard. A friend of the Williamses was walking through the Atlanta airport one day with her adopted Korean son. A stranger stopped her to comment, "Don't you expect he'll give you trouble when he's older?"

Give her an *A* for honesty. Often, fears about maladjustment, excessive teen rebellion, and eventual rejection in favor of birth parents give adoption a far riskier reputation than it deserves. A study by two researchers at Drew University found that adopted teens are every bit as emotionally stable as teens raised by birth parents.

"The adopted may be different by being more positive rather than more negative than their non-adopted peers," Kathryn Marquis and Richard Detweiler found. The adopted teens they studied rated their parents as more nurturing, more comforting, more protective, and more predictable than did the teens who were born to their parents.

Raising the adopted child is no harder or easier than rearing a birth child. It simply brings with it an added dimension, a need for heightened awareness and carefully cultivated lines of communication. It means saying the word *adopted* even before the child can understand it, and not covering up or apologizing for the child's origins.

2:00 P.M. Sunday afternoon affords a slow-paced respite from the frenzied weekdays. Jill pulls a chair up to the kitchen table and clips recipes. Daughter Karyn is off to a friend's house. Andrea, the younger of the Korean sisters, paints alone at an easel in the playroom. In the library adjoining the playroom, three Filipino brothers are working puzzles. All around them are shelves filled with six thousand cataloged books, many of them on marriage and family.

In the living room, Bobby flips on the wide-screen television set to watch a ball game. The television is off limits except for news and sports—a rule that stirs surprisingly few complaints.

Two "homegrown" kids, Jimmy (the oldest) and Michael (the youngest), are spending the day at the Williamses' oceanfront condominium with Jill's par-

ents. The Korean twins, Thomas and Stephen, fish for bass and bluegill off a backyard dock that juts out into Lake Killarney; they are joined by Sarah, the older Korean sister, and David, the oldest Filipino.

A massive renovation of their ranch-style home made it possible for Pat and Jill to house a dozen children. The seven-month project commenced just after Thomas and Stephen joined the family, and it doubled their living space to eight thousand square feet. A much larger in-ground pool was added as well as a sun-bathed Florida room splashed with peach, ivory, and turquoise pastels.

Upstairs, eight bedrooms were added. Each is small and functional, furnished simply with bunk beds or a trundle bed and dresser. All but four of the children share bedrooms.

The playroom, where Andrea paints, contains bright posters, child-sized tables, and several easels for art projects. There is no avalanche of toys, not here and not in their bedrooms. Pat and Jill encourage creative play and physical activity: a daily mile-and-a-half jog, a swim in the pool, and team sports or classes to nurture what Pat calls "the red thread"—a natural ability woven into each person's being that needs to be called forth and developed.

Giving, sharing, and opening hearts to strangers are all part of the daily give-and-take. When the Williamses decide to adopt, the decision is not Pat and Jill's alone. Even before Sarah and Andrea came, the "homegrown" kids, ages 9, 6, and 4, were consulted. They were very enthusiastic. "At first, when you pick them up at the airport, it seems strange," Jimmy recalls. "Then you just remember that they are going to stay forever."

In this family, adoption is not some sort of extracurricular activity, taken up like golf or tennis, then abandoned when the novelty wears off. It is instead woven tightly into the fabric of faith that binds parents and children and siblings together. When adoption takes a bad rap in the media, it is often because the sole focus is on the pain of separating a child from his or her birth mother. "Genetic amputation," it has been called.

The image the Williamses prefer is a biblical one. The adopted child is indeed separated from flesh-and-blood relatives, and there may be much pain involved. But the child is then grafted into a new family, a real family. As in nature, the grafted branch grows strong, and it changes the very character of the plant that receives it.

So, too, is the adoptive family changed forever by adoption. That change, for the Williams children, often becomes real on the playground at school. Andrea and Sarah, for instance, sometimes face taunts from their classmates. "Here come the Chinese girls," a jeering youngster will say. When that happens, and Bobby or Karyn are in earshot, they appear instantly to share the insult and help deflect the pain. "They are my sisters," Bobby reminds the children.

As Christians, the Williamses view adoption as a God-honoring plan. In fact, it appears to be His idea in the first place. It is the way in which each human, through Jesus Christ, may become a true child of God. Paul's letter to the Ephesians puts it this way: ". . . In love he predestined us to be adopted as his sons through Jesus Christ, in accordance with his pleasure and will" (Ephesians 1:4, 5).

Adopted children, grafted into a family permanently and irrevocably, belong to a family no less than children born the usual way. Pat is fond of telling reporters, "We have twelve children, eight of which are adopted, but I forget which eight."

6:30 P.M. Stephen and Thomas load dishes from a light supper into the dishwasher. At an island in the kitchen's center, Pat stacks thirteen brown bags, readied for the lunches he packs each evening for himself and all twelve kids. He gets out a loaf and a half of bread, a five-pound container of peanut butter, and a bagful of apples from one of the kitchen's two refrigerators. For the next thirty minutes, he could pass for a short-order cook in any New York deli. He slaps on the peanut butter, halves the sandwich, bags it, and moves on to the next one.

"There is no à la carte," he explains. "You take what you get." This evening, Sarah and Andrea stand by, assisting their dad with sandwich duty. "They want to take over," Pat says, "so with great reluctance I'm training them."

Pat takes charge of ordering food in bulk, often from health food outlets. He buys twenty-four loaves of bread at a time, every three weeks. In the lower cupboards are forty-eight boxes of cereal, in four assortments—oat rings, corn flakes, raisin bran, and wheat squares. One of each kind is open, and the family goes through the equivalent of one box per day.

Before bed, the kids scribble in their diaries—a project Jill started one summer to keep them reading and writing. "How do you FEEL?" inquires a note on a kitchen chalkboard. "Write it in your diary." A chart on one of the refrigerators tracks with stickers each child's progress in journal keeping. It also records how many book pages each one has read. The one who "wins" receives a contribution to his or her savings account.

Adding children to their family in batches of two and four has meant making profound changes in their lives. It has meant stretching their financial and emotional resources to their limits. No longer do Pat and Jill dash off for a weekend alone. Carpooling with school friends or neighbors is next to impossible. "We don't carpool," Pat says. "We *bus*pool." Gathering this many children under one roof would surely strain the most rock-stable marriage. And theirs, just before the adoptions began, was anything but.

In *Rekindled,* their first book together, Pat and Jill tell the story of what they call "D day" in their marriage. One Sunday morning, Pat knew he was once again the target of one of Jill's "silent treatments." It was December 19, 1982, and the chill in the air had little to do with the season. The two of them appeared to have a perfect marriage and an abundantly full life together. Pat was a celebrity in Philadelphia, where he managed the pro-basketball 76ers. Jill was a noted violinist and vocalist, in demand at church functions and women's clubs.

At home, however, the happy-couple veneer had worn thin. Pat thought he had triggered the cold shoulder by nitpicking one Sunday morning before church. He had zinged Jill with a couple of cheap shots. "I hope you sing the hymns this morning. Haven't seen you studying your Bible recently." Pat didn't know it, but Jill was beyond caring. Ten years after their whirlwind courtship and marriage, she had given up. She was resigned to a life of married loneliness, sharing a roof and three children with this man, but not sharing his life, his dreams, or any shred of togetherness.

After church, Pat forced the issue, wanting to clear the air and get on with it. There were sports pages to catch up on, games to watch, phone calls waiting to be returned. "What's wrong?" he asked. The ice didn't melt. "Nothing," Jill said in a monotone. "Tell me what it is," Pat insisted. Finally, Jill leveled both barrels at him.

"I just don't care anymore," she whispered. "I hate this marriage. It's boring me to death. I give up."

Like a tidal wave, ten years' worth of slights, insults, snubs, and callousness flooded their tense conversation. Pat was stunned, and he groped for a quick fix. "What can I do?" he asked her.

Jill had no answer. What she wanted was *him;* an acknowledgment that she mattered enough to be drawn into the inner soul of her husband. She longed to be talked with, listened to, noticed, even admired occasionally. Instead, she told him, "You talk to me like I'm a Philadelphia sportswriter. You never share anything with me—your work, your Bible study, your dreams, your goals."

Their early conversations about adoption were a case in point. Ever since she'd been a little girl, Jill had dreamed of adopting children from Asia. She vividly remembers pretending that her doll collection and her stuffed animals were orphans, gathered under her special protection.

Jill grew up, and the dream persisted. She has no idea where it originated, or why. Shortly after they were married, she confided in Pat about her secret dream: She wanted to adopt a Korean orphan.

Pat wounded her with a barrage of ridicule. "It's a silly idea. Why would you want to do that? I'm not sure I could even love a child that wasn't my own." Pat remembers growing up in the forties, when *adoption* was a "bad word—like leprosy." He was gullible to all the myths and shopworn stereotypes. "It's just asking for trouble" he had heard people say. "Why take on someone else's problems?"

Jill didn't let the idea drop. After the war in Vietnam ended, Jill desperately wanted to adopt one of the babies brought over by the planeload. Pat told her she was being foolish. When they visited China in 1982 with eight NBA players, Jill badgered Pat to ask whether abandoned Chinese children could be adopted by Americans. Finally, she asked the question herself and learned it is virtually impossible to adopt a child from mainland China. Pat had heard enough. "Forget it, Jill," he said finally. "I don't even want to think about it."

On D day, Pat listened, really listened for perhaps the first time in ten years of marriage. The subject of adoption never came up. It appeared there was barely enough of a marriage left to accommodate Jimmy, Bobby, and Karyn.

Somehow, in the depth of her depression, Jill had gotten through to Pat. All the badgering, whining, and silent treatments of the last ten years had accomplished exactly nothing, but the stark picture of a wife who appeared to have died emotionally left Pat reeling. *She is emotionally dead,* Pat told himself. *And I killed her.*

A committed Christian, Pat turned immediately to his Bible and to prayer. "Remind me what I've done so I can set about changing it," he prayed. Like a newsreel, the images of times he'd been negligent, cutting, callous, and preoccupied came at him relentlessly. He wrote down every offense he could recall, and he asked God's forgiveness.

He recognized a pattern in his growing list. He was thoroughly selfish. Everything he did, whether it was jogging, speaking, working, even studying the Bible, was done to build himself up, in his eyes and in the sight of those around him. Everything and everyone else came second.

Pat was brokenhearted; Jill was exhausted and depressed. She had heard it all before, had seen Pat turn over innumerable "new leaves." But Pat knew things were different. He focused on his marriage all the energy and drive he usually reserved for the team. He immersed himself in a book on marriage, *Love-Life for Every Married Couple* by Ed Wheat (Zondervan, 1980).

In it he discovered principles for rebuilding a broken marriage, and he vowed to apply them until he won Jill back. He courted her that Christmas season as he never had before. And a chance encounter at a turkey farm jogged his memory of Jill's desire to adopt an Asian child. How strange it seemed, Pat recalls, to feel suddenly drawn toward adopting a child. He wasn't sure where to begin the process, but he was determined to try for the sake of his marriage.

9:00 P.M. The children are all asleep; the under-tens have been in bed since 7:30. Pat and Jill relax together in the Florida room, sharing stray items and observations about the week to come. They read the Bible and pray together, and collapse in bed by 10:00 P.M. Like every mother, Jill is feeling the pressure of constant demands. "If we didn't have twelve children," she muses, "I'd be traveling. Maybe France . . . or Hawaii."

Pat gazes at her with knowing eyes. "Yes, you'd probably be traveling if we didn't have twelve kids. But you would be miserable."

2

Andrea and Sarah Come Home

Three days before Christmas in 1982, Pat forced himself out the door to attend an office party with the Philadelphia 76ers staff. He left behind a wife who would barely talk to him, wouldn't look at him, and who recalls feeling emotionally numb—just no feeling there at all.

Pat had been praying constantly about his shipwrecked marriage, begging God for some answer, some glimmer of reconciliation, some foothold in the quicksand of their relationship. At the office party, Pat was stunned when his name was announced after a drawing for a big prize. He'd won an all-expense-paid trip for two to Disney World and EPCOT Center in Orlando, Florida.

Pat accepted the prize, then sensed immediately that God had just handed him a way to start winning Jill back. He hurried out of the room, practically in tears, and drove through the late afternoon darkness toward a turkey farm in Pemberton, New Jersey. Jill was expecting him to pick up a freshly dressed turkey for Christmas dinner.

Pat pulled his coat around him to keep out the chill as he stood in line. He continued to worry and pray about Jill, home staring at the television set. All at once, he focused on the couple ahead of him in line. The man held a tiny bundle of blankets, which he shifted up to his shoulder.

Out from under the blankets peeked a pair of dark, almond eyes. As Pat noticed the Asian infant and his Caucasian parents, he swallowed hard and his eyes again filled with tears. *What is happening, Lord?* Pat wondered. He felt God's answer deep inside: *This is no accident.*

Pat composed himself, then asked the couple about the baby. "How old is he?" The husband and wife were eager to tell about their new son, adopted from Korea through Holt International Children's Services. They acknowledged that the process is costly, the wait long and agonizing, but, they added, it was worth it all to finally hold in their arms their long-awaited child.

"Do you live around here?" Pat inquired. The couple named Moorestown, New Jersey, the Philadelphia suburb where Pat and Jill resided, and Pat eagerly wrote down their name and address. The young family casually invited Pat to bring his own family over for a visit sometime.

When he arrived home with the turkey, Pat burst into the house like a schoolboy with straight *A*'s. "You'll never guess what happened today, Jill." She didn't want to guess. Pat told her about the drawing, and how he won an expense-paid trip to Disney World.

Jill didn't say so, but the idea of a romantic weekend

alone with Pat held no appeal at all. She shrugged her shoulders and told him it was nice that he won.

"Guess what else happened," Pat persisted. Jill still wasn't interested in guessing. "At the turkey farm," Pat prodded. She just looked at him. "I was standing in line right behind a couple named Burkheimer. They've just adopted an orphan from Korea, and they live right here in Moorestown."

Pat was beginning to feel deflated as his day's surprises evoked no response at all from Jill. "I'm going to call the Burkheimers and see when we can visit them. I want you to see the baby."

Jill felt pestered beyond her limit. "Are you nuts?" she asked Pat. "You don't even know whether you have a wife left." Even so, she trudged to the kitchen and wrapped a package of shelled Georgia pecans for the Burkheimers, feeling light-years away from the Christmas spirit.

Pat, Jill, Jimmy, Bobby, and 4-year-old Karyn got in the car and drove two blocks to the Burkheimers'. Their Korean infant sat happily in a playpen, and the Williams children crowded around, making him laugh. Pat, meanwhile, pumped the couple for information. Whom do you call? How long does it take? Where do the children come from?

Jill acted cool, but cordial. "I felt as if I were up in the balcony watching," she remembers. She was utterly perplexed by Pat's sudden fixation on adoption. This was an idea he had ridiculed for years, scoffing at her fragile dream until it shattered. Now what was happening?

The next day, Pat telephoned Holt International in Eugene, Oregon, requesting an application to adopt and any information they could provide. He learned that the Korean government insists there be no more than forty years' difference in age between the oldest parent and the adopted child. Because he was 43, he and Jill would have to consider adopting a child no younger than 3 years old, a sibling group, or a hard-to-place child.

Pat is the first to acknowledge that his motivation for adopting was unusual. "I was trying to win my wife back, and I knew that her desire to adopt an Oriental child was one issue I had to deal with. I would have paddled to the Orient to win Jill back." It never entered his mind to consider the aspects of adoption that most couples weigh very carefully. "Adjusting to children who do not look like us, bonding with them, were the last things on my mind." Today, in her capacity as chairman of The Adoption Centre in Maitland, Florida, Jill cautions couples not to contemplate adoption at all unless their marriages are sound.

At the time, she was stunned by Pat's complete change of heart on a topic he had said was closed for good. Slowly, her desire to adopt came back to life as she perused the materials Holt sent and wrote a required autobiography. She still could not believe it would really happen.

One day, in typical Williams style, Pat convened a family meeting. He and Jill joined Jimmy, Bobby, and Karyn around the kitchen table, and Pat said, "We would like to adopt a baby from Korea. What do you think?"

The two boys lobbied hard for a brother, while Karyn wanted a sister. "Let's ask for one of each," Jill suggested, warming to the idea. "A brother and sister." By February 1, the application was finished and returned to Holt.

As spring approached, the thaw in Pat and Jill's marriage was nearly complete. Pat was a different husband and father, more keenly interested in spending time and energy with the family. And it was Pat who telephoned Holt every couple of weeks to check on the agency's progress. "Any news yet? Any siblings for us?"

At the beginning of June, their social worker in Trenton, New Jersey, Pat Keltie, finally had some news. "Holt has combed every orphanage in South Korea," she told Pat, "and can't come up with a brother-sister combination. But I do have a photo they sent showing two little sisters—and are they ever cute!"

The social worker scheduled a time to visit the Williams home, bringing with her a three-by-five black-and-white picture of two toddler girls, unsmiling and disheveled. They wore jumpers with frilly shoulder straps. Tags pinned on their dresses gave the girls' Korean names and case numbers. As Jill stared in fixed enchantment at the photos, Pat got out the camera. *Click!* He hadn't seen his wife so pleased in years.

"I was captivated by them," Jill remembers. "They were gorgeous, even though one of them had a horrendous haircut. Her hair was chopped off unevenly, as if someone had taken a dull butter knife to it."

One look at the photo was enough for the Williams children as well. "When are they coming?" Jimmy and Bobby chorused. The Williamses found themselves instantly attached to the young girls, named Yoo Jung and Yoo Jin. Nothing was known of their background; they had been abandoned in front of a police station in Seoul earlier in 1983.

Pat and Jill said yes to this offer from Holt, and the waiting began. They learned it would take at least three months, and maybe longer, for paperwork to be processed in Korea and filed with the U.S. Department of Immigration and Naturalization. Like several thousand other Korean orphans arriving annually in the United States for the past three decades, the girls would be escorted home by a social worker or volunteer.

Together, the Williamses chose names for the new sisters. Yoo Jung would be Andrea Michelle, and Yoo Jin, Sarah Elizabeth. Jill painted their bedroom a pale shade of peach, and stenciled a row of rust-colored teddy bears just below the ceiling. A collection of toddler-sized dresses hung in the closet, and fluffy teddy bears sat waiting on twin beds.

The social worker gave them a page full of everyday Korean expressions, translated phonetically. Together, they practiced the Korean words for Mommy, Daddy, our house, bed, shoe, yes, no, hot, cold, come here, let's go, don't cry, it's all right, hurt, stomachache, take a bath, wash your hands, thank you, let's play, and I love you. "I spoke fluent three-year-old Korean," Jill laughs.

As the summer dragged into autumn, Pat and Jill scheduled a family getaway to a summer home in Pennsylvania's Endless Mountains. It was the beginning of September, and a sense of change permeated the air. "We'll call you," the social worker had said, "after the girls get on the airplane."

Up in the mountains, Pat and Jill tried to take a weekend breather from the odd, anxiety-ridden sense of expectation an impending adoption brings. One evening, Jill drove from the summer home to a stable. She switched on the radio and only half listened to the music. As she pulled up to the stable, the news came on.

Jill snapped to attention at the terse report. "Korean Airlines Flight 007 has been shot down over the Pacific Ocean," an announcer said. "It appears there are no survivors."

If Jill had any lingering doubt about the adoption, it vanished in an instant. She stood frozen by the side of the car, her stomach contracting in the grip of fear. *What if ...* she worried, as she tried to breathe steadily. There was no way they could reach their social worker. Suddenly the two little girls, complete strangers to Pat and Jill save for one dog-eared photo, counted every bit as much as the rest of the Williams children. They were daughters, and their mother panicked.

Monday came, and the Williamses learned the details of the 007 tragedy. They received a reassuring call from Pat Keltie, telling them the girls still waited at their orphanage. "It won't be long," the social worker promised.

Three weeks later, the telephone rang and Jill answered. It was Pat, radiating the same exuberance he'd had after he saw the Burkheimer baby. "Tomorrow night, eight-fourteen, Northwest Airlines 008. That's it," he told Jill. Jill was frantically putting the finishing touches on Sarah and Andrea's room. She balanced precariously on a ladder, paintbrush in hand, while calling a favorite baby-sitter. "You must come to the airport," Jill told her.

The twenty-seven-hour trip included layovers in Seattle and Minneapolis before the plane finally touched down in Philadelphia on Wednesday, September 23, 1983. During the one-hour stop in Minneapolis, Jill's sister and brother-in-law drove to the airport there to get a firsthand look at their new nieces. Deb, Jill's sister, telephoned as soon as the girls were taken back on the airplane. "They looked so lost," she told Jill. "I felt so sorry for them, and all I wanted to do was hug them. They had no idea who we were or what we were doing there. They were totally exhausted."

Meanwhile, in Philadelphia, Pat Williams the sports celebrity was about to be upstaged by two jet-lagged tots. And all of Philadelphia's media were there to see it happen—along with the Williamses' nanny, two baby-sitters, Pat's mother, and the cofounder of Holt International, Bertha Holt, affectionately known to fifty thousand adopted Koreans as "Grandma."

"It was a big production," Pat remembers. "I was very proud of what we were doing, and I didn't want to hide it, so we invited all three network affiliates, the newspapers—everybody." In retrospect, it was a bit too much. Camera lights blazed throughout the Northwest gate, reporters, onlookers, and family friends milled about, and Jimmy, Bobby, and Karyn Williams stood in an anxious knot, holding gifts for the two girls.

Finally the plane rolled into view, as if in slow motion. The buzz of voices and camera equipment intensified as passengers filed off one by one. Andrea, age 2, and Sarah, 3, came last, carried by an off-duty flight attendant who had volunteered to serve as an escort. Blinded by the television floodlights, the flight attendant paused in confusion, asking, "Where's the mommy?" Jill couldn't hear her over the din, but she read the woman's lips.

"Right here," she said breathlessly, rushing forward to embrace Sarah. The escort started to hand Andrea to the Williamses' nanny, but a quick-witted television reporter shouted other directions: "Give her to the daddy!" In a melee of hugs, tears, and kisses, the two girls were welcomed into the fold of the Williams family. They clutched inflatable Mickey Mouses, given to them by a passenger during their first layover at the Tokyo airport. And they were as limp and unresponsive as little rag dolls, Jill remembers. They were numb with exhaustion and confusion.

Before he knew it, Pat fell in love. "I don't think the awesome reality of it hit until we were standing there at the airport. And then it hit hard. It was the same overwhelming sense of joy and responsibility that comes to you when a child is born. When we drove to the airport in the van that evening, we had three children. Driving home that night, we had five. That was the bottom line."

He later observed, "If I had known what an impact the adoption would have on all of us, we would have done it years ago. The minute I saw those girls, I felt exactly the same love for them as for our three homegrown children. I never imagined the reaction could be so intense. I was staggered by it."

Bertha Holt, posing for pictures with Pat, Jill, and their children, offered a sage bit of down-to-earth advice. "Don't worry about the Koreans; they'll be fine," Mrs. Holt said. "You take care of your American children. Everyone is going to pay attention to these little girls; make sure your birth children aren't neglected."

Jill soon learned the truth in Bertha Holt's words. "Everywhere we went people would say, 'Where did you get the cute little Chinese girls?' So I would make a point of introducing Karyn and telling how much she liked gymnastics, and singling out the boys as well. It was very important to keep them from feeling as if they had been replaced."

Pat and Jill gently carried the girls to the van in the airport parking lot. The girls fell asleep instantly on the drive home. Once there, Sarah and Andrea cooperated drowsily while Jill dressed them in pajamas. She put a diaper on 2-year-old Andrea, then took it off when Andrea began walking oddly, as if she had not worn a diaper in months.

At 11:00 P.M., the Williams family gathered around the television set to see the arrival on the news. Sarah and Andrea stared blankly at the screen, too worn-out to understand what they were seeing.

Jill tucked the girls into bed, and then fell deep asleep in her own bed. But not for long. At midnight, mournful wailing pierced the silence. Sarah was sitting awake on her bed. Jill grabbed her Korean phrase list and tried to reassure Sarah: "It's all right. Go to sleep now. Don't cry." In a moment, Andrea was awake, too.

Jill carried the girls into her bedroom, while Pat headed for the guest room to sleep. Andrea and Sarah, meanwhile, were ready for action. The time difference between the East Coast and Korea is fourteen hours, so at midnight in Philadelphia, it was mid-afternoon in Seoul. By 3:00 A.M., Jill surrendered to the rambunctiousness of the two sisters bouncing and fussing on her bed.

Wondering what in the world she had gotten herself into, Jill carried the two girls to the kitchen and switched on the light. "Are you hungry?" she asked in Korean. *"Pae go pooh nee?"*

"Yes," the girls said in unison. "Do you want a cookie? A banana? Milk?" Sarah and Andrea surveyed the possibilities. "Yes, yes, yes," they said to everything Jill set on the counter. They were ravenous!

"Suddenly, they were perfectly happy, having a tea party at three in the morning," Jill recalls. "They did not sleep at all for the rest of that night." The next day, Jimmy, Bobby, and Karyn stayed home from school to get acquainted with their new sisters. Sarah and Andrea each got a bath and a haircut, and tried on a few of the dozens of outfits friends and neighbors had dropped off.

They played outside and strolled around the neighborhood with the older children. "They were the happiest, giggliest girls ever," Jill says. "And the older children loved it. They kept asking, 'What's the Korean word?' for whatever they wanted to say." At lunchtime, Andrea and Sarah insisted on having their food packed in a bag. They sat on the floor in a corner, sharing their lunch from a sack.

Between meals, Andrea and Sarah each demanded a bag of crackers to carry around. They became very upset when Jill would not let them take their crackers to bed. Both girls were potty trained and never wet their beds. Andrea, who had turned 2 just three months before they arrived, would stand and cry when she had to go to the bathroom, but she never needed a diaper.

After a day or two, a sense of routine gradually returned to the household. Then a television crew called and asked if they could film a Williams family dinner, for a follow-up report. Jill prepared a simple meal of chicken and rice, and had her phrase list ready to try to explain to the girls what was happening.

The crew set up floodlights in the dining room and hoisted heavy cameras on their shoulders. Suddenly, Andrea burst into tears. The commotion and the strangeness of what was going on just got to her, and as she sobbed, mouthfuls of rice dribbled onto the table. Jill busily cleaned up and tried to calm her daughter. Then, with no warning, 4-year-old Karyn threw up on the table. "It was a total disaster," Jill says. The television reporter thought differently. "This is great," he told his cameramen.

Somehow, when the film was edited, the news spot

made the Williams family look happy and in control. Jill has no idea how they managed it. "After that," she says, "the media left us alone until Christmas."

When the girls ate at the table under less chaotic circumstances, their dainty table manners amazed Pat and Jill. "They ate beautifully, holding their spoons so carefully and not spilling," Jill observed. During the day, Sarah and Andrea played happily and did not cry. The nights were a different story.

Sarah awakened as often as a dozen times every night. Jill would go in and pat her, sing to her, rub her back, then wearily return to bed. After thirty minutes, the wailing would start again. Finally, Jill put a spare mattress in their room and slept on it with them. The late-night crying continued for six months.

One night, soon after Jill began sleeping in their room, she watched Sarah in the dim glow of the nightlight. As usual, Sarah awakened, crying, and sat up in bed. With both hands, she brushed frantically at her face and arms, as if her body were crawling with bugs. As Jill stared at her daughter, she remembered seeing tiny red welts all over Andrea soon after the girls arrived.

It dawned on her that Andrea must have slept through the night while bugs at the orphanage bit her. Sensitive Sarah woke up on cue to slap and scratch at them. Jill ached with sympathy for her daughters, and the sleepless nights seemed less agonizing. Pat took a turn sleeping on the mattress in Sarah and Andrea's room every other weekend.

Sarah and Andrea adjusted to America in much the same way as other adopted Asian children. During the months between the time they were abandoned and their placement with the Williams family, they had lived at a

Korean orphanage (not affiliated with Holt) that has a reputation for being unkempt. In most cases, orphaned Korean babies are cared for in well-scrutinized foster homes or spotlessly clean institutions. So Sarah's lingering fear of bugs in the night is not typical.

Children adopted from the Orient when they are past infancy often have trouble sleeping through the night. In Korea, most people do not sleep on beds. They spread a soft, quilted mattress on a floor warmed from beneath. Usually, several family members sleep together, and the youngest child generally sleeps next to the mother. Literature from Holt advises adoptive parents, "The child may be lonely and afraid if he or she is left alone in a bed with no adult nearby."

Mealtime customs are different, too. A Korean family usually eats sitting on the floor around a small table. The three meals of the day are very similar, consisting of rice along with side dishes which may include soup, meat or fish, and a variety of vegetables. A staple of the Korean diet is kimchi, or pickled cabbage. In her book *Oriental Children in American Homes,* author Frances Koh notes that adopted Korean children may love to eat dill pickles and sauerkraut because they taste like kimchi.[1]

Sarah and Andrea turn up their noses at kimchi, but they did bring with them a yen for strong-tasting food. Once, when Jill was slicing onions in the kitchen, both girls, drawn there by the pungent odor, stood next to Jill whining and begging for a taste. "You don't want this," Jill said with conviction, shooing them away.

They persisted, so Jill gave them each a slice of strong, raw onion. They loved it and came back for more.

Children who are adopted at an older age, and who have experienced hunger and poverty firsthand, may tend to eat everything in sight. It's as if they are not sure when—or if—the next meal will come. They also tend to hoard food, as Sarah and Andrea did with their bags of crackers; some may steal food persistently, even though they are well fed.

Some adoptive parents worry at first when their international infant or child seems subdued, faraway, even glazed. This is a common phenomenon. It is a way in which a child may cope with sudden, radical change in his life, grieving for the past even if it was an unpleasant one. His personality remains submerged for a time, while he comes to grips with all the new sights, sounds, and smells surrounding him.

A handbook for parents from Holt explains that children raised in orphanages often do not receive sufficient stimulation. "The child may look spiritless for a time," Holt cautions.

> Owing to the language barrier, he/she will attempt to read your mind but may misunderstand and not do exactly what you want. The child may also feel lonely and unhappy among his new brothers and sisters. In spite of all these problems, we earnestly believe that parental love is the most important key to the satisfactory development of a child.

Holt's purpose is to find permanent, loving homes for children who, for whatever reason, are not being cared for by their birth mothers or fathers. In addition to placing children overseas, Holt has worked hard since the mid-fifties to assist Korea in establishing an exemplary child welfare system. It is largely because of Holt International Children's Services that Korea has long been considered a model for other foreign adoption programs.

It all started in 1955, after the Korean War ended and American relief efforts joined the continuing military presence in South Korea. One of the organizations providing food, clothing, and shelter for war orphans and widows was World Vision, based in California. In an effort to raise funds for Korean assistance, World Vision president Bob Pierce traveled nationwide with documentary films on the war-ravaged land.

One evening in 1954, Harry and Bertha Holt left their Oregon farmhouse to hear Dr. Pierce speak at a local high school. At the meeting, they watched a film called *Other Sheep*. What they saw on the screen moved them profoundly—it "shattered our hearts," Bertha Holt wrote in her book, *The Seed From the East*.

> We saw before us the tragic plight of hundreds of illegitimate children ... GI babies ... children that had American fathers and Korean mothers ... children that had been hidden by remorseful mothers until it was no longer possible to keep their secret. Finally the children were allowed to roam the streets, where they were often beaten by other children who had never known Koreans with blond hair ... or blue eyes.[2]

Dr. Pierce explained to the audience that mixed-race children were singled out in Korean society as misfits. They often were subject to maltreatment, received inferior educations, and were relegated to the bottom rungs of society.

Harry and Bertha drove home to their six children, convinced they had to help. Together with their children, they decided to sponsor thirteen orphans at ten dollars each per month. Letters and gifts were sent to Korea, and in exchange, photos and information packets about the orphans arrived in the Holt's mailbox. Secretly, Bertha longed to adopt some of the children. She found herself eyeing each bedroom, mentally refurbishing it to accommodate another child or two.

Harry felt the same way, though he didn't tell his wife. When the truth came out, Bertha and Harry found they had independently decided the family could adopt eight GI babies. So Harry made plans to go to Korea. The Holt family is devoted in its Christian faith, and both Harry and Bertha felt this challenge was an insistent call from God. It was one they could not ignore.

Harry, 50 years old, arrived in Korea in early June. The sights of bombed-out streets in Seoul brought home the realities of the war. And a visit to an orphanage confirmed the desperation Harry had sensed in the World Vision presentation back in Oregon. At one orphanage, babies were dying of starvation and dehydration. A worker carried, on foot, some of the sickest ones to a hospital five miles away. All they had available to feed the babies was rice water. Harry urgently wrote home and told Bertha: "Sponsor ten babies at this orphanage immediately."

Harry did not return home until October that year. He combed the orphanages of South Korea, identifying babies and young children who desperately needed homes and were healthy enough to pass physical examinations and obtain passports.

While he waited for paperwork to be processed both in Korea and the United States permitting him to bring the children home, he cared for them and nursed them through bouts of dysentery, chronic worms, high fevers, colds, and—for the older ones—the emotional upsets of abandonment. The Korean press featured articles and interviews about his mission; meanwhile U.S. media were alerted to the story and began calling Bertha at the Oregon farmhouse for details.

Today in Korea, social mores are changing and old taboos are breaking down. Nonetheless, a young woman who becomes pregnant out of wedlock is still subject to family censure. In the 1950s, the plight of Korean women impregnated by American servicemen who may have lured them with promises of marriage and life in America was far worse. To his horror, Harry learned that babies who were half black and half Korean were particularly vilified. Reports circulated saying many of them were drowned.

After Harry returned to Oregon in October, bringing eight more children home to his family, he could not forget all the babies he had left behind. In the months that followed his return, five hundred couples in the United States wrote to the Holts asking how they could adopt a Korean orphan. By March 1956, Harry flew back to Korea, set up an office in Seoul, and began building an orphanage. Back home, one of the Holts' daughters began processing requests for adoption and scheduling home studies.

The Holt Adoption Program, as it was called then, soon had 75 mixed-race children in the Korean orphanage, ready to come to America. By the end of 1956, Holt had placed 191 orphans in the United States, and the following year, 287 children came home to adoptive parents. The processing of these adoptions was done by proxy, in Korea, rather than through established welfare channels in the United States. That changed in 1960, after officials of established adoption processes in America challenged Holt's practice of placing children specifically in Christian families.

As the work expanded, Harry Holt found a new location for a much larger orphanage and hospital. In 1961, Bertha and nine of her children (including all the adopted ones) moved to Korea to be with Harry, who had suffered multiple heart attacks and was in poor health.

In 1964, nine years after his first encounter with the problem of abandoned children in Korea, Harry Holt died. He was buried on a hillside above the orphanage he had worked so hard to build. The conviction that drove him and his family became, in 1970, the Holt organization's statement of purpose:

> Every child, of whatever nation or race, has the right to grow up with parents of his own. The silent call of homeless children is to all men of goodwill to see that neither apathy nor prejudice, neither custom nor geographical boundary shall prevent him from receiving his God-given right.

Today, Holt offers a variety of services in Korea, including counseling to prevent unwanted pregnancy, mother and child health services, adoption programs in Korea and abroad, a rehabilitation service for mentally retarded and physically handicapped children, a day-care center, and a scholarship program for underprivileged children. For all its adoptees in America, Holt offers Motherland Tours and a summer heritage camp to introduce aspects of Korean culture.

Beyond Korea, Holt works in cooperation with agencies in the Philippines, Thailand, India, and Latin America to place homeless children abroad. Holt is not the only agency in the United States placing Asian children in American homes, but its pioneering work made international adoption a realistic alternative for people who want to adopt. Bertha Holt still sends a letter of congratulations to each child adopted through the Holt program, including all the Williams children. Having her present at the airport when Andrea and Sarah arrived was a particularly special privilege for Pat and Jill.

Andrea and Sarah, like most international adoptees, learned English quickly and picked up the rhythms of life in the Williams household. By January, they were acting a bit restless, so Jill enrolled them in a Montessori school. Sarah attended three days a week, and Andrea two days a week. "They loved it; they blossomed," Jill says. "They soaked up everything like little sponges."

They remained strongly attached to each other. Each one made sure the other one had food to eat; they would hold hands, sing together, and constantly watch out for each other. "They act more like twins than real twins," Jill observes.

Jill, for her part, treats them as much like daughters as she does her birth daughter, Karyn. Only occasionally, a dark cloud will pass over Jill's sparkling countenance. What would have happened to these two little dolls, she can't help but wonder, if a distraught birth mother in Korea hadn't delivered her girls, safe and healthy, to a police station? And what about all the other children around the world who, for whatever reason, cannot remain with their blood relatives? As Jill has learned, there are many of them—far too many—out there waiting for an answer.

3
Who Are the Children?

Jill's deepening sense of attachment to Andrea and Sarah brought her into intimate contact with just two of the world's needy children. Instead of satisfying her, filling the void, easing the tug Jill felt toward international adoption, having Andrea and Sarah at home intensified her desire to learn more about these children and perhaps—just perhaps—provide a roof over the heads of a couple more.

In discovering a world she had never known before, Jill came to understand more clearly the purpose and rationale for adoption. She also began seeing some reasons why God apparently gave her a relentless urge to adopt.

Often, adoption is viewed as a solution for childless couples. Books about coping with infertility invariably discuss domestic and foreign adoption as options couples may consider.

Couples who discover that they are not able to conceive

a child or carry a pregnancy to term generally approach adoption seeking a healthy infant. Many of them find just the baby they are looking for, after some persistence and months or even years of waiting. They may locate a baby in the United States through a licensed adoption agency, or they may pursue international adoption as Pat and Jill did. Today, many couples are arranging adoptions independently, working directly with a birth mother or through a third party, often a lawyer.

There is much more to the adoption picture, Jill discovered, than childless couples seeking to adopt healthy infants. Even in the days when many young women with unwanted pregnancies placed babies for adoption, the reason most agencies existed was not to serve childless couples. They came into being instead to help homeless children find permanent homes. That remains their most important task, despite some new obstacles.

Adoption is changing. The number of unmarried pregnant women placing their babies for adoption has plummeted, so today only an estimated 5 percent of them do so. Many choose to raise their children, now that there is less social stigma attached to becoming a single parent. They may come under heavy pressure from classmates, boy friends, and even parents not to consider adoption as a possibility for their unborn child. Legalized abortion has resulted in the deaths of approximately 1.5 million unborn children every year. By most estimates, that number is matched, if not surpassed, by the number of couples waiting to adopt.

Meanwhile, the foster-care system in the United States shelters tens of thousands of children for years while they wait to return to their parents or to be released for adoption. If they move frequently from one foster family to another, failing to receive adequate attention and nurturing, they may have severe difficulty fitting into a family by the time they are freed for adoption.

Adopting couples are learning how important it is to remain flexible about what sort of child they could raise. Families who are unaffected by infertility—and in fact have honed their parenting skills already—make strong candidates to adopt waiting children. Some are drawn toward an older child who deeply desires a family, or a disabled child with a lot of love to give. As the Williamses have discovered twice over, bringing older children home is challenging but particularly rewarding.

It was their choice to locate children from other nations who needed a home. International adoption is a reality today in many countries largely because of the pioneering work of Holt. Yet even in the countries where channels exist to place children abroad, the tragedy of homelessness persists.

Just because adoption is changing does not mean it is a thing of the past. On the contrary, it is coming to be viewed more and more positively as one aspect of welfare services to assist homeless children. The reason it persists is because it works. "The fact of the matter is that children do better in families," says Susan Cox, director of development for Holt International Children's Services.

In the United States as well as abroad, it is important to understand adoption in context. On its own, it will not solve the problems posed by overpopulation, entrenched poverty, parental neglect, or abandonment. Instead, in nations that permit homeless children to be placed abroad, adoption is generally viewed as a temporary necessity until child welfare services can be expanded.

That is why reputable agencies work closely with foreign governments and their social welfare institutions to develop and maintain hospitals and orphanages for children who are unlikely to find permanent adoptive parents before they are grown.

The Holt organization models this sort of approach in Korea and elsewhere. The orphanage founded by Harry Holt at Il San, Korea, thrives today as a model facility for the handicapped, housing approximately three hundred. It is run by Harry and Bertha Holt's daughter, Molly, who is trained as a nurse with special expertise in cerebral palsy.

Children at Il San often are sponsored by concerned individuals in the United States and elsewhere who send monthly donations to provide basic care. Few of the children at Il San are available for adoption.

Susan Cox explains, "We think it's really important to enter a country out of love and respect for the children and the people. That means putting in place programs that meet the needs of children who will never be adopted.

"If you just gather up all the healthy, beautiful children and take them out of the country, and you are not providing services to families and children, then that is not appropriate. Holt has built its programs overseas based on relationships of mutual trust and respect."

The children of a developing country represent its greatest resource, but homeless children can be its greatest liability. As Susan Cox points out, "Children must be cared for. Someone must invest time and energy and resources and money in them. They don't just evolve into wonderful citizens and parents if they've never been parented. If they survive, they often have no social skills, no education, so another cycle repeats itself. It's a problem that grows with every generation."

Adoption offers at least some of these children a way out—an escape from poverty, uncertainty, the underclass. Holt's first priority is to try to keep the biological family together, particularly in cases where a child is being placed for adoption because of a sudden financial or family crisis.

If that is not possible, Holt attempts to find the child an adoptive home in the country of his birth. Finally, adoptive parents abroad are sought. "Children should not grow old waiting for the perfect family," Susan Cox says. "They should not wait for an inappropriately long time."

Children served by the process of adoption come in all races and colors, healthy and disabled, newborn, young, and older. This chapter will offer an overview of all the varieties of children who may be considered for adoption. It will introduce composite profiles of a few of the waiting children of America and the world.

Korea

Min-ho, age 10 months, is a charming, lively boy who needs a loving family. His birth weight was low, and he needed incubator care for three weeks. Although he was born prematurely, Min-ho is developing normally. He pulls himself to a stand, babbles in response to speech, and laughs often.

In recent years, Korean placements in the United States have accounted for more than half of all international adoptions here. Placement of Korean children in American homes peaked in 1986 when, according to figures from the U.S. Immigration and Naturalization Service, 6,188 of them came to this country. In 1987, there were 5,910 Korean children adopted by Americans.[1] Most of the Korean children placed for adoption throughout the sixties, seventies, and eighties were healthy infants under one year old. They received care in foster homes before being placed, which is far less expensive than providing institutional care. And children who have bonded to a "first mother," as the Koreans say, make a smoother transition to family life than babies who have been raised in an orphanage. The babies are cuddly and responsive because they have received plenty of affection and stimulation.

The Korean connection established in the 1950s by Harry and Bertha Holt set the stage for international adoption to become a reality, and it hastened the development of professional, compassionate child welfare services in Korea.

David Kim, president of Holt International, has worked for the organization since the mid-fifties, when he served as Harry Holt's translator. Neither of them expected the work to continue longer than a year or two. But the need was great, and those early overseas placements were amazingly successful. David Kim believes Holt's single most important contribution has been to help persuade the Korean government that children without families should not spend a lifetime in an institution.

In Korea, questions about the practice of placing children abroad have been raised. Adoption has come under fire in anti-American propaganda from North Korea, charging that the children are sold to raise money.

Even though such outrageous claims are groundless, they do fuel discomfort among Koreans about the practice. "Not many Koreans have had the opportunity to know adoption except from a distance," says Susan Cox. "There is certainly some anxiety in watching an American family adopt a Korean child, thinking, *How can that work?* Yet whenever a Korean family has seen the process of adoption more closely, and when it becomes apparent that the children are loved the same, they are very pleased that that child was able to have a family."

Korea has emerged as an economically competitive, modern nation, and it has experienced many social changes. As a result, there are fewer infants being placed overseas. As this book goes to press, Korean officials have announced plans to phase out international adoptions, for several reasons.

Korea's Confucian culture places a strong emphasis on blood ties and the importance of ancestry, so adoption of unrelated children has been traditionally opposed, or simply unheard of. Holt, along with other Korean agencies such as Eastern Child Welfare Society, has worked hard to change perceptions about adoption. Now they actively recruit Korean families for adoption. This effort brought a fifteenfold increase in adoptions by Korean families between 1970 and 1980, according to Byung Hoon Chun, president of Korea's Social Welfare Society.[2] In 1988, Holt Korea placed more than seven hundred children in adoptive homes in Korea.

Also, government efforts to educate young women about preventing unwanted pregnancies have begun to take effect, resulting in a marked decrease in the number of births to unmarried single women. And frequently, Korean women with unwanted pregnancies obtain abortions. Korea's economic success story has eased the grip of poverty for many Korean families. According to Susan

Cox, there are now practically no babies being placed for adoption because their parents cannot afford to raise them.

As Susan explains, "When intercountry adoption first began, it was a spontaneous response to the enormous needs of children right after the war. There has never been another time like that. Our mandate as an adoption agency is not to find children for families, but to find families for children. Finding adoptive homes in Korea is a process Holt is committed to, and it accounts for the fact that fewer children are coming to the United States."

The Philippines

Linda, 8, and Ariel, 10, are Amerasian siblings who would love to join a family. Linda is very sociable and gets along well with everyone in the group home where they live. Ariel is athletic—he enjoys running and climbing. This brother and sister are somewhat behind in their schoolwork because they attended school irregularly while they lived with their birth mother. The birth mother, who is unmarried, could no longer take care of them because of her own physical disability. This delightful brother and sister have been at their group home for two years, and their mother has recently signed papers releasing them for adoption.

Children available for adoption from the Philippines are older, or they come in groups of brothers and sisters who need to be placed together in one family. Lourdes G. Balanon, a welfare official in the Philippines, estimates there are eight thousand Filipino children living in child-care institutions, and millions more live on the streets or in extremely dangerous conditions.[3]

On the streets, life is brutal. Children are exposed to drug abuse, prostitution, infectious diseases, and physical abuse and exploitation.

Frequently, Filipino families adopt needy children, often reaching out to extended family members whose lives are in crisis. Balanon reports that 2,500 Filipino children were adopted in 1986. Overseas placements accounted for roughly 20 percent of these. That same year, according to INS, 634 Filipino children were adopted by families in the United States.[4]

"As a policy," Balanon writes, "foreign adoption is only resorted to when the needs of a child cannot be met in the Philippines." The plight of street children and institutionalized children may push Philippine authorities in the same direction as Korea: offering more family planning education, better support for unwed mothers, a foster-care network, and day-care centers, enabling single mothers to work.

Balanon emphasizes the Holt philosophy. She sees foreign adoption providing a focal point for assistance to children who are not adopted. "Adoption (and particularly foreign adoption) is to be seen not in isolation but as part of the total family and child welfare program."

Balanon raises an uncomfortable question—one which child welfare advocates raise in every nation where foreign adoption programs are proposed. Can these children thrive in another culture, where they may look different from their parents, siblings, and practically everyone they meet? Will they be considered "second-best" kids or "second-class" citizens?

No scientific studies have been done, since overseas

adoption is a relatively new phenomenon in the Philippines. Nonetheless, informal reports from social workers and adoptive families are overwhelmingly positive.

"The children have satisfactorily adjusted and integrated in their respective families, in school, and in the community," Balanon writes. "The Filipino children have survived and adjusted well in a considerably new environment."[5]

India

Sivaraj, 7, has spent most of his life on the streets of India. Considering the difficulties he has faced, he is remarkably bright and emotionally stable. He has suffered from malnutrition and is quite small for his age. However, he is doing well in school and especially enjoys learning to read. Sivaraj shows great potential and will have a bright future in a home of his own.

Crushing poverty in India's urban centers compels parents to abandon their children or place them in orphanages. Holt estimates that 10 million children there are living in institutions, most without any hope of being reunited with their birth parents.

In response, the Indian government is patterning an adoption program after the success story of South Korea. With an emphasis on finding Indian homes for abandoned children, the government is also freeing children to be placed abroad. In 1985, 496 Indian children found adoptive homes in America; in 1986, there were 588, and in 1987, the number jumped to 807.[6]

In 1979, Holt founded Bharatiya Samaj Seva Kendra (Indian Child Welfare Association) to begin offering comprehensive social services. Social workers associated with

Holt counsel birth parents who bring their children to Indian orphanages. They seek to find a way for the parents to provide for their children. When a child has no hope of returning home, efforts are made to place the child quickly with an adoptive family.

Other Asian nations also permit children to be adopted abroad, but far less frequently than Korea, the Philippines, and India. Between 1985 and 1987, according to the National Committee for Adoption, fewer than one hundred children came home to American families from each of the following countries: Japan, the People's Republic of China, Hong Kong, Taiwan, and Thailand.[7]

Closer to home, many American families interested in international adoption are turning to Central and South America. Colombia has been the leader in South America, permitting the placement of 724 children in the United States in 1987, 550 in 1986, and 622 in 1985.[8] Adoptions from Colombia have been postponed in some cases because of political uncertainties brought about by the war on drugs. Chile and Brazil have active programs as well. In Central America, El Salvador, Guatemala, and Honduras account for most adoptions, though other nations place some children.

Latin America

Esteban, 12, lives in a group home in Guatemala. He has a speech impediment and walks with a slight limp from an injury when he was younger. Esteban is very affectionate, and he tells his house parents that he longs to live with a real mother and father. He likes learning about nature and science, and he has made steady progress in his schoolwork since he came to the home two years ago. He will continue to need speech therapy.

It was in Guatemala that Jill saw for herself the terrible realities of urban poverty. She traveled there for four days in 1988 with her son Bobby, Lorraine Boisselle of The Adoption Centre, and Lorraine's adopted son, Rob, Jr.

At "the tracks," an encampment outside Guatemala City, they delivered donated goods to families scratching out an existence alongside a railroad track. Jill watched transfixed as youngsters clothed in layers of dirty rags played on the train tracks.

"The families live in shacks where the front door is maybe seven feet from the train tracks, the roof is made of cardboard, and the floors are dirt. When it rains they're washed out. Few of the shacks have doors, apart from a rag over the opening," Jill observed.

"I've never seen children so dirty and dressed in such rags. Their hair was matted, their noses running, their hands grimy. Twice while we were there, a train came through. It sounds a whistle, and the mothers come out of the shacks, pick up their children from the tracks, and take them into the houses. The train passes through, then the kids come back out again."

Jill, Bobby, Lorraine, and Rob spent one day at the tracks, handing out gifts of soap, toothpaste, toothbrushes, clothing, and toys. The day's highlight, however, was a hasty purchase Jill had stuffed in her purse just before the trip.

It was a bag of round, brightly colored balloons. As the Guatemalan kids crowded around, Jill and Bobby began blowing up balloons. Eager hands grabbed at these treasures, and children began racing toward home with their prize balloons. They would return in an instant asking for *"un otro,"* another one, for a brother or sister.

In Latin America, poverty is often the reason a baby or an older child is placed for adoption. Jill and Lorraine hoped to establish contact with a Guatemalan lawyer who could assist The Adoption Centre in placing abandoned children in American homes. It did not work out, and the experience left Jill and Lorraine wiser about how difficult it is to guard the best interests of children when independent entrepreneurs are in the driver's seat, rather than licensed agencies.

Jill and Lorraine spent most of one day meeting with a lawyer they believed they could trust. Talking through a translator, they described The Adoption Centre's goals and programs. There are plenty of American families who want to adopt, they told him, and these families are enthusiastic about adopting Guatemalan children.

The lawyer nodded eagerly, and agreed to assist The Adoption Centre by processing paperwork, in conformity with Guatemalan law, to release children for placement overseas. He accepted a good-faith deposit of several hundred dollars from Jill and Lorraine, and they left the country confident that they could begin assigning Guatemalan children to couples on their waiting list.

After several months had gone by, however, it became clear that no paperwork was being done. Letters flew back and forth, the lawyer assuring Jill and Lorraine that he was proceeding as they requested. Yet an unsettling feeling persisted, and Jill and Lorraine gradually realized they had been bamboozled. "He basically took our money and ran," Jill said.

It is not easy, as Jill and Lorraine discovered, to establish an adoption program in Latin America. Unlike Korea, Latin American nations tend not to have full-fledged programs in place to serve birth mothers, children, and families interested in adopting. At times, pregnant women and abandoned children have fallen victim to individuals who seek to buy babies and sell them on the black market.

Because of this, fear runs rampant in the streets, Jill learned. She was puzzled, at first, when mothers would quickly shelter their children from view whenever she took out her camera. As she became aware of the rumors surrounding foreign adoption and the actual threat from baby sellers, she grew more circumspect about taking photographs.

Because Latin American adoption has not been monitored as it has in Korea, many independent lawyers and others go into business to profit from adoption. "At whatever the cost, financially and emotionally, they will supply children to willing couples. It's a very risky business," Lorraine cautions.

The homeless children of Latin America—and families who seek to adopt them—are best served by established agencies with proven track records. Americans who adopt these endearing children through reputable channels often return again to adopt a second or third child. When it comes to building a family, they discover fulfillment doesn't hinge on nationality, physical condition, or age.

The United States

Samantha is 3 months old and has just been transferred into foster care from the hospital where she was born. She is biracial and was born with cocaine de-

pendency. Her mother relinquished parental rights before leaving the hospital. Samantha is small, weighing eight pounds. Her development appears to be normal—she follows an object with her eyes, turns her head at the sound of a bell, and kicks her legs energetically. Her prognosis is good, considering her difficult start in life.

When it became clear to Jill and Lorraine that a Guatemalan connection was not going to materialize immediately, they turned their attention to Florida's waiting children. They saw needs right in their own backyards that demanded solutions, including adoption.

In its first two years, The Adoption Centre placed more than one hundred children in permanent adoptive homes. Approximately one-third were from overseas, including the four Filipino boys adopted by the Williamses. (Holt works through local agencies such as The Adoption Centre to obtain home studies and provide postplacement services.) Another one-third were American children with special needs, and the remaining one-third were healthy infants born to young women who made a courageous choice to find a loving home for children they knew they could not raise.

There is no shortage of babies being born to unwed mothers in America, but today those babies are far less likely to be placed for adoption, particularly through an adoption agency. For a variety of reasons, there is little social stigma attached to single parenthood today. And, among young women in high school and college, peer pressure to keep a child can be overwhelming. "Give away your own flesh and blood?" they are asked. "How could you?"

Women who do explore the possibility of adoption frequently want to have more control over the circumstances of their child's placement than before. They may want to review written profiles of couples who want to adopt; they may insist on a particular characteristic for their child's adoptive family, or even request an open adoption, in which they would meet the adoptive couple and perhaps stay in touch through the years.

Traditionally, agencies have been reluctant to move toward more contact between birth mother and adopting parents. However, a clear trend toward increased participation by the birth mother in choosing adoptive parents is occurring, and some agencies—including The Adoption Centre—see it as a good thing.

"If we can give birth moms some peace of mind and a sense of control, in a situation where they have very little control, they will have an easier time of it," says Lorraine. As a result, every couple that applies to The Adoption Centre must be willing to participate in an open adoption.

"We are recruiting girls on that basis," Lorraine explains. "We tell them, 'No one is going to make you parent that child, and no one is going to make you release him for adoption. But please give that child life—do that much for him, and help us find someone else to raise him.' " As a result, The Adoption Centre places an unusually high percentage of children born to single mothers. Out of every one hundred pregnant women who seek counseling and assistance from Lorraine, forty of them plan for their babies to be adopted. The rate of placement at many agencies is far lower, in the range of 5 to 10 percent.

Lorraine works hard to convey a positive attitude toward birth mothers to couples applying for adoption. "Birth parents care about their children. They're making a decision that will affect them the rest of their lives."

Her enthusiasm toward increased involvement by birth mothers is based on personal, as well as professional, experience. The second-to-last child adopted by Lorraine and her husband, Robert, came into their home via an open adoption. The birth mother would not have agreed to release her child otherwise. Lorraine vividly recalls her first meeting with Sarah's mother.

"Our first meeting came after Sarah's birth, when she was still in foster care. I had a mixture of feelings; I was nervous and frightened. She was in her twenties, and had separated from her husband. She'd had an affair which resulted in Sarah, and then she and her husband got back together. Her husband had a lot of negative feelings about that baby girl."

Lorraine and Robert had adopted many children before Sarah came along, yet knowing the birth mother infused Lorraine with all the emotions of a "first-timer." "I knew my relationship with that child would be very special because I met her birth mother. That young woman handed Sarah to me. There is nothing else like it. Sarah is 6 years old now, and she is beginning to ask questions about babies and birth. I can say her birth mother's name, and tell her that that woman wanted me to raise her. I can tell her where she got her blue eyes."

Sarah's birth mother knows where the Boisselles live and has come to visit once or twice each year. Does Lorraine worry about Sarah being physically kidnapped or emotionally robbed out of the fold of her family by this other woman? Not at all. "She has never done anything inappropriate. She has a good head on her shoulders, and she knows we are not co-parents. She considers herself a friend of Sarah's, like an aunt. She takes no part in Sarah's parenting and doesn't want to."

At the same time, Lorraine is quick to caution against a fully open adoption if either the adopting parents or the birth mother feels even slightly insecure about it. "I know of only one other fully open adoption like ours," Lorraine says. "I'm a big believer in agencies being involved. At The Adoption Centre, if we feel a birth mother is not mature enough to exchange identifying information, we step in and assist her and the adopting couple in arriving at an acceptable level of openness." That may mean preserving confidentiality by not disclosing last names and telephone numbers, even if there is a face-to-face meeting.

By far the greatest challenge in adoption today is finding homes for children with acute needs. More and more babies who test positive for HIV, the AIDS virus, are being born and then abandoned in inner-city hospitals. Increasing numbers of newborns are addicted to crack cocaine at birth and need special medical attention. Often, they are abandoned as well. Finally, the children who present the most urgent need for stable homes are those caught in the U.S. foster-care system, living out childhoods devoid of permanent parental attention and love. Many of them remain trapped in a system that is not geared toward finding new homes for them.

AIDS Babies

There is perhaps no greater human tragedy than an infant born with the AIDS virus. One day at The Adoption Centre, Lorraine received a panicked telephone call from a local hospital. It was a young woman, unmarried, who had just given birth to a baby in deep distress.

The mother wanted to place her baby for adoption, but the agency she had been working with dropped her flat when a social worker saw the condition of the baby. The all-white baby boy was addicted to cocaine and was exceedingly small. The mother needed a ride home; Lorraine went to the hospital, took a look at the baby, and drove the mother home.

During her brief encounter with this mother, Lorraine strongly suspected the woman was a prostitute. After she dropped the woman off, she called the hospital. "Would you please do an AIDS test on that infant?" Lorraine requested. The little boy tested positive for the HIV virus, which causes AIDS.

Lorraine got on the telephone and recruited a permanent adoptive home for the boy, who has a 30 to 50 percent chance of developing AIDS. It was more difficult, says Lorraine, to find a suitable foster home while all the paperwork was being prepared.

Information about caring for HIV-positive babies is available from the National Adoption Information Clearinghouse in Washington, D.C., as well as a Christian advocacy group, Americans for a Sound AIDS Policy (ASAP) in Herndon, Virginia. (For more information, see the resource list at the end of this book.)

Boarder Babies

Another group of babies at severe risk are the "boarder babies," abandoned at birth by their drug-addicted mothers and left in the care of hospitals. After they have recovered sufficiently to be discharged, there is no place for them to go. And frequently, their mothers do not release the children for adoption. Because drug abuse hits hardest in America's inner cities, many of these children are black, Hispanic, or of mixed racial heritage.

In Washington, D.C., in 1989, more than one hundred such babies populated the nurseries of seven hospitals. Doctors and nurses bought them clothing and toys, named the children, and provided all the cuddling and attention they could muster in the course of a hectic work shift.

Meanwhile, the wheels of the city's understaffed child welfare department kept grinding slowly. Months and even years would go by before permanent homes were found. A series of articles in the *Washington Post* contained this account of two such babies:

> In one pediatric ward, chubby 6-month-old twin boys are still in residence even though their mother announced at their birth that she wanted to give them up for adoption. The mother, a cocaine user who has a lengthy history of substance abuse, has three other children in the child welfare system.[9]

An estimated 375,000 cocaine-addicted babies are being born each year, to mothers whose addiction has cost them the desire and motivation to rear a child. In New York City, around 400 boarder babies are born each month. In response, the city has aggressively recruited foster homes so the babies stay in hospitals less than one week, rather than for a month or more at a time.

Kids in Foster Care

The largest population of American children with special needs are those who are living in foster care, most often because they have been removed from homes where their parents neglect or abuse them. The goal of social welfare agencies has been to reunite these children with their birth parents as soon as possible, but that only happens about half the time. Often the children linger for years with no permanent solution. Sometimes the experience robs them of the ability to trust other people, to give and receive affection, to feel connected and valued.

Estimates of U.S. children in foster care range between 250,000 and 350,000, and between 36,000 and 50,000 of them are legally free for adoption. Of these, about two-thirds have physical or emotional disabilities, are members of racial minority groups, are older, or are waiting to be adopted along with their brothers or sisters.[10]

A task force on adoption appointed by President Reagan reports,

> Children with special needs are adoptable. However, the legal and administrative barriers, as well as inertia in the current foster care system, require focused attention and change. . . . There is a national consensus that the time a child waits for a permanent home must be shortened.[11]

Black Children

Finding homes for black infants and children has presented a continuing challenge to child welfare departments as well as adoption agencies. In some cases, the needs of these children have fallen victim to stereotyped ideas about what is best for them. After the Holt experiment of the 1950s demonstrated that white adopting couples eagerly welcomed children of a different race into their lives, some black children were placed with white families. It appeared to be working well. One of the best-known adopters of biracial children was novelist Pearl Buck. She wrote,

> The first few days, perhaps I did notice when I bathed her that her skin was darker than my own. The first day perhaps I felt strange. But caring for that little body, watching the keen quick mind awaken and develop, enjoying the vigor of the personality, soon made the child my own. Her flesh became my flesh by love, and we are mother and child.[12]

But the practice of transracial placements in the United States was halted in its tracks in 1972 by a fierce statement of protest from the National Association of Black Social Workers. In part, the lengthy statement said,

> Black children are taught, from an early age, highly sophisticated coping techniques to deal with racist practices perpetrated by individuals and institutions. . . . Only a Black family can transmit the emotional and sensitive subtleties of perception and reaction essential for a Black child's survival in a racist society.

In recent years, efforts to recruit black adoptive families have multiplied. One of the best-known and most effective of these efforts was started by Father George H. Clements, a Catholic priest in Chicago who has adopted three teenaged boys. In 1980, he began a campaign called "One Church, One Child," urging at least one black family in every church in the country to adopt a waiting child. Nine years after he began his campaign, an estimated 9,500 black children had been adopted into black homes in the United States.

Clements has spoken out in favor of transracial adoption as well. Same-race placements are clearly ideal, he has said. "But you cannot always have the ideal, and in lieu of the ideal, certainly I would opt for an Anglo couple, or whatever nationality, taking a child in."

Pressed by the growing inner-city problem of drug addiction, and spurred by the willingness of white families to adopt children of a different race, some agencies are reconsidering the taboo against interracial placements. The Adoption Centre is a case in point.

Lorraine finds it difficult to recruit Florida families of any race for black or biracial children. But she is adamant in her commitment to their birth mothers. She has established a link with several agencies in Vermont who know of families that are eager to take in black children.

Who are the children? They come in all possible variations, with one need in common: the need for a permanent home, complete with parents who have lifelong unconditional love to share.

Back at the Williams home, Pat and Jill were thinking a lot about children—the ones they had already. Sarah and Andrea were a handful, and the other three were sprouting rapidly into busy schoolchildren with unique interests and activities. Daughter Karyn was in love with dance and gymnastics, while Jimmy and Bobby showed surprising promise in team sports.

Welcoming more children into the fold was not exactly an event they planned to squeeze onto their crowded calendar. But more Williams children—surprising numbers of them—were on their way.

4

And Then There Were Eight

The months following Sarah and Andrea's arrival sped past in a blur of activity and adjustment. It had been three years since Pat and Jill had had toddlers in the house. All the demands and ploys for attention and alternate clinginess and independence of toddlerhood-times-two made Pat and Jill wonder, once in a while, if they were truly up to the challenge.

Jill, in particular, was feeling unusually exhausted. When she visited the doctor, wondering how to get her energy back, she was in for a real surprise: She was expecting another baby. In fact, the amused doctor told her, she had been pregnant for four months. As the time for delivery approached, she began explaining to Sarah and Andrea, ages 4 and 3, what was happening.

Not much occurs in the Williams household that does not involve everyone, and the impending birth was no exception. She asked her doctor, Brian Geary, if her five children—Jimmy, Bobby, Karyn, Sarah, and Andrea—could all be present in the delivery room. And Pat, too, of course.

He had been less than enthusiastic about attending the birth of his first child, but Jill persuaded him to be with her when Jimmy was born in 1974. After that, Pat's enthusiasm was unflagging. "I wouldn't miss them for the world," he said of the other three births.

Jill's doctor agreed. "Bring the whole team if you like," he said, referring to the Philadelphia 76ers. Pat and Jill turned down that invitation, but they signed up their children to attend three Saturday sessions about child delivery. All of this prompted a question in inquisitive 4-year-old Sarah's mind. "Mommy," she asked one day, "was I in your tummy?"

Jill took a deep breath. She had rehearsed her answer to this question many times, and the words came very naturally. "No, sweetheart. You were in another lady's tummy. Then she sent you to us, because she knew we would love you and give you a good home."

For the next five years, the subject never came up again. Jill, of course, is the only mother Sarah and Andrea have ever known. Telling the adoption story in a sensitive, positive, and personal way is important for every adoptive parent. It requires special sensitivity when the adopted child arrives home when he or she is older, bringing along vivid memories of another family, another home.

That was the case with Stephen and Thomas Williams, Korean twin boys who arrived when they were 6 years old. Pat and Jill's marriage had grown deeper and bloomed into a close, caring, and sharing relationship. Bringing Sarah and Andrea into the family, and then being blessed again with the birth of Michael, sealed the bond that was so nearly severed on D day in 1982.

In 1986, Pat took on the professional challenge of his life. He signed a contract with a group of businessmen to develop an expansion NBA team—now the Orlando Magic—in Florida. Also during 1986, Pat and Jill queried Holt about the possibility of another adoption, perhaps a child from the Philippines. Nothing came of that request, so in early January 1987, Pat telephoned Susan Cox at Holt to say hello and keep in touch.

Pat told Susan they were thinking of pursuing an adoption through another agency. Susan was dismayed. "You're one of our families," Susan told Pat. "Let's see what we can do."

Susan was well aware that the Williamses were interested in adopting again. In fact, they had come to mind just that morning, when a photograph of two brothers landed on her desk. "It's funny you should call today," Susan told Pat. "Yesterday it wasn't here, and tomorrow it will be gone, but today I have a photograph of Korean twin brothers who need a family."

A few days later, photographs and background information about the twins, named Sang Wan and Sang Hyung, arrived in the mail. It was time for another Williams family council meeting.

Sitting around the kitchen table, Pat, Jill, and the children peered at the two color photos, showing identical youngsters with unruly mops of black hair. They were not smiling, exactly; their expressions were uncertain. One of them wore a red jacket made by their mother.

Pat studied the photo, thinking, *These guys need haircuts . . . and family love to make 'em smile.* The idea of adopting twins was intriguing to the whole Williams clan, and Jimmy and Bobby favored adopting more brothers. Andrea and Sarah were delighted at the prospect of brothers from the country where they were born.

The paperwork provided minute details about the boys' health and activities. They sleep from 9:00 P.M. until 7:00 A.M., Pat and Jill read. They eat one bowl of rice at each meal, along with side dishes. They eat fruit and bread for snacks, count from one to ten, enjoy playing on a slide, a seesaw, and a swing at the orphanage playground. Sang Wan and Sang Hyung watch children's programs on television and enjoy picture books, the background sheet said.

"They prefer outdoor play to indoor life, so spend a lot of time in the playground and in the yard," the report concluded. "They are bright boys of good nature. They are cherished a lot by their Bomos." (Bomos are the women who care for children at the orphanages.)

By mid-January, all the paperwork was filed. Meanwhile, the Williams family moved into a comfortable three-bedroom home in Winter Park and planned, someday, to make a few minor renovations or move to a bigger home.

Jill busied herself by converting a sitting room into a bedroom. The room was connected by an open doorway with the nursery where Michael slept. She rooted through her files and dug out the old Korean phrase sheet. By the time Andrea and Sarah had been home for a few months, Jill found she no longer needed it. The girls soaked up the English language and quickly forgot Korean. Jill started working on the basics, once again.

She wondered what it would be like to receive into her home two sons who clearly remembered their birth mother and the extreme hardship that led to their placement for adoption. Andrea and Sarah had adapted so quickly, so naturally, to the Williamses' family life.

What happens when an older child changes not only his home, but his entire identity, language, culture? How will they take to American-style food, new names, schools, routines, other kids on the block?

"Everybody thought we were crazy," Jill remembers. "Here we are with six children, bursting at the seams of our house, and we're going to adopt again . . . twins this time." Adopting internationally requires filing an extraordinary amount of paperwork. Much of it is funneled through the U.S. Immigration and Naturalization Service (INS), which asks for proof of identification and a signed statement assuring the U.S. government that a particular child from abroad will be received into an American home as a full-fledged member of the family.

Part of the process includes fingerprinting and a statement assuring the agency that the couple has no criminal record. When Pat and Jill went to a police station to be fingerprinted and file the required forms, they waited more than an hour, with Sarah, Andrea, and Michael in tow. The woman who did the fingerprinting stared at the Williamses' background file, and looked up, dumbfounded. "You've got six kids already," she said. "What do you want with two more?"

Jill didn't answer; she was too busy keeping three kids corralled in the busy office. Pat was just a little annoyed at the woman's judgmental tone. *It's none of her business,* he thought. Then he realized there is a simple, direct—and truthful—answer to offer to all the people who think he and Jill are nuts. "The reason we are adopting again," Pat explained, "is because we want more children." Later

Pat realized the reasons behind their decision to adopt go even deeper.

Part of the commitment he and Jill made to each other as they worked to rebuild their marriage included living their lives God's way. God had so clearly nudged them in the direction of international adoption, Pat believed, and the task wasn't finished yet. *God created a void in our lives,* Pat thought, *and by doing so He is providing a home and family to children in need.* It's a good thing for adoptive parents to sense some urgency about the situation, Pat realized, because each day that passes for children who wait tends to diminish their chances of ever finding a permanent home.

At the end of February, Susan Cox called Pat with shattering news: Korea had just announced a new policy on adoptions, prohibiting families with more than four children from adopting any Korean children.

The news stabbed at Jill with the same fury as the radio report on Flight 007 had years earlier. Again, there wasn't any doubt. These two boys were her sons, and they might not come home because of some bureaucrat's decision.

Holt telexed Korea immediately to ask about the Williams case. The answer came back within days. Korea would allow the two boys to come, but no more exceptions. "You can adopt the two boys," Susan told Pat. "They are the last Korean children you can have." Pat was relieved, and thankful. "Wow," he told Jill. "God is really in the middle of this one!"

It seemed like only a matter of days, but two months went by before a telephone call came saying the boys were on their way to the airport, scheduled to arrive in Orlando on May 1.

The household pulsed with activity. Under the guidance of Andrea's artistic eye, the children made a huge poster to take to the airport. It said "Welcome Home Stephen and Thomas." As they waited at the airport on the morning of May 1, 1987, the scene was far calmer and more manageable than the circus surrounding Sarah and Andrea's arrival.

The Williamses' friend Cari Haught set up the arrival party, complete with a gift basketball from Jimmy and Bobby. One television station, several print reporters, a few friends from Pat's office, and Jill's father joined them, watching out the window for the airplane to taxi into view.

After all the passengers had filed out, a woman appeared at the end of the jetway with two rumpled boys, their faces drawn from exhaustion and bewilderment. She practically had to push them along—they were terrified, hiding behind her skirt. It was eighty-five degrees under an unforgiving Florida sun, yet it was obvious at first glance that Stephen and Thomas were wearing layer upon layer of clothing.

"They were stiff little soldiers," Jill recalls. "I knelt down to give them hugs, and they stood there rigid, their arms at their sides, staring blankly ahead." Jill spoke slowly and softly to them, in Korean. "I'm your mama. There is your daddy. We love you." Pat and Jill both cried as they sought a way of communicating with these little, scared boys. That day, Stephen and Thomas knew only two words in English, learned en route to America: *orange juice* and *ice cream*, words that sound similar to their Korean equivalents.

One of the boys had thrown up during the twenty-one-hour flight, and his clothing reeked. Pat and Jill stripped layers of flannel shirts, woolen pants, and long under-wear off the boys, and seated them in the van in their underpants for the drive home.

Stephen and Thomas rode in silence, expressionless, staring out the window at six lanes of traffic and a blur of fast-food restaurants, shopping centers, parks, and office buildings. When they reached the Williams home, Pat pulled up right by the front door, under a carport. Out tumbled six children, all eager to show their new broth-ers around. Stephen and Thomas filed out of the van gravely and marched toward the front door. There they stopped and methodically removed their shoes, lining them up in a neat row against the house.

Jill watched, amused and astonished. Then it hit her. This had all the earmarks of a great family tradition! Shoes would not wander off and hide, and the rug would escape muddy footprints. "Everybody!" she commanded. "Take your shoes off now and line them up like Thomas and Stephen did." All the kids complied, and Jill went inside to find some lightweight clothing for the boys. Af-ter they were dressed, she began fixing dinner.

Moments later, Pat startled Jill as he burst into the kitchen, hot and perspiring. "Jill, come out here. Bring the Korean dictionary." What in the world was going on? Jill patted her hands dry and hurried toward the door. There stood Thomas and Stephen in the backyard, clutch-ing baseball bats. They stared in confused delight at Pat, this fair-skinned, mustached, slender man gesturing and talking gibberish as he demonstrated how to swing a bat.

"How do you say *bat* and *ball*?" Pat queried over his shoulder to Jill. The twins had never hit a home run; in fact, they had never even seen a bat or ball. But Pat's first thought, as they arrived home from the airport, went something like this: *I wonder if these two can play ball. . . . I'll just get them warmed up before dinner is ready.*

Jill watched her husband and new sons, a wry smile playing at her lips. She wrote a list of appropriate expressions in phonetic Korean syllables: throw, catch, hit, run, don't run, let's go outside. "What were you planning to do if they couldn't play ball?" she asked Pat later. "Send them back?"

That evening, the exhausted twins slept soundly. After she tucked them in, Jill sat down next to Pat to bask in the glow of that day's miracle. "How are we going to tell them apart?" Pat asked sheepishly. They really were identical. Jill had already come up with a plan that would work at least temporarily. "Stephen is missing two of his baby teeth, so just remember *s is for space*. Thomas still has all his teeth, so think of *t for teeth*."

They laughed together at Jill's eagle-eyed observation, then peeked through bedroom doors at all eight of their children before heading for bed.

On their second night in Orlando, Stephen and Thomas did not sleep so soundly. Just after Jill had gone to sleep, she was jolted awake by a sound she recalled from the weeks following Sarah and Andrea's arrival. From the twins' bedroom came a mournful wailing, in stereo, with all the volume and intensity two 6-year-olds could muster with their mouths wide open.

Jill hurried to their bedside, concerned that Michael would awaken too and be frightened. She left the door open, so some light would come into the room. "Don't cry," she told them in Korean. "It's all right. Go to sleep." She held first one boy, then both, rocking them awkwardly as she sat on their bed.

Through their sobs, the boys were trying to say something, Jill realized. She could not hear the syllables clearly enough to look them up on her phrase sheet. "What is it?" she kept asking them in Korean, frustration gnawing at her. Were they sick? Had the other children treated them badly?

For four nights, the wailing continued, and Stephen and Thomas repeated their mystery words. Jill listened closely, trying to get them to calm down and speak to her quietly. Finally, as she studied her list of phonetically spelled Korean phrases, she recognized their words. "Moo so wo," they were saying. "Moo so wo." Moo so wo. She searched her tattered list, and found the phrase. Tears welled up as she read the translation. "I'm afraid," the boys were telling her. "I'm afraid."

She hugged the boys closely, for a long time. "Don't be afraid," Jill said softly in Korean. "I am your mommy. This is your home. I love you." She was overwhelmed with relief when she recognized their words. Of course they were afraid! Everything in their lives had changed suddenly, radically, in the twenty-four hours it took them to travel from Seoul to the East Coast.

Pat and Jill wanted to reassure the boys at a level they could understand, so they invited over a Korean couple who serve on The Adoption Centre's board. "Tell Stephen and Thomas that they will be here forever. That they are our sons," Jill said. In Korean, the couple told the boys what Jill had said, and asked them if they liked living in America.

Stephen and Thomas quickly agreed that the food at the Williams house was outstanding; they admired Jill's cooking right from the start. The Korean couple asked the boys about their life in Korea, and a few snatches of information came out. A large scar on Stephen's foot, he said, came from being hit by a taxi. The skin on the inside of Thomas's forearm was badly scarred, and he said it had happened when scalding tea spilled on him one time.

"My mommy sells drinks in a restaurant," Thomas said. "And my uncle sells strawberries. My grandma sells things in a store, and the old-old grandma couldn't take care of us." "Do you remember anything about your father?" the couple asked gently. "He was a busy worker," the boys replied.

The two boys did not understand all the circumstances that led to their birth mother's hardship. According to Holt files, she was a single woman who became involved with a married man. He was a stonemason and construction worker. "He made us a wooden toy," Stephen and Thomas said proudly.

Without a full-time father to provide for the family, the mother had to go to work. Caring for active twins proved too much for the woman who was probably their great-grandmother. Money was very tight, so the heartrending decision finally came. The boys would have to be placed somewhere else. "Everybody cried when we said good-bye," they told the Korean couple. "Mother told us what America would be like." The Koreans translated for the boys, as Pat, Jill, and the other children listened, wide-eyed.

As the Korean couple prepared to leave the Williamses, it was obvious that Stephen and Thomas still had a question on their minds. They conversed briefly with the couple, who told Pat and Jill, "They want to know if they will be staying here until they are big." Apparently, the idea that they would be there "forever" was meaningless to them. "Yes," the woman said firmly. "You will be here until you are very big." After that visit, the midnight wailing ceased. No more *"Moo so wo."*

About two months after Stephen and Thomas joined the family, the Williamses packed up for their annual summer visit to Word of Life, a Christian family camp on Schroon Lake in New York's Adirondack Mountains. Pat speaks at the camp annually.

As they drove to the airport, Jill puzzled over how to explain to Stephen and Thomas what was happening— and where they would be spending the next two weeks. The only time the boys had been to the airport since their arrival was to take Jill's father there after a visit. So when they boarded the airplane, Stephen asked in Korean, "Are we going to grandfather's house?"

Jill took a deep breath, and consulted her Korean phrase sheet. "No," she said. "We are going to a big school. You will eat there and sleep there and have fun." The boys were clearly bewildered, but they followed along obediently.

Jill walked the twins to their cabin and introduced them to their counselor. "This one is Thomas and this one is Stephen," she told the perplexed teenager.

"They don't speak any English. I'll see you at the end of the week." Jill wrote down a few Korean phrases for the counselor to use with the boys, and she told Thomas and Stephen she would be back for them. "This is your big brother," she said, introducing the counselor.

Also at Word of Life that week was Jin Park, a young Korean woman attending the Word of Life Bible Institute. She got to know the twins and talked with them daily in Korean. One evening, all the campers gathered for a worship service. Jin walked through the woods to collect Stephen and Thomas and take them to church. The two boys fidgeted during the service, but they seemed to enjoy the singing. At the end, an invitation to receive Christ as Savior was given, and Jin began explaining in Korean what was happening. In unison, Stephen and Thomas said they, too, wanted to believe in Jesus. There, in an upstate New York camp, with a fellow Korean by their side, the two Williams boys committed their lives to Christ.

By the time school began in the fall, Stephen and Thomas had mastered English and forgotten the Korean language. Jill enrolled them in First Academy, the Orlando Christian school her other children attended, and they were assigned to different first-grade classes so they would learn English more quickly. Thomas, it turned out, was in Andrea's class, and Stephen was in Sarah's.

"Not knowing their personalities," Jill said, "that turned out to be the best combination. Sarah and Stephen are the two aggressors, and it worked well to have them together." As it was, the twins adjusted quickly and comfortably to their classrooms, reassured by having a sister from home in each room.

Their personalities emerged as their lives took root in the family, and Pat and Jill marveled that they had not been able to tell the boys apart only months before. Both of the boys excel in sports, easing Pat's anxieties about their abilities with a bat and ball. Thomas, in particular, is rough and tough and extraordinarily absentminded.

One day Pat drove both of them to a soccer match. From the back of the van came a loud stomping noise. "What's going on back there?" Thomas replied that he was having trouble getting his shoes on. Pat thought nothing more about it. He couldn't wait to get out on the field and watch the boys run, passing the ball and kicking it toward the goal with amazing agility and accuracy.

But wait, Pat thought as he watched the boys play, *something isn't right here.* Thomas was limping—practically stumbling—as he practiced. Pat waved him over to the bleachers. "What's the matter, Bubba?" he asked, taking Thomas by the shoulders and looking him over. He focused on those troublesome shoes. They were Sarah's!

"The shoes were killing him. He had jammed his feet into them even though they were a good inch and a half too short," Pat laughs. With Thomas looking very sheepish—not to mention pained—Pat patiently lectured him about being more attentive to details.

"How many times have I told you to make sure you know exactly where your shoes are when you need them?" Pat concluded. Thomas, ever the literalist, gazed at his dad thoughtfully before replying. "Seventeen?" he asked.

One Saturday morning, two years after their arrival, Thomas and Stephen were finishing their chores. Together, they swept the kitchen floor, one wielding the broom, the other a dustpan. "I was pretty nervous when I came here," Stephen admits. "I couldn't understand what anyone said. The other kids could play ball and swim. I had never been swimming, so I was afraid to jump in the pool."

His memories of those first few fear-filled days are hazy now, but he does remember Jimmy, the oldest Williams boy, teaching him to play basketball. "We walked around and looked around a lot," he recalls.

The image that sticks in Jill's mind is one of two wild little colts, energetic as could be, but halting and, at times, awkward with the newness of it all. The fact that they came when they were school-age children, not infants, made a difference, Jill found.

"I did not bond with them in the same way that I bonded with younger ones," she says. "I missed their cute years. I know I love them like a parent, but the bonding is different."

Others who have adopted older children discover they face a unique, but usually rewarding, challenge. Claudia Jewett, author of an authoritative book on the subject entitled *Adopting the Older Child,* reassures parents that deep love and bonding will come about.

> The love I feel for the children who came to us at thirteen, fourteen, and seventeen is in no way less strong than the love I feel for the children who came to us at the younger ages of two, five, ten, and eleven. The love I feel for our adopted children is in no way less strong than the love I feel for the three children in our family who were born to us. It just doesn't make any difference. It is the caring and sharing that count—love is not prevented by the things and the time that you haven't shared.[1]

Elizabeth Hormann, author of *After the Adoption,* acknowledges that the bonding is different with older children. At the same time, it may be easier. School-age children separated from their birth families are often very eager to be adopted, and willing to make the new arrangement work. Mrs. Hormann points out they are less likely to fantasize about recovering or repairing the past.

The school-age child is far less predictable than an infant or toddler. To a large extent, his or her personality is formed. Past experiences shape the child's response to new circumstances. It is not surprising to see older adopted children regress, wanting to sit on laps for instance, or crawl, or wet their beds.

Some of these children may crave physical affection from parents; others may be distant and touchy. It is up to the parent to be observant and sensitive.

Elizabeth Hormann points out,

> Much of your bonding will take place as you share activities and talk with your child. The school-age child may express her need to be near you by "shadowing" you, by "being underfoot," by asking seemingly hundreds of questions. You can expect to spend much more time and effort with a child who is adopted at this point than you would with a child who had been living with you all along. There is a lot of catching up to do as you build your relationship, and usually a lot of making up for difficult experiences she had earlier.[2]

When the child is adopted cross-culturally, the adjustments are greater still. Frances Koh, an expert on Korean adoption, notes that Korean children past the age of 4 or 5 are stamped with the Confucian culture of their homeland. In many ways, it is exactly opposite from the taken-for-granted aspects of life in America.

Korean and other Oriental societies tend to value the group, not the individual, so dependency is fostered from an early age and independent expression is discouraged.

"Emotional passivity is fostered by strong parental authority and lack of verbal give-and-take," Frances Koh observes.[3] Korean children are generally indulged by their parents up to the age of 6; after that, discipline is administered very strictly.

At the Williamses', Thomas and Stephen performed well in school and on the playing field. Pat and Jill took each day's ups and downs as they came. Through it all, they were delighted with their new sons. But something had to happen with the house. Keeping the twins in a sitting room shared by baby Michael just would not work forever. So on November 6, 1987—six months after Stephen and Thomas arrived—all ten Williams family members moved out of their home and into a tiny, three-bedroom place with a postage-stamp yard. There they remained for the next seven months, while their house was renovated.

The expansion, which included adding a second floor and doubling the square footage from four thousand to eight thousand feet, was planned not only to accommodate their eight children. Already, the idea of adopting again—perhaps a daughter this time—had crossed both Pat's and Jill's minds.

Again, it began with a phone call to Holt. "I know we can't have any more kids from Korea," Pat said, "but what about the Philippines?"

"You won't believe this," said Betsy Guinn at Holt. "I have photos here of two different groups of brothers, available for adoption. I'll send them both your way."

Meanwhile, four Filipino brothers at Bethany Christian Home for Children in Mindanao were flipping through a copy of *Moody Monthly*. They paused and stared at a picture of the Williams family and an excerpt of their book *Rekindled,* featured in the Christian family magazine. "Could we go and live with this family?" they asked the woman they lived with.

Louise Lynip, the 75-year-old woman who runs Bethany, smiled at their innocence, concealing the pain that tugged at her insistently. Just who would take in these brothers, before it was too late? She had no idea that the boys' flight of fantasy about joining a unique Florida family was about to come true.

5

And Then There Were Twelve

In a Philippine courtroom in 1988, four skinny boys stood in a row before a judge's bench. A social worker, Rose Longcob, stood nearby, waiting quietly as the judge sifted through a stack of paperwork. "Has their natural mother relinquished her rights?" the judge asked. Rose said yes. The woman had last visited her four sons one month earlier, Rose told the judge, and she had signed an affidavit saying, "I do not have a permanent home or employment and have surrendered the four children because I am incapable of caring for them."

Turning to the four boys, the judge asked, "Do you understand what we are doing here?" Leifvan, the oldest at age 9, stared at the floor. Stiff with anxiety, he quickly nodded yes. "When did you last see your father?" the judge asked. Leifvan kept his eyes cast down. "I do not remember," he said.

Sighing, the judge executed an order declaring the boys

abandoned and neglected. *There are so many of these,* the judge thought. *What will become of them?* Straightening the papers, he dismissed Rose and the children. Now they were legal wards of the Philippine Department of Social Welfare and Development, living at Bethany Christian Home for Children. The four brothers had been at the group home, run by Louise Lynip, since 1986.

Before that, they had no place to call home. They had spent a lot of time on their own, on the streets of their rural village. Out there, the rules of survival were simple, if brutal. Leifvan had shouldered the responsibility of feeding his younger brothers, at an age when most boys are riding yellow buses to grade school. "If I didn't find food," he recalled years later, "we did not eat."

Life had not always been so hard. Leifvan could dimly remember different days, long ago. For several years, their mother and father had lived together although they never married. The father was a construction worker, who met the mother while he was out on a job, away from his home. After their fourth son was born, the truth came out: He had another wife in another city, where he used a different name.

The father left the family and went to Manila. He promised to send money and letters, but they never heard from him again. Because the family lived in extreme poverty even when the father was present, the boys had had little education or health care.

Their mother began seeing a different man, who was unemployed and indifferent to the boys. A social worker in the Philippines who reviewed their case wrote, "The attention of the mother was then focused on this man, and the children began to feel insecure, unwanted, and depressed." The mother's family had no interest in assisting her with the boys. For a period of time, they lived with their mother and grandmother. Later, it became apparent that the grandmother cruelly abused at least one of the boys.

When the mother's second common-law husband deserted her, she took her boys to the social welfare authorities, who placed them at Bethany. Eventually, she yielded her right to raise the boys and freed them to be placed with a family.

The social worker's write-up on them concludes,

> These children are really in need of a permanent substitute home where they could experience a wholesome way of living that they never experienced with their natural parents. They long to have a father and mother who could give them lifetime love and who could provide them their needs.

A background paper telling their story arrived at the Williams home shortly after Pat had called Holt to inquire about adopting a child—perhaps a daughter. With the report on the boys came four individual color photos, showing Leifvan, age 9; Marty, 8; Windell, 7; and Artem, 4. Pat and Jill stared at the smiling faces, framed by black hair. Each boy posed self-consciously on the porch of Bethany Christian Home, wearing tube socks and sneakers, identical dark shorts, and white shirts. Their eyes sparkled, and their faces reflected none of the hardship they had endured.

Together, Pat and Jill cried as they read the story. Holt also sent them photos and background on two other Filipino brothers, the older of whom was just about Jimmy's age. When they learned the two brothers would not be ready for placement for another year, Pat and Jill said no. Then they began searching their souls to discern whether there was room at home—and in their hearts—for four more children . . . all boys.

It was the toughest decision they have ever faced, coming hard on the heels of Thomas and Stephen's arrival and in the midst of their house renovation. One day Jill returned home after driving the children to school. She slammed the door and collapsed in a chair, not saying a word.

Pat had not yet left for work. "Something wrong?" he asked. Jill shook her head slowly, in disbelief. Not a day went by, it seemed, without the kids forgetting some critical item. It meant a second round-trip in the van, all the way into Orlando where the children attended a Christian school, The First Academy, affiliated with their church.

Today, it was Jimmy and Bobby. Both of them forgot their lunches. "I'll go deliver them," Pat said without hesitation. Later that day he made a cryptic entry in his journal. "Maybe no more kids. . . ."

Still, neither of them could get the four Filipinos off their minds. Long conversations with officials at Holt assured Pat and Jill that the boys were in good shape physically and emotionally, good candidates for placement, yet exceedingly hard to place because the oldest was going on 10 . . . and there were four of them.

Separating them into different adoptive homes would be considered only as an extreme last resort, since it is best to keep brothers and sisters together if at all possible. And the boys themselves were adamant; they wanted to stay together.

Pat and Jill wrestled with the decision for a full six weeks. "How will we drive the kids anywhere?" Jill would ask. "We just have an eight-passenger minivan. And think of all that laundry. . . ." Pat, whose living has always been made in the mercurial world of sports, was suddenly gripped by the reality of paying school tuition for twelve children. And what about college? "We were scared to death," Pat remembers.

Jill began praying about the decision. "I had a picture of myself married with lots of children . . . maybe even six. I never pictured twelve. But I feel called to adopt, even though I never would have asked for this many. The Lord just impressed adoption on our hearts, and we can't get away from it."

As she prayed, Jill listed all the reasons why they should say no to the four brothers. "Lord, we're doing great, everything is terrific, we don't need any more kids."

Practically speaking, it just wouldn't work. After all, the design for their new house was completed, and construction was under way. Housing four more boys . . . why, that would mean converting the kids' downstairs playroom into a bedroom; adding extra closets, maybe another bathroom.

Before she knew it, Jill had the blueprints out on the table, pencil in hand, discussing change orders with the builder. "Are you nuts, Mrs. Williams?" the bewildered builder, Donney Rex, asked.

And then there was Jimmy. The Williamses' oldest boy was 13, and suddenly more tuned in than ever to the opinions of his friends and classmates. Already, he endured a lot of teasing. "What do your parents think they're doing? Running an orphanage?" kids would ask.

He could just imagine what they'd say if he suddenly had four more brothers. Jimmy was a mature, self-possessed kid, but the taunts were getting to him.

Pat and Jill convened more than one family conference as they considered adopting the four brothers. Always, Jimmy voted no. "I didn't think I was up to it," Jimmy says. "The numbers just seemed too high." Jimmy feared the level of sacrifice that might be required to accommodate four more brothers. "He worried that the things he was used to, the activities he enjoyed, would be gone forever, ripped out of his life, because of the Filipinos," Pat realized. The rest of the children harbored no apparent qualms.

Bobby, in particular, never wavered in his enthusiasm. "I like having a big family," he announced. "There is always somebody to play with." The girls protested loudly that it was time to adopt another sister, but Sarah, Andrea, and Karyn had to admit the Filipino boys looked and sounded like good brothers.

Pat and Jill wrestled long and hard before replying to Holt. At ten-thirty one night, both of them tossed and turned in bed, trying to come to grips with the idea of twelve children. They got up, turned on the light, and stared—again—at the photographs of these vulnerable, small boys.

Then Pat got on the phone. "Lorraine," he said, "could you come over right away and talk this through with us?" Lorraine dragged herself out of bed, flipped off the television, and headed for the Williamses. She remembers finding them hunched over a table, with all the Philippine paperwork spread out before them. The house was dark except for a single light over the table.

Lorraine just listened while Pat and Jill said it all

again. "We're really struggling," Pat told her. "We feel the Lord is calling us to take these boys, but we have no idea how we'll do it." Added Jill, "The house additions are planned already, and besides, Jimmy doesn't want four more brothers."

Thinking back over the tough decisions her family had faced as they adopted thirteen children, Lorraine offered some advice. "Our oldest son has not been in favor of all of our adoptions," she said, "but we believe the parents need to make decisions like this. If you feel God is calling you to do this, then you need to be responsible to God. Jimmy can get through it. Just work with him."

Then came a pep talk. "You can do it," Lorraine assured them. "You run an organized, well-disciplined household, and your other adoptions have made you happier than your wildest dreams. I think you should go ahead, since you are so captivated by these boys."

Before he called Holt to say yes, Pat sat down alone with Jimmy. "Jim, your mom and I are going to adopt the four brothers. This is our call, and we hope you won't fight us on it. We believe the Lord is bringing us these boys, just as he brought you here and all the others. Besides," Pat added, "we are probably a last resort for these guys. Who else will adopt four brothers? We can do it."

Jimmy didn't have much to say, but he let his dad know it was okay. "I'm not going to fight you," he said with a smile.

From his office, Pat telephoned Holt. "The answer is yes. We would like to bring home the four Filipino brothers." He hung up the phone, feeling light-headed but overwhelmingly relieved. *It's scary*, he thought, *but I know it's right.*

In a matter of weeks, all the paperwork was completed

and filed. The waiting began. The boys could arrive as soon as May 1, Holt told Pat, but there were no guarantees. On June 6, the Williamses reoccupied their renovated house—complete with modifications for the four brothers. Jill put two sets of bunk beds in the downstairs playroom, just in case the Filipinos came before their bedrooms were finished.

Pat and Jill swore their kids to secrecy. When visitors asked about the bunk beds, Jill breezily replied that the kids liked to have friends stay overnight frequently (which is true), so they set up extra beds. No one suspected that another adoption was coming.

Back in Mindanao, Louise Lynip, the elderly woman who watched the boys at Bethany, picked up the mail one day and was delighted to find a copy of *Moody Monthly,* a Christian family magazine published in Chicago. As she thumbed through it, she came across an article about the Williams family. It was an excerpt from their book *Rekindled.*

The boys wanted to see what the day's mail had brought, and they looked with Louise at the magazine article. A large color photograph showed a beaming couple, surrounded by children. Some of those kids don't even look like the parents! the boys pointed out.

They begged Louise to read to them about this unusual couple. "Could we go and live with them too?" the youngest one, Artem, asked. They had no clue that thousands of miles away, the Williamses were studying photos of them and asking essentially the same question.

Finally, a representative of Holt contacted officials at Bethany Christian Home for Children. "There is a family in Florida," the woman said, "that wants to adopt the four brothers. Their name is Williams, and they have eight children, four of whom are adopted."

Louise radiated joy as she gathered the four boys and told them the news. Together, they studied their well-worn copy of *Moody Monthly,* with the Williamses' photo and story. The boys' impoverished upbringing prevented them from understanding exactly what this change in family identity meant to them, but they began dreaming and fantasizing nonetheless. None of them appeared to experience the fear and anxiety that gripped Stephen and Thomas before they came home.

Holt advised the Williamses to put together an album and send it to the boys, so they could get used to the names and faces of their new family. One day in the mail, Louise found a homemade booklet, brightly bound with floral wallpaper. It was filled with photos and messages from Pat, Jill, and all their children.

Leifvan turned the pages while his brothers crowded close to get a look. "We are your mother and father," Louise read as the boys studied the photo. "We are very excited that you are coming to be our boys. We'll have a great time together playing ball, swimming, and learning many new things. . . . Please come soon. We love you very much."

On the next page was a photo of Jimmy and a note telling how much he likes to surf, water-ski, and play basketball. "I am glad you are coming to live with us," he wrote. Bobby was unrestrained in his eagerness. "I can't wait until you come here to live with us," he wrote. "It's fun having a lot of kids to play with."

Stephen and Thomas wrote brief sentences, saying that they were adopted from Korea. "We are a big, happy family," wrote Andrea. At the end of the album were pictures of the Williamses' home and the lake in back of the house. Another photo showed the Williams family clustered around a globe. "We are looking on the globe for the Philippine islands," Jill wrote. "We have your picture on the table and we are talking about having you come to live with us."

Louise told the boys that their adoptive family had chosen new names for them. Leifvan sounded out his new name: "Da-vid." Marty decided he did not like the name chosen for him: Peter. Windell would be known as Brian; and little Artem would be called Samuel. Pat and Jill had considered using Marty's given name because it is so familiar in the United States. They decided to change it, however, since the other three boys were being renamed.

Summer dragged into fall, and the waiting continued. Finally, a letter came from Louise, telling Pat and Jill that she planned to take the boys to Manila on October 18. Because they expected to leave in a few days, the five of them made arrangements to stay at Holt's office there, sleeping on cots. Every evening, Louise would wash out the boys' clothing and hang it up to dry, draping underwear and socks over file cabinets and chairs.

Days went by, and then weeks, and the U.S. embassy would not budge, wouldn't release the boys to travel to the United States, because officials claimed that the brothers tested positive for tuberculosis. Finally, Louise obtained the test results and X rays, consulted two medical experts, and was told that the boys did not have tuberculosis.

The embassy insisted on retesting the boys, so Louise trooped them back to a clinic. A day later, a typhoon swept through Manila, flooding city streets with up to seven feet of water. The tuberculosis tests were swept away in the flood, so still the boys and Louise waited.

During the day, they watched television or walked the streets. In the evening, they went out with Louise for a simple dinner and some candy and then went home to the Holt office. This went on for nearly one month, before the U.S. embassy—prodded by a letter from Pat and Jill's U.S. senator, Bob Graham—approved their travel to America.

In early November, about a week before they came home, Louise telephoned the Williamses. "Would you like to speak to your boys?" she asked. Would they! It was early morning in Orlando, so Jill hurriedly gathered all the children out of bed. They all lay on the floor together in the master bedroom, with the speaker phone on. It was evening in Manila, and the Filipinos were getting ready for bed.

"Hello?" said Jill, tentatively. "We hope you will get to come home soon." On their end, the brothers stood practically on top of one another, twisting the telephone cord around their fingers and jockeying to listen. David said a few words, and then Sammy grabbed the receiver.

"Hi," he announced. Jill could tell this was her youngest boy, and she warmed to his engaging voice immediately. "You character," she said. "Put David back on the line." Sammy just laughed and held tight to the receiver, basking in the attention and the delight in his new mommy's voice.

Finally, on November 9, the phone call came. Louise and the boys were en route, scheduled to arrive the next day at 11:30 P.M. Pat was at work when Jill called with the news, so he gathered the Magic staff together and told them. They were shocked speechless.

So was Pat's mother—almost. "When do you plan to stop?" she asked Pat. "At twenty?" The product of a family with proud, historic roots, Pat's mother had trouble getting used to the idea that her only son was busy grafting all these new members—foreigners!—onto the cherished family tree. Even when Pat and Jill were awaiting Andrea and Sarah, Pat's mother told them bluntly, "You can't expect me to love them because they are not flesh-and-blood relatives." Pat wasn't rattled in the slightest. "I predict it will take you about thirty seconds to fall in love with them," he told his mother. She has warmed up to all the adoptees increasingly as the years have gone on.

Jill's parents, Emil and Mildred Paige, reacted differently. They warmly embraced the idea of four more grandchildren—all at once! In a letter to Pat and Jill, they wrote,

> We wish you God's best in connection with your first-round draft choice of four boys. . . . With the kind of love and concern you are giving all your children, we feel sure that all, including the adopted ones, will honor you and be a real credit to you and the Christian family everywhere.

Enclosed in a bulky envelope with the letter were four tie-dyed T-shirts for the boys.

The boys' flight from the Philippines to Orlando included a two-hour layover in Chicago, where the Paiges lived at the time. They drove to O'Hare to greet the four brothers. Off the plane they came, completely exhausted but happy to meet their new grandparents. The Paiges gave each boy an envelope with a dollar inside, and the brothers eagerly held the envelopes up to the light to see what was in them.

"They just kept clinging to us," Mildred recalls. "They understood who we were, and called us *grandma* and *grandpa.*" Then they boarded the airliner for the flight to Florida.

Meanwhile, late on the night of November 10, 1988, Pat, Jill, and their children gathered once again at an airport gate. Last off the plane came Louise Lynip, herding the four brothers along in front of her. The boys wore grins the size of melon slices as they looked at the faces they had long since memorized.

"Dad!" they said to Pat. And "Mam!" (instead of "Mom") to Jill. They quickly named all eight children, but they could not tell Stephen apart from Thomas. Their English was technically good, but the nuances of the language remained foreign to them. Their soft voices and singsong accents made them all the more endearing.

Jill drove all twelve children home in the van, while Pat and Louise waited for the luggage. There wasn't much. Each boy came with a single knapsack containing two shirts, a pair of slacks, underwear, and socks. They would not have had any extra clothes if they had not been delayed in Manila for so long. Louise felt compelled to clothe the boys more adequately during their long wait, so she bought them several items. The brothers also brought with them a memory book and some greeting cards from other children and house parents at Bethany.

Jill quickly learned how challenging it is to bring home four exuberant school-age boys. They entered the house and almost immediately began arm wrestling with their new brothers and sisters, holding impromptu push-up contests, and jumping on the furniture ... the formal sofa in the living room, and the overstuffed couches in the Florida room. Suddenly, they seemed to be everywhere. And out of control.

"In America we do not jump on the furniture," Jill said sternly. The boys obeyed at once. They were bursting with nervous energy, and the other Williams kids were getting wound up as well.

In a few moments, a pair of headlights glared through the window. Karyn, Sarah, and Andrea shouted, "Daddy's home."

The Filipino boys had a plan. "Hide, hide," they said. So all the children dove for cover—behind curtains, under cushions, jammed between the side of the piano and the wall.

Jill played along; when Pat and Louise came in, she said, "You should be very proud of me. I've put all the children to bed. They're all down and sleeping." Pat fell for it. "Wow," he remarked.

Right on cue, all the children jumped out and surprised him, shouting and laughing. Pat was buried in an avalanche of hugs. The Filipinos were home at last, and the Williams family began adjusting to these newly grafted limbs.

Jill put all four of them to bed in one room, in the bunk beds. Unlike the first two pairs of adopted children, these four boys went right to sleep that night and every night since then. The next day, the brothers ate like starving horses, and all the other children stayed home from school to get acquainted. The Filipinos stayed home for two weeks before Jill enrolled them in the same Christian school her other children attended.

The depth of the cultural chasm the boys had crossed

quickly became evident. Jimmy and Bobby took them fishing on the lake the first day, and the Filipinos insisted on making their own fishing rods out of sticks and strings. They wanted nothing to do with automatic rods and reels.

David collected scraps from around the house and made a kite, and Peter decided to plant a garden in the backyard. Jill came after each of them with her barber's scissors and electric razor, and when she was done, they all had been "buzzed."

The four boys gathered tentatively around the pool, watching Stephen and Thomas splash and shriek at each other. They couldn't swim, but they climbed in the shallow end and began splashing as well. And they rode bikes, played basketball, and got the obligatory lesson in baseball from Pat.

All at once, in the afternoon, the backyard seemed strangely quiet. Jill walked through the house quickly, glancing out the windows. There were Andrea and Sarah, playing quietly. Stephen and Thomas were out by the lake. Jimmy and Bobby and Karyn were indoors. The three youngest Filipinos were in the library. But where was David? Jill broke into a run as she headed for the front door, grabbing her purse and car keys.

She revved the engine of the van and pulled out of the neighborhood onto Lee Road. There, about a block and a half from home, one wiry boy with a fresh crew cut stormed down the sidewalk. Jill pulled into the parking lane next to him.

"David!" she called. "Where are you going?"

"I'm running away, Mam."

"Why?"

"Because Thomas hit me." Jill could see the hurt and

anger in David's eyes. So much was happening so fast that he felt he needed an escape of some sort.

"But, David," Jill said patiently, "where will you sleep tonight?"

David shifted uncomfortably from one foot to the other. "On the sidewalk?"

"And what will you eat for breakfast?" Jill persisted.

"I don't know."

Jill felt her irritation melt away, and she stepped out of the van to open the passenger door. "Get in the car and come home!"

This was a far cry from the earlier adoptions, Pat and Jill were beginning to realize. These boys were older and streetwise; they were used to doing whatever they wanted to do, whenever they wanted to do it. And David was used to being in charge. "Suddenly, he couldn't go anywhere without telling me," Jill says. "It was a very difficult adjustment."

David rode off on a bicycle one afternoon, and Jill had no idea where he went. *He's been here long enough to know better,* she reasoned, so she did not set off to search for him as she had on that first day. The other children all showed up, and Jill served dinner, but still no David. An hour after the dishes were done, he breezed into the driveway, turning lazy circles on his bike on the way to the garage. Jill's lips tightened as David headed toward the kitchen, expectantly. "You missed dinner, David. I'm sorry. You will have to wait until breakfast to eat."

Slowly, painfully, David began yielding his sense of leadership and independence to these new parents, who cared so consistently about where he was and what he was doing.

The hard realities of their family life in the Philippines

meant these brothers hadn't experienced normal childhoods. There were no toys, apart from what they made for themselves, no stimulation to learn and wonder, no attentive parent to observe and nurture a spark of individuality.

This became clear to Jill as she watched them play outdoors one day soon after they arrived. There was Peter, sawing branches off a tree with tools he had taken without permission from her toolbox. Then the four brothers lined up some toy trucks—old beat-up playthings of Michael's. She watched, fascinated, as the Filipino brothers tied strings on the trucks and pulled them around the yard.

"They needed to be little boys for a while, playing with pull toys," she realized. They worked simple puzzles by the hour and especially loved riding bikes. They habitually picked through trash bags by the curb, salvaging broken bits of plastic, metal, cardboard, or wire to fashion makeshift toys.

Jill's patience with the boys wore thin over simple matters of everyday hygiene. They were not accustomed to brushing their teeth, washing their hands, or chewing their food with mouths closed. Jill bit her tongue day after day as the boys sat at the table with black, grimy hands. Kindly she would remind them—again—that they must wash up first. "Breaking old habits and retraining these children was tremendously difficult. The older they are, the harder it is. I keep praying that by the time they're eighteen, they'll each remember one or two good habits!"

When it came time to enroll them in school, Jill met with the principal to explain their background. The two oldest boys had been working at a second-grade level, but the principal insisted on placing them by age in more advanced grades. Jill disagreed, but the principal wouldn't budge. "They'll catch on," he told her.

They didn't, and partway through their first school year, two of the boys, including David, were placed in lower grades. David liked it much better. "We told him we wanted him to be where he could do his best work," Jill says, and emotionally, David felt more at home as well.

Sammy moved from first grade to kindergarten, while Peter remained in fourth grade and Brian stayed in third grade. The following year, each boy repeated his grade at a different school, The Maitland Christian School, with six other Williams kids; after that they matched stride with their American classmates.

Pat and Jill wanted the four boys to learn to swim pronto, so their large backyard pool would not be a hazard for them. Jill took them to their first lesson at the pool where daughter Sarah worked out with the swim team. She was embarrassed to death. "The swim coaches kept trying to get their attention, and they were off splashing and giggling at the opposite end of the pool. All of them seemed so uncoordinated, flailing in the water."

At the end of the useless lesson, Jill walked well ahead of the boys on their way back to the van. She didn't want them to see how humiliated she felt at that moment. And she hoped none of the other swim team parents had seen her with these incredibly unruly boys.

In just a matter of months, however, coaches Harry and Kevin Meisel saw the Filipino boys in a whole new light. Not only had they learned to swim; they were as agile as a school of porpoises. They were winners. The coaches dubbed them "Brown Sugar," and got them signed up for swim team competitions.

Pat was bursting with pride, and he carved out time in his schedule to attend every possible meet. "Peter's got a great backstroke," he enthused. "And Brian won a state relay—he placed top among several hundred swimmers in freestyle. He got ribbons in three events, and it was only his second meet."

Pat and Jill had another reason to be proud. Jimmy, who had mustered all his teenage resources to block the adoption, had emerged as a true friend and brother to the Filipinos. "His school friends dropped all the nonsense about an orphanage," Jill says, once they met the Filipinos and got to know them. In fact, the "big kids" began to invite David and Peter to surf with them at the beach.

Jimmy recalls the early days with the Filipinos as wild ones. "We had to tell them five times over to do something. They would cheat or play dirty at sports or games, and they liked to do a lot of stuff on their own. In the Philippines, no one would do it for them."

Unfamiliar with their new names, the brothers continued to use their old names for several weeks. Meanwhile, it often appeared they were hard of hearing. "Brian," Pat would say. "Brian, BRIAN." Still no answer. Brian had heard his father just fine . . . he simply forgot to answer to that particular name.

In just one year after their arrival, radical changes were evident in all the boys, but particularly in David's behavior. He was thriving in school, pulling A's and B's and soaking up everything his teachers had to offer. In October, a new student entered David's class. Aaron seemed lonely, David thought, so he went out of his way to talk to the new boy, to sit by him at lunch. One day Aaron's mom invited David to spend the night.

David, with no prompting from Jill, wrote Aaron a thank-you note:

> Dear Aaron,
> Thank you for inviting me at your house. I have a lots of fun trading baseball cards, playing basketball in the rain, playing soccer in the backyard, and also when we're watching TV. . . . Aaron, you're the first friend who invites me at your house. I am your best friend.

Aaron was having difficulty with his history lessons, so David began tutoring him informally. "It's absolutely amazing," says Jill. "One year before this, David was a drowning man at school. Now he's the tutor."

Change was evident elsewhere in the Williams household, too. Not long after the Filipinos arrived, Jimmy knew he'd had an authentic change of heart. He showed the four brothers how to hook up an inner tube behind the family's motorboat and ride crazily across the water, bumping hard on the wake.

The Filipinos loved it, and they clearly looked up to their oldest brother. Already, David, Peter, Brian, and Sammy meant more to Jimmy than just four more pairs of shoes getting mixed up in front of the house. They weren't just numbers anymore, they were individuals; and more than that, they really were brothers. Jimmy grasped what his parents had tried to tell him even before the boys arrived: "They are part of us."

6
Preparing to
Adopt

By bringing an adopted child home, a couple builds a family. By growing in love for one another, to the point where the child and the parents feel irreplaceably linked, they become a family. At first, Jimmy seriously doubted his own ability to "become" family to the Filipinos. Similarly, many couples and individuals who consider adoption wonder, "Will it work?" Or perhaps more to the point, "Can I be a successful adoptive parent?"

Most adoptions succeed, but not all of them. The few placements that end when a child is removed from the adoptive home are known as *disruptions*. Generally, it happens before the adoption is finalized and the child becomes a legal member of the family. If it happens after an adoption is finalized, it is known as a *dissolution*.

There is no firm data on how many adoptions do not work out. Various studies show only a small fraction of adoptions disrupt or dissolve, while overall more than 90 percent succeed in establishing a true family bond.

When there is a threat of disruption, it often happens when an older child is placed. Children who have been abused, who have moved from home to home, and who have serious behavior disorders are more likely to be involved in placements that do not work.

Several factors have been linked with successful adoptions, even in cases where older, troubled children are involved. They include full, honest disclosure about the child to the adopting parents; a firm commitment on the part of both parents to make the adoption work; and thorough follow-up by the social worker after placing the child.

The track record of adoption is one of phenomenal success. In fact, it probably brings about stable, satisfying family relationships more predictably than blood ties. That is not surprising, considering how much thought, deliberation, planning, and dreaming go into an adoption before it happens!

Still, wondering whether adoption will work is a natural first step in preparing to adopt. Most adoption agencies look for particular qualifications in potential adoptive parents, as well as certain child-rearing attitudes and motives. A couple looking into adoption can expect to hear this question up front: "Why do you want to adopt a child?"

Motives

The natural jitters of any parent-to-be are intensified for potential adopters. They envision facing a formidable battalion of social workers, persuading them to entrust a child to their permanent care. "What if we fail? What if we're not good enough?"

It is the job of social workers and others who assist in arranging adoptions to guard the best interests of the children being placed. Yet it is not their job to put potential parents through a grand inquisition. The process for approving a couple for adoption is known as a *home study,* and its purpose is not to incite terror, but to assist a couple in determining what sort of child—if any—is right for them.

Early on, the question of motives will come up. It may be tempting for potential adopters to get defensive. "No one ever asks pregnant women why *they* want children," a couple may feel like shouting.

More likely, the couple may feel obliged to respond with uncharacteristic eloquence, weaving an elaborate rationale. Social workers have heard it all: adopting couples may want to please a parent or in-law; they may want a companion for a birth child, or someone to keep them company in old age. The reason most social workers are waiting to hear, however, is so obvious it may simply be overlooked.

At heart, the most authentic reason for wanting to adopt a child is because a person likes children. He or she enjoys their company, delights in their progress, is engaged by their games and antics. That is what social workers consider a valid motive, and one that will endure through difficult times.

Sentiments about rescuing a child out of the clutches of poverty are not going to impress an adoption agency, and they may even lead a social worker to wonder whether such idealistic people can possibly cope with the day-to-day rigors of child rearing.

In her classic book *Adopting the Older Child,* Claudia
Jewett addresses the confusing issue of motives.

> We didn't adopt out of pity, although compas-
> sion was there; we adopted because we deeply
> wanted a larger family and we felt that this was
> a good way to go about it. We didn't see adop-
> tion as a cause, although social consciousness
> was there; we adopted because we really like to
> be parents, and because we felt there was no
> need to reproduce ourselves again. We didn't
> adopt because we are noble, unusual people; we
> adopted in spite of our shortcomings, because
> we wanted each of the children who came to join
> us.[1]

For Pat and Jill, the motivation to adopt was admit-
tedly unusual. Jill appeared to possess an inexplicable
urge to adopt from the time she was a young girl. It was
as if adoption were in her genes. For Pat, it was simply
one more way of reaching out to an estranged wife. And
yet, once he experienced adoption, there was no stopping
him. If ever there was a testimony to the fact that adoption works, Pat's story is it.

For most people, the motivation to adopt comes after,
or during, a long struggle with infertility or multiple
miscarriages. A couple may discover, to their great surprise, that their reproductive systems do not work as they
are supposed to. This happens to about one in every six
couples in the United States today, and for a variety of
reasons, that number is increasing.

The infertile couple must grieve the loss of their reproductive abilities, and the loss of a "dream child" who will

never exist. They must cope with anger and depression and isolation—all the bad feelings that accompany grief. As they approach resolution, and the dark clouds begin to lift, they may find they are ready to move ahead confidently and energetically toward adoption.

Yet, as the Williams family so clearly demonstrates, adoption is not just for nonparents yearning to hold a baby in their arms. The real challenge of adoption presents itself in the form of waiting children and hard-to-place kids who may thrive best in a setting where there are other children. They may need seasoned, dedicated parents with a proven track record.

For parents like these, the motive to adopt is twofold. They like children and enjoy the challenges and rewards of raising them. In addition, they recognize the compelling need of waiting children to find homes *now,* before they spend an entire childhood in an institution or in foster care, without the stability and sense of belonging offered by a permanent family.

Why would anyone want to adopt a child bearing the scars of abuse and neglect? Jacqueline Plumez, in the book *Successful Adoption,* explains.

> Adopting one of these children is a big step and a big commitment. Parents who have done it will readily admit they often ask themselves why in the world they did such a foolish thing! But they also speak of the pride they take in their child's accomplishments, of the good feelings they get for providing the chance of a better life and of the love that grows as a homeless child is transformed into a son or daughter.
>
> There are stories of almost miraculous

changes in children. Many considered retarded
have become average learners. . . . Many withdrawn children learn to laugh and crippled children learn to walk given love, attention and
encouragement.[2]

Pat and Jill joke frequently about the two types of ques-
tioners they meet, over and over. The first is incredulous.
"*Why* have you adopted so many children?" they ask in
disbelief. The second is more thoughtful; generally, it is a
person who has already given adoption a long, hard look.
"How do you go about it?" people ask the Williamses.

Ordinarily, when they encounter a "why" question, Pat
and Jill stay diplomatically silent, or they simply say
they enjoy having a large family. There are days, of
course, when one of them feels like saying, "Why? I have
no idea why. This is the craziest thing we've ever done!"
Or Pat will surrender to his yen for one-liners: "We really
wanted to be able to field our own baseball team," he
says, deadpan. "And besides, a man who has twelve children is more content than a man who has twelve million
dollars. The man with twelve million dollars wants
more."

There is no single answer, because the Williams family
is growing and changing daily. Adopting children is not
like acquiring kitchen appliances and explaining the reason why in terms of wanting to become a more efficient
cook.

As Christians, Pat and Jill believe their attraction toward children is God-given. In that sense, their motive to
adopt is a response to God, a sensitivity toward serving
Him in a way in which they are uniquely equipped. It is

similar, then, to the impulse that guided Harry Holt in the early days of Korean adoption.

Yet the Williamses are quick to point out that parents do not need to be unusually gifted to consider adoption. In fact, in light of the numbers of children who wait, they have come to believe adoption is an opportunity for service, ministry, and personal enrichment that ought to be considered seriously by many more individuals and families.

Some have found in God's Word a way to articulate the reasons behind adoption. They see it as a plan that was His idea to begin with!

Adoption and the Bible

The Heidelberg Catechism poses an intriguing question about Jesus Christ: "Why is He called God's only begotten Son, since we also are children of God?" The answer indicates just how important the concept of adoption is to a Christian understanding of God's plan. "Because Christ alone is the eternal, natural Son of God, but we are children of God by adoption, through grace, for Christ's sake."

In the New Testament, the word *adoption* is used to mean "sonship," indicating a full and complete relationship that is in no way inferior to God's "birth children," the people of Israel. In his letter to the Galatians, Paul explains that gentile believers receive ". . . The full rights of sons." He adds, "Because you are sons, God sent the Spirit of his Son into our hearts, the Spirit who calls out, 'Abba, Father.' So you are no longer a slave, but a son; and since you are a son, God has made you also an heir" (Galatians 4:5–7).

Adoption is the way believers come into a relationship with God. By adoption, He is truly their Father in heaven, and they are truly sons and daughters and heirs along with Jesus. As mentioned in chapter 1, the letter to the Ephesians says, ". . . In love he predestined us to be adopted as his sons through Jesus Christ, in accordance with his pleasure and will" (Ephesians 1:4, 5).

The biblical imagery paints a compelling portrait of God's love being broad enough to encompass all of mankind, willing to adopt each person as a bona fide son or daughter. And the Bible makes it clear that it is a binding, lasting relationship. There is nothing tenuous or unstable about it. It is designed to last forever, even if a believer turns his back on God. That does not change the fact of adoption.

Similarly, human adoption is a picture of unconditional love and binding promise. Even though no human adoption will approach the perfection of God's plan, the very idea mirrors His love and commitment. An adopted child's identity is transformed because of the conscious decision made by the parents. The child then becomes firmly grafted on a branch of the family tree forever, his position and heritage guaranteed by the reality of adoption.

From a purely practical standpoint, adoption also squares with a biblical understanding of God's plan and purpose. Throughout the Bible, God sides with the poor, the people abandoned on the margins of life, "the least of these." God commanded His people to care for the poor, the widowed, the orphans; and early church leaders were likewise preoccupied with supplying the needs of the poor. When an "unwanted" child becomes a valued family member, God is honored and glorified. There is one less "least of these" in need.

Many of the couples who struggle with infertility see in adoption God's perfect answer for them. Many even reach the point where they can thank and praise God for a condition they at first found unbearable, because it resulted in the formation of a family that would not have happened any other way.

Because the Bible affords such a positive view of adoption, why is it that society has been reluctant—even embarrassed—to approve and embrace the idea? Many adopting couples find themselves wondering, "How did contemporary adoption get started, anyhow?"

History

Adoption happened frequently in the ancient world, and the practice is recorded in the Old Testament. Moses was discovered among the reeds by Pharaoh's daughter, who adopted him. Abraham, the father of the nation of Israel, longed for his promised heir. In accordance with custom, he adopted Eliezer, declaring him a son and heir, before Isaac was born.

It was extremely important in ancient societies to keep families intact. Adopting a son to carry on the family name, and perhaps the family business, was widespread among the early Greeks, Romans, Babylonians, and Egyptians.

In America, adoption is widely practiced and accepted because the value of bloodlines, or "breeding," has traditionally taken a distant backseat to an individual's own talents and character. Unlike European class systems, where a person would be valued just because he or she is born into the aristocracy, the American melting pot prides itself on affording opportunity and value to all, no matter how humble one's origins may be.

Because of this, it is puzzling to see how contradictory and varied state laws can be regarding adoption. Edmund Blair Bolles, writing in *The Penguin Adoption Handbook,* notes, "our laws and social workers treat adoption as though it were something extraordinary."

The key is British common law, out of which our own legal system emerged. The British did not recognize adoption, and placed great emphasis on blood ties. Bolles explains, "Property and titles passed directly to the oldest son. If there was no oldest son, the nearest male relation was awarded the land and title. If there were no male kin, the line ended and the title fell out of use. Under this system, adoption was forbidden."[3]

Informal adoption occurred frequently, to protect a family's inheritance. Yet adopted children received no legal protection.

In colonial America, tradesmen often used orphaned children as apprentices, a practice known as *indenture.* The practice was outlawed in the mid-1800s. At about the same time, Massachusetts became the first state to pass a law formalizing the adoption process.

It required written consent by the birth parents, joint petition by both adopting parents, a judge's decree of adoption, and legal separation of the child from the birth parents. Other state legislatures followed. By 1891, Michigan law required judges to investigate before decreeing an adoption; and Minnesota was the first state to require an adoption agency or state welfare office to recommend adoptive parents to the court after the parents were investigated.

Foreign adoption came about after World War II, when European orphans were brought to America. Then in the 1950s, as a result of the Korean War, the Holt experiment opened the floodgates for foreign adoption of all sorts.

Adoption in America is regulated at the state level, as are other matters of family law. Over the years, state laws have evolved toward better protection of the interests of children placed for adoption or awaiting adoptive homes. In most cases it is possible to adopt across state lines. Most states have signed the Interstate Compact, spelling out the rules and procedures to be followed when a child is born in one state and adopted by parents living in another. It is administered by the American Public Welfare Association in Washington, D.C.

Methods

Often, an acquaintance will tell Pat or Jill, "We would love to adopt a child. We've been praying about it for years." If their friend Lorraine is in earshot, she has a ready response: "Pray? You can pray forever, but have you applied? Have you filed any paperwork or completed a home study?" For couples ready to act on their desire to adopt, here are some guidelines:

1. For general information, contact the National Adoption Information Clearinghouse, a federally funded data base, at 1400 Eye Street, N.W., Suite 600, Washington, D.C. 20005. It provides helpful information sheets on all aspects of adoption, and it keeps on file abstracts of numerous articles and technical papers about adoption.

2. Get in touch with a local group of adoptive families. An adoption agency or social welfare agency listed in the telephone book may know how to contact one. Or write to NACAC, the North American Council on Adoptable Children, 1821 University Avenue, Suite N-498, St. Paul, MN 55104. They maintain a directory of such groups. Attend a meeting or a social event. Ask adoptive parents about their experiences; get suggestions from them.

3. From the adoptive families group or from a public social welfare agency, obtain a list of all the adoption agencies licensed to place children in your state. Call or write for an application and information about what sorts of children are available. Find out how long you will have to wait, how much you will have to pay, and whether the agency imposes restrictions such as age, number of years married, or religious affiliation.

4. Begin reading literature on adoption, drawing from the bibliography and resource list at the back of this book. Subscribe to a reputable national newsletter about adoption, such as "OURS," published by Adoptive Families of America, 3307 Highway 100 N, Suite 203A, Minneapolis, MN 55422.

5. Based on what you are learning about adoption, consider all the types of children who might fit into your family. Are you equipped to cope with

the needs of a physically challenged child? Do you live in an area where there are people from different ethnic backgrounds, enabling you to consider a child from another race or culture? Does your home have plenty of space for a group of brothers or sisters waiting to be placed together? What sort of child would blend into your extended family?

6. Identify any concerns or fears you may harbor concerning adoption. Take a class or arrange to meet with adoptive parents and children. Allow them to help you put your concerns in perspective. Discuss the pros and cons of an open adoption, and come to terms with your own feelings about contact with the birth mother and father now and in the future.

7. If you opt to work with an adoption agency, get an itemized statement of fees before you apply. Ask for references, including other adoptive parents, and call them. If you choose to adopt independently, scrutinize the track record of any lawyer or adoption facilitator you work with.

8. Don't be put off by the prospect of a *home study,* or a series of meetings with a social worker to assess your readiness to adopt. The process is a helpful one, offering you and your spouse a chance to talk through expectations, fears, hopes, and dreams. You and your housekeeping are not being placed under a microscope by officials bent on finding perfect homes. The home

study assures the adopted child, and the birth mother, of careful screening before placement, and it satisfies state requirements regarding adoption. Once an application has been accepted, rare is the couple who "flunks" a home study!

9. Often you will encounter a long wait between application and the beginning of your home study, and another long wait between home study approval and the assignment of a particular child. Keep in touch with other adoptive parents and with your agency throughout the waiting period. If possible, take a class on child care; begin anticipating the arrival of a child and preparing your home to receive a son or daughter.

10. When your long-awaited day arrives, you may have very little notice. Families who adopt children from overseas often are not telephoned until a day or two before the plane is airborne; domestically, the call may come just days ahead of the time you are expected to greet your new son or daughter at the agency's office. In the rush of excitement and last-minute preparations, make certain you do not overwhelm a new arrival with too much activity, too many outings or visitors in those first days home. Instead, let the visitors wait awhile. Get to know your child quietly, in the privacy of your home. As you begin to feel confident and competent as a parent, and as the child adjusts to the rhythms of life in

your home, there will be plenty of time to introduce him or her to family and friends.

11. As you adjust to the permanent change adoption
brings into your life, stay in touch with other
adoptive families. Familiarize yourself with
adoption literature for children and speak positively about adoption with your spouse and your
child. Savor the joy of building a family, and
becoming a family.

The adoption process today has been likened to a maze.
There is no sure, direct procedure for adopting a child,
and most couples explore many avenues simultaneously.
They should tell everyone they know that they are in
search of a child to adopt. More often than not, simple
word of mouth will result in the prospect of an independent adoption. If that possibility is permitted in both the
birth mother's state and the adopting couple's state, it is
an option they may choose to pursue.

Both in the United States and abroad, people exploring
adoption need to be wary of black-market situations. A
black-market adoption is one that is characterized by extremely high expenses, a "no-questions-asked" policy by
the person offering a child, and little or no information
about the child's origins. Unfortunately, baby-selling
schemes abound, preying on the current shortage of
healthy, white American infants available for adoption.

A black market continues to thrive in Latin America
as well. Without question, it should be avoided. People
interested in adoption will know they are toying with an
unsavory deal if their contact in Latin America will not
answer questions, especially about a particular child's

origin and whereabouts; if he demands "finder's fees" or exorbitant amounts of money in advance, or asks the couple to shade the truth about the procedure to immigration officials.

Instead, it is best to work with a licensed U.S. agency with good contacts abroad. People interested in adopting should not hesitate to ask intelligent questions about the entire scope of an agency's operation:

- How do the children come into their care?
- How do they define whether a child is legally free for adoption?
- How long have they been in existence?
- What services do they provide in the country for children and birth parents?
- Who is on the board of directors?
- Do they have annual, independent audits performed, and will they release a financial statement?
- Exactly how much will the adoption cost, and will the fees be outlined in writing, in advance?

If the answers are vague or unsatisfactory, or if the cost is far greater than what other, similar agencies are charging, a couple should look elsewhere. Susan Cox advises extreme caution: "If it sound too good to be true, it probably is."

Qualifications

It's a good thing Pat and Jill wanted to adopt internationally and were open to receiving older children into their home. As they quickly learned when they first contacted Holt, there are particular qualifications that determine what sort of child will be available for placement.

Most U.S. agencies are overwhelmed with applications from couples seeking healthy newborns. For this reason, many give priority to infertile couples. Often, a doctor's statement about the length and scope of infertility treatment is required. Many agencies strongly prefer couples who have been married at least one year, and sometimes as many as three years. And they often have age restrictions as well. In order for a baby to be placed in a home, at least one parent should be no more than 40 years old; sometimes the age limit is 35; sometimes both spouses must be under a certain age.

Korea has insisted that adoptive parents be no more than forty years older than the child they adopt; older couples may adopt older children or harder-to-place sibling groups. Also, the Korean regulations have prohibited placing a child with a single parent. In Latin America, restrictions such as these are much more varied, and generally more lenient.

The religious faith of an adopting couple may make a difference if they choose to work with an agency. Adoption agencies that are affiliated with a particular denomination or theological conviction usually give priority to like-minded prospective parents. For example, Bethany Christian Services is a national network of agencies in various states. Its social workers strongly prefer evangelical Christian couples who are pro-life, and who maintain an active membership in a pro-life church.

The expense of adopting varies considerably. Ordinarily there is no charge or only a minimal fee associated with adoptions through public welfare departments. If a child with special needs is adopted, there may be money available through grants or subsidies to pay for continuing medical care.

Fees charged by private agencies vary greatly, depending on how the agency is funded and what services it provides to birth mothers. Generally, the fee paid by adoptive parents does not cover all the expenses associated with the adoption, which include the birth mother's medical expenses, foster care for the infant before the adoption, home study and post-adoption visits by social workers, and legal fees. These additional costs may be covered by foundation funds, contributions, or church denominations that sponsor agencies.

Many private agencies charge a flat fee, up to around $20,000. Others have a sliding scale based on the adopting couple's income. Independent adoptions vary even more greatly, with some being relatively inexpensive. Others can grow very costly as legal fees mount up. Like many agencies, The Adoption Centre applies for grant monies, conducts fund-raising campaigns, and uses a sliding-scale fee structure. Adopting parents with higher incomes pay more, and that helps subsidize adoptions of "hard-to-place" children.

Applicants interested in adopting older, waiting children are charged no fee. Parents interested in healthy black or biracial children pay $5,000. For other special needs children, the fee is determined on a case-by-case basis.

Applicants for healthy, white babies pay an application fee and a home study fee. For placement, the sliding scale goes into effect:

Income up to $40,000	$9,500
$40,000–$60,000	$12,500
$60,000–$80,000	$15,500
Over $80,000	$18,500

The placement fee covers medical expenses and other costs for the birth mother and child, as well as services to the adopting couple, such as the home study and post-placement counseling.

Fees for adoption vary greatly from state to state and agency to agency. In practically every case, adopting a child is much more expensive than normal pregnancy and childbirth, which is generally covered by insurance. Some leading U.S. companies address this by offering reimbursement to employees who adopt. Often, these benefits are limited to adoptions done by licensed agencies. The amount of reimbursement is often pegged to the average amount other employees have received for pregnancy and delivery.

International adoptions are not necessarily more expensive. However, parents who are required to travel to the country of their child's birth may incur greater costs.

Agencies usually ask applicants to provide complete information about their savings, retirement plans, and other aspects of their family budget. Most agencies are not looking for vast wealth; instead, they want to be certain that the money available to a family is managed well.

Some agencies require one spouse to stay home with the child for a particular number of weeks or months. If both spouses will continue working outside the home, the social worker will want to know what sort of child care the couple plans to arrange.

Above: One of eight bedrooms in the second-story addition. All but four Williams children share their bedroom with one sibling.

Below: The whole family, plus two. Counterclockwise from upper right: Thomas, Andrea, Brian, Peter, Bobby, Jill (standing), Pat, Samantha (a foster child), Sarah, Jimmy, Nicole (a foster child), Karyn, Michael, David, Sammy, and Stephen.

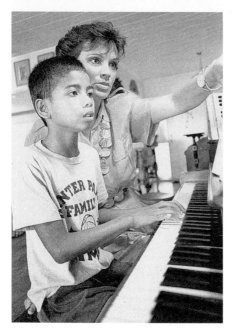

Jill coaches Peter on the piano.

Bobby shows off his baseball
card collection to Pat and Jimmy.

Jill with Karyn and Andrea, making a coil pot at a parent-child clay workshop.

Pat and Jill head out for their daily walk and talk.

Above: Everybody into the pool!

Below: Thomas and Sarah flank foster daughter Samantha, who lived with the Williams family for four months before returning to her birth father.

Future NBA draft picks in training.
Back row: Brian, Peter, Karyn, David,
Bobby. Front row: Thomas, Sammy,
Stephen.

Fancy footwork on the family's half-size
basketball court.

A lakeside family portrait. Back row: Michael, Karyn, Andrea, Peter, Bobby, Jill, and Pat. Sitting on hammock: Thomas, Sarah, Stephen. Front row, kneeling: David, Sammy, Brian, Jimmy.

Below: A quiet time in the children's playroom.

"Mom, where are my shoes?"

A series of meetings between an agency social worker and a couple wanting to adopt is scheduled to review these qualifications and assess whether the home is an appropriate place for a child to be raised. These meetings are the home study. Most of the meetings actually take place at the agency, with one or both prospective parents attending. Usually the social worker pays one visit to the home.

For the home study, each spouse prepares an autobiography or writes answers to numerous questions. Some of the questions delve into childhood experience, wanting to find out how upbringing will influence a person's style of parenting. Questions about discipline are common, and the couple must explain how they work out disagreements in the family.

Many adoptive couples find the process less scary—and more helpful—than they imagined. It offers an opportunity to indulge in some soul-searching, some dreaming, and some comparisons about life experience and expectations. All of these exercises cause the couple to focus sharply on the ways in which having a child will change their lives forever. It's a ready-made course in becoming a family, and it sustains adoptive parents through the early adjustments and beyond.

The Wait

Once a couple has applied for an adoption and completed a home study successfully, the wait begins. Adoptive couples agree there is nothing more trying than weeks and months of uncertainty about what sort of child will be joining the family—and when.

No matter how long the wait drags on, the couple keeps jumping nervously each time the telephone rings, and grows weary of well-meaning family and friends who badger them with an incessant question: "Any news yet?"

The waiting doesn't get any easier once a specific child has been assigned to a waiting couple. Having a photograph, a brief history, a medical report is often all it takes for a family to bond with a child to such an extent that they may be surprised at the intensity of their own emotions. That was the case for Pat and particularly Jill with each of their adoptions.

The Beginning

At last, *the* phone call comes, and a child is on his or her way to join a new family. In a frenzy of last-minute preparations, the parents burn up the accumulated nervous energy of the time spent waiting. Then they go to the agency, or a hospital, or an airport, or a lawyer's office to meet their new son or daughter.

The first few days and weeks at home are chaotic and at times uncertain, as everyone adjusts to new rhythms and routines. Just as a boat launched on choppy waters takes each bump hard at first, the family feels each disruption acutely. In time—a surprisingly short time, usually—the waters grow calmer and the boat sails more securely, more smoothly, more deliberately toward its destination.

Slowly, as a family bond is forged, the fact of adoption recedes, although it never disappears. It no longer holds the immediacy it did throughout all the months of preparation. Other tasks of parenting grow increasingly important, and the relationship becomes authentically one of parent and child.

An often-quoted verse, "To an Adopted" by Carol Lynn
Pearson, captures the essence of adoption:

I
Did not plant you.
True.
But when
The season is done—
When the alternate
Prayers for sun
And for rain
Are counted—
When the pain
Of weeding
And the pride of
Watching are through—
Then I will hold you
High to heaven.
A shining sheaf
Above the thousand
Seeds grown wild.

Not my planting.
But by heaven,
My harvest,
My child.

7

Twelve-Part Harmony

In a crowded roomful of couples with children, it would not be easy to pick out which parents had adopted and which had not. Adoptive parenting is certainly more similar to biological parenting than it is different. However, it is not exactly the same.

The process of grafting newly adopted children into a family brings with it some new aspects—aspects biological parents do not face. If the adopted child is older—old enough, perhaps, to remember the other family he left behind—the grafting process may be slower and require greater healing.

It is generally agreed that the most important task for parents who adopt is to provide ongoing assurance that the child belongs in the family. This happens in many ways, from expressions of physical affection to expectations that a child will conform to family rules and habits. Developing family unity, and instilling in the child a sense of belonging, is commonly called *bonding* or *attachment*.

It calls for flexibility and change on the part of all family members. The shoe incident on the day Stephen and Thomas arrived affords a good illustration of how the process begins. At first, all Jill thought of was the practical side of the matter: If the whole family practiced removing their shoes outdoors, it would make life easier all around. But her spontaneous willingness—even eagerness—to embrace a custom her adopted twins brought with them made it clear to everyone that those new arrivals belonged—and had brought with them new cultural aspects to be affirmed, not rejected.

True bonding does not happen overnight, and sometimes it takes many weeks and months. In the Williams family, real family affection developed for each set of adoptees even before they arrived. The rest of the family began incorporating the story of the toddlers, the twins, and the Filipinos into their lives and their own understanding of themselves as family.

Then when the children arrived, in various states of fear, shock, excitement, and inquisitiveness, they were welcomed enthusiastically. Pat and Jill and the other children knew *about* the new arrivals, but they didn't know *them*. Instant affection and authentic love? Yes. But real attachment, a secure sense of belonging, came later.

Why is bonding so critical? In her book *Raising Adopted Children,* Lois Melina explains,

> The attachment of parents and child does more
> than give the family a warm and fuzzy feeling—
> it creates order. The unattached child is a child

who doesn't care what people think, and therefore one who can do as he pleases. Obviously,
this can make life with the unattached child
chaotic and even dangerous.[1]

An absence of attachment on that first day home led
David to solve his quarrel with Thomas by simply running away. That was not the last time David stormed out
of the house. The Filipinos persisted for months in steal-
ing food and hoarding it in their dressers or between
mattress and bunkboard—a lousy idea in the unrelent-
ing heat of Orlando. They were not yet attached enough
to know, deep down, that there will always be enough
food for them.

Because the adopted child most often joins a family
later in life, a period of adjustment to new surroundings,
new sights and sounds, new rhythms, has to take place
before bonding is secure. Even babies as young as 6
months have been observed to "grieve" for a foster mother
or caretaker to whom they had become attached. They
may withdraw, shy away from touch, or cry a lot.

The older the child, the longer and rockier is the road
to attachment. Lois Melina notes, "All her past relationships with adults have ended in separation; she may be
worried that this one will too, and try to end it before she
gets too close. At the same time, she is drawn to the
parent."[2]

As the new adopted child adjusts, so does the rest of the
family. If another child is close to the same age as the
adopted arrival, he or she may feel particularly displaced
or threatened. That happened to Bobby, the second-oldest
homegrown Williams child, after David came along and
began to outshine him on the baseball field.

Parents usually discover they have some adjusting to do as well. Sometimes it may be as simple as recognizing cultural differences for what they are. When the Filipino boys first came home, for instance, it bugged Pat to pieces that David, in particular, would fix his eyes on the floor whenever he spoke to his mom or dad.

This isn't unusual among older adopted children, and in some cases it can be a sign that the child wants to keep the parent at arm's length. However, Pat and Jill learned that in the Philippines, children are taught to lower their eyes as a sign of respect for adults. There, it is disrespectful for a child to look an elder "in the eyes."

The harmony achieved by a couple or a family is inevitably altered when adoption introduces a new melody. The music of family familiarity must adapt to themes that echo different life experiences and a different genetic makeup. Sometimes it must accommodate the discordant notes of past abuse or neglect. It may be imperfect at times, but when harmony is restored—and attachment happens—a stronger, more unified family is the result.

Maintaining harmony in the Williams household means, of necessity, fine-tuning the details of daily life. It also means building relationships that endure the ups and downs of ordinary conflict among brothers and sisters. And it means Pat and Jill find ways daily to nurture their marriage and keep the lines of communication open.

As maestro of his family orchestra, Pat's baton is rarely still. That is why he and Jill take time each day to enjoy the calm of a morning walk before they face the music.

It is 6:30 A.M., and Pat and Jill are walking "the loop," a 1.5-mile route through their Winter Park neighborhood. For half an hour, they are alone, sort-

ing out the day's schedule, sharing bits of information and observations about their lives. It's catch-up time— a daily time they can't do without.

Pat is tuned into the kids' sports schedules, so he reminds Jill, "Three of them have to be at soccer right after school, and two have a swim meet."

Jill has a conflict: "I'm speaking at a women's luncheon from twelve to three. There's no way I can pick them up at three. Can you pick them up today?"

Oh, that's great, *Pat thinks.* I'm trying to run a ball team. *But this is a relatively slow, preseason day. "I think I can get away," he says.*

Jill is thinking ahead to the weekend. "Jimmy is invited to a party at a country club Friday night. Do you think he should go? He has a soccer game Saturday morning."

Now that Jimmy is 15, Jill is beginning to feel panicked about having him gone—off to college in just a couple years, then gone for good. "How much independence is too much?" she wonders aloud.

Pat's mind is still on sports. "David wants to play baseball in the fall, but there's a soccer coach who wants David on the team with some of the other kids. What do you think would be best for him? Oh—and before I forget—I'm invited to speak at a prayer breakfast next Wednesday. Does that fit with your calendar?"

"Speaking of breakfast," Jill says, "can we get together Thursday morning after I've dropped the kids off? I'm really feeling like we need some time together . . . sitting down."

"Hello, Lou," Pat and Jill say in unison as their jogging-suited neighbor passes them, pumping a can

*of macaroni in each hand. Pat catches a quick glimpse
of the family Chihuahua, Magic, galloping to catch
up. "Go home, Magic!" he commands.*

*"Karyn has to be at her dance class at five-thirty
three days a week," Jill remembers. "Andrea has to be
picked up from the art studio at five-thirty the same
days."*

*"Maybe Karyn could go early to the dance studio
and work on homework," Pat suggests.*

At the end of the loop, Jill walks up the long, curved
driveway to their house. Pat breaks into a jog and heads
out for a four-mile run. Indoors, the kids are helping
themselves to breakfast and getting ready for school. Jill
casts a critical eye in Peter's direction. "Is that the same
shirt you wore jogging?" Peter sets down his cereal box.
"Yes, ma'am." She reminds him once again to put his
sweaty clothing into the dirty clothes box and get out
something clean to wear after washing up.

Stephen pours oat rings into a paper bowl and takes a
spoon from a wicker basket holding a couple dozen teaspoons. He fishes through another basket on the table to
find the washcloth napkin numbered "8."

For quite a while, Jill resisted the idea of using paper
plates and bowls every day. Two things persuaded her to
give it a try. There was no way the dishwasher could
handle all the dishes generated by fourteen people daily,
eating breakfast and dinner at home. And the cost of
buying generic plates and bowls in bulk was reasonable.

Pat is ever alert for ways to simplify and streamline
their hectic lives—and besides, he reasons, the kids are
much more likely to load and unload the dishwasher

when it's their turn if there aren't mountains of dishes to be done.

The numbered napkins are another sign of streamlining. All the children's laundry is numbered, in order of their arrival in the family. So Jimmy is number 1, Bobby is 2, Karyn is 3, and so on. The Filipino boys are 9, 10, 11, and 12, beginning with the oldest.

Each week's meals are planned in advance, and Jill permits no commercial soft drinks or candy in the house. "We eat well, we get eight hours of rest at night, and I take a nap in the afternoon, when I can," Jill explains. She bakes muffins almost daily, and leftover bread gets used up in huge batches of French toast, often prepared by the girls. A typical monthly grocery bill is $1,400.

To her own surprise, Jill finds the day-to-day tasks very manageable. "I've gotten more done since I had eight or twelve children than when I had two or three. Leisure activities just go by the boards. I don't do any window-shopping, and I never read magazines. I keep good lists, and scratch off what I've accomplished. When my time is budgeted as it should be, then I know I can go out Tuesday evenings for a painting class or Wednesday mornings for photography, just for the fun of it. That's important for me. I regularly need to focus on other things. And in fact, Pat insists on it. When I have a particularly stressful few days, he will ask, 'Isn't it time for another painting class?' "

Running such a large family means tight financial budgeting as well as precise time management. "Truth is, we're broke," Pat says, only half joking. Adoption fees alone, with no tax break or insurance reimbursement, totalled $8,000 for Sarah and Andrea, $10,000 for Stephen and Thomas, and $10,000 for the Filipinos. Since then, routine expenses have taken a heavy toll. "Everything we have is invested in the new bedrooms, school tuition, and clothes." Sneakers, for instance, run about $1,200 a year for all twelve children. On top of that practically all the children need specialized sports shoes and Sunday "dress" shoes.

Often, because of the family's size, the Williamses receive discounts on food ordered in bulk. Fees for activities are sometimes lowered for a "group rate," and the Christian school where the Williams children were enrolled discounts tuition for having several children there. Nonetheless, tuition mounted up to $13,000 a year. Dental expenses for the Filipinos, in particular, were astronomical; routine checkups for all twelve Williams kids total $350 twice a year.

To compensate, school clothes consist of hand-me-downs and occasional purchases at K mart, not the local department store. The family's motorboat sat idle one summer, housed by the dock in the lake, needing repairs they couldn't afford at the time. The children know there is no money available for frivolous spending, and their enjoyment is centered instead on sports events and family times together. "We're not into designer jeans and the latest toys," Pat says. "There's not a whole lot we want."

Preparing for college debts presents the most daunting long-term financial challenge. Pat and Jill have established a special savings account earmarked for their children's education. Into it go all their earnings from speaking and singing engagements as well as book sales.

A demanding degree of discipline defines life at the Williamses. It pays off, but it is also the subject of much joking. "Living here is like going to a military academy," Pat says. The alternative is unthinkable. Chaos would reign if chores were not organized into manageable tasks.

As it is, even the youngest children can participate and gain a sense of accomplishment and belonging. Twice a week, for instance, it's laundry day. Often Jill will start a load or two before her mother comes in to finish the job.

Then it's up to the kids. Each one must find all the socks, underwear, shirts, and pants marked with his or her identifying number. Each child is responsible for folding and putting away the clean clothes. A twenty-pound box of concentrated laundry detergent lasts about a month. And the Williamses' heavy-duty washer and dryer work hard, averaging twenty loads per week.

Daily routines around the house flow smoothly now and are rarely disrupted, apart from the occasional school lunch left under the seat of the van. After-school activities pose a different challenge, as Pat and Jill's early morning conversation hints. "We could manage twenty children—easily," Pat says, adding one qualifier: "before three in the afternoon."

To manage all the kids' commitments to sports, art, or other lessons, the Williamses take it one day at a time. Both Pat and Jill have car phones, and frequently one will call the other in a panic. "There's no way I can get to the pool to pick up the boys," Jill will announce. Pat will change lanes instantly and head for the pool. Often, coaches, neighbors, and friends drive the children home. Even so, it isn't a foolproof system.

Once, no one remembered to pick Sarah up after swim practice. An hour later, when they realized what they'd done, Jill zoomed to the pool. There stood Sarah, shivering and crying on the sidewalk.

On Christmas Eve one year when a grandmother was visiting, Andrea was left behind when the van left for dinner at a friend's home. Her grandmother had told Andrea to go brush her hair; she obeyed, and meanwhile the rest of the family piled into the van and drove off.

At the dinner table, out of habit, Pat counted heads. No Andrea. "Where is Andrea?" he blurted. "Oh, she went back to comb her hair before we left," came a casual answer from one of her brothers. Fortunately, the drive home to pick her up was a short one.

"I can count from one to twelve faster than anyone in the world," Pat insists. "I find myself counting constantly, especially at the beach." Jill doesn't count—she groups them, four, four, and four. And she dresses them in look-alike T-shirts whenever six or more go anywhere together.

That strategy saved the day during a visit to Disney World. Once again, it was Andrea who was missing. Jill and five of the children climbed off a ride and gathered together at the exit. Jill's heart began pounding hard when one minute, then another, went by and Andrea didn't show up. Outside the confines of the ride milled hundreds of visitors, all moving by in quick confusion.

Jill didn't have to stop and think about what Andrea was wearing, because she had dressed all the children in black T-shirts—an unusual color for Disney visitors, she discovered. All at once, she saw a mop of dark hair atop a black shirt, wandering just outside the entrance to the ride. She swooped Andrea back into the fold.

Ferrying the kids to and from their activities on school-day afternoons places a relentless demand on Jill's time, as she logs between three and four hundred miles per week on the van. She believes her hours spent in the van are far from wasted. Often, she will have just one or two kids with her at a time, en route to pick up some of the others. Time in the van becomes a special occasion for Jill to talk at length with one child, maybe two, at a time.

All three of Jill's daughters are at an age when friends matter very much. If just one of the girls is with Jill, the conversation often dwells on the intricacies of finding and keeping good friends. "She isn't going to invite me to her birthday party. She doesn't like me," one of them will say to Jill. "Last week she liked me." Jill takes the opportunity to talk about what friendship really means. "You may not always like something a person does, but if you are her friend you keep on being her friend anyway."

Finding time with each child is a far greater challenge for Jill than keeping up with the daily schedule. It's easy to number laundry, plan meals, and assign chores. Smoothing ruffled feathers, deepening a relationship, understanding a preteen's moodiness—all require investments of time and energy that can't be scheduled in advance. Sometimes by the end of the week, Jill will feel miserable about not spending any one-on-one time with a particular child or two, especially the self-sufficient, undemanding, quiet ones like Andrea.

Pat and Jill tend to balance each other in terms of spending time with each child. "I have to keep reminding Pat to spend more time with the Americans," Jill remarks. "He has taken to the others; Stephen and Thomas were the pride of his life when they arrived because they were so good in baseball and soccer. Since I'm interested in music and entertainment, I enjoy Karyn and Bobby a lot—especially when, for four years in a row, they worked with Carol Lawrence in the EPCOT Christmas presentation, 'Holiday Splendor.' We spent hours driving back and forth for rehearsals and then being there for three shows each night during the two weeks of Christmas vacation. And I love seeing Sarah and Andrea learning to bake things in the kitchen, and Peter progressing on the piano. And of course, Michael, the 'baby,' is my special guy."

Bringing home the four Filipinos meant working harder than ever on relationships and discipline. David ran away not only on his first day home (after being hit by Thomas) but on another occasion as well. He had a hard time coming to grips with the fact that he was not the leader anymore—the one calling all the shots for himself and his brothers.

In the Philippines, he'd taken charge of the other three boys even before they entered the orphanage. When he came to the Williamses, "he did a lot of crying, sulking, and walking away," Jill remembers.

"I walked into his room one Sunday morning, and he was crying. I asked him what was wrong."

Between sobs, David replied, "Sammy won't listen to me. He won't obey me."

As Jill stood there wondering how to respond, it occurred to her that she and Pat had taken away his responsibility as leader the instant he entered their home. "That's a crushing blow," Jill realized. "He can't exert authority over anyone now, and to boot, he had to tell us where and when he's going someplace. He can't just go out and about."

Jill sat on the bed next to him and rubbed his back. She explained to him that she understood his feelings, but that he was still a boy. Like all boys, he needs to obey his parents. And that's not all, she told him. "The older children who have been here longer understand the rules. If I send someone to tell you to do something, like come for dinner, you do it. You might have to take orders from someone younger than you or from a girl."

David understood, and agreed to the rules, but sticking with a radical change in routine and identity at age 10 wasn't easy.

"All the Filipinos were unruly at first. They got spanked more than all the rest of our kids combined," says Jill. "We do spank them, but less and less now." Discipline often comes in the form of being sent to one's room or being grounded. Jill explains why: "We can't take away TV privileges because they don't watch it. We don't want to keep them out of their activities, because we've paid for lessons. So the worst punishment is having to lie down and take a nap."

Her attitude on discipline is an old-fashioned one, drawn from her years as a teacher. "The school year started in September," Jill says, "and I didn't smile until January."

During the first six months after their older adopted children arrived, Pat and Jill made their expectations clear, in no uncertain terms. "After that we lightened up," Jill explains. "We believe a parent cannot regain what is lost by being lenient early on. If these children thought we would not be true to our word, then we would never be able to discipline successfully."

Their success at getting the kids to obey astonishes casual acquaintances. A woman on the beach once saw Jill walking while all her kids were out jogging. As the kids came straggling past Jill, on their way back, the woman asked her, "How do you get them to go jogging?"

"I make them do it," Jill said. "I say do it, and they do it."

Others ask her, "How do you get them to cut their hair?"

Jill replies, "I say, 'sit down,' and I start cutting their hair. It probably saves us over a thousand dollars a year, and more importantly, they know we mean exactly what we say. We are 'the boss.' " At twelve minutes per head, Jill figures it is time well spent. The older boys and the girls, who need some extra styling, require about thirty minutes per head.

The kids know better than to talk back or fight. They tangle once in a while, but they don't fight. They're never allowed to hit; they are not allowed to touch except in love. "We never let full-blown fights start in the first place. We nip them in the bud," says Pat.

Jill is the perfectionist, the hawk, with eyes in the back of her head. "One boy even pushed my hair aside to check," she recalls. Pat is strict, too, but he injects a large dose of levity into matters of family discipline.

"Kids," he'll announce, "it's time for a talk." Particularly on a day when Jill feels she's been run ragged, Pat has a way of rallying the kids and restoring harmony.

"Children, life is easy. Life is not difficult. Here are some ways to make your life easy. Rule number one: When you leave the van, kiss your mother. It's not awful. Just close your eyes and hold your nose." Pat grins while Jill snaps him with a dish towel.

"Rule number two: Clean your room. It isn't that big. Straighten up the bathroom and put all your stuff away.

"Rule number three: Check the bulletin board for your chores, and do them. We are not asking you to paint the side of the house without a ladder. We're not asking you to reinvent the wheel or develop new software for Apple computers. You just need to do a few simple chores.

"The result? Your mother will be like putty. There's no telling what she'll do back."

When Jill is verging on burnout, she'll take a nap or get out by herself to the grocery store. "Then I'll come back and see these sheepish grins on the kids' faces. They will have gotten together and cleaned all their rooms or vacuumed. Sometimes they bring me breakfast in bed. And I get wonderful letters, really affectionate, especially from Sarah and Andrea. That makes it all worthwhile."

Patching broken relationships among the children proves more difficult; and sometimes it's even difficult to detect the root cause of a fractured friendship. One day Sarah did nothing but complain. "Mom, my hair's too short. Nobody likes me. I want to go live somewhere else." For half an hour, Jill endured the whining, checking her irritation. *What's at the bottom of this?* she wondered.

Finally, the truth came out. Sarah was jealous because Jill had taken Karyn on a special outing and left Sarah behind. "All the children have to understand that they cannot always do everything or get everything that everyone else does, or has," Jill says. "We work hard to treat them as individuals, and that means dealing with some envious, angry feelings at times if one feels short-changed. But we absolutely do not believe in being 'fair.' Our goal is to do what is best for each particular child at a certain time in his or her life. That may or may not be just what another kid got at the same stage of life. It is difficult but not impossible to tailor each child's individual experience."

The worst sibling difficulties occurred just after the Filipino boys arrived.

Bobby had been consumed with eagerness for his four new brothers to come home, and he enthusiastically

146

played with them and showed them around the house and the neighborhood. Then, as the Filipinos settled into some routines and activities, Bobby found himself doubly embarrassed by David, who was close to his age.

David began playing baseball on Bobby's Little League team. This new brother had a lot of ability, but he acted terribly immature and could not always grasp what the coaches or other players wanted him to do. His language skills were just not sophisticated enough to master the peculiar dialect of the baseball diamond.

Bobby was tugged in two equally uncomfortable directions. He felt responsible for David, as if he should be perpetually translating the banter of the ball field to this newcomer who was, after all, his brother. On the other hand, he watched with growing resentment as David readily handled the bat and ball, unfailingly catching the praise of the coaches.

Pat picked up the two of them after baseball one day. All the way home in the van, Bobby stared out the window, idly tapping his glove against the seat. He didn't say a word. David was full of talk about different plays. "Dad, I caught a fly ball today. It was the third out." Pat was all ears, but Bobby's uncharacteristic moodiness troubled him.

When they pulled into the driveway at home, David ran inside to change clothes. Pat swung around in the seat and blocked Bobby from climbing out. "What's on your mind?"

Bobby didn't want to answer. Yet he knew that old standby, "Nothing," would not get him off the hook. "I don't like David," he said resentfully. "He acts like a kid out there, and everyone laughs at *me* too." Pat sympathized with Bobby's feelings. "Bringing the Filipinos home is a shock to everyone's system," he said, "but they belong with us now. David is an excellent ballplayer. He really needs you to stick by him so he learns to fit in."

The problem resolved itself when David began playing on a different team. Apart from the rough patch on the ball field, Bobby genuinely glows when he talks about all of his brothers and sisters. He savors the benefits of plentiful playmates and the sense of specialness that marks all the Williams family members. That doesn't mean there are no difficult moments.

"Sometimes I feel like one person is getting all the attention," Bobby says. "If some kids get to go somewhere and I have to stay home, or if someone gets me in trouble, I just feel like saying, 'Oh, man, we've got too many kids!' " Bobby makes it clear that these are the exceptions. He has even thought about adoption as a way to build his future family.

Jimmy, the oldest, enjoys his brothers and sisters but has different plans for himself. Already looking ahead to college and independent living, he says, "I don't want to have a big family because I want to be really active. Dad doesn't go fishing or water-skiing, and I want to be able to do those things."

The Filipinos have brought what sometimes seems to be a fourfold share of troubles to the household. Yet, almost every other Williams child, asked to pick a favorite brother, named one of those four. David has excelled at working with his hands, making useful or amusing things out of scraps. He even built a rudimentary propeller for a boat.

Sammy, the youngest, is the entertainer. He has a ready answer for every question and a quick laugh. Peter has a quiet spirit, but will talk at length about the boys' experiences in the Philippines. And Brian is a charming, intelligent boy who apparently suffered severe abuse at the hand of his grandmother (see chapter 8). The residue of that experience is slowly wearing away, permitting Brian to sink his roots cleanly into his new family's depths of love and acceptance.

Pat's role as father is deeply challenged not just by the number of his children, but also by their need for extra nurturing. Yet, he is still the same ambitious, hard-driving sports executive he always was. Does he worry about slipping into the old patterns of self-preoccupation, subjecting his children to the same emotional neglect Jill experienced?

"It's a daily battle," he admits. "But at least I know the warning signs." Pat draws insight from a history lesson. Franklin D. Roosevelt was reared not to express emotion, Pat read in a biography. "He was taught to be 'above caring' by his mother," Pat says. "In many ways, that is how I was raised. There is an automatic masking of emotions that is unhealthy and keeps others at a distance, getting more and more frustrated.

"My challenge is to keep the kids talking." He does that by posing his famous "Question of the Day," and by staging silly, mock "interviews" with the kids. They love being in the limelight of their dad's life.

"Thomas," Pat barks out a name, and the summoned child comes running. "Tell me your full name, Thomas." Thomas complies. He is named Thomas Jonathan, "T.J.," after Stonewall Jackson.

"And tell me something else, Thomas Williams. Do you ever lose anything?"

Thomas grins self-consciously, weighing his reply.

"Stand up straight, shoulders back. That's good. Now,

where are your shoes today, young man? Repeat after me: I, Thomas Williams, promise never to leave my shoes on the beach again."

Thomas dissolves into giggles.

Pat and Jill's marriage has had to make its own adjustments to adoption and to the challenge of rearing a very large family. After the D-day incident, the low point of their marriage, Pat began spending time with Jill. It was focused time, not just sitting side by side on the sofa reading books "together."

Out of that has emerged a stronger, lasting bond that is not jeopardized by the stresses of so many children. Particularly when older children are placed for adoption, agencies are attuned to ways in which a couple or a family resolves conflict and crisis. Instead of being an impediment to adoption, the Williamses' marital struggle can be seen as preparation—unpleasant, ugly, but effective.

Adding so many children to the family has put a squeeze on the amount of time Pat and Jill can be alone together. They have found some ways that work for them. "We haven't gone on any big trips since we had six children," Jill says. "But I don't need a two-week vacation. Just give me one weekend away every couple months." Their most memorable getaway was a Civil War weekend.

During his years in Philadelphia, Pat had become captivated by stories of Civil War battles in the Pennsylvania countryside. Together, he and Jill visited Gettysburg, and Pat dreamed of tracing the path of the Union army into Virginia.

"He can tell you all the battles, all the situations," Jill says. "I'm not into the blood and guts, so I would

drag him into antique shops to look for books. I found one called The Gallant Mrs. Stonewall, *and after I read it, I was hooked on the people, the personalities, of the era."*

For four days, the two of them drove lazily south, through Manassas and Fredericksburg, surveying the battlefields and enjoying the countryside. Years later, in Orlando, they keep their interest alive.

"Look at this," Pat said one day, hauling an enormous painting into the house. It was a Mort Kunstler oil of General Robert E. Lee visiting the wounded, telling them, "It's all my fault," after the rout at Gettysburg. Several rooms in their home are decorated with Don Troiani Civil War prints, genuine Confederate money, and other paraphernalia.

Now that there are twelve children, even a two-day weekend away is a luxury Pat and Jill have not figured out how to manage. Finding sitters for an evening out is difficult, but it pales in comparison to finding someone who could drive the children to all their various events and activities during the day.

Instead, they find time for dinner or breakfast out once a week, just the two of them. It is essential for Jill to carve out time away from the house and the kids, and being with Pat helps her keep all the craziness in perspective.

"I was the firstborn, the perfectionist," Jill says. "I never broke a toy, never lost anything. So when these kids lose things and break things, it drives me crazy. Pat reminds me what it is like to be a kid. 'They're just being boys,' he tells me. When I begin to fuss about too many bikes on the lawn or games strewn around the living room, he reminds me that we're raising kids, not lawns or beautiful homes."

Jill does not take time to read newspapers or magazines, though she keeps a book in the van for times when she is waiting alone to pick children up. "Pat has become my reader. He goes through newspapers and magazines and marks things of interest to me. It may sound as if I'm submitting to a chauvinist, but it's part of his job to keep up with the media, and it's an enormous help to me to keep abreast of current events, both nationally and with our team."

At times, Jill watches her husband with wonder, recalling the rocky pre-1982 days of their marriage. "He's the only man in the world who can handle us," she says. "Even so, having twelve kids definitely puts a strain on our marriage. It's been tough. Sometimes I do get so overwhelmed that I wonder, *Can I really handle this?*"

The stress is twofold. Each day it builds, as the pressures of driving to and from activities collide with the need to get dinner ready—even if dinner is a simple meal of soup and bread. *Why in the world did we do this?* Jill thinks to herself as she races into the kitchen. It's a never-ending marathon, a treadmill of responsibility from which there appears to be no escape.

Beyond the daily struggle, there are times when she feels trapped, despondent at the prospect of having children living at home for another thirteen years—at least. Jill feels particularly anxious when she contemplates having a houseful of teenagers, instead of third and fourth graders.

Her sense of long-term suffocation is triggered by the same sorts of irritants that plague all moms—messy bedrooms, things left out in the rain, chores forgotten or half-done. Multiply a few of those per day times twelve, and it is no wonder that Jill feels stretched past her limit to endure.

"By five o'clock Friday afternoon, I'm ready to go anywhere all by myself and not tell anybody. Deep down, I would not really change a thing; but there are moments, after a hectic week, when I would give anything to be a normal, everyday housewife with two children and a baby-sitter around the corner. As it is, Pat and I can't do anything spontaneously. Everything has to be planned and thought out ahead of time from six different angles."

Pat often sends Jill off to their oceanfront condominium for a weekend by herself. "She needs to get her batteries recharged," he says, "and a weekend at the beach works wonders. There is one stipulation: She can't call home unless there is an emergency, and no one can call her." Jill returns on Sunday evening, renewed, relaxed, and unstressed.

Beyond the daytime challenges, Jill finds it especially difficult to set aside the worries and frustrations of the day at bedtime. "By the time it is nine or nine-thirty, I've collapsed into an unintelligible heap. And Pat—like any normal husband—is interested in sex. Usually, that is the last thing on my mind. Getting past the emotional barriers of sheer exhaustion is a real struggle."

For his part, Pat tries to keep up the little romantic reminders he vowed to introduce into their failing marriage in 1982—flowers, cards, attentive conversation, lots of hugs. But for Jill, the day flies past in such a mad blur of activity, she scarcely has a chance to notice—much less savor—his initiatives. Finally, Pat occasionally resorts to a blunter approach: "Jill, it's just got to happen!" he'll say, at bedtime.

Even intrusions on their sex life fall into perspective when Pat and Jill consider the rewards of seeing their large family move haltingly toward harmony. "We have made a commitment to these kids; we can't alter that," Pat says. "There are many, many rewards and joys. Seeing them blossom, flourish, achieve, succeed is so satisfying."

For Jill, encouragement comes unexpectedly. "When we're out at a restaurant, someone will comment on how well-behaved the children are, or what a beautiful family we have. They'll say, 'These children must be so grateful to have you as their parents.'"

To herself, Jill replies, *Get serious! These children are just like any others. They won't appreciate their parents until they hit 30!* Suddenly, the fact of attachment becomes clear to her. These children all belong to the family, so securely that they can grouse about their problems, act up, even storm out of a room if they don't like what they're being asked to do. *It's really happened,* Jill thinks in amazement. *We're really on the way to becoming a family.*

"Let's adopt one child from every country," Jill tells Pat during a flight of whimsy on their morning walk.

Pat can't believe his ears. Is this the same wife who doesn't know how she's going to manage to pick up children at art class and dance class at exactly the same time? "How about settling for one from every continent?" he suggests.

8
"Who Am I?"

A few weeks after the Filipino boys arrived home, Pat and Jill began to suspect that one of them—Brian—was having an especially difficult time adjusting. A phone call came one day from Brian's teacher, confirming their suspicion.

"Mrs. Williams? I want to talk with you about Brian. He refuses to speak in class, and he won't participate or work on any papers. Do you have any idea why?"

Jill wasn't sure how to reply, so she evaded the question. "Well, if you can be patient with him, we believe he'll do just fine. It might take him a little longer than the others to get used to all these changes in his life."

Jill sounded self-assured on the phone, but doubts plagued her. There were those wet sheets every morning on Brian's bed, and stolen candy in his dresser. "Pat, do you suppose something is troubling Brian?" Pat responded in his usual take-charge way. "Let's get in touch with Louise Lynip," he suggested. Louise is the elderly woman who cared for the boys in Mindanao and escorted them to Florida.

In a letter to Pat and Jill, Louise said she thought she could explain why Brian appeared to have so little self-esteem. She wrote,

> During the days that the mother and her four boys stayed with her family, her mother (the boys' grandmother) turned against her. Brian was the special object of her wrath and she was cruel to him. He must have been the most vulnerable in those days. . . . I know the Lord will give you the wisdom and love to help him trust adults.

Jill knew that adopting an older child often means confronting painful circumstances from the past. With Brian, she had to take the initiative. Jill arranged a time when she and Brian could be all alone together in the family's big kitchen.

Sitting at the table over some juice and cookies, Jill chatted with him about everyday matters. He was relaxed and talkative, basking in his mother's undivided attention. Then Jill asked kindly, "Could you tell me about your Filipino grandmother?"

The grandmother's son, a teenager, used to take away Brian's makeshift toys and his brothers' things as well, Jill learned. Whenever the four brothers managed to get things back from their uncle, he would complain to the grandmother. Then one of the four brothers would be punished. Usually, for some unknown reason, it was Brian. "Can you tell me what she did to you?"

Staring down at the table, Brian spoke in a whisper. "She tied a rope around my neck," he told Jill. "Then she dunked me in the well."

Big tears splashed onto the place mat, and Jill cried too. She wanted to keep him talking, so she asked another question. "Brian, when you wet your bed, are you angry at someone?" Brian didn't reply. "Are you angry at us? At your old grandmother?" He began nodding slowly. "Are you angry at Brian?" Jill persisted. Brian burst into racking sobs. Jill folded her arms around him, rocking him and crying along with him. "I love you, Brian. It will never happen again. You are our son forever."

From that moment on, it was as if a curtain dropped on Act I of Brian's life. He seemed to breathe more freely, to run more jauntily, to exhibit genuine joy and delight. In school, he began to participate and work on projects.

The bed-wetting incidents dropped dramatically, but did not end completely. Particularly if Brian had been disciplined during the day, he would wet his bed that night. Pat and Jill used a firm approach, making him do his own laundry the next morning, but never shaming him or belittling him.

Jill found he continued to need large doses of encouragement and understanding. Whenever Brian brought home a spelling paper from school, or an art project, Jill would take time to admire it. "Brian, that is a beautiful paper!"

Before her eyes, Brian would grab it back and rip it to shreds, as if he could not yet accept the idea of doing something right and being praised for it. He would draw away from the extra hugs Pat and Jill lavished on him. "He was still quick to throw a punch or a rock," Jill observed. "He was more volatile than the others."

As Brian matures, he will face the same identity issues every teenager confronts. For him, and other children bearing scars from the past, the tasks of defining "Who am I?" and feeling comfortable about it will most likely present more difficulties than they will for children like Jimmy, Bobby, and Karyn.

Brian is extremely fortunate to have caring parents to nudge him back into the mainstream of adjustment and activity when he strays emotionally. Their tasks as parents, Jill and Pat are discovering, are different as well—even with their other adopted children who have not shown any signs of early abuse or neglect.

Families formed by adoption need to make room in their lives for the realities of a child's past. John Aeby, writing in Holt's magazine, *Hi Families*, eloquently describes this truth.

> The events of our past are embedded in our memories. Like the small, center rings of oak trees, our histories are held fast in unchangeable hardwood at the cores of our beings. And even if those events are hidden under the layers of years, they have an influence upon who we are today.[1]

Sometimes, those "center rings" may be hidden in complete mystery. That is the case for Sarah and Andrea, who were abandoned. It is very unlikely that they would be able to track down any blood relatives if they ever chose to try. Yet, their abandonment and the time they spent at an orphanage is an essential part of the fabric of their lives.

Talking about it, coming to terms with it, and understanding their dual heritage as Korean Americans will be an important part of the sisters' coming of age. For twins Thomas and Stephen, the task will be still different. Their memories of Korea and their birth mother are largely positive, and were formed at a very young, impressionable age.

It will be important, Pat and Jill realize, to let the twins know their birth mother did not reject them because *they* were bad, or unacceptable, or unlovable. On the contrary, her decision to place them in a home where they would be well cared for represents a sacrifice born of love and concern.

The ways in which adopted children adjust have been studied for years, with mixed results. The age-old question of nature versus nurture fascinates students of human behavior, but for all their analysis, no firm conclusions have been drawn. The best evidence suggests that heredity *and* environment affect intelligence and behavior.

What is clear is that the overwhelming majority of people who are adopted—whether into same-race families or transracially—become well-adjusted, productive adults. The first Vietnamese child placed by Holt in the United States offers a striking illustration. Keri Mailinda Horn, a graduate of the University of Oregon in broadcast journalism, was born in Saigon and spent her first four and a half years in a French Catholic orphanage.

In an interview in *Hi Families,* she commented,

> Being adopted hasn't made me feel different. I feel very secure, very normal. Now that I am a young adult, I am beginning to realize that

my immediate family's background is different from a lot of families, but it's okay to be different.

Does Keri ever wonder about the past? Like most adopted children, she does.

Because I am mixed race and from Vietnam, I can't help looking at photos from around the world and especially photos of American soldiers and Vietnamese women and wondering about my birth parents. I'm not really searching for my birth parents. It's like I'm looking, but I'm not really looking.[2]

For the Williams children and people such as Keri, the question of *telling* them they are adopted is, of course, beside the point. Transracial adoptees grow up knowing they were not born into their families. When these families discuss adoption, other aspects of the story are emphasized.

The Filipino brothers brought with them one treasure that may help them untangle the threads of their early lives someday. A caring social worker in Mindanao, Rose Longcob, presented them with a sixteen-page "Memory Book" before they left the Philippines.

In the Memory Book, photos of the boys are accompanied by warmhearted captions. David is "shy but friendly and affectionate. He is known to friends as a good boy always," Rose wrote. Peter is "a lovable boy who has a sense of humor and is sports-minded," while Brian is "the intelligent brother who always wants to tease and prefers to play all the time." The youngest, Sammy, is "the apple of his brothers' eyes, vocal and lively."

Other pictures show the boys with their friends, participating in activities. When the memories of their early lives flicker with uncertainty, their Memory Book will shed light on who they were at the time they were adopted.

For same-race adoptive families, telling the adoption story is an ongoing task of parenting that sets them apart from birth families. This chapter will review some of the tasks of adoptive families and some proven methods for parents and adopted children to explore together the question, "Who am I?" Often, the storytelling begins in the toddler years, when a child asks:

Did I grow in your tummy?

It is not unusual for an adopted toddler to pose this question when the child becomes aware of pregnant women. Sarah asked Jill this question when she was four, just before Michael was born. Even before a question such as this surfaces, experts on adoption counsel parents to talk to the child about adoption, using the word in a warm, positive, and natural way.

Pat and Jill began using the word *adoption* as soon as Sarah and Andrea arrived. When they spoke or sang.at churches, they would bring all five children along and let them introduce themselves. After asking Sarah and Andrea to say their names and tell how old they were, Jill asked, "Why are you so special?" The girls replied, "Because I'm 'dopted."

Telling a baby, "We're so glad we adopted you!" or, "You are our sweetest adopted girl," lets the child begin to recognize the word very early on. Then when the "tummy" question comes up, it will be natural for the parents to respond factually and calmly.

"No, you grew in some other lady's tummy. She knew she could not take care of a baby then, so she made sure you went home to a new mommy and daddy who would love you always." That is, in essence, the way adoptive parents are advised to begin telling their child's story. It makes a positive statement about the birth mother, yet avoids confusing the child by saying something like, "The other lady loved you *so much,* she gave you away." An explanation like that may make a young child worry that if her adoptive parents love her *so much,* they might give her away too.

Also, focusing on the birth mother's inability to care for *any* baby takes the pressure off a child who may wonder if she was placed for adoption because she was bad or troublesome or particularly unlovable. It helps to emphasize circumstances, rather than whether the people involved were "good" or "bad."

Until they are well into their grade-school years, most adopted children cannot fully understand the motives and mechanics of adoption. Often, according to researchers, they go through a stage when they believe everyone is adopted or, if they came from overseas, that some children arrive at the hospital and some arrive at airports!

Young children will want to hear "their" story again and again, and many adoptive parents find it helps to compile a "Life Book" for their children. A Life Book is simply a scrapbook of mementos, photographs, and easy-to-understand comments that tell of the child's journey home.

It may include photos of the parents waiting to meet

their child; copies of paperwork describing the child and the institution or foster home where he lived; pictures of the parents greeting their child; a flag or tourist guide from the country where he was born; cards from baby showers; a copy of the child's new birth certificate or court order of adoption. And of course it will contain as well all the usual snapshots of first birthdays, family gatherings, playgroups, and outings.

In this way, the story of adoption is integrated from the beginning into the whole of the child's life. It is nothing for him to be ashamed of, and should instead be a source of pride and pleasure. It will not put an end to the questions, however.

Once the child begins to grasp the reality of "another mother," he may ask:

Why did she give me away?

When the child begins to wonder about the reasons for his adoption, social workers advise clarifying what he really knows and understands already. By asking the child questions, a mom or dad can discern how much and what to tell him. Another guideline for parents involves honesty.

In the days when adoption was cloaked in shame and secrecy, some parents were advised not to tell their children or to wait until a certain age, such as the early teens. Often, children were told that their birth parents died in an accident, or they were told the "chosen child" myth: "Daddy and I went to a big building with lots of little babies and picked *you* to be our special child!"

Today, gilding or obscuring the truth is strongly discouraged. Instead, parents are advised to collect and keep as much information as possible about the child's origins at the time of the adoption. As the child grows curious and can understand different aspects of the story, the parents should "tell it like it is," being sensitive to the child's feelings and level of maturity.

Even if some parts of the story are especially painful or frightening, the truth should be told anyway. In *OURS* magazine, the story of Heather, adopted from Colombia at the age of 11 weeks, shows how "bad news" can be handled sensitively.

From the time she was 3, Heather peppered her mom with questions about why she was adopted. Her mom consistently spoke of the birth mother as a caring, loving young woman. It was not until she turned 9 that her mother received paperwork from the adoption lawyer saying that Heather had been abandoned on a city street in Bogota when she was about a month old.

"How could she do this to me?" Heather screeched when she learned the truth. All her dreams of one day finding and meeting her birth mother shattered in an instant. At age 10, Heather wrote a school essay about her feelings:

> Sometimes I wish I knew my birth mother. Sometimes I wonder what would happen if I knew her. . . . All I know is Mrs. Carol Kellmann is my mother, the one who brought me up. If it weren't for the Kellmanns, I would still be there, waiting. I love my parents very much and if my birth mother does come back, Mom is my mom, not someone who hasn't seen me for 10 years.[3]

Adopted children who have grown up with positive images of their birth parents may find themselves torn with conflicting feelings. Particularly in the case of children adopted at an older age, such as twins Stephen and Thomas, they may wonder:

Can I love both my birth mom and my adoptive parents?

Research on adoption indicates that adoptees may tend to be preoccupied with a sense of rejection, or they may fantasize that their birth parents are perfectly wonderful people. One 39-year-old adoptee said, "I often thought I'd get a call from an attorney saying I'd come into a huge inheritance from my birth parents."

On a parallel track, the adoptee may worry about hurting his adoptive parents. Particularly when children are old enough to remember clearly another family, as with the Filipinos, they may be reluctant to bring up the subject for fear it will hurt the adoptive parents.

Experts on older-child adoption, including Claudia Jewett, recommend a candle ceremony to assure the child that growing attached to his adoptive family does not mean rejecting everything about his past. The family and, if possible, the newly adopted child's social worker meet in the home. Candles on a table represent each family or person the child as lived with. The adopted child lights the first candle and uses it to light the others, as the social worker describes his early life, noting any particularly close or warm relationships.

It is pointed out that all the candles can remain burning at the same time. No candle has to be snuffed out in order for another one to be lit. In the same way, a child's love may continue to burn for a previous birth family or foster family. But that will not prevent him from loving and bonding with his permanent, adoptive family.

For the adopted child with no recollection of a birth mother, feelings may range from pity to gratitude to anger. The majority of adopted children do not search for their birth parents, but virtually all who are adopted harbor some curiosity, and some eventually will ask:

Can I find my birth mother, and meet her?

The prospect of having a child search for a birth parent concerns many couples who consider adoption. Often, they are reassured to learn that a child who searches for blood relatives—and even develops a relationship with them—usually continues to regard his adoptive family as his "real" family.

Jacqueline Plumez, in her book *Successful Adoption,* notes,

> The relationship between adoptive parents and children seems almost always to be enhanced by the search, especially if the adoptive parents are supportive. Most adoptees, however, are afraid to tell their parents that they want to search. They fear hurting the parents or losing their love. It is a relief when parents understand and accept the adoptee's yearning for information.[4]

One way to ease the difficulty from the start is for adoptive parents to make certain they or their adoption agency have access to original records. They may want the agency to ask the birth mother whether she ever wants to be in touch with her child again.

If the answer is no, or if the adoptive parents have no clue how the birth mother feels a decade or more after the adoption, they should caution a child who wants to search. A birth mother who was unmarried and pregnant during her school years may have gone on to marry and raise a family of her own. She may not welcome the intrusion of a child from her past—a past that is best left alone.

There is no way of knowing exactly how many of the estimated 500,000 adoptees in the United States have searched for birth parents. A well-regarded ten-year research project in Scotland, however, found that only 1.5 adult adoptees per thousand applied for copies of their original birth certificates. Of those who did apply, 60 percent wanted to meet a birth parent; the others just sought information on their heritage.

Many adoptees fantasize about inheriting a fortune from birth relatives, and others may idealize their blood relatives as "perfect parents." The flip side of this tendency is a gripping fear that the adoptee may find something overwhelmingly negative in his background.

According to Jacqueline Plumez,

> Searchers usually find that they had birth mothers with very good and caring reasons for not keeping their babies. Most adoptees will find they were born illegitimate, that their birth parents knew each other for a while, cared about each other, but did not feel able to provide a stable home or marriage for the child.[5]

There is one nagging question that may plague an adoptee coming to grips with his or her identity. It is magnified by society's tendency to highlight negative aspects of adoption:

Is there something wrong with me? Will I "go bad"?

Whenever someone who is arrested for a crime happens to be adopted, that fact is mentioned prominently in newspaper accounts. Far less often do people discover how many ordinary—and not-so-ordinary—law-abiding adoptees there are. Former president Gerald R. Ford, Olympic diving champion Greg Louganis, and business entrepreneur Dave Thomas, the founder of Wendy's Restaurants, are just a few examples cited in public service announcements sponsored by the National Committee for Adoption.

Old myths about "bad blood" have prompted some psychologists to refer to *adoption syndrome,* a collection of unfavorable personality traits and emotional disturbances. This term got its start in 1984, when psychiatrist David Kirschner used it as a defense in court. His client was an adopted 14-year-old who set fire to his parents' home and burned them to death. The boy was found guilty despite his defense attorney's original argument.

Kirschner and other researchers claim disproportionate numbers of adoptees seek counseling or mental health assistance. Psychologist David M. Brodzinsky, at Rutgers University, is widely recognized in this field. He notes that studies show 84 percent of all adoptions are successful, while 16 percent may be considered unsuccessful. Only 1 or 2 percent of all U.S. children under the age of 18 are unrelated adoptees, yet between 4 and 5 percent of minors referred to guidance clinics or mental health facilities are adopted.

"On the average, adopted children are more likely to manifest psychological problems than nonadopted children," Brodzinsky writes. But that does not mean it is necessarily because they are adopted. Brodzinsky goes on to offer some explanations that center on the adoptive family's ways of adjusting, rather than the fact of adoption itself.

He theorizes, "The degree to which adoptive parents and their children acknowledge the unique challenges in their life, and the way in which they attempt to cope with them, largely determine their pattern of adjustment."

Once the child reaches an age of understanding and begins coping with identity issues, Brodzinsky says the adoptee will most likely enter a normal process of grieving over the loss of biological ties to parents. When a school-age adopted child acts up, or is labeled difficult or disturbed by teachers or other observers, it may reflect the fact that the child is grieving, says Brodzinsky. Parents who recognize that and permit the child to finish grieving help speed his progress toward stability and adjustment.

Brodzinsky writes,

> Adoptive parents, then, need to recognize that as their children become more aware of what it means to be adopted, a certain amount of confusion and uncertainty is bound to be manifested. . . . Instead of ignoring their children's concerns or treating them as insignificant, which could very well foster feelings of inade-

quacy or inferiority, it is important for parents to acknowledge to their children that they recognize and accept their concerns, and encourage them to explore and resolve what one 9-year-old boy called "the master question of my life—why was I given up for adoption?"[6]

There is no reason for an adoptive family to harbor fears about a child "going bad" just because he or she is adopted. Nonetheless, the ordinary turbulence of adolescence may pose a rougher passage for an adopted child. Facing the hard questions squarely, and not shrinking from them, helps assure normal adjustment and maturity.

In the Williams family, coming to grips with feelings and identity issues is encouraged daily. Jill reminds the children to write in their diaries, keeping a running log of important thoughts and discoveries. Among their adopted children, another key question is certain to be posed, sooner or later:

Can I be Asian and American at the same time?

Making the choice to adopt a child of a different race or nationality means choosing to forge a new family identity. That adds another aspect to the special tasks of adoptive parenting. Interracial families attract undue attention wherever they go, and parents need to be prepared to answer or deflect remarks from strangers.

Helping a child feel good about his racial or ethnic heritage is essential. That may take the form of finding positive role models from the child's ethnic group: Connie Chung on television or Michael Jordan on the basketball court. It means skipping ethnic jokes of all sorts and developing sensitivity about language and stereotypes.

Lois Melina, author of *Raising Adopted Children*, points out, "It isn't unusual for transracially adopted children to sometimes wish they were the same color as their parents. Most likely this is not a rejection of their racial identity, but a desire to be like the people around them."[7] A parent's admiring comments about the adopted child's features or coloring go a long way toward affirming the beauty and value of being different.

Usually, parents who adopt from Asia or Latin America either bring with them or develop a deep admiration for the culture of their child's birth. Often they travel to the region of the child's birth and get to know Asian or Hispanic individuals. They may agree to keep aspects of that culture alive in their home, but they may wonder how to go about it.

Some U.S. adoption agencies and adoptive parents' groups offer "culture classes" and social opportunities to participate in meals, sporting events, or even language training. Holt reaches out to its adoptive families in two ways: a summer heritage camp program and an annual Motherland Tour of Korea for adoptees who have graduated from high school.

The tours of Korea began first, when Holt president David Kim heard parents and adoptees ask over and over, "What's it like in Korea?" Many of the adoptees who toured Korea came home with a wistful yearning. "I wish we could have known about Korea as we were growing up," they told David Kim. "I feel so proud of the Korean part of me now." In response Holt began its heritage camps.

The program is open to all Holt adoptees as well as

Korean adoptees placed by other agencies. Camp is the place where many international adoptees come to grips, for the first time, with their shared ethnic identity.

"Without exception, what is most important to the campers is the chance to be with kids who are 'just like me,'" Susan Cox says. "I hear those words over and over again."

Finding others with similar feelings and experiences makes a real difference for people adopted across cultural and racial lines. One Holt adoptee, at age 27, reflected on her experience in a letter to the agency:

> Show me one Oriental who has not been teased.
> I was hurt and I cried a lot. Sometimes the pain
> doesn't go away. I still remember, but it's some-
> thing we have to live with and accept just be-
> cause we look special. No matter if you are
> white or black, other kids will still find some-
> thing they can use as a reason for making fun of
> you. Just remember that God made you special
> and that's what counts.[8]

When adopted children set out to discover "Who am I?" they may have a longer list of questions to grapple with than birth children. Coming to terms with the past may take a while. It may mean accepting and even embracing aspects of a previous life that are uncomfortable, sad, downright painful. Susan Cox, who was among the first Korean children placed for adoption by Harry Holt, observes, "You are an adoptee forever. That's neither good nor bad. It just is. You must acknowledge that, accept it, and find out where that balance fits in your own life."

It is a process that can either be helped or hindered by adoptive parents. Pat and Jill are taking it one day at a time, searching for ways to continue affirming each child as a unique and valued individual. The payoff comes unexpectedly, at times. One spring day, it came in the form of a note from Brian to Jill. In painstaking third-grade penmanship, with each capital *T* carefully embellished, the note said:

Dear Mom,
    Thank you mom for taking me To school and feeding me and I like it. And Thank you for putting me To Bed at night and Thank you for taking me to swimming and you are the Best mom I have ever had and Thank you for being the best mom. The end.

                                                    From Brian

9

The Red Thread

When it comes to sports enthusiasm, Jimmy and Bobby Williams are already in the big leagues. That was exactly what Pat expected from his birth children, and it is something he encourages every chance he gets. It's not at all surprising.

Pat grew up in Wilmington, Delaware, where his father coached football and baseball at a private prep school, Tower Hill. When he turned three, Pat received a baseball glove for his birthday. Growing up, he eagerly tracked favorite teams and players, memorizing all the statistics and papering his wall with photos of baseball heroes.

His father yearned for Pat—his only son—to become a professional athlete. Pat went to Wake Forest University on a baseball scholarship; he was first-string catcher on the team. His father rarely missed a game.

Pat held fast to his dream of entering professional

sports and got a chance to play baseball with a minor league team in Florida. He quickly realized he had no future on the playing field, but he possessed the self-confidence to laugh about it. "I just got word about a scouting report," he would say. "They told the home office, 'Williams may not be big, but he's slow.' "

Different aspects of professional sports opened up to Pat, and he quickly hit his stride doing special promotions, generating big turnouts at games, and making the fans feel they were being treated royally. "My whole life is athletics," Pat readily admits. He would consider it his *red thread*, a term he and Jill use to designate a particular area of ability and interest in a person's life.

The red thread is the one aptitude that stands out among all the rest; it weaves the fabric of a person's life into a cohesive and interesting whole, standing out in sharp relief against the duller grays and browns of pursuits that are less exciting and satisfying.

It's not surprising at all when a particular "thread," such as sports, weaves its way from one generation to the next—from Pat's father to Pat to Jimmy and Bobby. But what about the adopted child? For Pat and Jill, the red thread principle is—if anything—more important for the adopted children. Identifying, nurturing, and encouraging an area of keen desire and skill is the cornerstone of parenting, Williams style.

As Pat and Jill are discovering, one of the thrills of adopting a child is watching a personality unfold. For adoptive parents, there are always surprises in store. Will a child become a gifted pianist, or a talented artist? Is he good with his hands—able to fix and build things? Is there a particular attraction toward reading, writing, and studying? With an adopted child, there's no telling.

Emphasizing the red thread theme accomplishes two important goals in adoptive parenting, particularly in a family where there are children both by birth and by adoption. It is a "leveler," a way in which all the children are made to feel equal. And it stresses the positive. So often in adoption, there are real or imagined negatives associated with a child's history. By concentrating on interests and abilities *now,* parents wisely unshackle the child—and often themselves—from brooding over the past.

Pat and Jill believe that finding and strengthening each child's red thread is critical to the development of self-esteem, confidence, and competence through the teen years and into adulthood. Says Pat, "If they reach their teen years and have no aspect of their lives that they enjoy or excel in, then we've failed. That's when kids tend to turn to thrills, drugs, all these false idols of our age."

Their thoughts on this made a deep impression on their friends at Holt. Susan Cox details some of the traits she observed in Pat and Jill—traits that add up to success in an adoptive family. "The Williamses are very flexible. They anticipate a child's abilities and help the child be his or her best at whatever it is.

"To maintain individual personalities in a family as large as theirs is really a gift, and it represents a deep commitment on their part. They don't expect one child to be the same as all the rest. They allow individuality to blossom in each child."

"Train Up a Child ..."

For Pat and Jill, the red thread concept has a biblical, as well as a practical, basis. The words of Proverbs 22:6 are familiar to most Christian parents: "Train up a child in the way he should go, even when he is old he will not depart from it" (NAS). The words may be understood and applied in a variety of ways. Often, the verse is interpreted in a way that suggests a "Father Knows Best" approach—lay down the law, and teach the kid to walk in lockstep with it. Then, even if he rebels, he will return to the fold eventually, like the Prodigal Son.

A different interpretation is suggested by Pat and Jill's favorite Bible teacher, Chuck Swindoll. In his Bible study guide entitled *You and Your Child,* he illuminates a more child-centered understanding. Getting to know the child as an individual is the key to "training" him, Swindoll writes, because only then will parents be truly effective.

Swindoll paraphrases the Proverbs verse this way: "If you want your training to be meaningful and wise, be observant and discover your child's way, and adapt your training accordingly." Jill puts it a little differently: "Better to build a child right than to have to rebuild an adult."

He explains that each child comes with an individual temperament and personality.

> One may be creative; another, practical. One may be intelligent; another, just average. One may be outgoing; another, withdrawn. . . . The short-sighted parent, however, overlooks this, focusing only on the immediate task of making the children conform, shaping them up. The result? When the parent starts barking "shape up or ship out," the child starts saving up for a boat ticket. Invariably, parents make two common mistakes. First, they use the same approach with all their children. Secondly, they compare them with other children.[1]

On their morning walks, when Pat and Jill discuss opportunities and challenges their children face, they try to sort out the individual "bents" that make each child unique. Finding that red thread is not a one-time event; in fact, the sorting-out process may take years, and it may involve some unexpected tangles along the way.

Finding the Thread

Naturally, it would not bother Pat at all if every one of his dozen children lived and breathed sports. He has to check his own inclination to push them too hard in that direction. Jill's own red thread is music: playing the violin and singing professionally. She does yearn for at least *one* child to play the piano, and so far, soft-spoken Peter is the only one who shows much interest.

A parent's own skills and interests make a deep impression on children, and frequently determine a life direction. Pat and Jill are learning, though, that there is no sure way to predict what will engage a child, whether the child is adopted or born to them. Birth daughter Karyn is a case in point.

Beginning at the age of 3, she loved gymnastics and would practice tirelessly. Her commitment to gymnastics had all the earmarks of an aptitude that could last a lifetime. So Pat and Jill drove her to the gym, gave her lessons, encouraged her through the difficulties of being too small to successfully navigate the uneven parallel bars. Her coaches loved her and were enthused about her potential.

Suddenly, just before she turned 10, Karyn burned out on gymnastics. "She hit the wall," Pat says. Gymnastics practice was lasting until 10:00 P.M., and Karyn was bone-tired every morning after a workout. She stretched her petite arms and legs to their limits, trying to master the uneven bars. Finally, discouragement settled in like a long autumn storm. The old exhilaration and sense of accomplishment vanished.

One evening, while the others went ice-skating, Pat took Karyn to the gym, then out to Pizza Hut for a father-daughter date. He had sensed that gymnastics had become a burden for her, and they talked about it. There was no retribution, no blaming or belittling. "We'll just have to try out some new activities, Karyn," Pat told her.

Casting about for a pursuit Karyn might enjoy more, Jill noticed one day that tryouts were scheduled for a stage performance at Disney World. At the audition, Karyn radiated joy and stage presence, and she won the spot. For the next four years, she and Bobby both appeared in a Christmas special, "Holiday Splendor," at EPCOT Center. Her first taste of singing and acting left her hungering for more. Jill is continuing to scout for opportunities for Karyn to perform.

Pat and Jill make no secret of their search for a red thread, and each child is encouraged strongly to be a part of the process—to let the family know what he or she most wants to do. Often, Pat will use his "Question of the Day" time at breakfast or dinner to stimulate some creative thought about new areas of interest.

"Who's your favorite hero?" he will ask. "If you could choose to be one person from the Bible, who would it be?" "If you could be anyplace in the world today, where would you be?" Stretching their imaginations, waiting patiently for answers, and affirming what each child says is a critical part of parenting in the Williams family. Sometimes, there is a surprise in store.

From the time Sarah and Andrea arrived home, they have been inseparable. Yet, they have very different aptitudes and personalities. Andrea sits and paints or colors for hours on end, and has done so since she was 3 years old. There is little question in Jill's mind that Andrea's red thread will involve some aspect of art. Jill is delighted. "Andrea was secure enough to be saying, in her own way, that she is not interested in sports."

Sarah had no clear-cut area of interest, so Pat and Jill encouraged her to try a variety of sports activities. Nothing seemed to click, until one day, during a family discussion, Sarah announced, "I want to be a swimmer." She had shown little interest in swimming before; in fact, she had been afraid of the water.

Making up her own mind, in her own good time, was all it took. "From that day on, Sarah has loved swimming," Jill observes. She joined the swim team, and before long, she had developed one of the best butterfly strokes on the team. "They think she's going to be one of the premier butterflyers in Florida for her age," Jill says proudly.

When twins Stephen and Thomas arrived, Pat succumbed to his curiosity about their sports abilities and had them playing baseball within minutes of arriving home. They have loved baseball ever since, and they also play soccer very well.

Pat tried out all four Filipinos on the family's half-size outdoor basketball court when they arrived. They liked it, and David in particular showed some real aptitude. Brian took to swimming, and Peter just might satisfy Jill's longing for a child who is oriented toward music. "They all love to sing," Jill says. "And Peter can draw very well, but he complained when I sent him to art class with Andrea."

The youngest Williams children, Sammy and Michael, are still too little to blossom in any one special area. Pat and Jill agree it is wrong to push children too far, too fast. The early years are carefree, centered on building strong, trusting relationships in a relaxed, unpressured environment.

Pat and Jill consider themselves students of their children, learning daily what makes them tick. Identifying a red thread for each child is a way to build self-esteem, keep the kids active, and celebrate the uniqueness of each family member. The process does not end, though, once a thread appears.

Strengthening the Thread

Just eight and a half months after Stephen and Thomas arrived, Pat drove them to Little League tryouts one Sunday afternoon. The boys were uncharacteristically quiet as the van pulled up to the playing field. A creeping sense of uncertainty must have gripped them, as they watched other parents and youngsters emerge, cocky and self-assured, from other cars.

Pat was feeling a little shaky himself. Were these two ready for Little League? All the expectations of the coach, the teammates? The intensity of competition? Pat wasn't exactly sure, but he did know that the twins played ball incessantly and enthusiastically at home.

He settled into a bleacher seat to watch. "Knock 'em dead, guys," he called to the twins. Pat scratched his head. *Do they know what that means?* he wondered.

All at once, Stephen stepped up to the plate. Pat held

his breath, waiting for the pitch. It was a fastball, right over the plate. Stephen took command of the bat and swung it with authority. *Smack!* The ball was a goner. Pat was ecstatic. "Atta boy!" he shouted. When the twins took field positions, they played as if they'd been training for Little League since infancy.

Strengthening and encouraging a child's area of interest and skill is critical, Pat and Jill believe. As parents, they spend an extraordinary amount of time doing just that. "I don't care whether it's baseball or needlepoint," Pat says, "but each child needs to gain a sense of accomplishment, even mastery, in some area of life."

There are several ways in which they work at strengthening a child's red thread. One is focused, individual attention. Pat's trip to Pizza Hut with Karyn to discuss her troubles with gymnastics is a good example. Taking along a stopwatch to the kids' swim meets is another. Pat and Jill are not "see you later" parents—dropping the kids off and paying scant attention to what they are doing. Their enthusiasm and their presence communicate to each child a sense of personal importance and specialness.

Another way to strengthen a child's red thread is through role models. Pat and Jill have an extensive network of friends and acquaintances in the world of professional sports as well as in music, publishing, and Christian circles. By linking up their children with adults who have similar special aptitudes, Pat and Jill offer their children a chance to "try on" different adult identities and see the benefits of working hard at what they want to become.

"We are constantly trying to get the kids together with older players or sports figures they can look up to," Pat says. "One is Boyd Coffie, the baseball coach at Rollins College. He has really taken an interest in Bobby and lets him work out with the Rollins College team. And the Doyle brothers, Denny and his twin brothers, Blake and Brian, are baseball players Stephen and Thomas admire. Blake and Brian run a baseball school that the kids have attended. Whenever I ask 'Who is your hero?' I can count on Stephen or Thomas answering, 'The Doyle brothers.' "

Similarly, actress Carol Lawrence has influenced Karyn and Bobby during their rehearsals and performances at EPCOT. Says Jill, "She is gracious, not bossy; she is the epitome of a star, telling the children in the production to relax and enjoy themselves." Karyn beams when she talks about performing side by side with Carol Lawrence. "She tells us what we need to work on," Karyn explains, "and she tells us when we're doing well."

Pat and Jill try hard to remain realistic in their expectations of each child. It does no good to push a child in an area where he will meet failure time after time. Adjusting the grade levels of the Filipinos was not easy, for instance. Some parents might feel it reflects badly on them to hold a child back. Yet the results were phenomenal.

When he repeated fourth grade, David would climb into the van at 3:00 P.M. fairly bursting with good news. "I got a ninety-eight!" he'd blurt, as Jill glowed with pride. Just one year after he had failed to complete a single paper satisfactorily, David was on his way to the head of the class. Even if he did not excel in school, Pat and Jill were determined to give him every chance to do his best and feel proud of himself.

After he met his friend Aaron and began tutoring him, David's self-esteem blossomed. Just twelve months after joining the Williams family, David already was modeling the same sort of caring, helpful behavior he sees daily at home.

Saturday Madness

The family's commitment to a red thread approach to parenting is not without its difficulties. It means a non-stop, hectic pace that would exhaust some parents—and children. Sometimes, on a particularly demanding weekend, even energetic Pat and Jill feel done in.

One Saturday in November, Jill begins warming up the Dodge Caravan at 8:15 A.M. to take Bobby and Karyn to EPCOT for Christmas rehearsals. On the way there, she telephones a sitter from the car phone, lining her up to stay with the younger children that night while she watches the Orlando Magic face the Philadelphia 76ers on the basketball court.

Jill stays at EPCOT, assisting Bobby and Karyn with costuming until early afternoon. At 2:15 she drops Bobby off at a baseball game, fretting because he has not had time for lunch.

Meanwhile, at home, Jimmy is left in charge of the two youngest, Michael and Sammy. Peter and Brian are under strict orders to be dressed and ready for soccer at 12:45; Andrea and Sarah occupy themselves with paints and projects.

Pat drives David, Stephen, and Thomas to the baseball field at 9:20 for Little League games. He brings along a book and the newspaper, counting on getting some reading done while he watches them play. No such luck.

As they arrive at the ball field, David and Thomas hop out of the van. Stephen begins rummaging through accumulated stuff on the floor of the van. "Who took my glove?" he asks. Pat sees this one coming a mile away. "Are you sure you had your glove with you when we left?" he asks. Sheepishly, Stephen says, "No."

Stephen climbs out of the van, and Pat does a U-turn, vanishing in a cloud of dust toward home. There, in the sports equipment box in the garage, is Stephen's glove. Back to the ball field goes Pat, only to find David waiting for him on the curb, the game already progressing without him. "What's your problem?" Pat inquires.

"I left my glove in the car," David says. Pat parks the van, finds David's glove on a distant backseat, and hands it to him. Sighing, Pat leans back against the headrest on the driver's seat. *It's going to be a long day,* he thinks.

When these three boys are finished with their games, back home they go to pick up Peter and Brian, who have soccer games at 1:00 P.M. Sarah plays in a soccer game that day as well.

At 3:15, Jill pulls into the driveway with Karyn. Sarah greets her at the door, saying, "Mom, we beat First Academy at soccer!" Pat grabs Jill for a quick hug and kiss on his way to a book signing—he has just published *Making Magic,* an account of how Orlando acquired its expansion basketball team.

Jill rests for an hour, then changes clothes. She prepares canned split pea soup and bread for dinner for the children, listening to a chorus of stories about their day. The sitter arrives and Jill gives quick instructions. At 5:00 P.M., she swings by the baseball field to pick up Bobby. Leaving the car running, she goes to the bleachers and watches Bobby steal a base as the game comes to an end.

Back at the car, Jill takes an EPCOT parking pass off

her dashboard and replaces it with an arena pass. At 6:30 she meets with a group of players' wives. She organized the group and held the first meeting at her home to offer support and friendship to women whose husbands are on the road often.

Jill's parents are at the game, and so are Lorraine Boisselle and her husband, Robert. The Magic win handily after a five-game losing streak, and Jill finds she is blissfully caught up in the excitement of every point scored. "I really lose myself in those games. It is a great stress-reliever and a way of taking my mind completely off the family for a time."

During the game, Jimmy and Bobby are darting on and off the court, working as ball boys. Pat occupies his usual spot: standing in a stairwell at one corner of the court, nervously taking in each detail of the game.

After the game, Jill drives home in the van. Pat stays behind to rehash the details with local sports reporters and congratulate the players. At 10:30 P.M. Jill dials Domino's on the car phone. "Two small pizzas, both with extra cheese. Put sausage on one and green pepper and onion on the other."

Jimmy and Bobby wait at the arena to come home with their dad. After the pizzas are consumed, Pat and Jill, bone-tired, reluctantly agree to skip church in the morning. Services from their church are broadcast live on television, so they'll catch morning worship in their living room. The younger children can go with Jill's parents in the morning. They sleep soundly. And so do all dozen children.

The Whole Fabric

Finding and nurturing a red thread is an important theme in the Williams home, but it is not the only one.

There is a larger fabric of concerns and goals for each child, in which the red thread is perhaps the most prominent strand.

Pat maps out his hopes for each child this way: "I want them to be strong spiritually and trust in Christ and grow in their faith. I want them to be able to handle their schoolwork responsibly, and to be disciplined. I want them to do what has to be done, when it has to be done, and I want it done right every time they do something."

Jill balances Pat's concerns with her own set of priorities for all the children. She wants to encourage them to express themselves and sort out their feelings, so she nudges them frequently to read books and to write in their journals. Part of her reasoning is based on her own experience as a newlywed with a notoriously uncommunicative husband. Jill says, "I want the boys to know what they're feeling so that when they are married and their wives say, 'Talk to us,' they'll be able to do it."

Staying in touch with feelings and recording thoughts and dreams may be particularly helpful to adopted children. The fabric of their lives contains some loose ends from a previous history, whether they remember it or not. And the red thread principle, in Pat's view, is critical for adopted kids. "The real challenge of adoption," he says, "is to take kids who appear to have few skills and no future, and build into their lives some opportunity. Seeing them respond is the greatest reward."

Raising an adopted child is on the whole very similar to raising a birth child. Yet there is a constant added dimension as well. Questions about the child's adoption, birth parents, and identity begin coming even in the preschool years. Often a child's curiosity intensifies greatly by the age of 12 or 13. Adoptive parents need to know what to expect and how to respond. Most important, they need to remain ready and open to discussions about adoption throughout their lives.

Being a student of the child, knowing his natural bents and inclinations, gives a parent the perception that is necessary to keep lines of communication open. The fact of adoption may not be the most important thread in an adopted child's life, but it is one that is embroidered into practically every aspect of the child's identity and sense of self-worth.

By birth and by adoption, Pat and Jill have formed their family. It no longer matters that some limbs on the family tree originated with Pat and Jill, while others were grafted at various stages of growth and development. From the moment they were grafted, those added limbs began drawing their sustenance from the new "tree."

The adopted children are becoming real Williamses— assuming family mannerisms, habits, values, and outlooks on life. Similarly, Pat and Jill have assumed new identities. Their family is part-Korean and part-Filipino, and will be from now on. Embracing the differences and acknowledging the difficulties help make it work, yet it has to happen one day at a time. The creation of something new, renewed, growing, and changing is the essence of adoption. Pat and Jill have learned that adoption forms real families, forms them forever.

Framed in the entryway of the Williams home is this verse, entitled "Children Among the Thorns."

> Some would gather money
> Along the path of life;
> Some would gather roses,
> And rest from worldly strife.

But we would gather children
From among the thorns of sin.
We would seek dark almond eyes,
And a carefree, toothless grin.

For money cannot enter
In the land of endless day,
And the roses that are gathered,
Soon will wilt and fade away.

But oh, the laughing children,
As we cross the sunset sea,
And the gates swing wide to heaven,
We can take them in, you see!

Epilogue

Children who need homes do not tend to show up when it is most convenient. Their backgrounds may be troubling indeed, and they may require unusually large quantities of parental attention, love, discipline, and patience at the outset. For some families, however, the challenge these children represent and the joy they bring make it easy to say yes. Pat and Jill learned these lessons when the Filipinos arrived, and they were in for another education just one year later.

It came at Christmastime, after Jill spoke to a group of church women. "There are so many children in our home that we don't give a lot of gifts," Jill explained. "Instead, we emphasize Jesus' birthday. Since this is His birthday, here is what I would like to give Jesus.

"I'd like to give Him myself—my feet, to walk where Jesus wants me to go. I'd like to give Him my hands—to have working hands busy for Him. I'd like to give Him my voice, and sing praise to Him this Christmas." Jill had no idea just how God would put her hands and feet and heart to work that holiday season.

One chaotic December day, Jill was teaching music at Maitland Christian School, getting students prepared for their Christmas program. In the midst of rehearsals, she was summoned to the telephone. It was Lorraine Boisselle. "I need to see you," Lorraine said in a voice that would brook no compromise. "I'll be at your house at one o'clock."

Jill finished the rehearsal, sent the children back to their classrooms, and dashed home. Lorraine drove up with two toddler girls, Nicole and Samantha, sucking on bottles. The younger one, at age 2, wore a pacifier on a string around her neck.

The girls' mother had come to Lorraine that morning, desperate and confused. Her husband was in jail, and she said she could not take care of her five children. There was an 8-year-old son, 5- and 6-year-old girls, and these two darlings—just the same age and size of Sarah and Andrea when they had arrived home. The mother told Lorraine she wanted to sign over all the children to the adoption agency. Lorraine agreed to provide temporary shelter for them until the family's circumstances could be assessed fully.

"I've found places for the others," Lorraine said, rubbing the ear that had been planted to the telephone receiver all morning. "But I have no place to send these two girls. They need someplace to stay tonight, and probably for several weeks until we come up with some solution." Lorraine referred the woman to public agencies that could help her, and even set up an appointment.

Jill tried to hug the two girls gently and stroked their

matted hair. They screamed and shrank back against Lorraine. Together, Jill and Lorraine bathed the girls, commenting quietly about their strangely bloated stomachs. Then they gave the two thorough lice shampoos—something they obviously needed.

The Williamses' family doctor, Steve Selznick, paid a rare house call to see the two girls. At first glance, he could tell they were suffering from malnutrition. Also both of them were wheezing and coughing, rubbing red eyes and wiping runny noses with their little hands, so Dr. Selznick put them on antibiotics.

Pat knew nothing of the day's events until he was on his way home. He placed his usual afternoon "checkup" call to Jill from the car phone. She sounded breathless, then she started to laugh. "Are you sitting down?" she asked. "Of course," said Pat. "I'm in the car."

"Promise you won't get mad?" Pat promised. Jill paused a second. "We have two more children," she announced. Pat pushed the disconnect button in bemused silence. He pulled into the driveway, and there was Jill, flanked by 2-year-old Samantha and sister Nicole, 3.

At dinner, when Pat asked everyone to hold hands for grace, Nicole and Samantha burst out laughing. Prayer was clearly not a part of the girls' early upbringing.

That evening, a fully orchestrated lobbying campaign was under way in the Williams household. "Mom, I think they should stay here. When can we adopt them?" asked Sarah, then Andrea, then a few of the boys. David and Peter entertained the two sisters in the library, while Jill made up a bed for the two of them to share.

After five weeks at the Williams home, Nicole and Samantha were well-fed, relaxed, and more in tune with activities appropriate to their ages. Jill had discarded their bottles and was beginning to potty train them. Sarah and Andrea labored each afternoon to teach them colors and numbers.

Hints at their earlier life-style popped out unexpectedly. Riding in the Caravan one day, Samantha pointed to a police car and yelled, "Cops!"

Will Nicole and Samantha boost the Williams family roster by two, leaving Pat and Jill with fourteen children to raise? It is possible—even a welcome possibility in this impossible household. More likely, a solution will be developed to return the children, eventually, to the care of their mother and father when he is released from prison.

Temporary care for children in need is part of the adoption picture as well, whether it's foster care for children before they are placed for adoption, or crisis care for a family that is trying to pick up the pieces of a broken life. To their own amazement, Pat and Jill found themselves opening their door and their hearts to these two tiny, bedraggled strangers.

In just a day, Pat and Jill had become "Mom" and "Dad." And the girls became "Niki" and "Sam." Jill sat rocking a sleepy Samantha one evening at bedtime, stroking her blonde, Shirley Temple curls and marveling at how soft and sweet-smelling the formerly lice-ridden hair had become.

It wasn't exactly the same as rocking Karyn, or Sarah, or Andrea, or even baby Michael; yet the feeling was unmistakable. Jill knew she could love Sam and Niki as a mother. Yet how uncertain and vulnerable their lives are, Jill mused. She knew she had to guard against growing too attached, for now. Maybe it would be best to reunite them with their birth parents, and hope that the safety net of Florida's social services won't let them down.

Samantha stirred, staring at Jill with a fixed gaze and a contented smile, innocent and oblivious of the turmoil surrounding her parents, the finality of decisions soon to be made about her life. Jill fought back tears, and silently committed Sam's life to the Lord.

•   •   •

Weeks later, Lorraine telephoned from The Adoption Centre. "Their dad is out of jail," she told Jill. "He's here at the office, and he wants his daughters back." Their mother had relinquished her rights to raise the children, but the father refused to sign the papers that would free them to be adopted. Lorraine had no choice but to send Sam and Niki home at his request.

Sarah, Andrea, and Karyn helped Jill pack two suitcases full of clothing and belongings. Heavy with sorrow, they worked in slow motion and mostly in silence.

Willing herself to stay calm and cheerful, Jill picked the girls up from nursery school. She bathed Sam and Niki, dressed them, brushed their hair. She knew she could not manage to make the ten-minute drive to Lorraine's office, so she called Pat. "You've got to come home and do this," she said. Pat arrived home at 1:00 P.M., and it was time to say good-bye. The Williams family formed a circle and held hands. It was a school holiday, so all the children were at home.

Pat prayed for the girls' protection, health, and spiritual growth. He thanked the Lord earnestly for bringing Sam and Niki into their lives. Then each of the twelve children kissed and hugged the confused little sisters. Pat whisked them into his car and handed each of them a bag of cookies. At Lorraine's suggestion, Pat met her at a post office so he would not have to see their father face-to-face.

Pat and Jill have no idea whether they will ever see the girls again, or learn what has become of them. After the other children were in bed that evening, Jill ached to hold and rock Samantha as she had shortly before Lorraine called. As she sought comfort and peace about their future, Jill recalled the words of Psalm 139:13–16.

For you created my inmost being; you knit me together in my mother's womb. I praise you because I am fearfully and wonderfully made; your works are wonderful, I know that full well. My frame was not hidden from you when I was made in the secret place. When I was woven together in the depths of the earth, your eyes saw my unformed body. All the days ordained for me were written in your book before one of them came to be.

Source Notes

Chapter 1: *Eight Grafted Limbs*

1. Bob Morris, "A Quiz Much Easier to Digest Than Turkey," in the *Orlando Sentinel,* 25 November 1988, p. C-1.

Chapter 2: *Andrea and Sarah Come Home*

1. Frances M. Koh, *Oriental Children in American Homes* (Minneapolis: East-West Press, 1981), p. 4.
2. Bertha Holt, *The Seed From the East* (Eugene, Ore.: Industrial Publishing Co., 1956), p. 21.

Chapter 3: *Who Are the Children?*

1. *Adoption Factbook,* Table 13. "Immigrant orphans (foreign adoptees) admitted to the United

States by country or region of birth, fiscal years 1985–1987" (Washington, D.C.: National Committee for Adoption, 1989), p. 101.

2. Byung Hoon Chun, "Adoption and Korea," in *Child Welfare,* Vol. 68, No. 2, p. 256.
3. Lourdes G. Balanon, "Foreign Adoption in the Philippines: Issues and Opportunities," in *Child Welfare,* Vol. 68, No. 2, p. 241.
4. *Adoption Factbook,* p. 101.
5. Balanon, "Foreign Adoption in the Philippines," p. 251.
6. *Adoption Factbook,* p. 101.
7. Ibid.
8. Marcia Slacum Greene, " 'Boarder Babies' Linger in Hospitals," in the *Washington Post,* 11 September 1989, p. A-7.
9. *America's Waiting Children: A Report to the President from the Interagency Task Force on Adoption,* Government Printing Office No. 711AB, April 1988, p. 1.
10. Ibid., pp. 2, 26.
11. Pearl Buck, *Children for Adoption* (New York: Random House, 1964).

Chapter 4: And Then There Were Eight

1. Claudia L. Jewett, *Adopting the Older Child* (Boston, Mass.: The Harvard Common Press, 1978), p. 14.
2. Elizabeth Hormann, *After the Adoption* (Old Tappan, N.J.: Fleming H. Revell Co., 1987), p. 92.
3. Frances Koh, *Oriental Children in American*

Homes (Minneapolis: East-West Press, 1981), p. 31.

Chapter 6: *Preparing to Adopt*

1. Claudia L. Jewett, *Adopting the Older Child* (Boston, Mass.: The Harvard Common Press, 1978), Introduction.
2. Jacqueline Hornor Plumez, *Successful Adoption* (New York: Harmony Books, 1982), p. 49.
3. Edmund Blair Bolles, *The Penguin Adoption Handbook* (New York: The Viking Press, 1984), p. 23.

Chapter 7: *Twelve-Part Harmony*

1. Lois Ruskai Melina, *Raising Adopted Children* (New York: Harper & Row, 1986), p. 50.
2. Ibid., p. 48.

Chapter 8: *"Who Am I?"*

1. John Aeby, "Dear Readers," in *Hi Families,* Vol. 31, No. 5, p. 2.
2. *Hi Families,* Vol. 31, No. 5, p. 15.
3. Heather Kellmann, "A Different Land," in *OURS,* Jan.–Feb. 1989, p. 25.
4. Jacqueline Hornor Plumez, *Successful Adoption* (New York: Harmony Books, 1982), p. 128.
5. Ibid., p. 131.
6. David M. Brodzinsky, "Adjustment to Adoption: A Psychosocial Perspective," *Clinical Psychology Review,* 1987, Vol. 7, pp. 25–47.

7. Lois Ruskai Melina, *Raising Adopted Children* (New York: Harper & Row, 1986), p. 175.
8. Cathy Jimenez, "Thank You, Lord," in *Hi Families,* Vol. 28, No. 5, p. 15.

Chapter 9: The Red Thread

1. Charles R. Swindoll, *You and Your Child* (Fullerton, Calif.: Insight for Living, 1986), p. 3.

Recommended Readings and Resources

Books

Arms, Suzanne. *To Love and Let Go*. New York: Knopf, 1986.

Bolles, Edmund Blair. *The Penguin Adoption Handbook*. New York: The Viking Press, 1984.

Feigelman, William, and Arnold R. Silverman. *Chosen Children: New Patterns of Adoptive Relationships*. New York: Praeger, 1983.

Gilman, Lois. *The Adoption Resource Book*. New York: Harper & Row, 1984.

Hormann, Elizabeth. *After the Adoption*. Old Tappan, N.J.: Fleming H. Revell Company, 1987.

Hunt, Angela Elwell. *The Adoption Option: Exploring the Adoption Experience for Christian Families*. Wheaton, Ill.: SP Publications, Inc., 1989.

Jewett, Claudia L. *Adopting the Older Child*. Boston, Mass.: The Harvard Common Press, 1978.

————. *Helping Children Cope with Separation and Loss.* Boston, Mass.: The Harvard Common Press, 1982.

Johnston, Patricia Irwin. *An Adoptor's Advocate.* Fort Wayne, Ind.: Perspectives Press, 1984.

Kirk, H. David. *Shared Fate: A Theory and Method of Adoptive Relationships.* Port Angles, Wash.: Ben-Simon Publications, 1984.

Koh, Frances. *Oriental Children in American Homes.* Minneapolis: East-West Press, 1981.

Krementz, Jill. *How It Feels to Be Adopted.* New York: Knopf, 1982.

Livingston, Carol. *Why Was I Adopted?* Secaucus, N.J.: Lyle Stewart, 1978.

Margolies, Marjorie, and Ruth Gruber. *They Came to Stay.* New York: Coward, McCann and Geoghegan, Inc., 1976.

Melina, Lois Ruskai. *Raising the Adopted Child: A Manual for Adoptive Parents.* New York: Harper & Row, 1986.

Menning, Barbara Eck. *Infertility: A Guide for Childless Couples.* Englewood Cliffs, N.J.: Prentice-Hall, 1977.

Plumez, Jacqueline Hornor. *Successful Adoption: A Guide to Finding a Child and Raising a Family.* New York: Harmony Books, 1982.

Newsletters and Organizations

AASK America Adoption Exchange
Aid to Adoption of Special Kids
595 Market Street
San Francisco, California 94105
(415) 451-1748

Adopted Child
(Newsletter edited by Lois R. Melina, P.O. Box 9362, Moscow, Idaho 83843)

Adoptive Families of America, Inc.
(formerly OURS, Inc.)
3333 Highway 100 North
Minneapolis, Minnesota 55422
(612) 535-4829
(Membership organization providing information and referral to adoptive parents' groups. Publisher of *OURS* magazine)

Committee for Single Adoptive Parents
P.O. Box 15084
Chevy Chase, Maryland 20815
(202) 966-6367
(Publishes "The Handbook for Single Adoptive Parents")

Holt International Children's Services
P.O. Box 2880
Eugene, Oregon 97402
(503) 687-2202

International Concerns Committee for Children
911 Cypress Drive
Boulder, Colorado 80303
(303) 494-8333
(Has sponsorship program for orphans abroad and an information service on adoptable children living overseas and in the United States)

Latin American Parents Association
P.O. Box 72
Seaford, New York 11783
(718) 236-8689
(Provides information on sources and procedures for Latin American adoptions)

National Adoption Center
1218 Chestnut Street
Philadelphia, Pennsylvania 19107
(Publishes a bibliography of books on adoption for children; has a computer matching service for waiting children and families)

National Adoption Information Clearinghouse
1400 Eye Street, N.W., #600
Washington, D.C. 20005
(202) 842-1919
(Federally funded database with abstracts of articles on adoption. Free monographs available on all aspects of adoption)

National Committee for Adoption
1930 17th Street, N.W.
Washington, D.C. 20009
(202) 328-1200
(Lobbying organization and publisher of *Adoption Factbook,* a comprehensive collection of adoption statistics)

NACAC
North American Council on Adoptable Children
1821 University Ave. #S-275
St. Paul, Minnesota 55104
(612) 644-3036
(Nonprofit coalition which holds an annual conference
and publishes a newsletter, "Adoptalk")

One Church/One Child
607 East Oakwood Blvd.
Chicago, Illinois 60653
(312) 624-5375
(Father George Clement's adoption program for black
children)

Resolve, Inc.
5 Water Street
Arlington, Massachusetts 02174
(617) 643-2424
(National infertility support organization)

DOG OWNER'S
HOME VETERINARY HANDBOOK

A healthy puppy makes for a happy puppy - and a happy owner.
Kathy Giffin and her 3-months old Great Pyrenees.

Dog Owner's HOME VETERINARY Handbook

by

DELBERT G. CARLSON, D.V.M.
and JAMES M. GIFFIN, M.D.

FIRST EDITION

HOWELL
BOOK HOUSE

Howell Book House
Macmillan Publishing Company
866 Third Avenue, New York, NY 10022

Collier Macmillan Canada, Inc.
1200 Eglinton Avenue East, Suite 200
Don Mills, Ontario M3C 3N1

Library of Congress Cataloguing in Publication Data

Carlson, Delbert G
   Dog owner's home veterinary handbook.

   Includes index.
   1. Dogs—Diseases—Handbooks, manuals, etc.
I. Giffin, James M., joint author.   II. Title.
SF991.C25   636.7'089   80-13912

ISBN 0-87605-764-4

20   19   18   17   16   15

Printed in the United States of America

*Dedicated
with love
to our families*

The Authors

Dr. Delbert G. Carlson

DELBERT G. CARLSON, D.V.M.

Dr. Del Carlson, a practicing veterinarian with a long-standing experience in the medical and surgical care of dogs, makes his home in Springfield, Missouri. He received his medical degree from the University of Minnesota Veterinary School in 1954 and interned at the Rawley Memorial Hospital in Springfield, Massachusetts.

He and Mrs. Carlson have found the time to raise and show horses throughout the Midwest, breed Afghan Hounds and Borzois, and put five children through college. He is an avid fly fisherman.

Dr. Carlson is a member of the Missouri Veterinary Medical Association and a past-president of the Greene County Humane Society.

Dr. James M. Giffin

JAMES M. GIFFIN, M.D.

Dr. Jim Giffin is the co-author of the award-winning book, *The Complete Great Pyrenees* (Howell Book House, Inc.) He and Mrs. Giffin founded their Elysee Great Pyrenees Kennel in 1969 and became active in showing and judging the breed. They finished several champions and campaigned a Best in Show winner.

Dr. Giffin received his medical degree from Yale University School of Medicine in 1961 and completed his surgical residency at Barnes Hospital in St. Louis. He served as Chief of Surgery at the 45th Surgical Hospital in Vietnam.

His family interests include skiing, fishing, and hiking with the dogs in the mountains neighboring his home in Delta, Colorado.

Dr. Giffin has served on the Board of Directors of the Great Pyrenees Club of America, Inc.

**Finding it quick in
DOG OWNER'S HOME VETERINARY HANDBOOK:**

A special INDEX OF SIGNS AND SYMPTOMS is on the inside front cover page for fast referral. Consult this if your dog exhibits unexplained behavior. It will help you locate his problem.

The detailed TABLE OF CONTENTS outlines the organs and the systems which are the usual sites of disease. If you can locate the problem anatomically, consult it first.

The GENERAL INDEX begins on Page 359, and gives you a comprehensive guide to the book's medical information. (Where a page number is in boldface, it indicates a more detailed coverage of the subject.)

CROSS-REFERENCES note pertinent supplementary information. Where the reference is in caps and small caps (SKIN), it identifies a chapter title; in italics, it identifies a subdivision of a chapter.

Contents

Introduction

A Roman historian once spoke of a tribe of Ethiopians who made a dog their King. All were obliged to obey him. "When he barks," he said, "they know he is angry. And when he scratches himself, they know he is not."

Modern veterinary diagnosticians are no less concerned about the interpretation of a dog's behavior than were the Ethiopians of old. To the extent that a dog can't tell you what is on his mind, he can't give you a long list of symptoms to mull over. Instead, you have to study the ailing animal; and then come to some conclusion as to what might be wrong with him.

In writing this book, we have attempted to describe in the dog signs and symptoms which will help the owner arrive at a preliminary diagnosis—so he can weigh the severity of the problem. Some health problems are not potentially serious and can be treated at home. Others are not. Knowing when to call your veterinarian can be of great importance. Delays can be costly.

At the same time we have sought to provide guidance for the acute or emergency situations that common sense dictates you should handle on your own. Life-saving procedures such as *Artificial Respiration, Heart Massage,* the treatment of *Bloat,* management of *Obstetrical Emergencies, Poisonings,* and the like are illustrated and explained in a step-by-step fashion.

A Veterinary Handbook is not intended to be a substitute for professional care. Book advice can never be as helpful or as safe as medical assistance. No text can replace the interview and physical examination, during which the veterinarian elicits the sort of information which leads to a speedy and accurate diagnosis. But the knowledge provided in this book will enable you to work in better understanding and more effective cooperation with your veterinarian. You'll be more alert to the symptoms of disease and better able to describe them for him.

xvii

In this book you will find the basics of health care and disease prevention for the young and the old. A well-cared-for dog suffers fewer illnesses and infirmities as he grows older.

Chapters on *Sex and Reproduction, Pregnancy and Whelping,* and *Pediatrics* provide comprehensive coverage on matters of importance to all dog breeders.

The combined efforts of many people make this book possible.

The Infectious Disease chapter was prepared with the assistance of Frances Rogers Ippensen, A.B., M.S. (in Biological Sciences). Mrs. Ippensen has taught anatomy, physiology, microbiology and chemistry at the University of Illinois, the University of Cincinnati, and the Cook County School of Nursing. She owns and manages a top Labrador Retriever kennel.

We are indebted to Dr. James Clawson for his splendid photographs showing techniques in handling and medicating dogs.

Krist Carlson and Jamie Giffin assisted us with much of the taking, developing, and processing of the photographs depicting canine ailments.

Rose Floyd and Sydney Giffin Wiley created the many fine drawings.

Patti Herzog and Gene Boxx deserve our sincere thanks for their long and devoted service in the typing of the manuscript.

Recognition would not be complete without mentioning the many researchers, clinicians, and educators whose works have served as a source for our information. Among them are *Current Veterinary Therapy* (edited by Robert W. Kirk, D.V.M.); *Small Animal Dermatology* (George W. Muller, D.V.M. and Robert W. Kirk, D.V.M.); *Canine Ophthalmology* (William G. Magrane, D.V.M.); and the numerous contributors to *The Veterinary Clinics of North America* (W. B. Saunders Company).

We are indeed grateful to Elsworth S. Howell who gave us the opportunity to produce this work.

— DELBERT G. CARLSON
— JAMES M. GIFFIN

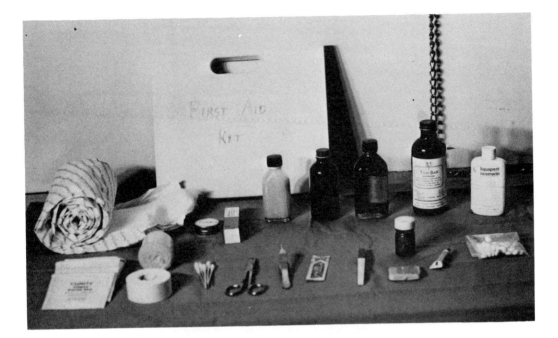

HOME EMERGENCY and MEDICAL KIT

1. Container
2. Cotton roll
3. Gauze pad—3 x 3
4. Gauze roll—3"
5. 1" roll adhesive tape
6. Q-Tips
7. Tweezers (thumb forceps)
8. Scalpel and scissors
9. Thermometer
10. Hydrogen peroxide (3%)
11. Pepto-Bismol
12. Furacin ointment
13. Panolog ear drops
14. Charcoal suspension
15. Kaopectate
16. Milk of Magnesia
17. Dramamine
18. Aspirin
19. Gastric tube

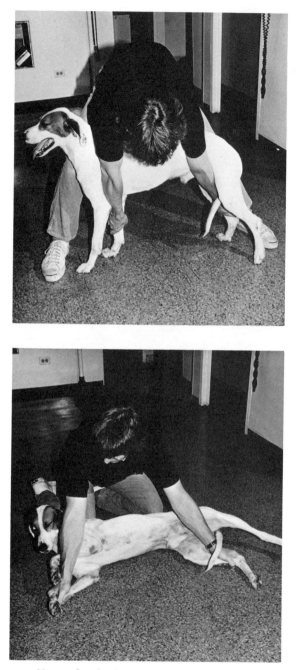

How to lay the dog on his side. —*J. Clawson*

1

Emergencies

ARTIFICIAL RESPIRATION and HEART MASSAGE

Artificial respiration is an emergency procedure used to assist breathing in an unconscious dog. Heart massage is used when no heart beat can be heard or felt. When combined with artificial respiration, it is called *cardiopulmonary resuscitation*. As cessation of breathing is soon followed by heart stoppage, and vice versa, cardiopulmonary resuscitation frequently is required to sustain life. Heart massage by itself provides for both movement of air and pumping of blood. For best results, combine heart massage with forced mouth to nose breathing. This requires two people, one to administer heart massage and one to give mouth to nose breathing.

The following emergencies may require artificial respiration and/or heart massage:

Shock	Head Injury
Poisoning	Electric Shock
Prolonged Seizure	Obstructed Airways (Choking)
Coma	Sudden Death

Artificial Respiration

Two methods are used. The *chest compression* technique consists of applying force to the chest wall, which pushes air out and allows the elastic recoil of the chest to draw air back in. It is the easiest to perform.

Mouth to nose forced respiration is used when the compression technique is ineffective, or when the chest is punctured *(pneumothorax)*.

3

Steps in Chest Compression

1. Feel for pulse or heart beat.
2. Open mouth and clear away secretions. Check for a foreign body. If found, remove if possible. If impossible to reach, execute the *Heimlich* maneuver (see RESPIRATORY SYSTEM: *Object in the Voice Box).*
3. Lay the dog on a flat surface with his *right* side down.
4. Place both hands on his chest and press down sharply. Release quickly. If properly performed, you should be able to hear air moving in and out. If you can't, proceed with mouth to nose resuscitation.
5. Continue until the dog breathes on his own, or as long as the heart beats.

Steps in Mouth to Nose Resuscitation:

1. Perform steps 1 and 2 in *Chest Compression.*
2. Pull the tongue forward and close the mouth. Seal the lips with your hand.
3. Place your mouth over the dog's nose and blow in steadily for three seconds. The chest will expand. Release to let the air come back out.
4. Continue until the dog breathes on his own, or as long as the heart beats.

Heart Massage

Steps in Small Dogs and Puppies:

1. Perform steps 1 and 2 in *Chest Compression.*
2. Lay the dog on his side. Place your thumb on one side of his sternum (*see* P. 224) and your fingers on the other, just behind the elbows.
3. Compress the chest firmly six times. Wait five seconds to let the chest expand; then repeat.
4. Continue until the heart beats on its own, or until no heart beat is felt for five minutes.

Steps in Larger Dogs:

1. Repeat steps 1 and 2 in *Chest Compression.*
2. Lay the dog on a flat surface with his *right* side down.
3. Place the heel of your hand on his rib cage just behind the elbow (over the heart).
4. Compress the chest firmly six times. Wait five seconds to let the chest expand; then, repeat.
5. Continue until the heart beats on its own, or until no heart beat is felt for five minutes.

The *chest compression* technique for giving artificial respiration.

Heart Massage. Note the placement of the hands behind the elbow and over the heart. Heart massage alone provides for movement of air as well as pumping of blood. —*J. Clawson*

BURNS

Burns are caused by heat, chemicals, electric shocks, and radiation. Sunburn is an example of radiation burn. It occurs on the nose of dogs with insufficient pigment (see SKIN: *Collie Nose),* and on the skin of white-coated dogs who are sheared in summer.

Skin damage depends upon the length and intensity of exposure. With a superficial burn, you will see redness in the skin, sometimes blisters, perhaps slight swelling, and the burn is tender. With deep burns, the skin appears white, the hair will come out easily when pulled, and pain is severe. If more than 15 percent of the body surface is involved in a deep burn, the outlook is poor. In such cases fluid seeps from the damaged area. This can lead to shock.

Treatment: Apply cold water soaks or ice packs to small burns for 20 minutes to relieve pain. Clip away hair and wash gently with a surgical soap. Blot dry. Apply a topical antibiotic ointment *(furacin).* Protect the area from rubbing by applying a loose-fitting gauze dress.

Treat chemical burns by flushing them with copious amounts of water. Acid on the skin is neutralized by rinsing with baking soda (four tablespoons to a pint of water). Alkali is neutralized by rinsing with a weak vinegar solution (two tablespoons to a pint of water). Blot dry and apply antibiotic ointment. Bandage loosely.

COLD EXPOSURE

Hypothermia: (Abnormal Low Temperature)

Prolonged exposure to cold results in a drop in body temperature. It is most likely to occur when a dog is wet. It is seen most often in Toy breeds and those with short hair. Hypothermia also occurs in shock, after a long anesthetic, and in newborn pups. Prolonged chilling burns up the available energy and predisposes to low blood sugar.

The signs of hypothermia are: violent shivering followed by listlessness and apathy; a rectal temperature below 97 degrees F (which is diagnostic); and finally, collapse and coma.

Treatment: Wrap your dog in a blanket or coat and carry him into the house. If he is wet (having fallen into ice water), give him a warm bath. Rub him vigorously with towels to dry his skin.

Warm chilled dogs by applying warm water packs to the axilla (armpit), chest and abdomen. The temperature of the packs should be about that of a baby bottle (warm to the wrist). Continue to change the packs until the rectal temperature reaches 100 degrees F. Warming with a hair dryer or air comb works well.

As the dog begins to move about, give him some honey or glucose (four tablespoons of sugar added to a pint of water).

How to warm a chilled puppy is discussed in PEDIATRICS: *Warming a Chilled Puppy*.

Frostbite

Frostbite affects the toes, ears, and scrotum. The skin at first is pale white. With the return of circulation, it becomes red and swollen. It may peel. Eventually, it looks much like a burn, with a line of demarcation between the live and dead tissue. Dead skin separates in one to three weeks.

Treatment: Warm frostbitten parts with warm water soaks as described above. Prevent infection by applying an antibiotic. Cover with a bandage as described in *Bandaging*, at end of this chapter.

DEHYDRATION

Dehydration is excess loss of body fluids. Usually it involves loss of both water and *electrolytes* (which are minerals such as sodium, chloride, potassium). During illness, dehydration may be due to an inadequate fluid intake. Fever increases the loss of water. This becomes significant if the dog does not drink enough to offset it. Other common causes of dehydration are prolonged vomiting and diarrhea.

One sign of dehydration is loss of skin elasticity. When the skin along the back is picked up into a fold, it should spring back into place. In dehydration, the skin stays up in a ridge. Another sign is dryness of the mouth. Late signs are sunken eyeballs and circulatory collapses.

Treatment: If your dog is noticeably dehydrated, he should receive veterinary attention. Treatment is directed at replacing fluids and preventing further losses.

In mild cases without vomiting, fluids can be given by mouth. If the dog won't drink, he can be given an electrolyte solution by bottle or syringe into his cheek pouch (see APPENDIX). Balanced electrolyte solutions for treating dehydration in children are available at drug stores. Ringer's lactate, mixed half and half with 5% Dextrose in water, and a solution called Pedialyte, are suitable for dogs. They are given at the rate of two to four cc per pound body weight per hour depending on the severity of the dehydration (or as directed by your veterinarian).

The treatment of dehydration in infant puppies is discussed in PEDIATRICS: *Common Feeding Problems*.

DROWNING and SUFFOCATION

Conditions which prevent oxygen from getting into the lungs and blood cause *asphyxiation*. They are: carbon monoxide poisoning; inhalation of toxic fumes (smoke, gasoline, propane, refrigerants, solvents); drowning; and smothering (which can happen when a dog is left too long in an airtight space). Other causes are foreign bodies in the airways and injuries to the chest which interfere with breathing.

The symptoms of oxygen lack are: straining to breathe; gasping for breath (often with the head extended); extreme anxiety; and weakness progressing to loss of consciousness as the dog begins to succumb. The pupils begin to dilate. The tongue and mucus membranes turn blue, which is a reflection of insufficient oxygen in the blood. One exception to the blue color is carbon monoxide poisoning, in which the membranes are a bright red.

Treatment: The most important consideration is to provide your dog with fresh air to breathe. (Better yet, give him oxygen, if available.) If respirations are shallow or absent, begin immediately by giving mouth to nose respiration.

If he has an open wound into his chest, which you can diagnose if you hear air sucking in and out as he breathes, seal off the chest by pinching the skin together over the wound.

When the situation is one of drowning, turn the dog upside down, suspend him by his legs, and let the water run out of his windpipe. Then position the dog with his head lower than his chest (on a slope, or with a roll beneath his chest) and begin artificial respiration. Mouth to nose forced respiration may be required. With heart stoppage, heart massage should be attempted. Continue efforts to resuscitate until the dog breathes on his own or until no heart beat is felt for five minutes. (See *Artificial Respiration and Heart Massage* in this chapter.)

Once the immediate crisis is over, veterinary aid should be sought. Pneumonia from inhalation is a frequent complication.

ELECTRIC SHOCKS and BURNS

Electric shocks occur in puppies who chew on electric cords. Occasionally, a dog comes into contact with a downed wire or is struck by lightning. Burns of the mouth from electric cords are discussed in the chapter ORAL CAVITY. Dogs who receive an electric shock may be burned. They may show signs of circulatory collapse and difficulty breathing. Electric current damages the capillaries of the lungs and leads to the accumulation of fluid in the air sacs *(pulmonary edema)*.

Treatment: If your dog is unconscious and not breathing, administer artificial respiration. Pulmonary edema has to be treated by a veterinarian.

HANDLING and RESTRAINT

Any dog in pain, or severely injured, cannot be held responsible for his actions. No matter how docile your dog may be, you should recognize that under certain circumstances he may turn and bite. This is an understandable reflex. You should take proper precautions, so as not to be injured.

Apprehension is another cause of panic and aggressive behavior. If you plan to give your dog an injection, or must do something to him which is apt to cause pain, approach him with quiet confidence and a minimum of fanfare. Dogs are quick to sense anxiety in their owners.

If there is a possibility your dog may bite, take precautions *before* doing anything which might excite or hurt him. When a dog is properly restrained, usually he settles down and accepts the treatment. A good assistant is a real asset.

There are several good ways to restrain a dog. They are illustrated in the photographs. An emergency muzzle can be made from tape, a necktie, silk stocking, piece of linen, or anything suitable at hand. A good muzzle can be made by looping a leash around the jaws and fastening the end to a door knob. Pillows and blankets around the neck are good for short procedures such as giving a shot, but an assistant is required to hold them in place.

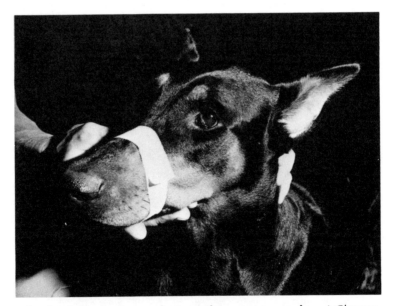

A strip of adhesive tape makes a good temporary muzzle. —*J. Clawson*

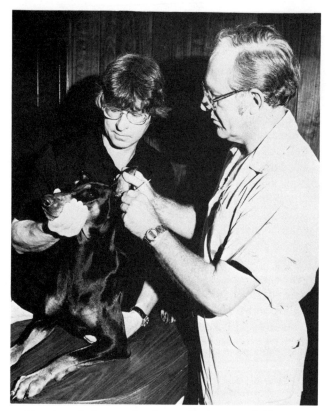

How to restrain your dog for medical care. —*J. Clawson*

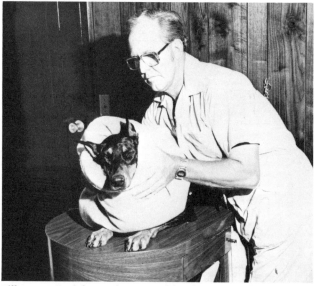

Pillows around the neck are good for short procedures such as giving a shot. —*J. Clawson*

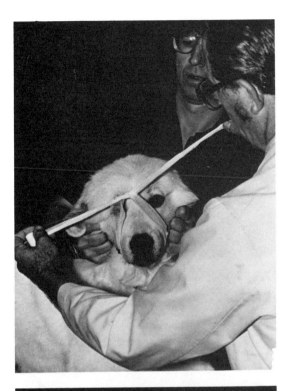

A piece of linen can be used in an emergency. It should be tied behind the head to keep the dog from pawing it off.
—J. Clawson

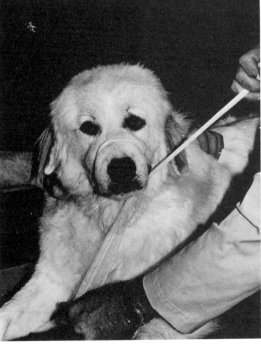

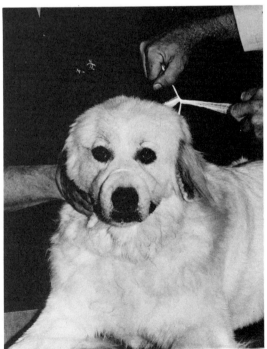

Lifting a small dog who must be restrained.

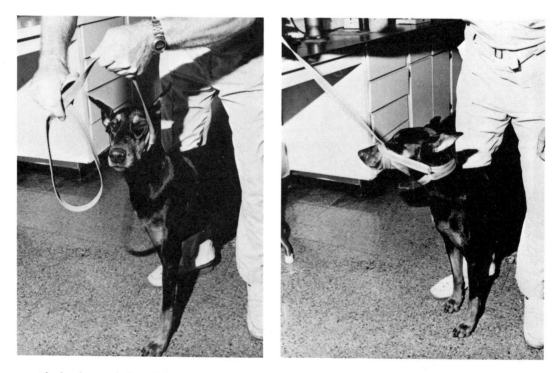

The leash muzzle is useful when you don't have an assistant. Tie the end to a door knob.

—*J. Clawson*

HEAT STROKE (Overheating)

Heat stroke is an emergency which requires immediate recognition and prompt treatment. Dogs do not tolerate high temperatures as well as humans. They depend upon rapid breathing to exchange warm air for cool air. Accordingly, when air temperature is close to body temperature, cooling by rapid breathing is not an efficient process. Dogs with airway disease also have difficulty with excess heat.

Common situations which predispose to overheating or heat stroke in dogs are:

1. Being left in a car in hot weather.
2. Being confined on concrete runs; chained without shade in hot weather.
3. Being of a short-nosed breed, especially a Bulldog or Pug.
4. Being muzzled while put under a dryer (this can happen in a grooming parlor).
5. Suffering from airway disease or any condition which impairs breathing.

Heat stroke begins with rapid frantic noisy breathing. The tongue and mucus membranes are bright red; the saliva is thick and tenacious; and the dog frequently vomits. His rectal temperature is high, sometimes over 106 degrees F. The cause of the problem usually is evident by the typical appearance of the dog; it can be confirmed by taking his temperature.

If the condition is allowed to go unchecked, the dog becomes unsteady and staggers; he has diarrhea which often is bloody and he becomes progressively weaker. Coma and death ensue.

Treatment: Emergency measures must begin at once. Mild cases respond to moving the dog to a cooler surrounding, such as an air-conditioned building or car. If his temperature is over 104 degrees F, or if unsteady on his feet, he should be cooled by immersing him in a tub of cold water. If this is impossible, hose him down with a garden hose. For a temperature over 106 degrees F, or if he is near to collapse, give him a cold water enema. A more rapid temperature drop is imperative.

Heat stroke can be associated with swelling of the throat. This aggravates the problem. A cortisone injection by your veterinarian may be required to treat this.

Prevention:
1. Do not expose dogs with airway disease or impaired breathing to prolonged heat.
2. Restrict exercise during the heat of the day in summer.
3. Breed dogs in air-conditioned quarters.
4. Crate a dog only in an open wire cage.
5. Provide shade and cool water to dogs living outdoors in runs.

HOW TO INDUCE VOMITING

DO NOT induce vomiting if your dog:

1. Swallows an acid, alkali, solvent, or heavy duty cleaner;
2. Is severely depressed or comatose;
3. Swallows a petroleum product;
4. Swallows tranquilizers (which prevent vomiting);
5. Swallows sharp objects (which could lodge in his esophagus or perforate his stomach);
6. Or if more than two hours have passed since the poison was swallowed.

Induce vomiting by giving:

1. Syrup of ipecac (1 teaspoonful per 10 pounds body weight);
2. Hydrogen peroxide 3% (one to three teaspoonfuls every 10 minutes; repeat three times);
3. One-half to one teaspoonful of salt, placed at the back of the tongue.

INSECT STINGS

The stings of *bees, wasps, yellow jackets,* and *ants,* all cause painful swelling at the site of the sting. If an animal is stung many times, he could go into shock as a result of absorbed toxins. Rarely, hypersensitivity reactions develop in dogs who have been stung before (see SKIN: *Allergies*).

The stings of *Black widow* and *Missouri brown* spiders, and *tarantulas,* also are toxic to animals. The signs are sharp pain at the sting site. Later the dog can develop chills, fever, labored breathing. Shock can occur.

The stings of *centipedes* and *scorpions* cause local reaction and at times a severe illness. The bites heal slowly.

The bite of a female wood *tick* rarely can cause a paralysis (see NERVOUS SYSTEM: *Tick Paralysis*). Other common insect parasites are discussed in the SKIN chapter.

Treatment of insect bites:
1. Identify the insect.
2. Remove a stinger when accessible with tweezers. (Only bees leave their stingers behind.)
3. Make a paste of baking soda and apply it directly to the sting.
4. Ice packs relieve swelling and pain.
5. Calamine lotion relieves itching.

If there are signs of generalized toxicity, take your dog to the veterinarian.

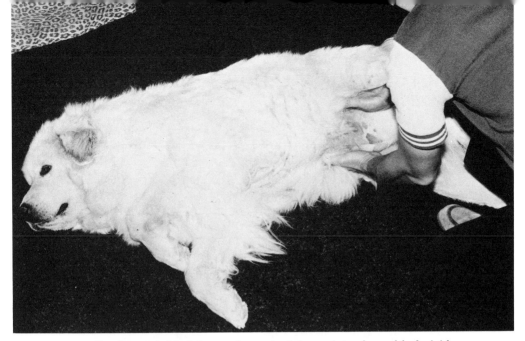

Feeling for a painful abdomen. An *acute abdomen* is tender and feels rigid.

PAINFUL ABDOMEN (Acute Abdomen)

The acute abdomen is an emergency that may lead to the death of the individual unless treatment is started as soon as possible.

This condition is characterized by the *sudden onset* of abdominal pain along with vomiting; retching; extreme restlessness and inability to find a comfortable position; whining and crying; grunting; and labored breathing. The abdomen is extremely painful when pressed on. A characteristic position sometimes is seen in which the dog rests his chest against the floor with his rump up in the air (prayer position). As his condition advances, his pulse becomes weak and thready, his mucus membranes pale, and he goes into shock.

One of the following may be the cause:

Urinary stones
Trauma to the abdomen with internal injury
Rupture of the bladder
Torsion of the stomach and intestines (bloat)
Poisoning
Rupture of the pregnant uterus
Peritonitis
Acute pancreatitis
Intestinal obstruction

A dog with an acute abdomen is critically ill. He should have immediate veterinary attention.

POISONING

General Remarks

A poison is any substance harmful to the body. Animal baits are palatable poisons that encourage ingestion. This makes them an obvious choice for intentional poisoning.

Dogs by nature are curious and have a tendency to hunt small game, or explore out of the way places such as wood piles, weed thickets, and storage ports. This puts them into contact with insects, dead animals and toxic plants. It also means that in many cases of suspected poisoning the actual agent will be unknown. The great variety of potentially poisonous plants and shrubs makes identification difficult or impossible — unless the owner has direct knowledge that his dog has eaten a certain plant or product. Most cases suspected of being malicious poisoning actually are not.

In some types of vegetation only certain parts of the plant are toxic. In others, all parts are poisonous. Ingestion causes a wide range of symptoms. They include: mouth irritation; drooling; vomiting; diarrhea; hallucinations; seizures; coma; and death. Other plant substances cause skin rash. Some toxic plants have specific pharmological actions which are used in medicines.

Tables of toxic plants, shrubs, and trees are included for reference.

POISONOUS HOUSEPLANTS

Toxic Houseplants

A.   That give rash after contact with the skin or mouth:

Chrysanthemum	Poinsettia
Creeping fig	Pot mum
Wheeping fig	Spider mum

} might produce dermatitis

B.   Irritating (toxic oxalates), especially the mouth gets swollen; tongue pain; sore lips:

Arrowhead vine	Majesty
Boston ivy	Neththytis
Colodium	Ivy
Drunk Cane	Pathos
Emerald Duke	Red princess
Heart leaf (Philodendrum)	Saddle leaf (Philodendrum)
Marble Queen	Split leaf (Philodendrum)

C.   Toxic plants — may contain wide variety of poisons. Most cause vomiting, abdominal pain, cramps. Some cause tremors, heart and respiratory and/or kidney problems, which are difficult for owner to interpret:

Amaryllis	Elephant ears	Pot mum
Asparagus fern	Glocal Ivy	Ripple Ivy
Azalea	Heart Ivy	Spider mum
Bird of paradise	Ivy	Sprangeri Fern
Creeping Charlie	Jerusaleum Cherry	Umbrella plant
Crown of thorns	Needlepoint Ivy	

OUTDOOR PLANTS WITH TOXIC EFFECTS

A. *Outdoor plants* that produce vomiting and diarrhea in some cases:

Delphinium	Poke weed	Indian Tobacco
Daffodil	Bittersweet woody	Wisteria
Castor bean	Ground cherry	Soap berry
Indian Turnip	Fox glove	
Skunk Cabbage	Larkspur	

B. *Trees and shrubs* which are poisonous and may produce vomiting, abdominal pain, and in some cases diarrhea:

Horse Chestnut	Western Yew	Apricot, almond
Buckeye	English Holly	Peach, cherry
Rain Tree	Privet	Wild cherry
Monkey Pod	Mock orange	Japanese plum
American Yew	Bird of Paradise bush	Balsam pear
English Yew	Black locust	

C. *Outdoor plants* with varied toxic effect:

Rhubarb	Buttercup	Moonseed
Spinach	Nightshade	May apple
Sunburned potatoes	Poison Hemolock	Dutchman's breeches
Tomato vine	Jimson weed	Mescal bean
Loco weed	Pig Weed	Angel's Trumpet
Lupine	Water Hemlock	Jasmine
Dologeton	Mushrooms	Matrimony vine

D. *Hallucinogens:*

Marijuana	Periwinkle
Morning glory	Peyote
Nutmeg	Loco weed

E. *Convulsions:*

China berry	Nux vomica
Coriaria	Water Hemlock
Moonweed	

If you think that your dog may have been poisoned, the first thing to do is try to identify the poison. Most products containing chemicals are labeled for identification. Read the label. If this does not give you a clue to its possible toxicity, call the emergency room of your local hospital and ask for information from the *Poison Control Center.*

The first step in treatment is to eliminate the poison from your dog's stomach by making him vòmit (see *How to Induce Vomiting* earlier in this chapter). The second step is to delay absorption of the poison from his intestinal tract by coating it with a substance which binds it. This is followed by a laxative to speed its elimination.

How to Delay or Prevent Absorption:
1. Mix activated charcoal with water (1 gram to 4 cc). Give one teaspoonful per two pounds body weight.
2. Thirty minutes later, give sodium sulphate (glauber's salt), one teaspoonful per 10 pounds body weight, or Milk of Magnesia, one teaspoonful per 5 pounds body weight.

NOTE: If these agents are not available, coat the bowel with milk, egg whites, vegetable oil; and give a warm water enema.

If your dog has a poisonous substance on his skin or coat, wash it well with soap and water or give him a complete bath in *lukewarm* (not cold) water, as described in the SKIN chapter. Even if the substance is not irritating to the skin, it should be removed. Otherwise he may lick it off and swallow it. Soak gasoline and oil stains with mineral or vegetable oil. Work in well. Then wash with a mild detergent, such as Ivory soap.

If your dog begins to show signs of nervous system involvement, he is in deep trouble. At this point, your main objective is to *get your dog to a veterinarian as quickly as possible.* Try to bring with you a sample of vomitus, or better yet the poison in its original container. Do not delay to administer first aid—unless it is life saving. If the dog is convulsing, unconscious, or not breathing, see *Shock* and *Artificial Respiration.* (Also see NERVOUS SYSTEM: *Fits: Loss of Consciousness.)*

The poisons discussed below are included because they are among the most frequently seen by veterinarians.

Strychnine

Strychnine is used as a rat, mouse, and mole poison. It is available commercially as coated pellets dyed purple, red, or green. Signs of poisoning are so typical that the diagnosis can be made almost at once. Onset is sudden (less than two hours). The first signs are agitation, excitability, and apprehension. They are followed rather quickly by intensely painful tetanic seizures which last about 60 seconds, during which the dog throws back his head, can't breathe, and turns blue. The slightest stimulation, such as tapping the dog or clapping the hands, starts a seizure. This characteristic response is used to make the diagnosis. Other signs associated with nervous system involvement are: tremors; champing; drooling; uncoordinated muscle spasms; collapse; and paddling of the legs.

Seizures due to strychnine and other central nervous system toxins sometimes are misdiagnosed as epilepsy. This would be a mistake, as immediate veterinary attention is necessary. Epileptic seizures are self-limited; the signs always appear in a certain order, and each attack is the same. They are over before the dog can get to a veterinarian. Usually they are not considered emergencies (see NERVOUS SYSTEM: *Epilepsy*).

Treatment: If your dog is showing signs of poisoning and hasn't vomited, induce vomiting as discussed above.

With signs of central nervous involvement, don't take time to induce vomiting. It is important to avoid loud noises or unnecessary handling which could trigger a seizure. Cover your dog with a coat or blanket and drive him to the nearest veterinary clinic.

Sodium Fluroacetate (1080)

This chemical, used as a rat poison, is mixed with cereal, bran, and other rat feeds. It is so potent that cats and dogs can be poisoned just by eating the dead rodent. The onset is sudden and begins with vomiting followed by excitation, straining to urinate or defecate, an aimless staggering gait, atypical fits or true convulsions, and then collapse. Seizures are not triggered by external stimuli as are those of strychnine poisoning.

Treatment: Immediately after the dog ingests the poison, induce vomiting. Care and handling is the same as for strychnine.

Arsenic

Arsenic is combined with metaldehyde in slug and snail baits, and may appear in ant poisons, weed killers, and insecticides. Arsenic is also a common impurity found in many chemicals. Death can occur quickly before there is time to observe the symptoms. In more protracted cases the signs are: thirst; drooling; vomiting; staggering; intense abdominal pain; cramps; diarrhea; paralysis and death. The breath of the dog will have a strong smell of garlic.

Treatment: Induce vomiting. A specific antidote is available. It requires professional use.

Metaldehyde

This poison (often combined with arsenic) is used commonly in rat, snail, and slug baits. The signs of toxicity are: excitation; drooling and slobbering; uncoordinated gait; muscle tremors; and weakness which leads to inability to stand in a few hours. The tremors are not triggered by external stimuli.

Treatment: Immediately after the dog ingests the poison, induce vomiting. The care and handling are the same as for strychnine.

Lead

Lead is found in insecticides and is a base for many paints used commercially. Intoxication occurs primarily in puppies and young dogs who chew on substances coated with a lead paint. Other sources of lead are: lineoleum; batteries; plumbing materials; putty; lead foil; solder; golf balls; and some roofing materials. Lead poisoning can occur in older dogs after ingestion of insecticides containing lead. A chronic form does occur.

Acute poisoning begins with abdominal colic and vomiting. A variety of central nervous system signs are possible. They include: fits; uncoordinated gait; excitation; continuous barking; attacks of hysteria; weakness; stupor; and blindness. Chewing and champing fits might be mistaken for the encephalitis of distemper, especially in young dogs.

Treatment: When ingestion is recent, induce vomiting. Otherwise, coat the bowel as described above. Specific antidotes are available through your veterinarian.

Phosphorus

This chemical is present in rat and roach poisons, fireworks, matches and match boxes. A poisoned dog may have garlic odor to his breath. The first signs of intoxication are vomiting and diarrhea. They may be followed by a free interval — then by recurrent vomiting; cramps; pain in the abdomen; convulsions and coma.

There is no specific antidote. Treat as you would for strychnine.

Zinc Phosphide

This substance also is found in rat poisons. Intoxication causes central nervous system depression; labored breathing; vomiting (often of blood); weakness; convulsions and death. There is no specific antidote. Treat as you would for strychnine.

Warfarin (Decon; Pindone)

Warfarin is incorporated into grain feeds for use as a rat and mouse poison. It causes death by interfering with the blood clotting mechanism. This leads to spontaneous bleeding. There are no observable signs of warfarin poisoning until the dog begins to pass blood in his stool or urine, bleeds from his nose, or develops hemorrhages beneath his gums and skin. He may be found dead with no apparent cause. A single dose of warfarin is not as serious as repeated doses.

Treatment: Induce vomiting. Vitamin K is a specific antidote. It is given intramuscularly (or in cases where there are no symptoms it can be given by mouth as a preventative) in a dose of 10 to 20 mg, depending on the size of the dog.

Anti-freeze *(Ethylene glycol)*

Poisoning with anti-freeze is not uncommon because ethylene glycol has a sweet taste that appeals to dogs and cats. In dogs, a toxic dose is ½ teaspoonful per pound body weight. Signs of toxicity, which appear suddenly, are: vomiting; uncoordinated gait (seems "drunk"); weakness; mental depression; coma; and death in 12 to 36 hours. Convulsions are unusual. Dogs that recover from the acute phase may have damage to the kidneys and go on to kidney failure.

Treatment: Induce vomiting. Coat the bowel to prevent further absorption. Intensive care in animal hospital may prevent kidney complications.

Organophosphates and Carbamates

These substances are used on dogs to kill fleas and other parasites. The common ones are *dichlorvos, ectoral, malathion,* and *sevin,* but there are others. They also are used in garden sprays and in some dewormers. Improper application of insecticides to the dog can lead to absorption of a toxic dose through the skin. These drugs effect the nervous system primarily. *Insecticides* are discussed in the SKIN chapter.

Chlorinated Hydrocarbons

These compounds, like the organophosphates, are incorporated into some insecticide preparations for use on the dog. The common products in veterinary use are *chloradane, toxaphene, lindane,* and *methoxychlor.*

Corrosives (Acid and Alkali)

Corrosives and caustics are found in household cleaners, drain decloggers, and commercial solvents. They cause burns of the mouth, esophagus and stomach. Severe cases are associated with acute perforation, or late stricture, of the esophagus and stomach.

Treatment: If acid is ingested, rinse out your dog's mouth. Give him an antacid (Milk of Magnesia or Pepto-Bismol) at the rate of one to two teaspoons per five pounds body weight. If an alkali, use vinegar or lemon juice. Vinegar is mixed one part to four parts of water. The amount to give is judged by the size of the dog. Do not induce vomiting; this could result in rupture of the stomach or burns of the esophagus.

Petroleum Products (Gasoline, Kerosene, Turpentine)

These volatile liquids can cause pneumonia if aspirated or inhaled. The signs of toxicity are vomiting, difficulty of breathing, tremors, convulsions, coma. Death is by respiratory failure.

Treatment: Do not induce vomiting. Administer an ounce or two of mineral oil, olive oil, or vegetable oil by mouth; then follow it in 30 minutes with glauber's salt. Be prepared to administer artificial respiration.

Garbage Poisoning (Food Poisoning)

Food poisoning is common, as dogs are notorious scavengers and come into contact with carrion, decomposing foods, animal manure, and other noxious substances (some of which are listed in DIGESTIVE SYSTEM: *Common Causes of Diarrhea*). Signs of poisoning begin with vomiting and pain in the abdomen; they are followed in severe cases by diarrhea (often bloody), in two to six hours. If the problem is complicated by bacterial infection, shock may develop. Mild cases recover in a day or two.

Treatment: Induce vomiting. Afterwards, coat the intestines to delay or prevent absorption. The condition may require antibiotics. (See also NERVOUS SYSTEM: *Botulism*.)

Toad Poisoning

Since all toads have a bad taste, dogs who mouth them slobber, spit and drool. In southern states a tropical toad *(Bufo marinus)* secretes a potent toxin which appears to affect the heart and circulation of dogs, bringing on death in as short a time as 15 minutes. There are 12 species of "Bufo" toads distributed world-wide.

Symptoms in dogs depend upon the toxicity of the toad and the amount of poison absorbed. Signs vary from merely slobbering to convulsions and death.

Treatment: Flush your dog's mouth out with a garden hose and attempt to induce vomiting. Be prepared to administer artificial respiration.

People Medicines

Veterinarians frequently are called because a dog has swallowed pills intended for his owner, or has eaten too many of his own pills. (Some dog pills are flavored to encourage dogs to eat them.) Drugs most often involved are antihistamines, sleeping pills, diet pills, heart preparations, and vitamins.

Treatment: Induce vomiting and coat the bowel as described above to prevent further absorption. Discuss possible side effects of the drug with your veterinarian.

SNAKE BITES

If your dog is bitten by a snake, there may be no cause for concern as the majority of snakes are nonpoisonous. The bites of harmless snakes show teeth marks in the shape of a horseshoe — but there are no fang marks.

In the United States, there are four poisonous varieties: Cotton mouth moccasins; Rattlesnakes; Copperheads; and Coral snakes. The diagnosis of poison snake bite is made by the appearance of the bite; the behavior of the animal; and by identification of the species of snake. (Kill it first, if possible.)

Pit Vipers *(Rattlesnakes–Moccasins–Copperheads)*

Identify these species by their large arrow-shaped heads, pits below and between the eyes, elliptical pupils, rough scales, and the presence of fangs in the upper jaws.

The bite: There are two puncture wounds in the skin (fang marks). Signs of local reaction appear *quickly* and include swelling; excruciating pain; redness; and hemorrhages in the skin.

Behavior of the animal: Signs and symptoms depend on the size and species of the snake, location of the bite, and amount of toxin absorbed into the system. The first signs are extreme restlessness, panting, drooling, and weakness. They are followed by diarrhea, collapse, sometimes seizures; shock; and death in severe cases.

Coral Snake

Identify this snake by its rather small size, small head with black nose, and vivid colored bands of red, yellow, white and black — the red and yellow bands always next to each other. Fangs are present in the upper jaw.

The bite: There is less severe local reaction but the pain is excruciating. Look for the fang marks.

Behavior of the animal: Coral snake venom primarily is neurotoxic. Signs include: vomiting; diarrhea; urinary incontinence; paralysis; convulsions and coma.

Treatment of All Bites:

First identify the snake and look at the bite. If it appears your dog is bitten by a poisonous snake, proceed as follows:

1. Restrain the dog. Snake bites are extremely painful.
2. Apply a flat tourniquet above the bite. It should not be as tight as an arterial tourniquet (see *Wounds*), but should be tight enough to keep venous blood from returning to the heart.
3. Using a knife or razor blade, make parallel cuts ¼" deep through the fang marks. On a leg, make them up and down. Blood should ooze from the wound. If not, loosen the tourniquet.
4. Apply mouth suction unless you have a cut or open sore in your mouth. Spit out the blood. If poison is swallowed, the stomach will inactivate it. Continue for 30 minutes.
5. Loosen the tourniquet for 30 seconds every half hour.
6. KEEP THE DOG QUIET. Excitement, exercise, struggling, increase the rate of absorption. Carry him to your veterinarian.

Specific antivenoms are available through veterinarians. Snake bites become infected. Antibiotics and dressings are indicated.

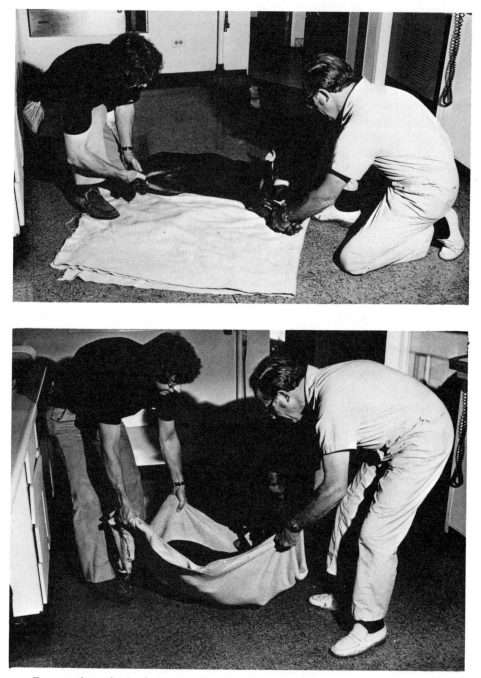

Transporting a dog in shock. Muzzle only when absolutely necessary. —*J. Clawson*

SHOCK

Shock is lack of adequate blood flow to meet the body's needs. Adequate blood flow requires effective heart pumping, open intact vessels, and sufficient blood volume to maintain flow and pressure. Any condition adversely affecting the heart, vessels, or blood volume, can induce shock.

At first the body attempts to compensate for the inadequate circulation by speeding up the heart, constricting the skin vessels, and maintaining fluid in the circulation by reducing output of urine. This becomes increasingly difficult to do when the vital organs aren't getting enough oxygen to carry on these activities. After a time, shock becomes self-perpetuating. Prolonged shock causes death.

Common causes of shock are: dehydration (prolonged vomiting and diarrhea); heat stroke; severe infections; poisoning; and hemorrhage. Being hit by a car is the most common cause of traumatic shock in the dog.

The signs of shock, which are due to the effects of poor circulation and the adjustments made to compensate for this, are: a drop in body temperature; shivering; listlessness and mental depression; weakness; cold feet and legs; pale skin and mucus membranes; and a weak faint pulse.

Treatment: First evaluate the dog. Is he breathing? Does he have a heart beat? What are the extent of his injuries? Is he in shock? If so, proceed as follows:

1. If not breathing, proceed with *artificial respiration.*
2. If no heart beat or pulse, administer *heart massage.*
3. If unconscious, check to be sure his airway is open; clear secretions from his mouth with your fingers; pull out his tongue to keep his airway clear of secretions. Keep his head lower than his body.
4. Control bleeding (as described under *Wounds* in section that follows).
5. To prevent further aggravation of shock:
   a) Calm him, and speak soothingly.
   b) Let him assume the most comfortable position; he will adopt the one of least pain. Don't force him to lie down — it may make breathing more difficult.
   c) When possible, splint or support broken bones before moving the dog (see MUSCULOSKELETAL SYSTEM).
   d) Cover him with a coat or blanket. Do not wrap tightly.
   e) Transport large dogs on a flat surface or in a hammock stretcher. Carry small dogs with injured parts protected.
   f) Muzzle only when absolutely necessary. It may impair breathing.

WOUNDS

In the care of wounds, the two most important objectives are first to stop the bleeding, and then to prevent infection. Since wounds are painful to the dog, be prepared to restrain or muzzle before you treat the wound.

Control of Bleeding

Bleeding may be *arterial* (the spurting of bright red blood), or *venous* (oozing of dark red blood), or sometimes both. Do not wipe a wound which has stopped bleeding. This will dislodge the clot. Don't pour peroxide on a fresh wound. Bleeding then will be difficult to control.

The two methods used to control bleeding are the pressure dressing and the tourniquet:

The Pressure Dressing: Take several pieces of clean or sterile gauze, place them over the wound, and bandage snugly. Watch for swelling of the limb below the pressure pack. This indicates impaired circulation. The bandage must be loosened or removed.

An alternate method to control bleeding is to apply pressure over the artery in the groin or axilla. (See CIRCULATORY SYSTEM: *Pulse*). Often this will control bleeding long enough to permit an assistant to apply a pressure dressing.

If material is not available for bandaging, place a pad on the wound and press it firmly. Hold in place until help arrives.

The Tourniquet: A tourniquet may be needed to control a spurting artery. It can be applied to the leg or tail above the wound (between the wound and the heart). Take a piece of cloth or gauze roll and loop it around the limb. Then tighten it by hand, or with a stick inserted beneath the loop and twisted around until bleeding is controlled. If you see the end of the artery, you might attempt to pick it up with tweezers and tie it off with a piece of cotton thread. When possible, this should be left to a trained practitioner.

A tourniquet should be loosened every 30 minutes for two to three minutes, to let blood flow into the limb.

Treating the Wound

All wounds are contaminated with dirt and bacteria. Proper care and handling will prevent some infections. Before handling a wound, make sure your hands and instruments are clean. Starting at the edges of a fresh wound, clip the hair back to enlarge the area. Cleanse the edges of the wound with a damp gauze or pad. Irrigate the wound with clean tap water. Apply antibiotic ointment. Bandage as described below.

Older wounds with a covering of pus and scab are cleansed with 3% hydrogen peroxide solution or a surgical soap. Blot dry. Apply antibiotic ointment and bandage as described below.

Dressings over infected wounds should be changed frequently to aid in the drainage of pus, and to allow you to apply fresh ointment.

Fresh lacerations over ½ inch long should be sutured to prevent infection, minimize scarring, and speed healing.

Wounds over 12 hours old are quite likely to be infected. Suturing is questionable.

Bites are heavily contaminated wounds. Often they are puncture wounds. They are quite likely to get infected. They should not be sutured. Antibiotics are indicated.

With all animal bites, the possibility of rabies should be kept in mind (see INFECTIOUS DISEASES: *Rabies*).

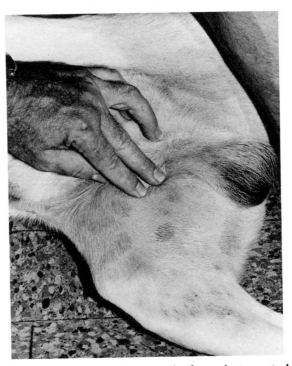

Apply pressure over the artery in the groin to control arterial bleeding in the leg.   *—J. Clawson*

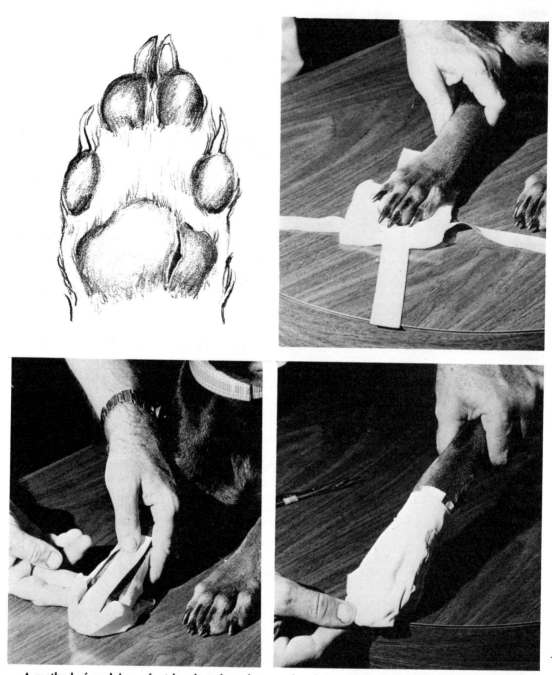

A method of applying a foot bandage for a lacerated pad. Tape loosely to allow good circulation.
—*J. Clawson*

Bandaging

The equipment you will need is listed in the *Home Emergency and Medical Kit*, at beginning of this chapter.

Foot and Leg Bandages. To bandage the foot, place several sterile gauze pads over the wound. Insert cotton balls between the toes and hold in place with adhesive tape looped around the bottom of the foot and back across the top until the foot is snugly wrapped.

For leg wounds, begin by wrapping the foot as described. Then cover the wound with several sterile gauze pads and hold in place with strips of adhesive tape. Wrap the tape around the leg but don't overlap it, so that the tape sticks to the hair. This keeps the dressing from sliding up and down, as often happens when a roll gauze bandage is used. Flex the knee and foot several times to be sure the bandage is not too tight and there is good circulation and movement at the joints.

When a dressing is to be left in place for some time, check on it every few hours to be sure the foot is not swelling. If there is any question about the sensation, or circulation to the foot, loosen the dressing.

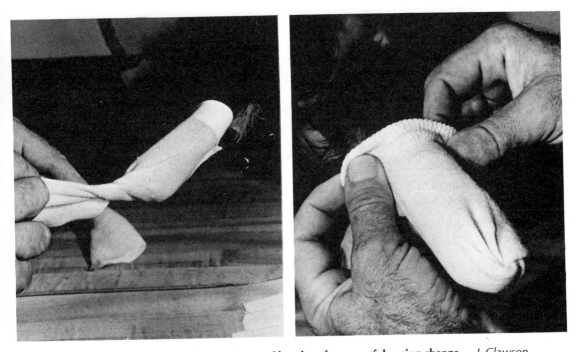

A sock slipped over a gauze square is a good bandage for ease of dressing change. —*J. Clawson*

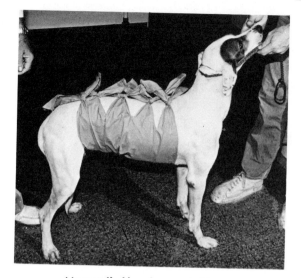

Many-tailed bandage. —*J. Clawson*

Many-Tailed Bandage. This bandage is used to protect the skin of the neck or abdomen from scratching and biting, and to hold dressings in place. It is made by taking a rectangular piece of linen and cutting the sides to make tails. Tie the tails together over the back to hold it in place.

A many-tailed bandage may be used to keep puppies from nursing infected breasts.

Eye Bandage. At times your veterinarian may prescribe an eye bandage in the treatment of an eye ailment. Place a sterile gauze square over the affected eye and hold it in place by taping around the head with one inch adhesive. Be careful not to get the tape too tight. Apply the dressing so that the ears are free.

You may be required to change the dressing from time to time to apply medication to the eye.

The ear bandage is discussed in the chapter EARS.

Elizabethan Collar. An Elizabethan Collar, named for the high neck ruff popular in the reign of Queen Elizabeth, is a useful device to keep a dog from scratching at his ears, and biting at a wound or skin problem. They are recommended for certain disorders discussed in the SKIN chapter. They can be purchased from some veterinarians or pet stores, or can be made from plastic and cardboard. Plastic flower pots, waste baskets and buckets work well! The size of the collar is tailored to the dog. Cut just enough out of the bottom to let the dog's head slip through, then fasten the device to his leather collar by strings passed through holes punched in the sides of the plastic. The neck of the collar should be short enough to let the dog eat and drink. Most dogs adjust to them quite well after a few minutes. Others won't eat or drink with the collar in place. In that case, temporarily remove the collar.

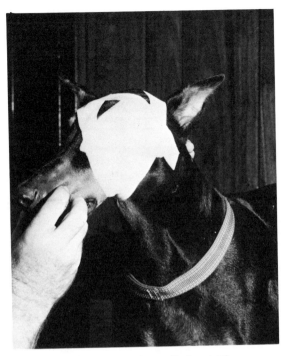

Eye bandage, properly applied. —*J. Clawson*

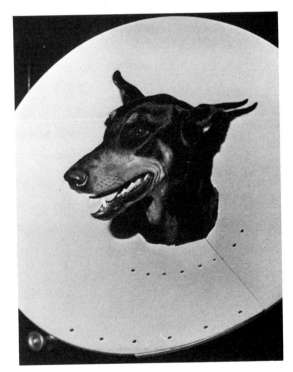

Elizabethan collar. —*J. Clawson*

Typical appearance of a puppy suffering from intestinal parasites.

2

Worms (Intestinal Parasites)

GENERAL INFORMATION

Most owners believe that if a dog is found to have parasites in his stool, then he must be suffering from a disease state.

This is not necessarily the case. Most dogs are infested at one time or another with intestinal parasites. Some are born with them and others acquire them later in life. When they recover, they develop a certain amount of immunity. This helps to keep the worms in check.

One should distinguish a disease state from the mere presence of a parasite. For example, demodectic mange mites live on the skin and in most dogs they produce no disease and require no treatment. The same may be true of intestinal parasites.

If worms are causing disease, there should be some change in the appearance of the stool. In turn, this is reflected by a decline in the general health of the dog. You should note decreased appetite, loss of weight, upset stomach, anemia, mucus and/or blood in the feces.

Dogs are capable of developing a resistance to certain worms—those having a larvae phase which migrates in their tissues (roundworms, hookworms and threadworms). The effect is on the maturation cycle. The larvae remain dormant as cysts in the tissues instead of becoming adults in the intestine. Whipworms and tapeworms have no migratory stage and thus cause little build-up of immunity.

Resistance to roundworms appears age related. Experimentally, it is difficult to induce a heavy infestation (over 10 worms in the gut) in dogs over six months of age.

Immunosuppressive drugs such as cortisone have been shown to activate large numbers of hookworm larvae lying dormant in the dog's tissue. Stressful events such as trauma, surgery, severe disease, and emotional upsets (i.e., shipping a puppy), also can activate dormant larvae. This leads to the appearance of parasites in the stool.

33

DEWORMING AGENTS

DRUG	TYPE OF WORM INVOLVED					COMMENTS
	Hook	Round	Whip	Tape	Thread	
Caricide (Diethylcarbamazine)	—	***	—	—	—	Do not use if animal has heartworms.
Piperazine	—	***	—	—	—	Do not overdose the animal.
Canopar (Themium Closylate)	****	?	—	—	—	Do not use in a nursing bitch. Use one size of pill only. It may induce some vomiting.
Task (Dichlorvos)	****	****	****	—	—	You cannot use this if the animal has heartworms. Do not use with insecticides.
DNP (Disophenol)	****	—	—	—	—	Use with caution in anemic dogs or those with respiratory problems. Do not overdose.
Milibis V (Glycobiorsol)	—	—	**	—	—	It is expensive and may cause vomiting.
Whipicide (Phthalofyne)	—	—	*	—	—	It makes some dogs wobbly and has a bad odor.
Nemural (Drocarbil)	—	—	—	*	—	Often causes diarrhea, vomiting and cramps.
Yomesan (Niclosamide)	—	—	—	**	—	Vomiting occurs frequently.
Scolaban (Bunamidine)	—	—	—	****	—	
Thiabendazole	—	—	—	—	****	Some vomiting occurs.
Vermiplex (2.2 Methylenebis) Methylbenzene	****	****	—	**	—	Some vomiting occurs.
Telmintic (Mebendazole)	****	****	****	*	—	Reports indicate a wide margin of safety. Give to the animal for three to five days.
Nemex (Pyrantel pamoate)	****	****	—	—	—	Can be given to nursing puppies. Liquid.
Droncit (Praziquantel)	—	—	—	****	—	Available as pill or injection.

**** Excellent   *** Good   ** Fair   * Poor   — No effect

During pregnancy, round and hookworm larvae are activated and migrate to the unborn puppies. Accordingly, a heavy parasite problem may appear in a litter even when the mother was effectively dewormed. This can happen because none of the deworming agents are effective against larvae encysted in the tissue.

Deworming Your Dog

Puppies

Most puppies are infested with roundworms. Other worms may be present, too. It is advisable to have your veterinarian check your puppy's stool before treating him for roundworms. Otherwise, other worms may go undetected.

Worm infestations are particularly harmful in puppies subjected to overfeeding, chilling, close confinement, and a sudden change in diet. Stressful conditions such as these should be corrected before administering a deworming agent.

Puppies should be dewormed at two to three weeks of age and again at five to six weeks. If eggs or worms are still found in the stool, subsequent courses should be given.

There are a number of patent dewormers on the market. No one preparation is advisable for all occasions. If you decide to use one of these preparations, be sure it is safe and effective; follow the recommendations supplied by the manufacturer.

Adults

Many veterinarians recommend that adult dogs be dewormed only when there are specific signs of an infestation. A stool examination is the most effective way of making an exact diagnosis and choosing the best agent.

Most dogs carry *roundworms* as encysted larvae but intestinal infestation by the adult worm in the healthy dog is a rare occurrence. *Hookworms* are likely to be a problem during periods of stress. Routine deworming may catch an intestinal phase but is not effective against encysted larvae. When *whipworms* are present, usually several courses of treatment are required to eliminate the infestation. *Tapeworms* are common in the dog but the worm segments are easy to detect in the stool. Fortunately they cause very little difficulty. *Threadworms* are not common. Very few agents are effective against this parasite.

However, many kennel owners believe that their dogs are kept in better condition if they deworm them once or twice a year. In such cases, Telmintic is a good choice. It has a wide spectrum of activity and few ill effects.

Problems may be caused by over-worming with harsh preparations. They are stressful to the dog, irritate his intestines, and actually may lower his resistance to the worms.

Consult the accompanying table to learn about some of the currently recommended deworming agents. Certain dewormers should not be given to dogs with coexistent illnesses, such as heartworms. Others can react adversely with drugs your dog has taken recently. It is not safe to use certain drugs on breeding animals or those who are pregnant. It is best to check with your veterinarian before using one of those preparations.

The Brood Bitch

Before breeding your female have her stool checked. If parasites are found, she should receive a thorough deworming. This will not protect her puppies from all worm infestation. However, it will help to put her in the best condition for a healthy pregnancy.

How to Control Worms

The life cycles of most canine worms are such that the possibility of reinfestation is great. To keep worms under control, you must destroy eggs or larvae *before* they infest the dog. This means good sanitation and maintaining clean dry quarters for your dog.

Dogs should not be kenneled on dirt runs. A water-tight surface, such as cement, is the easiest to keep clean. Hose it down daily and allow it to dry thoroughly. Disinfect with boiling water and lysol. Gravel is a good substitute. Usually it provides good drainage and it is easy to remove stools from gravel. Gravel can be disinfected with lime, salt or borax. Remove stools from the pens daily.

Lawns should be cut short and watered only when necessary. Stools in the yard should be removed at least once a week.

Fleas, lice, mice and other rodents are intermediate hosts for the tapeworm. It is necessary to get rid of these pests in order to control this disease (see *Premises Control*).

Dogs should not be allowed to roam and hunt. They could catch and devour raw meat, ingest carrion or parts of dead animals. Be sure to cook thoroughly all fresh meat before feeding it to your dog (see *Tapeworms*).

Kennels that have continuous problems with worms often have other problems, too. They include skin, bowel and respiratory difficulties. Steps should be taken to improve the management of the kennel, especially sanitation measures.

Heartworm preparations, given to prevent dirofilaria immitis, also are partially effective against roundworms (Caricide), and round and hook-worms (Styrid-Caricide). These agents are given daily in low dosages. The effect lasts only as long as you give the medication. Used in this manner, they serve mainly to *prevent* infection.

DISEASES CAUSED BY CERTAIN WORMS

Roundworms *(Ascarids)*

Adult roundworms, which live in the intestine, are one to seven inches long. A female may lay 200,000 eggs in a day. These eggs are protected by a hard shell. They are extremely hardy and can live for months or years in the soil.

Dogs acquire the disease through contact with soil containing the eggs. Eggs, entering via the oral route, hatch in the intestine. Larvae are carried to the lungs by the bloodstream. Here, they become mobile, crawl up the windpipe and are swallowed (this may cause bouts of coughing and gagging). They return to the intestine and develop into adults. This sequence occurs mainly in the young puppy.

In the older dog, only a few larvae return to the intestine. The others encyst in tissue and remain dormant. During the late stages of pregnancy, these dormant larvae are released, re-enter the circulation and are carried to the unborn puppies. Circulating larvae also get to puppies via the breast milk.

Deworming the dam before or during pregnancy does not prevent roundworm infestation of unborn puppies; medications do not work on encysted larvae. Accordingly, many puppies are born with roundworms.

Roundworms do not cause much difficulty in adult dogs. A severe infestation in puppies, however, can lead to death. Puppies with a heavy roundworm infestation have a pot-bellied appearance and a dull coat. The usual signs are vomiting (sometimes of worms), diarrhea, loss of weight and failure to thrive. Worms may be passed in the stool. Typically, they look like white earthworms or strands of spaghetti which are alive and moving.

Roundworms can cause a disease in humans called *visceral larva migrans*. A few cases are reported each year, usually from areas with a mild climate. There is often a history of dirt-eating (of soil contaminated by the eggs). Children are most likely to be affected. Because man is not the normal host, the immature worms do not become adults. Instead, they migrate into tissues and wander aimlessly, causing fever, anemia, liver enlargement, pneumonia and other ill effects. Usually, the disease runs its course in about a year. It is prevented most effectively by controlling infestation in the dog through periodic deworming and good sanitation (see *Parasite Control*).

Treatment: A Piperazine component (Antepar) is the safest dewormer for roundworms and for this reason is the agent of choice for puppies. Puppies should be dewormed by three weeks of age to prevent contamination of their quarters by roundworm eggs. A second course should be given two to three weeks later to kill any adult worms which were in the larvae stage at the first deworming.

Piperazine dewormers can be obtained from your veterinarian or a pet shop. You do not have to fast your dog before using this agent. Be sure to follow the directions of the manufacturer in regard to dosage.

Dichlorvos (Task) is effective against roundworms, hookworms, and whipworms. It is somewhat harsher than Piperazine. It should not be given to heartworm positive dogs. Dogs who have been treated with insecticides, and those wearing a flea collar, should not be treated within a week. Use under veterinary guidance.

Telmintic (Mebendazole) is effective against roundworms, hookworms, tapeworms and whipworms. Its disadvantage is that it must be given for three to five consecutive days. It should be used under veterinary guidance.

Caricide and Styrid-Caricide given in low doses to prevent heartworms also keep roundworms under control. It is advisable to treat first with a more effective agent and then to maintain a worm-free state with these products. Styrid-Caricide also helps control hookworms.

Hookworms *(Ancylostoma)*

Hookworms are small thin worms about one-fourth to one-half inch long. They fasten to the wall of the small intestine and draw blood from the host.

The dog acquires the disease through contact with larvae in contaminated soil or feces. The immature worms migrate to the intestine where they become adults. In about two weeks, the dog begins to pass eggs in the feces.

Unborn puppies can acquire hookworms while still in the uterus. Newborns can acquire the disease from the milk of an infected dam. They may sicken and die rapidly.

The typical signs of *acute* hookworm infestation are anemia and diarrhea. Stools characteristically are bloody, wine-dark or tarry-black. Usually this condition affects puppies at two to eight weeks of age. Occasionally it is seen in older dogs.

Chronic hookworm infection usually is not a problem in the adult dog. When it occurs, the signs are diarrhea, anemia, weight loss and progressive weakness. The diagnosis is made by finding the eggs in the feces.

Many puppies and adults who recover from the disease become carriers via cysts in the tissue. During periods of stress or some other illness, a new outbreak can occur as the larvae are released.

A disease in humans called *cutaneous larvae migrans* (creeping eruption) is caused by the hookworm (A. brasiliense). It is due to penetration of the skin by larvae present in the soil. It causes lumps, streaks beneath the skin, and itching. The condition is self-limited.

Treatment: A number of agents are effective against hookworms. Canopar is effective against hookworms only. Dichlorvos, Telmintic, and Styrid-Caricide are effective against other worms as well (see *Roundworms*). Disophenol (DNP) is a hookworm preparation which must be given by subcutaneous injection. Consult your veterinarian before using any of these agents.

Puppies with acute signs and symptoms require intensive veterinary management.

Tapeworms *(Cestodes)*

These worms also live in the small intestine. The scolex (head) of the parasite fastens itself to the wall of the gut by hooks and suckers. The body is composed of segments containing the egg packets. Tapeworms vary in length from less than an inch to several feet. To cure tapeworm infection, the scolex must be killed and purged.

The body segments containing the eggs are passed in the feces. Fresh moist segments are capable of moving. They are about a quarter of an inch long. Sometimes you will see them adhering to the fur about your dog's anus or in his stool. When dry, they resemble kernels of rice.

Dogs can acquire several different kinds of tapeworm. One is due to eating uncooked meat or discarded animal parts. Another is acquired by eating raw fresh fish. Commonly, the disease is transmitted by the flea. The dog must bite or swallow the flea which harbors the immature tapeworms in its intestine. Fleas acquire the parasite by eating tapeworm eggs.

Apart from a change in the texture and condition of the coat, the common tapeworm rarely causes significiant ill effects. Severe infestations can cause a mild diarrhea, loss of appetite, or reduction in weight. Unless there is a heavy infection, probably you will not notice tapeworm segments in the feces.

Children can acquire a tapeworm if they accidentally swallow an infective flea.

A more serious disease in man is caused by the tapeworm *Echinococcus granulosus*. This disease is found in cattle, sheep, deer, elk, pigs, horses and other domestic livestock. The dog acquires the infection by eating uncooked meat or the carcass of an animal infected with Echinococcus granulosus larvae. Man acquires the disease directly by contact with eggs present in the feces of the dog.

The eggs do not produce worms in humans, as man is not a natural host. Instead, they produce large cysts in the liver, lungs and brain. These cysts are called *hydatids*. A serious or even fatal illness can result.

Prevention: The common dog tapeworm can be prevented by controlling fleas and other insects (see *Premises Control*).

Echinococcus granulosus is found in the southern, western and southwestern United States, in areas where sheep and cattle are common. A number of cases are reported each year. Dogs should not be permitted to have access to dead animals or offal. Do not give your dog uncooked meat or raw game to eat.

If you live in a rural area where Echinococcus granulosus could be a problem, ask your veterinarian to check your dog's stools for tapeworms twice a year. This species of tapeworm can be identified only after the head has been recovered by effective deworming. Accordingly, dogs infected with a tapeworm of unknown type must be handled with extreme caution to avoid fecal contamination of the hands and food, until a definite diagnosis is forthcoming.

Treatment: Niclosamide (Yomesan) is effective against all the common dog tapeworms. Other suitable remedies are Nemural, Scolaban, and Telmintic. Use under veterinary guidance.

Whipworms *(Trichuris vulpis)*

The adult whipworm is two to three inches long. It is thread-like for the most part but is thicker at one end. This gives it the appearance of a whip.

The adult lives in the first part of the large intestine (cecum). It fastens itself to the wall of the gut. The female lays fewer eggs than most worms. Infestations are frequently light. Therefore, it is sometimes difficult to detect the presence of whipworms, even after several stool examinations.

Heavy infestations do occur in dogs where the soil is badly contaminated with eggs. These dogs lose weight, appear unthrifty and frequently have diarrhea. Periodic stool checks may be advisable in such areas to identify the presence of these worms.

Treatment: A number of preparations are effective against whipworms. They include Milibis, Dichlorvos, Telmintic, and Whipcide. Repeated stool checks are required to assure success, as false negatives are common. Usually several courses of treatment are required to eliminate the infestation.

Threadworms *(Strongyloides stercoralis)*

Threadworms are small round worms which live in the intestine and are able to infect both man and dogs. Eggs and/or larvae are passed in the feces. The life cycle of the threadworm is complex. The disease may be acquired by ingestion of the larvae or direct penetration of the skin of the body by larvae present in contaminated soil.

Puppies with threadworms may suffer from profuse watery diarrhea and signs of lung infection. The disease might be mistaken for distemper.

The hazard to human health is variable. There are several geographically separate strains which vary in their ability to infect man. Humans living in tropical climates are affected most commonly. Only a few cases are reported in temperate zones.

Treatment: At present, the deworming agent of choice is Thiabendazole. It must be given once a day for five days, and repeated monthly as required. Several negative stool examinations should be obtained before concluding that your dog is free of threadworms.

3

Infectious Diseases

GENERAL INFORMATION

Infectious diseases are caused by bacteria, viruses, protozoa and fungi which invade the body of a susceptible host and cause an illness.

Infectious diseases are often transmitted from one animal to another by contact with infected urine, feces and other bodily secretions; or inhalation of germ-laden droplets in the air. A few are transmitted via the genital tract when dogs mate. Others are acquired by contact with spores in the soil which get into the body through a break in the skin.

Bacteria are single-celled germs, while the virus, the tiniest germ known and even more basic than a cell, is simply a package of molecules. Although germs exist virtually everywhere, only a few cause infection. Fewer still are contagious — i.e., capable of being transmitted from one animal to another. Many infectious agents are able to survive for long periods outside of the host animal. This information is especially useful in controlling the spread of infectious diseases.

Antibodies and Immunity

An animal who is *immune* to a specific germ has chemical substances in his system called antibodies which attack and destroy that germ before it can cause an illness.

Natural immunity exists which is species-related. A dog does not catch a disease which is specific for a horse, and vice versa. Some infectious diseases are not specific. They are capable of causing illness in several species of animals.

If an animal is susceptible to an infectious disease and is exposed, he will become ill and begin to make antibodies against that particular germ. When he recovers, these antibodies afford protection against reinfection. They continue to do so for a variable length of time. He has acquired *active immunity*.

Active immunity can be induced artificially by vaccination. Through vaccination the animal is exposed to heat-killed germs, live or attenuated germs rendered incapable of disease, or toxins and germ products. They stimulate the production of antibodies which are specific for the vaccine.

Since active immunity tends to wane with the passage of time, booster shots should be given at regular intervals to maintain a high level of antibody in the system.

Antibodies are produced by the *reticuloendothelial system*. It is made up of white blood cells, lymph nodes, special cells in the bone marrow, spleen, liver and lung. The special cells act along with antibodies and other substances in the blood to attack and destroy germs.

Antibodies are highly specific. They destroy only the type of germ that stimulated their production. Some drugs depress or prevent antibody production. They are called *immunosuppressive* drugs. Cortisone is such a drug.

Run-down, malnourished, debilitated dogs may not be capable of responding to a challenge by developing antibodies or building immunity to germs. Such dogs can be vaccinated but should be revaccinated when in a better state of health.

Puppies under two weeks of age may not be able to develop antibodies because of physical immaturity.

There is another type of immunity called *passive immunity*. It is acquired from one animal to another. A classic example is the immunity puppies acquire from the colostrum, or first milk of the dam. Puppies are best able to absorb these special proteins through their intestines during the first 24 to 36 hours after birth. The length of protection is dependent upon the antibody level in the blood of the dam when the pups were born. Dams vaccinated within a few months have the highest levels. The maximum length of protection is 16 weeks. If the dam was never vaccinated against a disease, her pups would receive no protection against it.

Passive antibodies can "tie-up" vaccines given to stimulate active immunity, rendering them ineffective. This is one reason why vaccinations do not always "take" in very young puppies.

Another method of providing passive antibodies is to inject a dog with a serum from another dog who has a high level of type-specific antibody. Antitoxins and antivenoms are examples of such *immune serums*.

VACCINATIONS

Vaccines are highly effective in preventing certain infectious diseases in dogs, but failures do occur. They can be due to improper handling and storage, incorrect administration, or the inability of the dog to respond. Trying to stretch out the vaccine by dividing one ampule between two dogs is another reason for failure to take.

If a dog is already exposed, vaccinating him will not alter the course of the disease.

Because each pup is an individual case and proper handling and administration of the vaccine is so important, vaccination should be given only by those familiar with the techniques. When you go to your veterinarian for a booster shot, your dog will get a physical check-up. The veterinarian may detect some important change that you have overlooked.

Young puppies are highly susceptible to certain infectious diseases and should be vaccinated against them as soon as they are old enough to build an immunity. These diseases are distemper, infectious hepatitis and lepto-spirosis. Rabies is another problem which continues to be a serious threat to the dog.

To be effective, vaccinations must be kept current (see the *Vaccination Schedule*).

Distemper Vaccine

The first distemper shot should be given shortly after weaning and before a puppy is placed in a new home where he will be exposed to other dogs. Many veterinarians recommend that six-week-old puppies be vaccinated with the combination *canine distemper-measles vaccine*. A high percent of puppies do not get a satisfactory take from a distemper shot due to circulating maternal antibodies which block out the inactivated distemper virus in the vaccine. The measles virus, which is quite similar to the distemper virus, is not so affected. It is able to stimulate antibodies which protect against distemper but it does not cause any disease in dogs as it does in humans. This combination vaccine has been found to build temporary immunity to distemper in most young puppies. But beyond 15 weeks of age, the combination vaccine is not nearly as effective as distemper vaccine alone. At this point one should switch over to one of the standard distemper preparations (the DHL shot). Booster shots are required.

Infectious Hepatitis Vaccine

Your veterinarian will probably recommend a vaccine containing one of the adenovirus preparations (CAV-1 or CAV-2). It protects against hepatitis and the adenovirus implicated in the kennel cough complex. Clouding of the clear window of the eye may occur one to two weeks after vaccination in a few cases (see *Blue Eye*). Hepatitis vaccines are incorporated into the DHL shot. Booster shots are required.

Leptospirosis Vaccine

Leptospira bacterin protects against two bacteria that cause lepto-spirosis. The first shot should be given at three to four months of age.

Leptospira vaccine is incorporated into the DHL shot. Booster shots are required.

In areas where the disease is endemic, vaccinations at eight and ten weeks of age often are indicated. Since immunity to leptospira vaccine may be short-lived, in high risk areas a booster dose may be advisable as often as every six months.

Rabies Vaccine

There are two general types of rabies vaccines. One is a modified live virus preparation and the other is an inactivated virus. *All vaccines must be given in the muscle.* Care must be taken to be sure the product is made specifically for dogs.

The live virus vaccines provide longer-lasting immunity. The first injection should be given at three to six months of age, the second at one year, and then injections annually or every three years thereafter, depending upon the strain of vaccine.

If a dog is vaccinated before three months of age he should be re-vaccinated at six months.

Parainfluenza Vaccine (CPI) — Kennel Cough

The parainfluenza is one of the germs implicated in the kennel cough complex. CPI vaccine will protect against this virus, while hepatitis vaccine will protect against two of the adenoviruses. For routine immunization, see *Vaccination Schedule.*

Bordetella bronchiseptica vaccine (bacterin) is available and is of aid in the control of another agent implicated in the kennel cough complex. Show dogs and dogs living in kennels may benefit from this additional protection. Discuss this with your veterinarian. Two initial vaccinations are given, three to four weeks apart. Repeat annually.

Parvovirus Vaccine

Canine origin vaccines have largely replaced those of feline origin. Both inactivated and modified live virus vaccines result in effective levels of parvovirus antibody. The live virus preparation appears to generate high levels of protection over longer periods of time. Initial vaccination consists of two doses given three to four weeks apart, then an annual booster. For maximum protection in high risk areas, vaccinate at two week intervals until the puppy is 16 weeks of age.

Vaccination Schedule

This suggested vaccination schedule should provide adequate protection at minimum cost. It should be modified under the following circumstances:

1. If the mother dies during delivery, puppies receive no colostrum. Special immunization procedures will be required. They are discussed in the chapter, PEDIATRICS.

2.   Females who have not been immunized within a year should be given a DHLPP booster shot *before* being bred.

3.   Live virus vaccines should not be given to pregnant bitches because of potential harmful effects on the fetus. Do not vaccinate a pregnant female until you have discussed it with your veterinarian.

4.   Some strains of rabies vaccine require booster shots at one year intervals, others at three years. Follow the recommendations of the manufacturer of the vaccine or those of your veterinarian.

5.   Parainfluenza and leptospirosis vaccinations are indicated *more frequently* in endemic areas, areas in which the disease is constantly present. See *Parainfluenza* and *Leptospirosis*.

VACCINATION SCHEDULE

Age of Dog	Vaccine Recommended
At 5–8 weeks	Canine distemper-measles-CPI
At 14–16 weeks	DHLPP (distemper, hepatitis, lepto, parainfluenza, parvovirus) Rabies
At 12 months and annually	DHLPP
At 12 months	Rabies
At three year intervals	Rabies

CANINE BACTERIAL DISEASES

Brucellosis

This disease is caused by a bacteria called *Brucella canis*. It was first isolated at Cornell University in 1966. Brucellosis is an important cause of reproductive failure in dogs. It is the leading cause of late abortions (45 to 55 days gestation). It may be at fault when a bitch delivers stillborn puppies, or puppies which sicken and die shortly after birth. It can produce sterility in a dog and bitch without causing obvious signs of disease.

Dogs with active infection may show enlargement of the lymph nodes in the groin or beneath the jaw in association with a febrile illness. Joints may become swollen and painful. The testicles of the male may swell up, then go on to atrophy as the sperm-producing cells are destroyed. In others the disease goes unsuspected until there is evidence of reproductive failure. These animals are in a subclinical or "carrier" state, but are able to transmit infection. In the male, bacteria may be found in the prostate gland, and in the female in the uterus and vagina.

The most common mode of transmission is by sexual intercourse. In a kennel it can spread from dog to dog through contact with infected secretions.

A rapid serum agglutination slide test is available as a screening procedure to see if a dog has the disease. It can be done in most veterinary clinics with results back the same day. It should be done on all dogs before mating. The stud's owner should always request a veterinarian's certificate showing that the visiting bitch has been tested and found free of brucellosis before the dogs are allowed to run together. False positives do occur. They indicate the need for more detailed laboratory studies and cultures.

Treatment: At present there is no effective vaccine or treatment for the prevention and cure of brucellosis in dogs. Long-term treatment with antibiotics may be undertaken but relapse is likely to occur when the drugs are stopped. Pet dogs should be castrated or spayed to keep them from transmitting the disease.

To control the spread of brucellosis in the kennel, all animals must be screened and infected ones removed from the premises. Follow-up tests must be run every three months to identify new cases.

Leptospirosis

Canine leptospirosis is a disease caused by a bacteria called a *spirochete*. There are two spirochetes that commonly affect the dog. They also cause disease in other animals including cattle, sheep, wild animals, rats and man. The disease is spread in the urine of an infected animal. Rats appear to be one of the main reservoirs of the infection.

Spirochetes enter a dog's system through a break in his skin. They may gain entrance via the alimentary route when he drinks water or eats food contaminated by infected urine.

In the majority of cases the disease is mild or subclinical. In areas where it is prevalent serological studies have shown that many dogs are positive reactors—i.e., they have been exposed to the disease but have developed antibodies against it.

Signs of illness appear within 5 to 15 days. Fever is present in the early stage of the disease. It is accompanied by listlessness, loss of appetite and depression.

Leptospirosis can affect many systems but the primary signs are those associated with kidney involvement. They include a "hunched-up" gait due to pain in the kidney area; the formation of ulcers on the mucus membranes of the mouth and tongue; the appearance of a thick brown coating on the tongue; bleeding from the mouth or the passage of bloody stools; and severe thirst with increased urination.

The whites of the eyes may turn yellow. This indicates liver involvement.

Persistent vomiting and diarrhea are common. Dogs have difficulty eating and swallowing due to sores in the mouth.

Treatment: A presumptive diagnosis can be made on the basis of the dog's clinical signs and physical findings. This can be confirmed by finding spirochetes in his urine or blood and by blood tests.

Severely ill dogs cannot be treated at home and should be hospitalized for public health reasons and to provide more intensive care. Antibiotic combinations are effective against spirochetes when given by intramuscular injection for seven to ten days. Supportive measures include control of vomiting and diarrhea, replacement of fluids, and maintenance of nutrition. Complete kidney failure can be treated by peritoneal dialysis.

Some dogs go on to a chronic or progressive type of kidney failure long after the illness has passed. They become "carriers" and shed bacteria in their urine for as long as a year.

Spirochetes cause a disease in humans called *Weil's disease*. Precautions should be taken when handling sick dogs or cleaning up their quarters to avoid contact with infected secretions.

It is advisable to vaccinate dogs in areas where leptospirosis is a problem (see *Vaccinations*).

Tetanus (Lockjaw)

This disease can affect almost all animals including man. It is not contagious. It is caused by a bacteria called *Clostridium tetani*. Dogs possess some natural resistance to this infection, more so than does man.

Bacteria enter the skin via an open wound, such as a puncture. The rusty nail is the classical example. But any cut or injury to the full-thickness of the skin can act as a point of entry.

The tetanus bacteria is found commonly in soil contaminated by horse and cow manure. It is found in the intestinal tract of most animals where it does not cause a disease.

Symptoms appear as early as a few days after the injury but can be delayed for as long as several weeks. Tetanus bacteria grow best in tissues where the oxygen level is low (anaerobic conditions). The ideal environment is a deep wound which has sealed over, or one in which there is devitalized tissue heavily contaminated with filth. The bacteria make a toxin which affects the nervous system.

Signs of disease are due to the neurotoxin. They include spastic contractions and rigid extension of the legs; difficulty opening the mouth and swallowing; retraction of the lips and eyeballs. Folds in the forehead may cause the ears to stand erect. Muscle spasms are triggered by almost anything that stimulates the dog.

Treatment: Tetanus cannot be treated at home. Fatalities can be avoided by prompt veterinary attention. Tetanus antitoxins, antibiotics, sedatives, intravenous fluids, and care of the wound alter the course for the better.

The disease can be prevented by prompt attention to tetanus-prone wounds (see *Wounds*). Since natural resistance is high in dogs, routine vaccination of all dogs is not necessary. However, vaccination of herding dogs and those that live around livestock may be indicated.

Tuberculosis

This disease is caused by the *tubercle bacillus*. It affects man and all domestic animals. While there has been a steady decline in the incidence of tuberculosis, it has not been completely wiped out.

Dogs may infect humans and vice versa. The disease is still a problem in cows and other livestock. They may infect the dog also.

Tuberculosis is mainly a lung infection. However, it can affect other organ systems as well. The symptoms depend upon the site of infection. A common finding is low grade fever with chronic wasting and loss of condition in spite of good care and feeding.

Respiratory tuberculosis causes a chronic cough, labored breathing, shortness of breath and the production of bloody sputum.

Treatment: A typical x-ray and the finding of tubercle bacilli in sputum or other secretions of the dog makes the diagnosis. There are reports of successful treatment in dogs hospitalized over a long period of time and treated with certain antibiotics. However, the uncertainty of treatment, plus the obvious hazard to human health, makes euthanasia the wisest choice.

CANINE VIRUS DISEASES

Distemper

Distemper is a highly contagious disease which is caused by a virus similar to the germ that causes measles in people. World-wide, it is the leading cause of infectious disease deaths in dogs.

The distemper virus can live for many years in a frozen state. During spring, virus protected by freezing temperatures thaws out. Perhaps this accounts for the higher incidence of distemper during spring months.

Distemper is present wherever there are susceptible animals. It is probable that all dogs are exposed to it sometime in their lives. The disease is most common in unvaccinated puppies three to eight months of age. These pups have lost the protection of maternal antibodies. However, older dogs can acquire the disease, too.

Among infected dogs, about half show little in the way of illness. In others, the illness is mild. In some cases, the illness is severe or fatal. The overall condition of the dog has a lot to do with the seriousness of his illness. The disease is more acute in poorly nourished and ill-kept dogs.

The distemper virus has a special affinity for attacking epithelial cells. These are the cells that line the surfaces of the body including the skin, conjunctival membranes of the eye, breathing tubes, and mucus membranes of the intestinal tract. The brain is also affected.

The disease takes a variety of forms. Secondary infections and complications are common. They are sometimes the cause of death.

Typically, the signs of first stage distemper appear 3 to 15 days after exposure.

First stage. The disease begins with a fever of 103 to 105 degrees, loss of appetite, listlessness and a watery discharge from the eyes and nose. This symptom complex may be mistaken for a "cold". But dogs do not catch "colds" as people do. Therefore the signs should not be taken lightly.

Within a few days the discharge changes from watery to thick, yellow and sticky. This is an important indicator of the fact that your dog is suffering from distemper. The nose and eye discharge is accompanied by a pronounced dry cough. Pus blisters may appear on the abdomen. Diarrhea is a frequent problem and can cause severe dehydration.

During the next one to two weeks, the dog continues to run a fever but appears to get better for a day or two, then seems to get worse. The course of first stage distemper is up and down. The outcome will depend upon whether there is a step-wise improvement or gradual worsening.

Second stage. Two or three weeks after the onset of the disease some dogs develop signs of brain involvement which begin as brief attacks of slobbering, head-shaking and chewing movements as if he had a bad taste in the mouth. Later, epileptic-like seizures can occur. The dog runs around in circles, falls over and kicks his feet wildly. Afterwards he may appear confused, even shy away from his owner or wander about aimlessly. These are signs of *encephalitis*.

Another sign of brain involvement is *chorea*. Instead of having seizures, a dog with chorea starts to twitch or jerk. These movements can affect any part of the body but are more common in the head. They are first seen when the dog is relaxed or sleeping. Later they become continuous day and night. Pain accompanies the chorea-like motions and dogs whine and cry, especially at night. Should the dog recover, the jerking continues for life, but tends to be less severe as time passes.

Dogs with brain involvement usually do not survive the initial illness.

Hard-pad is a form of distemper in which the virus attacks the skin of the feet and nose, causing a thick horny-like skin to form on the nose, and callus-like pads to form on the feet. It begins about 15 days after the onset of the infection.

At one time hard-pad and encephalitis were thought to be diseases separate from distemper. They are now recognized to be due to different manifestations of the distemper virus.

Treatment: Because of the complexity of the disease treatment should be under veterinary supervision.

There is no antibiotic effective against the virus of distemper. Antibiotics are indicated, however, to avoid secondary bacterial complications. Intravenous fluids are employed to correct dehydration. Diarrhea should be controlled with appropriate drugs. Anticonvulsants and sedatives help to manage seizures.

The success of treatment depends upon how soon the owner realizes his dog is sick and seeks professional help.

Prevention: Distemper vaccinations must be kept current in all dogs (see *Vaccination Schedule*).

Brood bitches should be given a booster vaccination before they are. bred. This assures that their pups will be well protected by a high maternal antibody titer.

The use of distemper antiserum no longer is recommended.

Callus-like pads on the foot of a dog recovering from *hard-pad distemper*.

Herpes Virus of Puppies

Herpes infection is due to a contagious virus which attacks puppies at one to three weeks of age. The onset is sudden. The principal sign is a tight, painfully distended abdomen in puppies who cry continuously. Nothing seems to relieve their distress. After a brief illness lasting about 24 hours they usually succumb.

The disease is discussed in the PEDIATRICS chapter.

Infectious Canine Hepatitis

Infectious canine hepatitis is a highly contagious viral disease transmitted only to dogs. It should not be confused with hepatitis in man. Primarily it affects the liver, kidneys and lining of the blood vessels.

Infectious canine hepatitis presents a variety of signs and symptoms which range from those of a mild or subclinical infection at one extreme to a rapidly fatal one at the other. At times, it is difficult to distinguish the disease from distemper.

A few days after a dog is exposed, virus multiplies in the dog's tissues and is shed in his stool, saliva and urine. At this stage, the disease is most contagious. It is spread to other dogs coming into contact with the sick dog or his urine, stool and saliva. Convalescent dogs, and those that have recovered, may shed virus in the urine, sometimes for months.

The most severe cases occur in puppies during the first few months of life; but dogs of all ages are susceptible.

In the *fatal fulminating form* the dog suddenly becomes ill, develops bloody diarrhea, collapses and dies. Puppies may die suddenly without obvious illness.

In the *acute form* the dog runs a fever which may reach 106 degrees F. He passes bloody diarrhea and may vomit blood. He refuses to eat. Movement is painful. He may show a "tucked-up" belly which is caused by painful swelling of the liver. Light may hurt his eyes so that he squints and tears. Tonsillitis, bleeding beneath the gums and under the skin, and yellowing of the whites of the eyes (jaundice) may occur.

In *mild or subclinical cases* the dog simply appears lethargic or below his normal condition. There is loss of appetite. A blood test may help make the diagnosis.

After the acute symptoms have subsided, about 25 percent of dogs develop a characteristic clouding of the cornea of one or both eyes. It is called *blue eye*. In most dogs it clears spontaneously in a few days. If it persists, it should be treated by a veterinarian. Rarely the eye remains permanently clouded.

Blue eye can occur after vaccination against infectious hepatitis, too. This happens to only a small percentage of dogs. To learn more about blue eye, see the chapter on *Eyes*.

Treatment: Infectious hepatitis usually is recognized by the typical clinical picture. It is confirmed by blood tests.

Acute cases should be hospitalized for intensive veterinary care. Large doses of Vitamin B complex and Vitamin B_{12} often are given in the convalescent stage.

The disease can be prevented by proper vaccination. These vaccinations must be kept current in all dogs (see *Vaccination Schedule*).

Rabies

Rabies is a fatal disease that occurs in nearly all warm blooded animals although rarely among rodents. The main source of infection for humans is a bite from an infected dog or cat. However foxes, skunks, bats and other wild animals can serve as a reservoir for the disease, thereby accounting for sporadic cases. Any wild animal that allows you to approach it without running away from you is acting abnormally. Rabies should be suspected. Do not pet or handle such an animal.

The virus, which is present in infected saliva, usually enters at the site of a bite. Saliva on an open wound or mucus membrane also constitutes exposure to rabies. Animals suspected of having rabies should be handled with great care — or preferably not at all!

The average *incubation* period is two to three weeks but can be as long as several months. The virus travels to the brain along nerve networks. The further the bite is from the brain, the longer the incubation period. Virus then travels back along nerves to the mouth where it enters the saliva.

The signs and symptoms of rabies are due to encephalitis (inflammation of the brain). The first signs are quite subtle and consist of personality changes. Affectionate and sociable pets may become irritable and aggressive. Shy and less out-going pets may become overly affectionate. Soon the animal becomes withdrawn and stares off into space. He avoids light, which hurts his eyes (photophobia) and seeks seclusion. Finally he resists handling. Fever, vomiting and diarrhea are common.

There are two characteristic forms of encephalitis. One is the so-called "furious" form and the other is the "paralytic" form. A rabid animal may show signs of one or a combination of both forms.

The *furious form* is the "mad dog" type of rabies. Here the animal becomes frenzied and vicious, attacking anything that moves. The muscles of the face are in spasm, drawing the lips back to expose the teeth. When running free he shows no fear and snaps and bites at any animal in his path.

In the *paralytic form* the muscles of the head become paralyzed causing the mouth to drop open and the tongue to hang out. The swallowing muscles become paralyzed which causes drooling, coughing spells and pawing at the mouth. As encephalitis progresses, the animal loses control of his movements, staggers about, collapses and is unable to get up.

Public Health Considerations: The World Health Organization has established certain guidelines for practioniers to follow in the appropriate management of people who are exposed to a potentially rabid animal. The treatment schedule depends upon the nature of the exposure (lick, bite), severity of the injury, and the condition of the animal at the time of exposure and during a subsequent observation period of ten days.

If there is the slightest possibility that a dog or cat is rabid, and if there has been any sort of human contact, *impound the animal immediately and consult your physician and veterinarian.* This holds true even if the animal is known to be vaccinated for rabies. Depending upon the nature of the exposure, a victim of a biting animal may have to undergo a series of injections—either antirabies serum, rabies vaccine, or both. Often these injections are started at once but can be stopped if the animal remains healthy.

As an alternative in the case of a wild animal or feral dog or cat whose owner is unknown, the animal can be killed immediately. Should he escape, there is no way to prove that the animal was not rabid. In most cases a full course of treatment will have to be given.

When an animal is killed or dies during confinement, its brain is removed and sent to a laboratory equipped to diagnose rabies from special antibody studies. *Animals suspected of rabies should not be destroyed if instead they can be confined.* If the animal does not die of rabies, it may not be possible to recover virus from its brain. Then a full course of rabies treatment may have to be given to the victim. When an animal escapes there is no way to prove it was not rabid. In most cases a full course of treatment will have to be given.

Treatment: There is no effective treatment for dogs. To protect the health of your pet be sure he is vaccinated at three to six months of age. Then follow the procedure of your veterinarian to keep his vaccinations current.

Infectious Tracheobronchitis *(Kennel Cough)*

This is a highly contagious disease of dogs that spreads rapidly through a kennel. A harsh spastic cough is the characteristic sign of the illness. The cough may persist for many weeks and become a chronic problem due to replacement of the virus by secondary bacterial invaders. Chronic bronchitis is a common sequel to kennel cough.

A number of viruses have been implicated in the kennel cough complex. They include adenovirus types 1 and 2, herpes virus in the adult, and parainfluenza virus. Immunization of your dog with hepatitis vaccine (as found in the DHL shot) protects against adenovirus. Parainfluenza vaccine (CPI) protects against canine parainfluenza virus.

To learn more about tracheobronchitis, see the chapter on THE RESPIRATORY SYSTEM.

Canine Parvovirus (CPV)

This disease appeared suddenly in the United States in the summer of 1978, after which it spread rapidly throughout North America, Great Britain, Australia, South Africa and Europe.

CPV was first thought to be a disease which attacked the gastrointestinal tract primarily, producing vomiting and diarrhea. Both the *Corona* and *Parvo* viruses were implicated. It is now recognized that while both viruses do produce an illness in dogs, the Corona virus seems to cause a milder disorder, especially in adults.

Parvovirus has a special affinity for attacking rapidly reproducing cells—such as those lining the gastrointestinal tract; bone marrow; lymph nodes and heart. The virus, which is highly contagious, is transmitted from one dog to another via contaminated droplets and feces. It can be carried on the dog's hair and feet, as well as on contaminated cages, shoes and other objects. Dogs of all ages are affected, but the highest mortality occurs among puppies less than five months of age. Two main syndromes are recognized:

Diarrhea Syndrome (Enteritis): After an incubation period of seven to 14 days, the first signs are severe depression with loss of appetite, followed by vomiting. The dog appears to be in extreme pain, with a tucked-up abdomen. Within 24 hours he develops a high fever (up to 106 degrees F) and a profuse diarrhea which is frequently bloody. Mouth inflammation *(Stomatitis)* can occur. Almost no other canine disease produces such devastating symptoms.

Cardiac Syndrome (Myocarditis): This form of CPV affects the muscle of the heart, especially in puppies less than three months of age. Puppies with myocarditis stop nursing, cry out and gasp for breath. Death can occur suddenly, or in several days. Puppies who recover sometimes develop a chronic form of congestive heart failure which leads to death in weeks or months. While myocarditis can occur without enteritis, it might appear three to six weeks after a dog has apparently recovered from enteritis.

Treatment: Success of treatment is variable, depending on the form and severity of CPV infection as well as the age of the dog. It includes fluid and electrolyte replacement, medication to control diarrhea and vomiting, and administration of broad spectrum antibiotics to prevent secondary bacterial infections. In all but mild cases, hospitalization for intensive management is essential. Dogs who recover are immune to the disease.

The quarters of an infected dog should be cleaned and thoroughly disinfected. This is an extremely hardy virus that resists most household cleaners. The best disinfectant is Clorax (one part to 30 parts of water).

CPV can be prevented by an appropriate vaccination schedule. Parvovirus vaccinations must be kept current in all dogs (see *Vaccinations*).

FUNGUS DISEASES

Fungus diseases may be divided into two groups. In the first, the fungus affects just the skin or mucus membranes. Examples are ringworm and yeast stomatitis. They are discussed elsewhere. In the second the disease can be widespread, in which case it is called systemic.

Systemic fungal diseases are not common in the dog. They tend to occur in chronically ill or poorly nourished animals. Prolonged treatment with steroids and/or antibiotics can change an animal's pattern of resistance and allow a fungus infection to get established. Occasionally, a dog in good health can come down with one of the systemic fungal diseases.

Norcardiosis, histoplasmosis, blastomycosis and coccidioidomycosis are diseases caused by fungi that live in soil and organic material. Spores, which resist heat and can live for long periods without water, gain entrance through the respiratory system or through the skin at the site of a puncture. Respiratory signs resemble those of tuberculosis. They are: chronic cough, recurrent bouts of pneumonia, difficulty in breathing, weight loss, muscle wasting and lethargy. Up and down fever may be present.

Fungal diseases are difficult to recognize and treat. X-rays, biopsies, and fungus cultures are used to make the diagnosis in systemic cases. A fungus infection should be suspected when an unexplained illness fails to respond to a full course of antibiotics.

Systemic fungus infections do not respond to conventional antibiotics and require intensive veterinary management. Most fungi that cause disease in dogs also can cause illness in man. When the disease is systemic, euthanasia is often recommended.

The following systemic fungal diseases can occur in the dog:

Norcardiosis, Actinomycosis, Cryptococcosis. These are respiratory or skin infections occurring in dogs often under a year of age. They also affect the lymph nodes, brain, kidney and other organs. Large tumorous masses which discharge a material that looks like sulfa granules can appear on the legs or body.

Histoplasmosis. This is a disease caused by a fungus found in the central United States near the Great Lakes, the Appalachian Mountains, and the valleys of the Mississippi, Ohio, and St. Lawrence rivers. Spores are found in soil contaminated by the dung of chickens and other birds, or bats. In the majority of dogs the signs are those of a mild respiratory illness. There is a systemic form which attacks lymph nodes, small intestine and other organs. The principal signs are fever, weight loss, muscle wasting, enlargement of the tonsils and a prolonged diarrhea which may become bloody.

Do not kennel dogs in chicken coops, caves, or other places where birds and bats roost.

Blastomycosis. This disease is found in the same geographic distribution as histoplasmosis. The skin form is characterized by nodules and abscesses which ulcerate and drain. The systemic form is similar to histoplasmosis. The disease is difficult to treat and presents a hazard to human health.

Coccidioidomycosis. In most dogs this is a mild respiratory infection, but the systemic form can spread to virtually all organs of the body. It is found in dry dusty parts of the southwestern United States and in California. This is not the same disease as coccidiosis, which is caused by a protozoan. The signs of systemic illness resemble those of histoplasmosis.

PROTOZOAN DISEASES

Protozoans are one-celled animals. They are not visible to the naked eye but may be seen under the microscope. A fresh stool specimen is required to find the parasites. They are responsible for six major infectious diseases in dogs, as discussed below.

The life cycle of protozoans is complicated. Basically, infection results from the ingestion of the cyst form *(oocyst)*. Cysts invade the lining of the bowel where they mature into adult forms and are shed in the feces. Under favorable conditions they develop into the infective form.

Coccidiosis

This is a common protozoan disease found usually in young dogs, although adult dogs are not immune. It is especially severe in litters of nursing puppies. It is a serious problem in the southern United States but can occur in the northern states. Usually it occurs in connection with filth, overcrowding, poor sanitation, and the housing of dogs in cold damp quarters.

Puppies can acquire the infection from contaminated premises, or from their mother if she is a carrier. When kennel sanitation is poor, puppies reinfect themselves from their own feces. The disease spreads rapidly through a kennel.

Five to seven days after the ingestion of oocysts, infective cysts appear in the feces. The entire cycle is complete in a week. The first signs can be a mild diarrhea which progresses until the feces become mucus-like and tinged with blood. There is loss of appetite, weakness, dehydration and anemia. Often this is accompanied by a cough, runny nose and a discharge from the eyes — much like distemper.

Coccidia can be found in the stools of puppies without causing problems until some stress factor such as an outbreak of roundworms or shipping reduces their resistance. Dogs that recover can become carriers. They remain in good health but can suffer relapses when afflicted with some other disease, such as distemper. Carriers and dogs with active infection can be identified by finding adult oocysts in a microscopic slide of fresh stool.

Treatment: Stop the diarrhea with a Neomycin-Kaopectate antidiarrhea preparation. A severely dehydrated or anemic dog may need to be hospitalized for fluid replacement and blood.

Supportive treatment is important since in most cases the acute phase of the illness lasts a few days, perhaps ten days, and is followed by recovery in uncomplicated cases.

Sulfonamides and antibiotics have been used to treat coccidiosis. Response is slow once the signs of disease are apparent. Currently a drug called amprolium, used in the treatment of this disease in poultry, is the agent of choice in the United States. It is effective against only one stage in the life cycle of the protozoan. Therefore, it must be continued until all protozoan that reach this stage are destroyed. Mix it with the dog's food or water at a rate of 50 to 100 mg/lb body weight per day. This eliminates oocysts from the stools in seven to twelve days. In kennels where coccidiosis is a problem, amprolium is used on all six-week-old puppies before they are sold or shipped.

Known carriers should be isolated and treated. At the same time their quarters and runs should be washed down daily with lysol and *boiling* water to destroy oocysts. Otherwise they will reinfect themselves.

Toxoplasmosis

This protozoan disease affects all animals including man. Cats by far are the more common source of the infection, but the disease can occur in the dog. The exact mode of transmission is unknown. Possibly it is due to ingestion of oocysts in contaminated soil, or the eating of wild game or uncooked meat. Transmission through the placenta from mother to offspring is possible.

Toxoplasmosis often is asymptomatic. When symptomatic it affects the brain, lymphatic system and lungs. Young puppies with toxoplasmosis may show signs of pneumonia, hepatitis and encephalitis. Serological blood tests are necessary to confirm the diagnosis.

About half the human adult population shows serological evidence of having been exposed in the past. The disease is a real hazard to human health when a pregnant woman without prior immunity is exposed to the disease. Birth defects, largely involving the central nervous system, do occur.

Treatment: This disease is difficult to recognize. Effective medications are available for the dog but should be used under veterinary supervision.

Public health measures in regard to cats are ineffective because cats roam freely and hunt raw meat. It is easier to control the disease in dogs. They can be fenced and supervised.

Few people are willing to give up owning a pet because of an infrequent disease. A blood test can be requested to see if an animal has acquired immunity through prior exposure. A pet with an immune antibody level is safer than one without.

Trichomoniasis

This is a protozoan infection caused by a species of trichomonas often associated with a mucoid (and occasionally bloody) diarrhea in puppies. Commonly it is found in accordance with poor kennel sanitation. Prolonged infection leads to weak, debilitated, stunted puppies with rough hair coat. The diagnosis is made by finding the protozoan in fresh stool smears.

Treatment: The infection responds well to Flagyl. The dose is 30 mg per pound body weight per day for five days.

Giardiasis

This illness is caused by a protozoan of the Giardia species. The disease in dogs has received little recognition in the past, although it has grown steadily more common. Usually it occurs in young dogs. The principal sign is diarrhea, occasionally mixed with mucus and blood. Diagnosis is made by finding the protozoan in saline smears of fresh stool. Smears from rectal swabs are satisfactory.

Treatment, which is highly effective, is the same as for trichomoniasis.

Piroplasmosis

This is a disease which is also called Canine Babesiosis. It is due to a protozoan which destroys red blood cells. Characteristic signs are anemia, fever, enlargement of the spleen and liver and changes in the blood chemistries due to interference with bone marrow and liver function.

Piroplasmosis is transmitted by the common brown dog tick. It is best prevented by keeping your dog free of ticks. To learn how to control ticks on your dog, see the chapter on SKIN.

Medications effective against piroplasmosis are available through your veterinarian.

4

Skin

GENERAL REMARKS

Skin disease is a common problem in dogs and the condition of the skin can often tell you a great deal about your dog's general health and condition.

Unlike the skin of people, your dog's skin is thinner and more sensitive to injury. It is easily damaged by careless or rough handling with the wrong kind of grooming equipment, and once the surface of the skin is broken and disturbed by trauma or some sort of skin disorder, the condition tends to spread rather easily and becomes a major problem to the dog and his owner.

There are many functions served by the skin. Without an intact skin, water from the dog's tissues would quickly evaporate, draining him of body heat and water and leading to his death from cold and dehydration. Skin is a barrier which keeps out bacteria and other foreign agents. It is involved in the synthesis of essential vitamins. It provides sensation to the surface of the body. It gives form to the body and insulates the dog against extremes of heat and cold.

The outer skin layer is the *epidermis*. It is a scaly layer which varies in thickness in different parts of the dog's body. It is thick and tough over the nose and feet pads and is thin and most susceptible to injury in the crease of the groin and beneath the arms.

The *dermis* is the next layer inward and its main purpose is to supply nourishment to the epidermis. It also gives rise to the *skin appendages* which are the hair follicles, sebaceous glands, eccrine glands, and toenails. They are modifications of the epidermis to serve special functions.

In man, the skin is well supplied with sweat glands and blood vessels which regulate the loss of heat from the body. *Dogs do not have sweat glands,* except for those found in the dermis of the feet pads. The sebaceous glands are important in that they secrete an oil which coats the hair and waterproofs the coat, allowing it to shed water. Water-going breeds depend upon skin oils to waterproof their coats. Skin oil is influenced by hormone levels in the blood. Large amounts of circulating estrogen (the female hormone) reduce oil production, while small amounts of androgen (the male hormone) increase it.

The color of your dog's skin may vary from pink to light brown, or it may be dark with patches of black. The dark pigment is called melanin and is produced by cells in the skin called melanocytes.

BASIC COAT CARE

Growing a Coat

The growth of a dog's coat is controlled by a number of factors. Some dogs, by selective breeding, carry a more abundant or more stylish coat.

Dog hair, unlike scalp hair found in people, does not grow continuously. Dog hair grows in cycles. It grows for a short period, then rests. Then it dies and is shed before the cycle begins again. The coat of the average dog takes about 130 days to grow, but there is wide variation within the breeds. The Afghan, for example, grows its coat for about 18 months before it is shed.

Too much female hormone in the system may slow the growth of coat hair. Too little thyroid hormone in the system often impairs the growth, texture, and luster of a dog's coat. Ill health, a run-down condition, hormone imbalance, vitamin deficiency, or parasites on the dog or within his system may cause the coat to be too thin and brittle. If you suspect that your dog's coat is below par, you should take him to your veterinarian for a general checkup.

Environmental factors have a definite influence on the thickness and abundance of a dog's coat. Dogs living outdoors continuously in cold weather grow a heavy coat for insulation and protection. Some additional fat in the diet is indicated in winter to build up the subcutaneous layer of fat and provide more warmth for dogs living outdoors. Bacon grease may be added to the diet, as this also improves the palatability of the food and encourages the appetite. An alternative is to feed natural corn oil, which is well tolerated by the digestive tract of dogs and adds calories. Give about one or two teaspoonfuls a day to the average size dog.

Nutritional supplements, reported to build coat and improve skin health and hair sheen, are of questionable value in the healthy well-nourished dog.

Shedding

Most dogs shed or "blow" their coats at least once a year. Bitches sometimes blow their coats after heat, during pregnancy, or after nursing.

Some dogs have a double coat composed of a long outer coat of guard hair and an under coat of soft woolly hair. When a dog with a double coat begins to shed, his appearance may be quite alarming and at first suggest a skin disease. This is because the inner coat is shed in a mosaic or patchy fashion giving rise to a moth-eaten look. However, this is perfectly normal. Dogs do not shed their coats evenly or in waves.

Coat loss is occasionally precipitated by sudden physical stress or illness, pregnancy, or changes in the internal balance of hormones. Stressful conditions causing hair to drop out first appear where hair grows the fastest, on the body and flanks; as opposed to the hair on the legs which grows the slowest.

Many people believe that it is the seasonal change in temperature which governs when a dog sheds his coat. But, in fact, shedding is influenced more by changes in surrounding light. The more exposure to light, the greater the shedding. This is why house dogs, exposed to long hours of artificial light, seem to shed excessively.

When shedding begins you should attempt to remove as much of the dead hair as possible by daily brushing, or—in some breeds with thick double coats—by a bath which first loosens the dead hair and then makes it easier to remove by thorough brushing. Dead hair next to the skin is irritating to the dog. It often leads to an itch-scratch cycle which damages the skin and may cause further skin problems.

HOW TO AVOID COAT AND SKIN PROBLEMS

Grooming

Brushing your dog for a few minutes each day will help to keep him free of problems of the skin and hair. Establish a routine and try to adhere to it. If you are grooming a puppy, keep the sessions relatively brief and try to make it a pleasurable experience for him. If he grows to dislike the basic routine, then a simple procedure is made most difficult.

Grooming tools that are especially useful are listed below. Your choice will depend upon the breed of dog you own and the nature of his coat.

Grooming Table. It is important that a table be solid with a non-slippery surface. The correct height of the table is that at which you can work on your dog comfortably without having to bend.
Nail Clippers. Pet stores sell several kinds of nail clippers. We prefer those that have two cutting edges.
Comb. Buy a metal dog comb with smooth round teeth which is especially designed to avoid trauma to the skin.
Carder. This is a square board with a short handle and fine wire teeth which are bent. Insert the teeth into the hair next to the skin; then twist and pull out. A carder is used to remove dead hair and mats.
Brush. A brush with natural bristles, or a soft wire pin brush, is recommended. Long hair is usually brushed against the grain and short hair is brushed with the lay of the coat.

Accustom the puppy to a thorough grooming once a week. This requires adequate exposure and a good assistant. —*J. Clawson*

When trimming the nails, avoid the quick. A nail clipper having two cutting edges works best. —*J. Clawson*

Hound Glove. This is used on short-coated breeds to remove dead hair and polish the coat.

Stripping Comb. This type of comb is used to pluck dead hair and dress the coat.

Toweling. Toweling is used in short-haired breeds to remove loose dead hair. It tends to tangle long hair.

File.

When brushing your dog, use special care to see that any soft woolly hair behind the ears is completely brushed out. This is one area where lumps of fur form if neglected. If such lumps are present, use sharp scissors and *carefully* cut away from the skin into the fur ball in narrow strips; then tease these out with your fingers. Slide a comb under the mat and cut on top to avoid cutting skin.

Groom under the ear flaps whenever your dog has been in tall grass, weeds, and brush. Foreign material, particularly plant matter, can enter the ear canal by first clinging to the hair surrounding the outer opening. To remove dirt and debris see *Cleaning the Ears*.

Routine inspection of the teeth will tell you if there is any build up of tartar or calculus. To learn how to remove calculus, see *Care of Your Dog's Teeth*.

If the toenails have not been worn down through activity, they should be filed or trimmed. Pay special attention to the front *dewclaws,* and the rear ones if present. As these claws do not touch the ground, they are not worn down and may grow back into the pads when neglected.

Before you clip your dog's nails, look carefully and identify the pink part of the nail (quick). Avoid cutting into the quick, as this part contains nerves and blood vessels. Should the nail begin to bleed, hold pressure over it with a cotton ball. The blood will clot in a few minutes. If it persists, a styptic (such as used for shaving) can be used.

Inspection of the anal sacs may disclose a build up of secretions. To care for the anal sacs, see *Anal Glands or Sacs*.

There are several good books which go into considerable detail about grooming for the show ring. *How to Trim, Groom and Show Your Dog* (Howell Book House, Inc.) is one of them. Most breed books provide more information on this subject. You may wish to consult one of them if you own a breed of dog that requires special grooming care.

Bathing

Over-bathing a dog can remove natural oils which are essential to the health of his coat. It is difficult to lay down specific guidelines on bathing since this varies widely among dogs with different coat types.

In general, dogs with *undercoats,* such as the German Shepherd and Great Pyrenees, are best bathed in spring and fall, and at other times may be kept clean with a dry shampoo and brushing.

When bathing, rinse the dog thoroughly to remove soap and residue from his coat.
—*Joyce Stannard*

Dogs with long *silky* coats, such as the Afghan, should be bathed about once a year; spaniels, on the other hand, are bathed as often as every six weeks. The addition of one teaspoonful per quart of water of Alpha-Keri to the rinse is often effective in adding luster to the coat.

Curly and *woolly* coated breeds, such as the Poodle and Bedlington, may have to be bathed as often as every four to six weeks and should be brushed every day.

Smooth coated breeds, such as the Beagle and Doberman, should be bathed only when necessary. The coat should be maintained by brushing to a shiny slickness with a hand towel or hound glove.

Wire coated breeds, including the Welsh Terrier and Airedale, are usually bathed every eight weeks.

Bathing is often restricted to an occasional bath for a specific purpose.

It is not necessary and may even be undesirable to bathe before every dog show. There are certain risks to bathing. If, for example, your dog is about to shed, the bath will hasten the shedding and loss of the coat. However, when the coat is badly stained or has a strong odor, when it appears lumpy in spite of a thorough brushing, the only solution is a complete bath.

How to Give Your Dog a Bath:

First brush out the coat and remove any knots or mats; matted hair tends to "set" when wet. Plug the ears with cotton to keep out water. Instill ointment into the eyes to prevent soap burn. A drop of mineral oil in each eye works well (see *How to Apply Eye Medicine*).

The next question is what shampoo to use. Most human shampoos are on the acid side. This is because human skin is more acid than a dog's. Some human shampoos are on the alkaline side and may be suitable for use on your dog. You should check this with your veterinarian first. Coconut oil shampoo is safe to use on dogs.

In general, it is far better to use a good commercial dog shampoo.

Next, wet your dog thoroughly, using a nozzle and spray. Then lather and rinse the head carefully, keeping the soap and water out of the eyes and ears. After the whole dog has been lathered and rinsed, relather and rerinse his legs, feet and other areas of stubborn stain.

The secret of getting a clean dog with a healthy skin is to rinse and rinse until all soap and residue has been removed from the coat. Use a spray hose and nozzle. Soap which has been left behind dulls the coat and irritates the skin.

Special rinses are sometimes recommended to bring out the coat for show purposes. Do not use vinegar, lemon or bleach rinses. They are either too acidic or too basic and will damage the coat and skin. Alpha-Keri bath oil may be added to the final rinse to give luster to the coat. Use one teaspoonful per quart of water.

Now dry the coat gently with towels, or if your dog does not object to it, dry him with an air comb. Remember, a dog's coat takes several hours to dry and he should be kept indoors until completely dry to avoid chilling.

Some dogs with an oily coat are prone to collect dirt. In such cases, some method of dry cleaning the coat between baths is desirable. A number of products have been used successfully as dry shampoos. Calcium carbonate, talcum or baby powder, Fuller's earth, and cornstarch are all effective. They can be used frequently without danger of removing essential oils or damaging the coat or skin. To remove excess powder from your dog, start at the bottom with a soft bristle brush. Brush against the lay of hair, being careful to get down to the skin. Brush the whole dog. If you are planning to show your dog, you must remove all traces of powder before you enter the ring for judging. Otherwise, if the judge finds artificial substances on the coat of your dog, he may dismiss him from the ring.

Special Bath Problems:

Skunk Oil: Skunk odor may be removed from your dog's coat by soaking it in tomato juice and then giving him a bath as described above. An alternative is to make up a dilute solution of ammonia in water. Use it as a rinse and follow it with a complete bath.

Tar. Trim away excess coat containing tar when feasible. Soak the tarry parts of the coat in vegetable oil overnight. Then give your dog a complete bath. Do not use petroleum solvents, such as gasoline, kerosene, or turpentine; they are extremely harmful to the skin.

WHAT TO DO IF YOUR DOG HAS A SKIN PROBLEM

If your dog begins to scratch at himself all the time, or if he licks, paws, bites at his skin and rubs up against things to relive his discomfort, then you are faced with an *itchy skin disorder* and should attempt to determine the cause. See *Table I.*

There is another group of skin conditions which have to do with the appearance of the coat and hair. These diseases do not cause your dog much discomfort—at least not at first. *Hair loss* is the main sign. It may appear as impaired growth of new hair. Or you may notice patchy losses of hair from specific areas on the body. At times, you may notice that the coat does not look or feel right. It may be coarse and brittle, dull and lifeless. Skin changes are often present. To determine the possible cause, see *Table II, a and b.*

When your dog has a painful skin condition and you can see pus and other signs of infection on or beneath the skin, then your dog is suffering from *pyoderma.* Some pyodermas are late developments of other skin ailments. Others are specific skin diseases that occur by themselves. See *Table III.*

During the course of grooming, playing with or handling your dog, you may discover a *lump or bump* on or beneath the skin. To learn what it might be, see *Table IV*.

If you suspect that your dog is suffering from a skin ailment, conduct a thorough examination of his skin and coat. On short-coated dogs, run a fine-toothed metal comb against the lay of the hair to expose the skin. On long-coated dogs use a pin brush. In many cases a typical finding makes the diagnosis obvious.

Unfortunately, this is not always the case. The diagnosis of a specific skin disease in a dog can be a difficult task. Early signs of skin disease are not easy to detect in heavy-coated dogs. The picture is sometimes complicated by biting and scratching at a constant itch or painful sore. History becomes important in trying to decide what could have caused the ailment in the first place.

Facts such as age, sex, breed, change in activity or diet, contact with other animals, emotional state, exposure to skin irritants, environmental influence, and the like, then become important points to consider.

AIDS IN THE DIAGNOSIS OF SKIN DISEASE
Table I
ITCHY SKIN DISORDERS

Scabies *(Sarcoptic Mange):* The most common cause of *intense* itching. Small red spots like insect bites on the skin. Identify mites. *Typical crusty ear tips.*

Walking Dandruff *(Cheyletiella Mange):* Puppies two to twelve weeks. *Dry flakes* over the head, neck and back. Mild itching.

Fleas: Itching and scratching along the back, around the tail and hindquarters. Fleas and/or black and white gritty specks in the hair (flea feces and eggs). *Fleas very mobile.*

Lice: Found in poorly kept dogs with matted coats. *Not common.* Look for lice or nits beneath mats. May have bald spots.

Ticks: Large insects fasten onto the skin. *Blood ticks* may swell to pea-size. Cause irritation at the site of the bite. Can be difficult to remove intact. Often found beneath ear flaps and where hair is thin.

Damp Hay Itch *(Pelodera):* Severe itch caused by a worm larva. *Must have contact with damp marsh hay.*

Inhalation Allergy *(Canine Atopy):* Severe itching, face-rubbing and licking at paws (hay fever type symptoms). Often begins at the same time each year *(seasonal pollens).* Certain breeds more susceptible.

Flea Allergy Dermatitis: Follows flea infestation. Pimple-like rash along back and peri-anal area. *Scratching continues after fleas have been killed.*

Contact Dermatitis: Itching and skin irritation *at site of contact* with chemical, detergent, paint, dye, etc.

Allergic Contact Dermatitis: Requires *repeated or continuous contact* with allergen (i.e., flea collar). Rash may spread beyond area of contact.

Lick Sores *(Acral Pruritic Dermatitis):* Mainly in large, short-coated individuals left alone for long periods of time (boredom sores). Starts with licking at wrist or ankle.

AIDS IN THE DIAGNOSIS OF SKIN DISEASE

Table II-a

DISORDERS IN WHICH HAIR IS LOST OR GROWS POORLY: HORMONE RELATED DISORDERS

Thyroid Deficiency *(Hypothyroidism):* Males and females. *Coat is thin and scanty.* Hair is brittle and coarse and falls out easily. Skin is thick, sometimes darker.

Cortisone Excess *(Adrenal Gland Hyperfunction):* Can be due to prolonged medication with steroids, too. Males and females. *Hair lost in symmetrical pattern,* especially over the trunk. Skin thin.

Estrogen Excess *(Hyperestrinism):* Mainly in females. *Hair has greasy feel,* falls out along flanks and abdomen. Build-up of wax in ears. In males consider a testicle tumor, especially with a retained testicle. Loss of hair in genital area. Nipples enlarge. Dry skin and brittle hair.

Estrogen Deficiency *(Hypoestrinism):* Mainly spayed females. *Scanty hair growth* (thin coat). Skin is smooth and soft, like a baby's skin.

Acanthosis Nigrans: Hair loss begins in *armpit folds.* Black, thick, greasy, rancid-smelling skin. *Mainly in Dachshunds.*

Seborrhea: *Dry* type: similar to dandruff. *Greasy type:* hair and skin is oily; yellow brown greasy scales on skin. *Hair lost in circular patches,* resembles ringworm. Rancid odor.

Table II-b

DISORDERS IN WHICH HAIR IS LOST OR GROWS POORLY: OTHER DISORDERS

Collie Nose *(Nasal Solar Dermatitis):* Sunburn-type reaction affects lightly pigmented nose; *mainly in Collies and Shelties.* Loss of hair at junction of nose and muzzle. Can lead to severe ulceration.

Ringworm *(Fungus Infection):* Scaly, crusty or red circular patches one-half inch to two inches in size with hair loss at center and *red margin* at periphery of ring. Affects all parts of coat. Looks healthy unless complicated by scabs and crusts. Some cases involve a large area with hair loss.

Demodectic Mange (Two Forms):

Localized—Moth-eaten look due to hair loss around eyelids, mouth and front legs. Patches about one inch in diameter, fewer than five in number. *Dogs and bitches less than one year old.*

Generalized—Progression of the above. *Numerous patches enlarge and coalesce.* Severe skin problem complicated by *pyoderma.* Affects dogs of all ages, primarily young purebreds.

Calluses (Elbow Sores): *Gray, hairless, wrinkled pads of skin* usually over elbow but can occur over any bony pressure point from lying on hard surface.

AIDS IN THE DIAGNOSIS OF SKIN DISEASE

Table III

PAINFUL SKIN DISORDERS WITH DRAINAGE OF PUS (PYODERMA)

Puppy Dermatitis *(Impetigo and Acne):* Puppies under 12 months. Not painful.
Impetigo—Pus-filled *blisters* or thin brown *crusts on hairless skin* of abdomen and groin.
Acne—Purplish-red bumps on chin and lower lip.

Hair Pore Infections *(Folliculitis):* Dogs of all ages, Schnauzers in particular. *Pimple-like bumps* or black-heads *along the back* and elsewhere. In severe cases, draining sinus tracts and hair loss.

Skin Wrinkle Infection *(Skin Fold Pyoderma):* Macerated *inflamed skin with a foul odor in characteristic locations:* lip fold, facial fold, vulvar fold and tail fold.

Hot Spots *(Acute Moist Dermatitis):* Mainly in heavy-coated dogs. Rapidly advancing *painful* inflamed patches of skin covered with a *wet surface exudate of pus* from which *hair is lost.* Skin is irritated from many causes. Disease progresses through self-maceration.

Cellulitis and Abscesses:
Cellulitis—Painful, hot, inflamed skin. Caused by wound infections, foreign bodies, breaks in the skin.
Abscesses—Pockets of pus beneath the skin. Painful swelling that comes to a head and drains.

Puppy Strangles (Juvenile Pyoderma): Puppies under 4 months. *Sudden painful swelling of lips, eyelids, ears and face.* Draining sores, crusts and sinus tracts.

AIDS IN THE DIAGNOSIS OF SKIN DISEASE

Table IV

LUMPS OR BUMPS ON OR BENEATH THE SKIN

Papillomas and Warts: Grow out from the skin and look like warts or pieces of chewing gum stuck to the skin. Can occur in the mouth. Not painful.

Hematomas: Collections of blood beneath skin, especially of the ears. Caused by trauma.

Tender Knots: Frequently found at the site of a shot or vaccination. Resolve spontaneously. Often painful.

Cysts: Smooth lumps beneath skin. May grow slowly. Can discharge cheesy material. Become infected. Otherwise not painful.

When a Lump May be a Cancer:
Rapid enlargement; appears hard and fixed to surrounding tissue; any lump growing from bone; a lump which starts to bleed; a mole which begins to spread and/or ulcerate; unexplained open sore which does not heal, especially on feet or legs.
Note: Only way to tell for sure is to remove and study under the microscope.
These conditions also are discussed in the chapter TUMORS AND CANCERS.

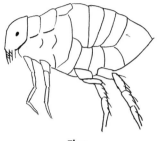

Flea.

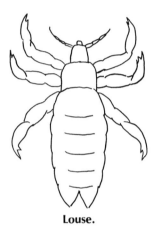

Louse.

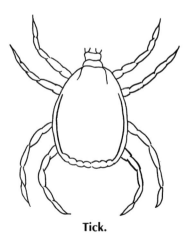

Tick.

—Rose Floyd

ITCHY SKIN DISORDERS

Insect Parasites

Scabies (Sarcoptic Mange)

This disease is caused by a microscopic spider-like creature called a mite. The diagnosis must be made by examining skin scrapings under a microscope, or in difficult cases by a skin biopsy (searching for mites).

Probably no other skin disease will cause your dog to scratch and bite at himself with such intensity. The intense itching is due to the female mites tunneling a few millimeters under the skin to lay their eggs. Mite eggs hatch in three to 10 days. The immature mites develop into adults and begin to lay eggs of their own. This whole cycle takes only 17 to 21 days.

Signs: At first you will see small red bumps that itch. They look very much like insect bites, which in fact they are. Later, because of scratching, rubbing and biting at the itch, the skin breaks down allowing serum to seep out. One sees scabs, crusts, and even patches of hair loss. In the final stages the skin becomes thick and darkly pigmented.

These mites seem to prefer the skin of the ears, elbows, legs and face. Early hair loss and crusts are often seen in these areas. Crusty ear tips, along with an intense itching, make the diagnosis almost certain (see EARS). If you rub the edge of your dog's ear between your fingers, he usually will begin to scratch himself on that side.

If your dog has scabies you may notice itching of your skin at the belt line. The mites have transferred from your dog to you. However, mites do not live over three weeks on human skin. The problem is self-limited if the dog is treated.

Treatment: Clip scabies-affected areas on long-haired dogs and bathe the entire animal in one of the insecticide dips (see *Insecticides*). Dips active against Sarcoptic Mange mites are: lime-sulphur, ronnel, and malathion. At least three dips are required at intervals of 10 days each. A fourth dip is often needed to catch late hatching eggs.

Dandruff shampoos such as Seleen are useful. They can be employed between insecticide dips to loosen scales.

Cortisone will help relieve severe itching. Sores that look infected from self-mutilation should be treated by a soothing topical antibiotic ointment (Panalog).

Walking Dandruff (Cheyletiella Mange)

This type of mange occurs in puppies primarily. It is caused by a large reddish mite that may infest kennels. It may be recognized by the presence of a heavy dandruff over the head, neck and back. It causes a mild itching. Walking dandruff is highly contagious. The mite lives on the surface of the skin and dies in a short time when off the host. The diagnosis is made by finding the mite on the puppy or in dandruff scrapings collected on paper and examined under a magnifying glass.

Treatment: All infected animals should be treated with an insecticide dip once a week for three to four weeks. Control is easily achieved by using the same methods as described for *Scabies*.

When the condition involves a kennel of dogs, the premises should be treated with an insecticide (see *Premises Control*). Dichlorvos fly strips aid in the control of Cheyletiella Mange mites.

Fleas

The flea is the most common parasite found on the skin of the dog. Fleas live by feeding on blood. While in most dogs flea bites cause only a mild itch, under certain circumstances a heavy infestation of fleas may cause a severe anemia or even the death of the animal. A flea is also the intermediate host of the dog tape worm.

Some dogs experience a marked hypersensitivity to the saliva of the flea. It leads to an intense itching and skin reaction (see *Flea Allergy*).

Signs: Flea infestation can be diagnosed by the finding of fleas on your dog; or by seeing salt and pepper-like, black and white grains about the size of sand in the coat. They are flea eggs and flea feces. Fecal material is made up of digested blood. When brushed onto a wet paper, it turns a reddish brown. Look for fleas on your dog's back and around his tail and hindquarters. Fleas are sometimes seen in the groin where it is warm and there is less hair. Itching is most pronounced in these areas.

The adult flea is a small, dark brown insect which can be seen with a naked eye. Although the flea has no wings and cannot fly, it does have powerful back legs and can jump great distances. Fleas move through the hair rapidly and are difficult to catch. Ticks and lice move slowly and are easier to pick off.

Life Cycle: In order to flourish, fleas need a warm humid environment. They are more common in summer, but occur all year around in pets living indoors. They mate on the skin of the dog where they lay their eggs. The eggs falls off and incubate on furniture, in carpets, cracks, and dog bedding. After a few days, the eggs hatch into larvae which feed on what debris is available. Then they spin a cocoon. Depending on environmental conditions, the larvae can take three weeks to two years to grow into adult fleas.

Treatment: Because fleas spend most of their life off the dog, treatment of an individual dog is only partly effective. It is most important to eradicate fleas in the environment as well. To learn how to control fleas on the premises, see *Premises Control*. (Insecticide sprays and powders especially effective in the *environmental* control of fleas are Lindane, 0.5% spray or 1.0% dust; Chlorodane, 0.5% solution; DDVP; and Sevin 5% dust).

A variety of products are available for killing fleas on the dog. Mild flea shampoos such as Fleavol, powders such as Diryl, or sprays such as Sprecto, remove fleas; but their effect is short-lasting and you will find it difficult to get adequate concentrations of insecticide over the whole animal. Sprays work best on dogs with short coats.

Scabies. The mites attack the skin of the ears, causing early hair loss, crusty skin, and *intense* itching.

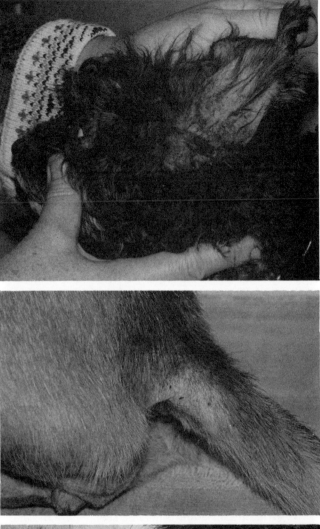

Fleas frequently are found around the dog's tail.

Lice frequently are found around the face and ears *(pediculosis)*.

Flea collars and medallions aid in flea control but cannot be relied upon to eradicate all fleas. They have little effect on dogs living outdoors.

Insecticide dips are by far the best method of ridding your dog of fleas. Dips especially active against fleas are Dermaton, Paramite, Kem Dip, and Para Dip. Before using one of these insecticide dips, be sure to read the section on *Insecticides*. For the control of fleas, dips should be utilized every two weeks until the dog is free of fleas by close inspection. Between dips, spray short-haired dogs and powder long-haired dogs, once or twice a week. One week after the last dip, put on a flea collar and change it every two months.

Occasionally, a dog is found to be sensitive to the chemicals in flea collars and develops a skin allergy (see *Allergic Contact Dermatitis*). Flea collar dermatitis sometimes can be prevented by airing the collar for 24 hours before putting it on the dog. The collar should fit loose enough so that you can get two or three fingers between it and your dog's neck.

CAUTION: Do not permit your dog to eat or chew his flea collar or medallion. It contains toxic chemicals. Flea collars impregnated with Dichlorvos should be removed one week before worming with Task (Dichlorvos) and should not be put back on until one week after worming. Otherwise, the additive effect of the insecticide in the flea collar and in the worm medication could be harmful to your dog.

Dogs with flea allergy dermatitis require special attention (see *Flea Allergy*).

Lice (Pediculosis)

Lice infestation is called pediculosis. Lice are not very common. They occur primarily in dogs who are run down and poorly cared for and are often found beneath matted hair and around the ears, head, neck, shoulders and anal area.

The usual picture is itching in an unkempt dog. Because of the constant irritation, bare spots may be seen where the hair has been rubbed off.

There are two types of lice. *Biting lice* feed on skin scales. *Sucking lice* feed on the dog's blood and can cause a severe anemia.

Adult lice are pale-colored insects about two to three millimeters long. They lay eggs called *nits*, which look like white grains of sand and are found attached to the hairs. They are difficult to brush off. Nits may look something like dandruff (seborrhea); but dogs with seborrhea do not itch as they do with lice. Inspection with a magnifying glass makes differentiation easy as nits are well-formed rounded eggs attached to hair shafts.

Treatment: Lice do not show much resistance to insecticides and do not live long off the dog. They can be killed by giving a thorough bath followed by an insecticide dip which is effective against fleas (see *Fleas*). Three to four dips must be given at 10 day intervals. In between, dust the dog with a 5% Sevin powder (see *Insecticides*).

Infected bedding should be destroyed and the dog's sleeping quarters disinfected (see *Premises Control*). Severely anemic dogs may require a blood transfusion; or a build up with vitamins, iron and a high protein diet.

Ticks

Most people who live in the country are familiar with ticks. The male tick is a small flat insect about the size of a match head. A "blood" tick is a female tick feeding on the dog. She may swell up to the size of a pea.

Ticks have a complicated life cycle. It involves three hosts including wild and domestic animals and man. The adult tick fastens onto the dog. Males and females mate at this time and the female feeds on the host. When you see a puffed-up tick (female) on your dog, look for a small male tick nearby.

There are several varieties of ticks that live on the dog. The brown dog tick is perhaps the most common. All are capable of transmitting some disease. Rocky Mountain spotted fever, Q-fever, tularemia and encephalitis are diseases transmitted by ticks. Ticks are capable of secreting a toxin which causes dogs to become paralyzed. This disorder is common in some parts of the United States (see NERVOUS SYSTEM: *Tick Paralysis*).

Ticks are usually found on the ears, neck, head and between the toes. Occasionally a dog is found with hundreds of ticks all over his body.

Treatment: When your dog has just a few ticks, the easiest thing to do is to remove them. First kill the tick by applying alcohol, gin, ether, or fingernail polish directly to the tick by means of a cotton-tipped applicator. After a few moments, grasp the dead tick as close to the skin as possible and apply steady traction until it releases its hold. If the head remains fixed to the skin, there is no need for concern. In most cases, this causes only a local reaction which clears up in a few days. Only rarely does a tick bite become infected. To learn how to treat ticks on your dog's ear, see EARS.

If your dog has many ticks, you will have to resort to a commercial insecticide preparation such as 4% Malathion powder; or a dip such as Ronnel 1% (Ectoral), or Kem Dip. Before using one of these preparations read the section on *Insecticides*. With heavy infestations, a multiple dipping procedure is required. Dip once a week for four to six weeks. At the same time be sure to treat the dog's sleeping quarters (see *Premises Control*). If your dog lives in the house, it may be best to use a professional exterminator.

For outdoor control of ticks it is advisable to cut tall grass, weeds, and brush. Spray or dust with Toxophene, Chlorodane, or Dieldrin. These products are toxic to pets. Use them with caution.

Damp Hay Itch *(Pelodera Dermatitis)*

This condition is caused by the larvae of a thread-like worm found on damp marsh hay. The larvae burrow into the skin of the dog's chest,

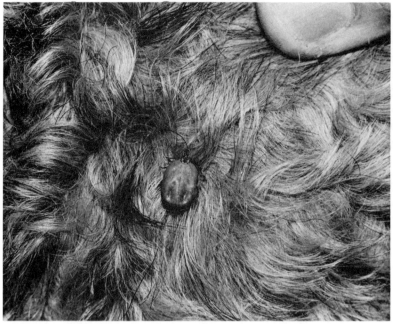

Engorged female tick. —*J. Clawson*

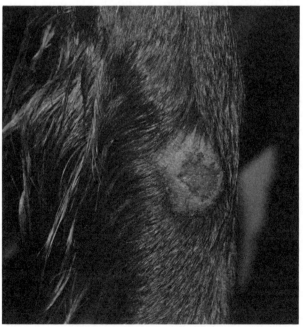

Lick sores are due to boredom.

abdomen and feet, causing raised pimple-like bumps. Later, you may see raw crusted and inflamed areas where the dog has scratched and infected his skin.

The disease is found among dogs living outdoors, or housed on damp marsh hay. The diagnosis is made by examining skin scrapings under the microscope.

Treatment: Kill worm larvae by dipping your dog in an insecticide solution such as Dermaton or Paramite once a week until he is free from itching. Bathe infected areas with a mild soap such as pHisoHex: then apply a topical ointment (i.e., Neosporin Ointment) three times a day. Change your dog's bedding from hay to cedar shavings, cloth, or paper shreds. Spray sleeping quarters with an insecticide solution (see *Insecticides*).

Lick Sores *(Acral Pruritic Dermatitis)*

In this condition a sore at the ankle or wrist is caused by a constant licking at that spot. It is also called a "boredom" sore because it occurs in dogs left alone without company or something to interest them for long periods. It is most common in dogs who are middle-aged and therefore less active. It tends to occur among bird dogs, Labradors, Danes, Dobermans, and other large short-coated breeds.

As the dog begins to lick at his wrist or ankle the hair is rubbed off. The surface of the skin then gets red and shiny-looking and begins to itch. This leads to further maceration of the skin which continues the cycle. Eventually the sore becomes raised, thick and hard, and insensitive to pressure. But it remains clean and fresh-looking from constant cleansing. Often it is just one leg that is involved.

Treatment: The most important step in treating this condition is to get your dog interested in something else. Take him for a walk every day, bring him into the house, or perhaps get him another pet to keep him company. Cortisone relieves the itching but will probably be licked off right away. It can also be administered by injection directly into the sore. In stubborn cases x-ray treatment and cobra-venom injections have been tried.

Insecticides

Insecticides are used as powders, dusts, sprays and dips for the elimination of insects on the dog. They are also used to disinfect bedding, houses, kennels, runs, gardens, garages, and other spots where a dog might reinfect himself by coming into contact with the adult insect or its inter-mediate forms.

Insecticides are poisons!

If you decide to use an insecticide preparation, be sure to follow the directions of the manufacturer. Otherwise, poisonings are likely to occur from improper exposure.

There are four classes of insecticides in current use. They are: *chlorinated hydrocarbons* (Lindane, Chlordane); *organophosphates* (Dichlorvos, also called Task; and Ronnel, also called Ectoral); *methylcarbamates* (Diryl, Sevin); and *Pyrethrins*.

Commercial preparations for powdering, spraying and dipping your dog are available through many pet stores and agricultural supply outlets for control of fleas, lice, mites, ticks and other parasites. They all contain insecticides of the classes listed above.

When you purchase one of these products, be sure that it is made *especially for dogs*. Preparations manufactured for sheep and livestock can irritate the skin of dogs or even cause the death of the animal through toxic reactions.

Lysol and other household disinfectants are not suitable for washing your dog and should not be used because, like insecticides, they are absorbed through the skin and can cause illness or death.

An overdose of an insecticide could cause your dog to twitch at the mouth, foam, collapse, convulse and fall into a coma. Other signs of insecticide toxicity are diarrhea, asthmatic wheezing, a staggering gait and muscle twitching and jerking.

If you suspect that your dog is suffering from an insecticide reaction, give him a bath in warm soapy water to remove residual compounds from his coat and keep him quiet. Contact your veterinarian.

Dipping

The object of a dip is to rid your dog of insect parasites. Choose a dip which is recommended by your veterinarian or, if you decide to wash your dog with a commercial preparation, check the label to be sure that it is effective against the insect in question. Insecticides active against fleas, mites, lice, ticks and Pelodera are listed under the discussion of these parasites.

CAUTION: Some worm medicines contain similar chemicals. If your dog has just been wormed, there could be a sudden build up of chemicals in his system from powdering, dipping or spraying with an insecticide. Check with your veterinarian before applying an insecticide to a dog which has been wormed within a week.

Dipping your dog is not difficult if you first wash him with a gentle commercial dog shampoo. Then, while his coat is still wet, rinse him thoroughly with an insecticide dip made up according to the directions on the package. Apply eye ointment to the eyes and plug the ears with cotton so you can treat the head and ears with the dip also.

Most insecticide dips have to be repeated three or four times at intervals of seven to 10 days. This varies according to the insect and the severity of the infestation.

Premises Control

The object of premises control is to rid the environment of insects, eggs, larvae and other intermediate stages. Otherwise your dog will reinfect himself.

Treat all animals likely to come in contact with your dog or his living quarters.

Destroy infected bedding and scrub your dog's quarters with a strong household disinfectant. A thorough housecleaning which includes vacuuming of carpets, spraying of furniture, application of insecticide to corners and cracks, will help to eliminate the insect, its eggs and larvae. This usually has to be done two or three times. With heavy infestation, it is sometimes better to enlist the services of a professional exterminator.

Insect bombs such as Vet Fog are suitable for use in dog houses and homes and may be used safely in closed spaces. Be sure to remove all pets and read instructions carefully. Some of the insecticide dips can be used as sprays on gardens, lawns and kennels. Use according to the method of dilution suggested by the manufacturer.

Dichlorvos fly strips kill fleas by a vapor blanket effect if properly placed. Attach a strip three or four feet above a dog's bed or, if he lives in a dog house, attach half of the strip to the inside of the roof and half beneath the floor.

A dog's sleeping quarters should receive at least two treatments spaced two weeks apart. Eggs and cocoons are resistant to insecticides and can remain dormant for several months.

Sevin is an insecticide powder which can be purchased rather inexpensively from garden and agricultural supply stores. It comes in different concentrations. Be sure that you purchase the *five percent* dust. It can be used safely in kennel runs and dog houses, on lawns and shrubs; it will not hurt your dog if light powder adheres to his coat. Dust liberally in and around sleeping quarters, kennels, and dog houses by means of a shaker can. Force dust into crevices and cracks. It is effective against fleas, ants and lice. It is partially effective against ticks.

ALLERGIES

General Information

An allergic reaction is an unpleasant side effect caused by the dog's *immune system*. Without an immune system, an animal would not be able to build up any resistance to viruses, bacteria, foreign proteins, and other irritating substances which get into his system. In the allergic dog, substances such as pollens, molds, house dust, insect bites, certain foods and chemicals, trigger a reaction typified by itching and occasionally sneezing, coughing, tearing, or vomiting and diarrhea.

In order for a dog to become allergic to something in his surroundings, he must be exposed to it at least twice. What he is allergic to is called the *allergen*. The way in which his body responds to that allergen is called a *hypersensitivity reaction* (or allergic reaction). *Anaphylactic shock* is a life-threatening type of allergic reaction. It is discussed on page 346.

About 15% of people and 10% of dogs over-react to allergens. They have this extra-sensitivity and are called *atopic*. It is hereditary.

There are two kinds of hypersensitivity reactions. That of the *immediate type* occurs shortly after exposure and produces hives and itching (urticaria). *Hives* can be recognized by wheal formation and hair which sticks out in little patches, especially around the face. Frequently you will see swelling of the eyelids. Hives, often caused by insect bites, usually disappear within 24 hours.

The *delayed reaction* produces itching which occurs hours or days afterward. Flea allergy dermatitis is an example of both types: there may be both an immediate and delayed response. This explains why a dog may continue to itch even after a successful flea-dipping.

Canine allergy is one of the major causes of skin ailment in the dog.

Inhalant Allergy *(Canine Atopic Dermatitis)*

If your dog starts to scratch at his skin about the same time each year he may be suffering from a skin allergy due to breathing pollens. It is called canine atopy. It is similar to hay fever in humans.

Severe itching is the leading sign. It often is accompanied by licking at a runny nose, rubbing an itchy face on the carpet, sneezing, watering at the eyes, and lapping at the paws (look for characteristic brownish stains on the feet). Areas where the hair has been rubbed off may be found beneath the arms and along the flanks. The skin is red and scratched. It sometimes feels warmer than normal. In a small percentage of cases you may notice droplets of water on the skin.

Canine atopy seldom occurs in dogs younger than six months of age and usually begins in dogs one to three years old. There is a hereditary basis in most cases. Commonly it is found in Wirehaired Fox Terriers, West Highland White Terriers, Dalmatians, and Poodles; but all breeds are affected.

In the typical case, signs first appear in August and September (the ragweed season). Later other pollens begin to influence the picture: tree pollens in March and April; then grass pollens in May, June and early July. Finally, the dog starts to react to wool, house dust, molds, feathers, kapok and other irritants. With prolonged exposure and multiple allergens, the condition becomes a year-around problem.

In order to see if your dog has an inhalation allergy, your veterinarian may wish to hospitalize him and see if he gets better. If his symptoms come back after he goes home, then it is quite certain that he is allergic to something in the environment. Skin tests with various allergens help to identify causative agents.

Canine atopy can be confused with flea allergy, contact dermatitis, and irritations of the ears and eyes.

Treatment: You should try to keep your dog away from whatever it is that he is allergic to. If it is just feathers or kapok, this may be possible. However, the atopic dog usually has many different allergies and it is not feasible to protect him from them all. It may be possible for your veterinarian to give him a course of injections to desensitize him.

Cortisone also is effective and helps to control his symptoms. It should be administered only under medical supervision because of serious side effects.

Flea Allergy Dermatitis

All dogs with fleas experience flea bites. But a certain percentage of dogs are allergic to flea saliva and break out in a rash. This is a hypersensitivity reaction of both immediate and delayed type and itching occurs even after fleas have been eliminated. It is characterized by a severe itching along the back and around the tail, in the perianal area and hindquarters. Dogs often scoot or back up against something they can rub their bottoms against. If the cause is undetected the itching becomes generalized.

With close observation of skin you will notice fleas and small red pimple-like bumps. They may form crusts and become infected. After a time, the skin gets thick and pigmented, and the hair drops out.

Treatment: Kill fleas with dips and insecticides (see *Fleas*). Cortisone tablets or injections block the allergic reaction and relieve the itch. They should be used only with veterinary supervision because of potential side effects. Treat sores with a topical antibiotic ointment (Panolog).

Desensitization is not of much value in delayed allergies of this type.

Contact and Allergic Contact Dermatitis

Contact dermatitis and allergic contact dermatitis are two different conditions discussed together because they produce similar appearing reactions. Both are caused by contact with a chemical. Whereas any dog coming into contact with irritating chemicals develops a skin irritation, in some cases only dogs allergic to a substance show a skin response. A dog does not break out with an *allergic* dermatitis until he has been exposed to an allergen repeatedly.

A contact dermatitis of either type causes itchy red bumps along with redness and inflammation of the skin. You may notice moist weepy spots, crusts, blisters, ulcerations and pus.

Common contact *irritants* are acids and alkalis, insecticides, detergents, solvents, soaps and petroleum by-products.

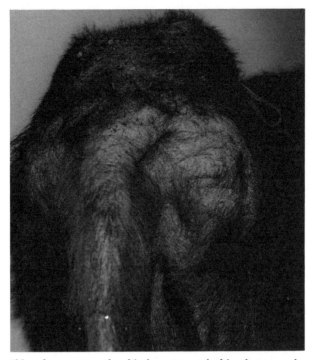

Skin changes on the hindquarters of this dog are due to hypersensitivity to flea saliva *(flea allergy dermatitis)*.

Hyperestrinism. Excess female hormone caused enlargement of the vulva.

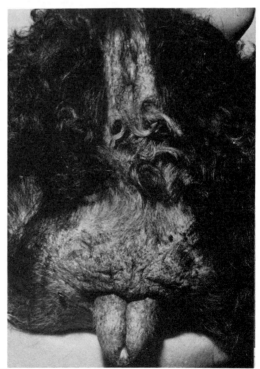

Common contact *allergens* are flea powders and collars, poison ivy nad poison oak, plastic and rubber dishes, and dyes found in indoor-outdoor carpets.

You will find contact dermatitis on the feet, chin, abdomen, groin and scrotum (areas likely to come in contact with chemicals). Since dogs lie on their hocks and stifles, these areas are affected,too.

Flea collar allergy causes local itching and redness followed by loss of hair, skin ulceration, and crust formation beneath the collar (see *Fleas*). This condition may spread to other areas.

Food dish dermatitis affects the nose.

Skin disease easily mistaken for contact and allergic contact dermatitis are canine atopy, ringworm and seborrhea.

Treatment: First identify the skin allergen causing the problem and then keep your dog away from it. Treat infected areas with an appropriate antibiotic. Cortisone is of value because it stops the itching, biting and scratching. It should be used only under a veterinarian's supervision.

DISORDERS IN WHICH HAIR IS LOST OR GROWS POORLY

General Information

The outstanding sign of these non-irritative skin disorders is skin change without itch or pain. The exception to this is the dog whose primary disease has been complicated by a secondary infection of the skin (see *Pyoderma*).

Hormone induced skin diseases usually are seen in dogs over five years of age but are not common. They develop slowly, progress gradually, and can be a lifetime problem.

Characteristically, hormone disorders cause symmetrical changes over the body, one side being the mirror image of the other. The typical changes are first loss of hair, and then darkening of the skin. The diagnosis is often difficult, the response to treatment is slow, and professional help is required for diagnosis and long-term therapy.

Thyroid Deficiency *(Hypothyroidism)*

This condition is due to inadequate output of thyroid hormone from the thyroid gland in the neck. Thyroid deficiency causes the coat to become thin and scanty. The hair is coarse and brittle and falls out easily. The skin gets thick, tough, and dark in color.

Since the rate of metabolism is under the influence of the thyroid, a deficiency of thyroid hormone in the system slows down energy production. In the dog, the signs of thyroid deficiency are lethargy, obesity, drooping of the eyelids, mental dullness, and irregular heat cycles. These signs develop gradually and may take months to become evident. If your dog has a mild thyroid deficiency he may show little or no signs of it. You might begin to

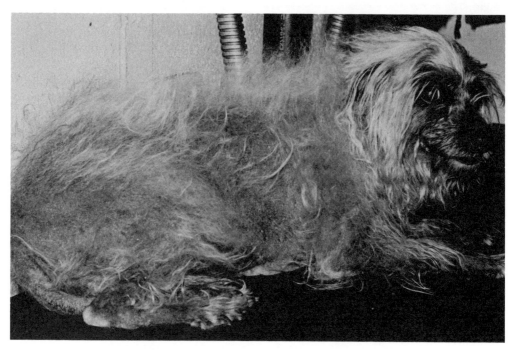

Before treatment of a hormone imbalance *(cortisone excess).*
Note loss of hair over the body in a symmetrical pattern.

After treatment the coat looks a lot better.

suspect this only in connection with an infertility problem. Diagnosis requires a thyroid blood test.

Treatment: Hypothyroidism is easy to treat with thyroid hormone given daily. Usually it is permanent and requires lifetime treatment.

Cortisone Excess *(Adrenal Hyperfunction)*

This condition is due to overproduction of cortisone by the adrenal glands located on top of the kidney. If your dog is getting cortisone by mouth or by injections, after a time he could get the same effect as if his adrenal glands were making too much cortisone.

The effect on the coat is loss of hair in a symmetrical pattern over the body with darkening of the underlying skin. Small "blackheads" may be found on the abdomen. There is a pot-bellied look. Dogs with cortisone excess gain weight and retain fluid.

Treatment: If your dog is getting cortisone by tablet or injection, your veterinarian may want to reduce the dosage or stop the medication altogether. If it is due to overproduction, the administration of drugs to reduce cortisone production by the adrenal glands may be needed.

Estrogen Excess *(Hyperestrinism)*

An excess of female hormone can occur in both males and females. In females it is due to cystic ovaries which manufacture too much estrogen. Often there is a history of infertility, false pregnancy or enlargement of the vulva.

The effect on the skin is to stimulate oil production and cause greasy hair. Wax builds up in the ear canals. Hair falls out along the flanks and abdomen. The skin in the groin and axilla becomes thickened and tough (like pigskin).

In the male estrogen excess can be due to a tumor of the testicle. This is a rare condition.

Treatment: The female should be spayed. Castration should be performed on males. Some testicular tumors are malignant.

Estrogen Deficiency *(Hypoestrinism)*

This is a mild skin condition which occurs in older female dogs who were spayed as puppies. There is a gradual lack of hair growth over the under surface of the belly and around the vulva, later involving the lower chest and neck. The skin becomes soft, smooth and nearly hairless. Females with the condition shed very little and do not collect much dirt. They make good house pets.

Treatment: Your female dog will regrow her coat if you give her small doses of stilbesterol over an extended period of time.

Dry flaky skin *(secondary seborrhea)*.

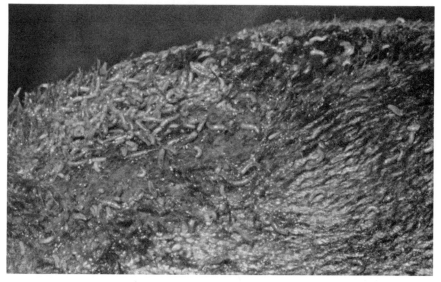

Maggots are the larvae of blow flies. They hatch on dirty and infected skin.

Acanthosis Nigrans

Acanthosis Nigrans literally means "thickened black skin". The disease affects the armpit folds and those of the groin. It is found most commonly in Dachshunds. The exact cause is unknown.

As the disease progresses an extreme dark black pigmentation and the development of a greasy rancid discharge on the surface of the skin, occurs. Bacterial infection is common. Eventually the process may extend over a considerable area, covering the brisket and extending onto and around the legs. This disease causes considerable distress to the dog and his owner.

Treatment: There is no available cure but with continuous management the dog can be kept comfortable. Keep the skin surface clean with an antiseborrheal shampoo (Seleen) to remove excess oil and bacteria. Cortisone preparations such as Panolog aid in controlling the skin irritation. Weight reduction, to reduce friction in the skin folds, is advisable. Antibiotics are prescribed when the skin is infected.

This condition should be treated by a veterinarian.

Seborrhea

Two types of seborrhea exist in the dog. The *secondary type* of seborrhea is similar to dandruff. It is flaky and scaly, and easy to lift off the skin. It is usually not a disease in itself. Instead, it is found associated with other conditions such as allergic dermatitis, mange, and hormone skin disorders. If your dog has a severe scratching problem and you see dandruff, you probably have not found the cause and should keep looking for it.

The other type of seborrhea is called *primary* seborrhea. Its cause is unknown. Cocker and Springer Spaniels are affected more often than other breeds. Primary seborrhea is due to excess production of skin oil (sebum). It leads to greasy deposits of yellowish brown scales on the skin and hair, giving the dog a rancid, unpleasant odor. The hair may look as if it had lice nits attached to it. Skin patches may resemble ringworm (distinguished by culture); mange (distinguished by skin scrapings); or hormone imbalance (see *Estrogen Excess*).

The areas frequently involved by primary seborrhea are the elbows, hocks, and hair along the border of the ear. Small circular patches (having a pigmented oily center and a red halo-like outer rim) sometimes are found over the face and chest.

Treatment: Primary seborrhea is incurable but manageable. Sebum dissolving shampoos (Seleen, Pragmatar, Sebbafon and Sebulex) give good results when used to cleanse the skin of oil and scales. How often to shampoo depends upon the individual case; usually once a week is enough. Leave shampoo on the skin for 10 minutes and then rinse well. Creams and ointments (Thiomar Creame and Pragmatar Ointment) applied to individual

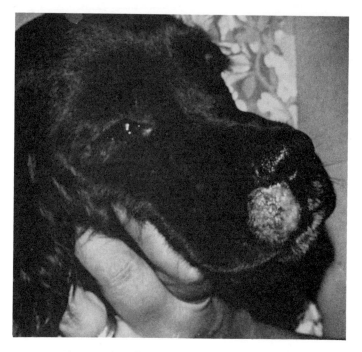

Ringworm on the muzzle of a Cocker Spaniel.

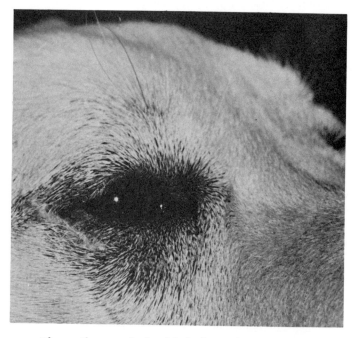

The moth-eaten look of hair loss around the eyes
is characteristic of *localized demodectic mange*.

skin spots help to keep them in check. Cortisone is used to control itching and redness. Topical and oral antibiotics are used for the treatment of secondary bacterial infection.

Collie Nose *(Nasal Solar Dermatitis)*

This skin condition, which usually affects Collies, Shetland Sheepdogs, and related dogs, is discussed in the chapter NOSE.

Ringworm *(Fungus Infection of Skin)*

Ringworm is not a worm but a plant-like growth which lives on the surface of the skin. The majority of cases are caused by the fungus *Microsporum canis*.

Ringworm gets its name from its appearance—a rapidly spreading circle having hair loss at the center and a red ring at the margins. This skin disease is transmitted to dogs by other animals and man, or to dogs by contact with spores in the soil. Humans can pick up ringworm from dogs and vice versa. Children should avoid handling dogs with ringworm, as they are especially likely to catch the disease. Adults seem relatively resistant.

Ringworm grows in circular patches one-half inch to two inches in size. Although simple ringworm is not an itchy condition, scabs and crusts can form, leading to draining sores. Cases do occur in which skin involvement is extensive. Ringworm also invades toenails. When the nails grow out they are usually deformed.

Mild cases of ringworm, with just hair loss and local scaliness, often resemble localized demodectic mange or dry seborrhea. A diagnosis of ringworm can be made if the skin glows green under ultra-violet light. This test is positive in only about one-half the cases. Microscopic examination of skin scrapings, and fungus cultures, are more certain.

Treatment: Clip away the infected hair at the margins of the ringworm patch and bathe the skin with Weldol or Betadine shampoo to remove dead scales. One or two small patches can be treated with a fungistatic solution (Tinactin) which can be purchased at a drug store without a prescription. For more extensive involvement, or patches that do not seem to be getting better with topical solutions, your veterinarian may wish to prescribe a drug called Griesofulvin (Fulvicin). It is given by mouth in a daily dose of 10 to 20 milligrams per pound, or at weekly intervals in a larger dose. It should not be given to pregnant females as it could be dangerous to unborn puppies. It is also a good idea to give a single large dose (100 milligrams per pound) as a preventative to other animals on the premises who are not infected but have been exposed. Infected sores should be treated with a topical antibiotic ointment (Panolog).

Demodectic Mange

Demodectic Mange is a disease included here because the signs are those of hair loss without itch. It occurs among dogs three to 12 months of age and is caused by a tiny mite, Demodex Canis, too small to be seen without a microscope.

Most dogs have some Demodex mites living in the pores of their skin. They acquire them early in life, from their mothers. This mite is usually present without causing symptoms.

All the factors responsible for skin disease in the presence of this mite are not yet fully understood. It has been shown that Demodex mites are able to produce a substance which lowers dogs' natural resistance to them, allowing them to multiply on the host. A number of kennels have observed that certain females have a higher incidence of Demodex mange in their litters than other mothers. This suggests that in some purebred dogs there is lowered immunity to the mite.

The disease is more common in short-haired dogs with oily skins. Symptoms appear at puberty. At this time sebum, which the mites feed on, is increasing in amount.

Demodectic mange may take one of two forms:

Localized form. This occurs in dogs up to a year of age. It starts out as thinning of the hair around the eyelids, the corners of the mouth, or on the front legs, giving a moth-eaten appearance to these areas. It progresses to patches of hair loss about one inch in diameter (which may be confused with ringworm). If more than five patches are present, the disease could be progressing to the generalized form. After one or two months the hair begins to grow back in. In three months the majority of cases are healed.

Treatment: A solution of 4% Ronnel in propylene glycol, or a topical preparation such as Canex or Goodwinol, can be used to shorten the course of the disease. Many cures of Demodectic mange attributed to drugs actually have been spontaneous recoveries. Watch closely to be sure that the localized form is not progressing to the generalized type.

Generalized form. This disease begins as a localized case but instead of improving it gets worse. Numerous patches appear on the head, legs and trunk. The patches coalesce to form large areas. Hair follicles become plugged with mites and debris. Skin breaks down to form sores, crusts and draining sinus tracts—presenting a most severe and disabling condition.

Treatment: Treatment of the generalized form is prolonged and response is slow, requiring frequent changes in medications.

Clip away all infected hair to facilitate topical therapy of the skin. Wash the whole dog with Betadine shampoo to remove scales and debris.

With rubber gloves, apply 4% Ronnel in propylene glycol to one-third of your dog's body each day. If more than one-third of the skin is treated, he is likely to develop signs of organophosphate poisoning (see *Insecticides*). Treat until skin scrapings are negative.

Cultures from infected skin sores will determine the most effective antibiotic. Cortisone has been used cautiously to treat severe skin irritations. However, it may depress a dog's immunity to the mites, making his condition worse.

This form of Demodectic mange should be treated under veterinary supervision.

Calluses *(Pressure Sores)*

Calluses are gray, hairless, thickened pads of wrinkled skin overlying bony pressure points. They are caused by constant pressure from lying on hard surfaces. The most common site is the elbow, but calluses can occur on the outside of the hocks, the buttocks, and the sides of the legs. They are much more common in heavy dogs and dogs kenneled on cement floors.

If the pressure problem goes unchecked, the surface of the skin can break down, forming a running sore with serum draining from the hair pores. This becomes a most difficult problem to treat.

Treatment: Provide your dog with a soft surface to sleep on so as to take the pressure off the callus and distribute it over a greater area. Foam rubber pads, or several thicknesses of bedding, or padded rugs may be used. An infected callus should be treated in the same way as an abscess (see *Pyoderma*).

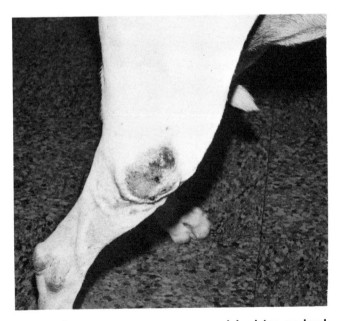

Callus. These pressure sores are caused by lying on hard surfaces, such as concrete.

PYODERMA (Pus On or Beneath the Skin)

General Information

Pyoderma is a pus-forming bacterial infection of the skin. Many cases of pyoderma are caused by maceration. When a dog rubs, chews, or scratches at a persistent irritant to his skin, it become infected. The infection, then, gets started only because some other problem was there first. This should always be kept in mind. Look for other signs of skin disease before concluding that pyoderma is the *only* problem your dog has.

Puppy Dermatitis *(Impetigo and Acne)*

This is a mild surface skin infection found in young dogs under 12 months of age. There are two typical conditions: impetigo and acne.

Impetigo (or milk rash) can be recognized by finding pus-filled blisters on the hairless parts of the abdomen and groin. These rupture easily, leaving thin brown crusts.

Acne is found on the chin and lower lip, or occasionally in the genital area, the perineum or groin. It is identified by finding purplish-red bumps which come to a head and drain pus (like pimples or blackheads). Blockage of skin pores by excess sebum or keratin is a predisposing cause. It is more common among dogs with oily skins.

Treatment: Both infections can be controlled by twice daily cleansing of the skin with a dilute solution of hydrogen peroxide or surgical soap (pHisoHex), followed by the use of a topical antibiotic (Panolog). When sebum is a problem, the skin should be cleansed with one of the seborrhea shampoos (Seleen, Thiomar, Sebutone, or Selsun Blue).

Acne usually clears up as a dog matures. However in certain breeds, including the Doberman, Boxer and Bulldog, the disease can persist as the dog grows older. If your dog does not seem to be improving with local care, see your veterinarian.

Hair Pore Infection *(Folliculitis)*

In this condition pimple-like bumps or blackheads are found along the back, the sides of the body, and the stifles. It is more common in shorthaired dogs and affects dogs of all ages. Some cases may be due to grooming too vigorously, causing injury to the skin.

Once established, the infection bores down into the hair pores and causes a deep-seated disease in which draining sinus tracts appear and the hair is lost in small patches.

A condition called "Schnauzer bumps" is common in Miniature Schnauzers. Dogs suffering from this condition have many large blackheads running down the middle of their backs.

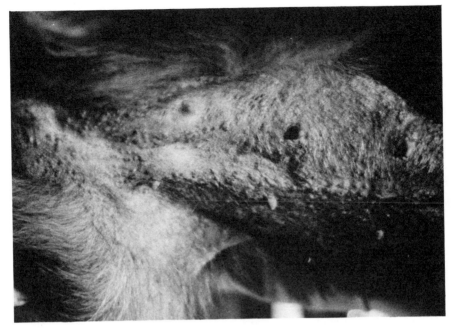

Hair pore infection on the abdomen *(folliculitis)*.

Treatment: Mild cases are treated in the same way as acne. Treatment is sometimes prolonged, requiring the addition of oral antibiotics. Pustules or small abscesses should be left alone. If you squeeze them you might cause the infection to spread downward into the tissues.

Skin Wrinkle Infection *(Skin Fold Pyoderma)*

Skin wrinkles and folds provide an ideal location for the growth of bacteria. This infection can be found as lip-fold pyoderma in spaniels and St. Bernards, as face fold pyoderma in Pekingese, as vulvar fold pyoderma in overweight females, and as tail fold pyoderma in Bulldogs (screw tails).

The signs are irritation and inflammation of the skin. The moist skin becomes infected and gives off a foul odor.

Treatment: Relief is obtained by clipping away hair and bathing the skin with a surgical soap (Weldol or pHisoHex). An antibiotic-steroid cream (Panolog) is effective against itching and scratching. Surgical removal is the method of choice when the condition is slow to respond to topical treatment.

Hot Spots *(Acute Moist Dermatitis)*

Hot spots are warm, painful, swollen patches of skin which exude pus and give off a foul odor. These circular patches appear suddenly and enlarge

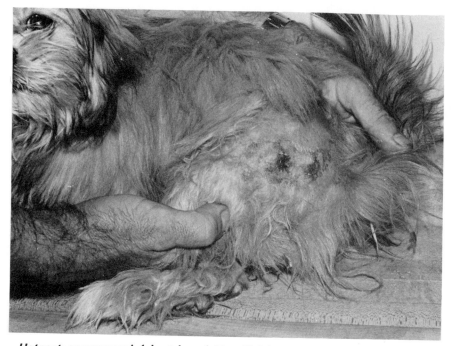

Hot spots are warm painful patches of skin which become infected and exude pus.

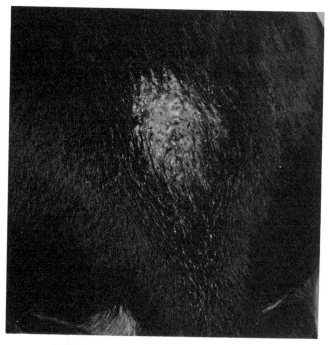

Cellulitis involves the deep layers of the skin.

rapidly, often within a few hours, attaining several inches in size. Hair is lost rapidly.

A hot spot, also called *pyotraumatic dermatitis,* is a bacterial skin infection which progresses through self-mutilation. Fleas, ear and anal gland problems, skin irritants, allergies, and other factors are probably responsible for initiating the cycle.

Hot spots are more common among breeds with heavy coats. They appear on the neck, ears, chest, back, rump and flanks. In breeds having a double coat, hot spots are more common just before shedding, particularly in the wet season when dead moist hair is trapped next to the skin.

Treatment: Clip hair away to let in air. Gently cleanse the skin with a surgical soap (pHisoHex or Weldol) or dilute hydrogen peroxide. Many dogs exhibit considerable pain and should be sedated or tranquilized to facilitate handling, and to prevent psychic trauma.

A product called *Sulfadene* is available at pet stores and works well when applied to the skin. Topical antibiotic-steroid creams (Panolog and Neosynolar) aid in reducing irritation. Apply them three times a day to achieve good results. Oral antibiotics and steroids might be indicated. Dogs should be prevented from licking and biting at their sores. Use restraints or an Elizabethan collar. Underlying skin problems should be identified and treated along with the hot spots.

Cellulitis and Abscesses

Cellulitis is an inflammation which involves the deep layers of the skin. Most cases are caused by a break in the skin which lets bacteria get established. Infection can be avoided in most fresh wounds if proper care is taken of them within the first few hours.

The signs of cellulitis of the skin are *pain* (tenderness to pressure), *warmth* (it feels hotter than normal), *firmness* (it's not as soft as it should be), and change in color (it appears *redder* than it should be). As the infection spreads out from the wound into the subdermal lymphatic system, you may see red streaks in the skin and be able to feel enlarged lymph glands in the groin, armpit, or neck.

A *skin abscess* is a localized pocket of pus beneath the surface of the skin. Pimples, pustules, furuncles, and boils are examples. The signs are the same as those for cellulitis except that an abscess is fluctuant (it feels like fluid under pressure).

If hot moist packs are applied to an area of cellulitis, the heat and moisture assist the natural defenses of the body to surround the infection and make it come to a head. The skin over the top of an abscess thins out and ruptures, allowing the pus to be evacuated. Then the pocket heals from below.

Treatment: Localize the infection by clipping away the hair and applying warm soaks three times a day. Saline soaks, made up to a teaspoonful of salt in a quart of water, make a suitable poultice.

Pimples, pustules, furuncles, boils and other small abscesses which do not drain spontaneously need to be lanced with a sterile needle or scalpel. Flush the cavity with dilute hydrogen peroxide to keep it open and draining until it heals from below.

Antibiotics are indicated in the treatment of wound infections, cellulitis and abscesses. Most skin bacteria responds well to penicillin, Keflex, Erythromycin or Chloromycetin, but cultures and antibiotic sensitivity tests may be indicated to select the drug of choice.

Foreign bodies (such as splinters) beneath the skin must be removed with forceps as they are a continuous source of infection.

Puppy Strangles *(Juvenile Pyoderma)*

This condition occurs in puppies under four months of age. It can be recognized by a sudden painful swelling of the lips, eyelids, ears and face, along with draining sores, crusts and sinus tracts. The lymph nodes beneath the chin swell up and these pups are quite sick and should be seen by a veterinarian promptly.

Treatment: Your veterinarian will probably want to prescribe moist hot packs to soften crusts and promote drainage. Treatment includes the use of selected antibiotics and in some cases steroids.

DO NOT attempt to express the pus from the sores as this increases the likelihood of scarring.

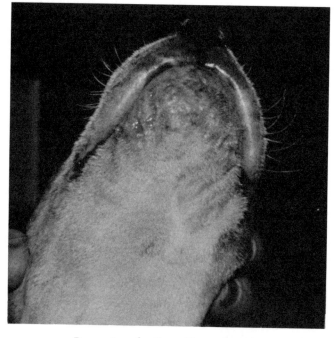

Puppy strangles *(juvenile pyoderma).*

LUMPS AND BUMPS
(TUMORS ON OR BENEATH THE SKIN)

Any sort of lump, bump or growth found on or beneath the skin is by definition a tumor (which literally means "a swelling"). Tumors are classified as *benign* when they are not a cancer—and *malignant* when they are.

Classically, a benign growth is one that grows slowly, is surrounded by a capsule, is not invasive and doesn't spread to other parts. However, there is no good way to tell whether a tumor is benign or malignant without removing it and examining it with a microscope. If the tumor is found to be benign, then it won't come back if it has been completely removed.

Cancers usually enlarge rapidly (a few weeks or month). They are not encapsulated. They appear to infiltrate into the surrounding tissues and they may ulcerate the skin and bleed. A hard mass which appears fixed to bone (or could be a growth of the bone itself) is a cause for concern. The same is true for pigmented lumps or flat moles which start to enlarge and then spread out and begin to bleed *(Melanomas)*.

A hard gray (or pink) open sore which does not heal, especially on the feet and legs, should be regarded with suspicion. This could be a skin cancer.

Any unexplained lump, bump or open sore on your dog should be checked by your veterinarian. Most cancers are not painful. So do not delay because your dog does not seem to be feeling uncomfortable. To learn more about common surface growths, see the chapter on TUMORS AND CANCERS.

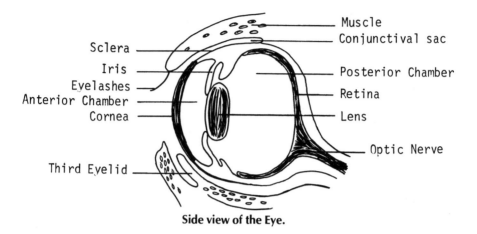

Side view of the Eye.

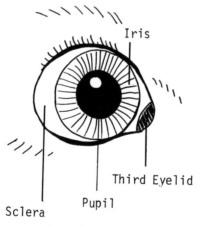

Front view of the Eye.

—Rose Floyd

5

Eyes

HOW A DOG SEES

The eye is an organ with several parts, all of which are important to your dog's health and well-being. The eyeball itself is seated in a cushion of fat which protects it in its bony socket. Seven muscles are fixed to the globe. They stabilize the eye and govern its movements.

As you look at the front of your dog's eye, you will see that the surface is rimmed by a narrow margin of white (sclera) much less conspicuous than your own. Most of the eye is pigmented. This pigment is found in the *iris*, a layer of smooth muscle that controls the size of the *pupil,* much as a shutter does a camera. The pupil is located in the center of the iris. Both the iris and the pupil are covered by a layer of thick transparent clear cells, the *cornea* or window of the eye. The inner eye has two chambers. The *anterior chamber* is found between the cornea and the *lens; the posterior chamber,* containing a clear jelly, is the larger central cavity of the eye between the lens and the *retina.*

Light enters the eye by passing first through the cornea and anterior chamber and then through the pupil and the lens. The iris expands and contracts, depending upon the brightness of the light. Light then traverses the posterior chamber and is received by the retina. Here it is converted into nerve impulses which pass via the optic nerve to the brain.

A number of investigators have concluded that dogs are near-sighted and have rather poor visual accommodation. That is, they cannot see things sharply and in focus. We might compare a dog's vision to that of a middle-aged man who has to wear bifocals. The dog's retina does not have many specialized cells which distinguish colors. Instead, he sees only black and white and various shades of gray (color blind).

On the other hand, the dog has a larger pupil and a wider visual field than man does; he also has more photoreceptors in his retina for the detection of light. Thus he sees very well in the dark. Because of his wide field of vision, he is quite adept at following moving objects. On the whole, he is supplied with a type of vision which is best suited to his needs.

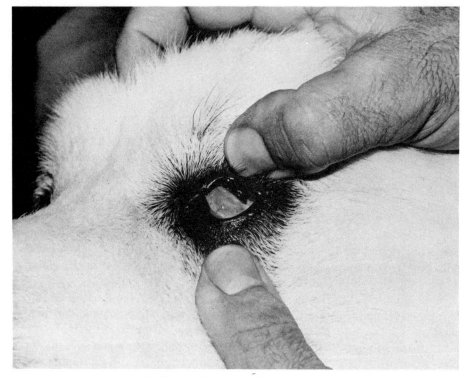

A third eyelid is normal. —*J. Clawson*

The eyelids are tight folds of skin which support the front of the globe. Actually they do not make contact with the surface of the eye because there is a thin layer of tears between them. On the upper lids eyelashes are always present. They are not present on the lower lids. The borders of the lids should meet when the eye is closed.

Tears serve two functions. First, they cleanse and lubricate the surface of the eyeball. The blink reflex assures that the moisture will be evenly spread out and your dog's eyes will not dry out. Tears also contain immune substances which prevent bacteria from gaining a foothold.

You may have noticed that your dog has a rather prominent layer of tissue (or well-developed membrane) at the inner corner of his eye, resting on the eyeball. This is the third eyelid or haw *(nictating membrane)*. It is an added protective device not found in man. Like a windshield wiper, the third eyelid is capable of sweeping across the surface of the eye, cleansing and lubricating it. In some dogs the third eyelid is more visible than in others. This depends to a certain extent upon its size and whether or not it's pigmented. Some breed standards call for a visible haw; others for it to be scarcely apparent.

When the third eyelid is drawn across the surface of the eye it gives the impression that the eyeball has "rolled back" into its socket. But in fact this is not the case; the eyeball hasn't really moved at all. You can demonstrate this by applying gentle pressure to the globe so as to recess the eye slightly, making the membrane come forward and across.

The conjunctiva is a slippery layer of tissue which covers the white of the eye and reflects back to cover the inner surface of the lids. It does not cover the cornea. In certain breeds it may be pigmented or spotted. If you look closely you can see small vessels running through the conjunctiva. It will appear red when the eye is irritated.

Tears are secreted by glands found in the eyelids, in the nictating membrane, and in the conjunctiva. A normal accumulation of tears is removed by evaporation. Excess tears are pooled near the nasal corner of the eye and carried via a drainage system to the back of the nose.

WHAT TO DO IF YOUR DOG HAS AN EYE PROBLEM

If your dog has matter in his eye and if his eye waters, if he squints, paws at his eye and gives evidence that his eye is painful, then you are faced with an eye problem. The first thing to do is examine the eye to see if you can determine the cause.

How to Examine His Eye

This requires a good light. To examine the eyeball, place one thumb against the skin of the cheek below the eye and the other thumb against the ridge of bone above. Gently draw down on the lower thumb and apply counter traction with the other. Due to the mobility of the skin of a dog's face, the lower lid will sag out and you can look in and see the conjunctival sac and most of the cornea behind it. Reverse the procedure to examine the eye behind the upper lid.

The Foreign Body

One of the most common causes for a foreign body in the eye (dust, grass seed, dirt and specks of vegetable matter), is allowing the dog to ride with his head out a car window. The first sign is tearing and watering of the affected eye, along with signs of irritation and blinking and squinting. Examine the eye to see if you can see a piece of foreign material behind the upper and lower lids. If not, the foreign body may be caught behind the third eyelid, in which case most dogs with a painful eye will not allow you to lift it without some form of anesthesia.

If the foreign body can be seen, it can be gently removed with a blunt-nosed tweezer, such as women use to pluck their eyebrows. Alternately, a cotton-tip swab, moistened first, can be used to gently swab the eye. The foreign body may adhere to it. Finally, if there is quite a bit of dirt in the eye, the eye should be irrigated with a salt-water solution (one

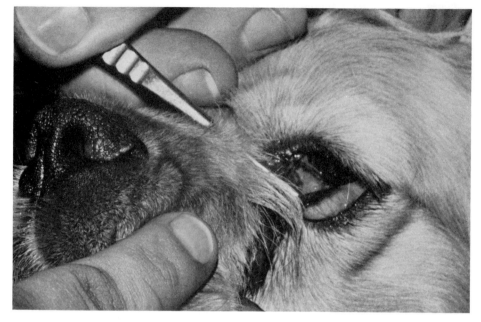

Foreign bodies can be removed with blunt-nosed tweezers.

teaspoonful of salt to a pint of water), soaking a wad of cotton and and squeezing it into the eye.

A foreign body such as a thorn, which has penetrated the surface of the eye, should be removed by a veterinarian.

If you believe you have successfully removed the foreign particle, finish the job by applying an antibiotic ophthalmic ointment to the eye (Neosporin).

If the dog persists in rubbing his eye after the treatment, the foreign body may still be in the eye, or a corneal abrasion may have occurred. Obtain professional assistance.

How to Apply Eye Medicine:

Pull the lower eyclid down and apply the ointment to the inner surface of the eyelid. Direct application to the eyeball will be resisted by the dog and may be hazardous should he jerk his head. Eyedrops may be applied directly to the eyeball.

Rub the eyelid gently over the eyeball to disperse the medicine.

When medicating an eye for any reason, DO NOT use preparations which are old, out of date, or not specifically labeled *for ophthalmologic use*.

Minor eye problems should not be neglected in the hope that they will clear up by themselves. If there is any doubt about the diagnosis, and particularly if the eye has been doctored at home but has shown no improvement in 24 hours, call your veterinarian.

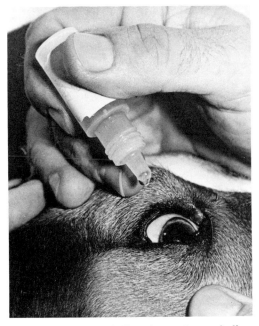

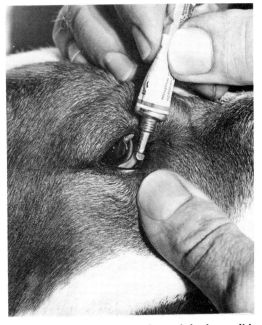

Drops are applied directly to the eyeball.   **Apply ointment to inner surface of the lower lid.**

—J. Clawson

Prolonged administration of antibiotics in the eye may lead to fungal infection.

Eye out of its Socket (An Emergency)

Prolapse of the eyeball is a common occurrence in dogs with large bulging eyes such as Bostons, Pugs, Pekingese, Maltese, and Spaniels. It is generally due to bites and other trauma. Struggling with these individuals while attempting to hold and restrain them for any reason can cause the eye to bulge out so far that the eyelids snap behind the eyeball instead of in front of it. This prevents it from returning to the socket.

This is an emergency. Replacement of the eyeball must be accomplished at once. Shortly after the dislocation takes place, swelling behind the eye makes it extremely difficult to manipulate the eye back into its normal position. To replace the eye, lubricate it with vaseline and attempt to lift the eyelids out and over the eyeball while maintaining gentle pressure on the globe with a wad of moist cotton. If the eye cannot be easily replaced, cover it with a wet cloth and seek professional assistance.

Caution: Do not make repeated unsuccessful attempts to manipulate a dislocated eye as this causes further swelling and inevitably leads to greater eyeball injury.

Other Causes of Eye Displacement. Infections and tumors in the space behind the eyeball push the globe forward so that it bulges out. Tumors are slow-growing and relatively painless. Retrobulbar abscess is an extremely painful condition of rapid onset. The head about the eye is usually swollen and exquisitely tender. Dogs with retrobulbar infection experience great pain when attempting to eat, as the muscles of mastication exert pressure on the eyeball when the mouth is opened. These abscesses are treated by incision and drainage.

Hemorrhage behind the eye is seen with head trauma and may occur spontaneously in some of the bleeding disorders. It also causes eye displacement.

EYELIDS

Sudden Swelling *(Chemosis)*

A sudden swelling of the eyelids may be due to an allergic reaction. These include insect bites, hives, inhaled irritants and allergens in medications. These lids look fluid-filled and soft. In fact, water has passed out of the circulation into the tissues in response to the allergy. Often the dog rubs his muzzle (itching). The condition may be accompanied by hives in which the hair stands out in an erect manner in little patches over the body. Puffy eyelids are seen in skin allergies (see ALLERGIES).

This is not a serious problem. It is of short duration and improves when the allergic agent is removed. Simple cases may be treated with drops or eye ointment containing a corticosteroid (Neocortef).

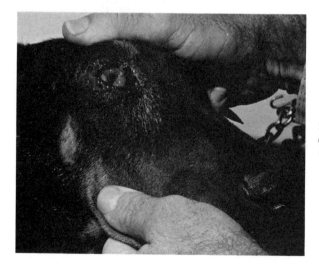

Sudden swelling of the eyelids *(chemosis)* may be due to an allergic reaction.

Bacterial infection of the eyelids *(blepharitis)*.

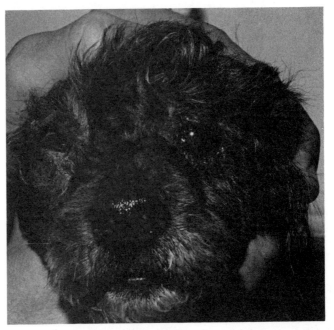

Hair loss around the eye, due to demodectic mange.

Inflamed Eyelids *(Blepharitis)*

Blepharitis is a name given to a variety of conditions in which the eyelid becomes thick, reddened and inflamed-looking. Usually you will find crusty accumulations and pus adherent to the lid margins.

Staphalococcal blepharitis is identified by finding small white pimples (abscesses) on the rim of the eyelids. This is due to a specific bacteria. These abscesses rupture and cause itching and redness. Quite often the glands under the neck enlarge.

This condition occurs most commonly in Poodles. It is not a serious problem and can be treated with Neomycin Ophthalmic Ointment and oral Ampicillin.

Hair Loss around the Eye *(Demodectic Mange)*

In young dogs suffering from demodectic mange the hair about the eyelids sometimes falls out, giving a moth-eaten look. When the roots of the hair become secondarily infected with bacteria a crust forms on the skin. Skin scrapings viewed under the microscope will show the true cause of the problem to be demodectic mites.

Treatment consists of the use of an insecticide (Goodwinol Ointment) applied to the infected part three times daily. Be careful not to get any of the mange ointment into the eye. As a safeguard, mineral oil should be applied to the eye first.

Stys *(Hordeolum)*

The eyelid contains numerous glands that open along its margin (Meibomian glands). They secrete an oil substance which acts as a barrier to the tears, keeping them from overflowing the lids, much as a grease barrier holds back water. Obstruction of the ducts of these glands, or an infection, will result in a swollen, reddened, tender pus pocket on the eyelid. It is referred to as a sty.

A sty may be brought to a head with hot compresses and may rupture spontaneously. In most cases it will need to be punctured with a small sterile needle. Afterwards an antibiotic ophthalmic preparation should be applied (Neosporin).

Whiteheads *(Plugged Meibomian Glands)*

Primarily this is a problem among white-coated dogs such as the white Poodle. It is not serious. The main reason for treating it is that it is unsightly. As you look at the rim of the eyelid you will see several large white bumps along its margin. They are due to an accumulation of glandular secretions. They may be expressed by placing the end of a spoon (bowl) under the eyelid

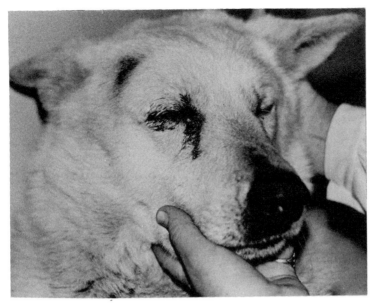

Severe squinting *(blepharospasm)*.

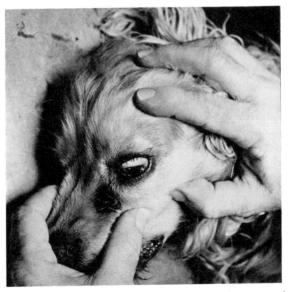

Extra eyelashes on the upper lid irritate the eye and cause tearing *(distichiasis)*.

and pressing against the whitehead with your thumb. Infection is usually not a problem. When present the glands should be expressed and the eye treated with antibiotic eye ointment.

Severe Squinting *(Blepharospasm)*

Spasms of the muscles around the eye are induced by eye irritation. The irritant causes tightening of the muscles of the eyelid which rolls the lid against the cornea or conjunctiva. Having once rolled in, the rough margins of the lids and the hairs rub against the eyeball causing further pain and spasm.

Anesthetic drops may be applied to the eyeball to relieve the pain and break the cycle. The relief is temporary unless the inciting factor has been removed.

Eye Irritation from Hairs

There are a number of eye problems in which eye irritation is caused by hair rubbing against the eyeball.

Extra Eyelashes (Distichiasis): This is a congenital condition in which an extra row of lashes grow from the lid margins and rub against the cornea. The irritation may not be severe enough to cause symptoms until the dog is mature. This condition occurs most often in Poodles, Cocker Spaniels and Pekingese — but all breeds can be affected. The hairs may be burned out with an electric needle or removed by surgery.

Facial Hair: This is a condition seen in short-muzzled breeds such as the Pekingese, Shih Tzu, Lhasa Apso, and Bulldog in which the hair on the nasal fold grows up against the eyeball. In the Old English Sheepdog, the Schnauzer, and other breeds with long facial hair, it is this hair which falls in against the eye causing the irritation. The offending hairs should be removed by clipping, or is some cases by plucking. Those requiring attention can often be identified because they are stained and discolored by the tears.

Eyelid Rolled Inward *(Entropion)*

This is the most common congenital defect of the eyelids. It may also be caused by injury or long-standing disease of the lids. Some cases are complicated by blepharospasm.

Breeds commonly affected are the Chow, Irish Setter, Golden Retriever, Chesapeake Bay Retriever, Great Dane, Great Pyrenees, Saint Bernard and Bulldog. Most commonly it affects the lower eyelid. In Bloodhounds and Saint Bernards, and in other breeds with large heads and loose facial skin, entropion can be found in the upper lid as well. The condition requires surgical correction.

Dogs with long hair about the face are subject to eye irritation *(trichiasis).* —*Sydney Wiley*

Ectropion. When the lower eyelids roll out, the eyes are exposed to irritants. —*Sydney Wiley*

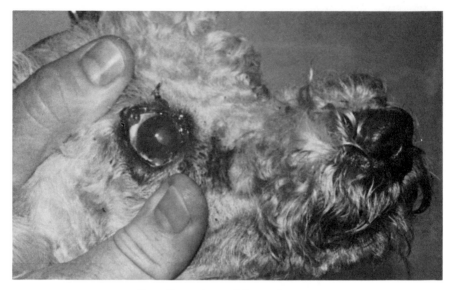

Growths on the eyelids —*adenomas.*

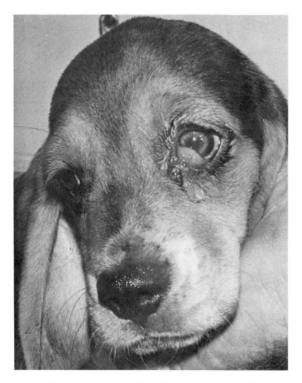

Cherry eye. **An infected tear gland on the inner surface of the third eyelid enlarges.**

Eyelid Rolled Outward *(Ectropion)*

In this condition the lower eyelid rolls out from the face exposing the eye to irritation. This condition is usually seen in dogs with loose facial skin such as hounds, spaniels, and Saint Bernards. It can be seen in older dogs in whom the facial skin has lost its tone and sags. You may notice this temporarily in hunting dogs after a long day in the field. Plastic surgery may be necessary to tighten the lid and protect the eye.

Tumors

The adenoma is the most common tumor of the eyelid. It has a cauliflower-like appearance and, like most growths of the eyelid, usually is found in the older dog. It should be removed. Otherwise, it will continue to grow, irritate the eye, and interfere with closing the lids. There are other tumors of the eyelid, some of which are malignant.

THE THIRD EYELID (NICTATING MEMBRANE)

When the third membrane is visible over the surface of the eye, it is said to be protruding or prolapsing. A protruding third eyelid can be due to one of three causes: sunken eyeball, an irritation of the eye, or a congenital defect.

Congenital prolapse is only important in that the dog has an unsightly appearance. Removal of the eyelid is seldom required for this condition.

A sunken eyeball causes the membrane to protrude. This may be the result of malnutrition or prolonged illness in which the fat pad at the back of the eye is reduced in size. Dehydration also gives a sunken eye. The dog may also protrude the third eyelid in order to protect an irritated eye.

A protruding third eyelid gives the "haws", which to dog trainers and handlers is frequently undesirable in that it gives the animal a somewhat haggard look. Most dog standards require that the "haws" (if mentioned at all) be scarcely apparent. In Bloodhounds, a visible "haw" is called for in the breed standard.

Eversion of the Cartilage

This is a congenital condition among Weimaraners, Great Danes, Golden Retrievers and Saint Bernards. The third eyelid appears to roll back upon itself like a dry leaf. Corneal irritation occurs in some cases. These should be treated surgically.

Cherry Eye

This is a condition in which the tear gland on the inner surface of the third eyelid enlarges due to infection. As it swells it is forced out from beneath the lid, exposing a red, cherry-like growth at the nasal corner of the eye. It occurs most commonly in Cocker Spaniels, Beagles, Boston Terriers and Bulldogs. Usually it must be removed surgically. A few cases may respond to antibiotics.

THE OUTER EYE

Conjunctivitis

This is an inflammation of the lining membrane that covers the inner sides of the eyelids and the surface of the eyeball up to the cornea. Commonly it is accompanied by a discharge from the eye. If the discharge is clear or watery *(Serous Conjunctivitis),* one of the following may be the cause: foreign bodies, misdirected hairs, physical irritants (such as wind and riding with his head out the window), and various allergens.

A discharge which looks like pus and presents a thick, tenacious appearance, often crusting over the eyelids, suggests a bacterial problem *(Purulent Conjunctivitis).* Cultures may be required to identify the bacteria, and to determine the most effective antibiotic for treatment. Where this condition persists for a long time it becomes chronic. A deep-seated infection is difficult to clear up. In such cases, one should consider the possibility that the tearing system has been affected. Repeated cleansing of the eye, correction of any underlying problem, and specific antibiotics tailored to cultures and sensitivities, form the primary approach to this problem.

Treatment: Mild irritative forms of conjunctivitis can be treated at home. The eye should be cleansed with a dilute solution of boric acid made up for ophthalmic use. This can be purchased over-the-counter. Use as directed for people. You should expect to see definite improvement within 24 hours. If not, you should have your dog examined by a veterinarian. A foreign body or other serious eye distrubance may be in the making.

Follicular Conjunctivitis: This is a condition in which the back side of the nictating membrane and the eyelids enlarge to form a rough cobblestone surface, giving an irritated look to the eye membranes. The eye discharge is mucoid. This type of conjunctivitis is frequently caused by an allergy or an infection. Occasionally, after the inciting factor has been removed, the follicles remain enlarged and the roughened surface of the conjunctiva acts as an irritation to the eye. This roughened surface must be removed by a cauterizing process in which copper sulfate crystals are applied to the affected parts. This causes the tissue to slough. A smooth membrane regenerates.

Conjunctivitis due to a fungal or parasitic infection is rare and requires laboratory aid for diagnosis.

Conjunctivitis of the Newborn (Ophthalmia Neonatorium): The eyelids of puppies do not open until they are 10 to 14 days old. There is a closed space behind the lids which can become infected if bacteria gain entrance to it via the bloodstream or through a small scratch about the eye. The eyelids look red, swollen and puffy, and there may be a discharge. Any discharge is abnormal.

The eyelids must be pried open to allow the pus to drain out. Otherwise there may be permanent damage to the forepart of the eye. Once the eyelids have been bluntly separated, pus will drain out in large drops. The eye should be flushed with boric acid eye wash and medicated with antibiotic drops. The eyelids must then be bathed several times a day so that they do not paste shut again. Drops should be applied four times daily.

Hair Growing from the Eyeball *(Dermoid Cyst)*

A dermoid cyst is a growth which usually is noted close to the outer corner of the eye. It contains follicles from which hairs grow. The hair often appears to grow out of the surface of the eye itself. The dermoid is not a malignant tumor, but it should be removed because of the irritating effects of its hairs.

THE TEARING MECHANISM

Diseases of the tearing mechanism fall into two separate categories. First is the *Dry Eye* (due to a lack of tears), and second is the *Watery Eye* (in which there is an overflow of tears).

The Dry Eye *(Keratoconjunctivitis Sicca)*

The appearance of the eye is characteristic. Instead of the bright, glistening sheen and shine which is seen in the normal eye, the Dry Eye presents a dull lack-luster appearance. There is a thick, stringy discharge which is difficult to clear away. Later, as the eye become infected, the conjunctiva looks reddened and inflamed. A purulent discharge may complicate the picture.

This is a disease principally of the older dog. Inadequate tear production is its cause. One of three mechanisms will be responsible:

(1) *The nerves to the tear glands are at fault.* In response to drying and eye irritation, they fail to stimulate the glands in the eyelids to secrete enough tears. Another sign of malfunction of this nerve complex is a dry nostril on the same side. The dog will sometimes lick at his nose to keep it moist. Quite often it is this sign, rather than the eye sign, which brings the matter to the owner's attention.

(2) *The tear glands themselves are at fault.* They have been partially or completely destroyed by an infection. The virus of canine distemper does this to

Purulent conjunctivitis is difficult to clear up.

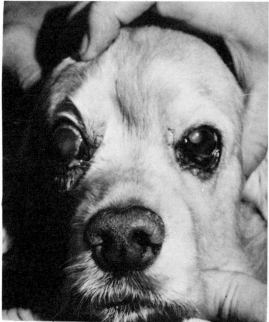

Inflammation of the cornea of the right eye. In this case it was due to lack of tears *(keratoconjunctiva sicca)*.

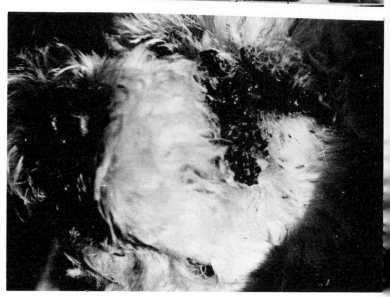

Poodle eye. The skin is infected from constant wetness.

tear glands. Usually the damage is permanent. Other diseases, notably chronic kidney ailments and uterine infections, may cause temporary depression of tear gland activity.

(3) *Finally, the tear glands and the nerves are working, but the small ducts which carry the tears from the lacrimal glands into the eye are plugged.* Scarring of the lids from long-standing infection (chronic purulent conjunctivitis) is one cause of this.

A combination of the above may be involved in any specific case. In most cases it is difficult to determine just what was the original cause of the condition.

The Dry Eye is a serious ailment in the dog. One can anticipate that there will be major complications unless the condition is treated in its early stages. The usual complication takes the form of a secondary deep-seated infection which eventually presents the problem of a corneal ulcer.

Treatment is directed towards re-establishing the flow of tears. It may be possible in certain cases to do this with drugs. At the same time antibiotics and steroids are used to control infection and inflammation.

If tears cannot be stimulated, then they will have to be supplied artificially. Artificial tears are available at drugstores but they have to be instilled almost hourly and are not convenient for most owners to use. In severe cases an operation may be contemplated. It involves transplanting one of the salivary ducts (from the mouth) up into the corner of the eye. The saliva will then take the place of the tears and keep the eye lubricated.

The Watery Eye *(Epiphora)*

In this category are a great many conditions in which a watery or mucous discharge from the eye overflows the lids and runs down the sides of the face, causing eye stains. There is a constant wetness to the area and the skin may actually become inflamed and secondarily infected, adding to the unsightliness and the dog's discomfort.

Dogs do not experience emotional tearing. They do not cry as people do, so this is not a factor to be considered as one of the causes.

Irritative diseases of the lids, entropion, as well as various forms of conjunctivitis and foreign bodies, can cause a runny eye. They have been discussed. All are characterized by excessive tear production in response to a painful eye. Other causes of tearing are discussed below.

Inadequate Tear Drainage (Nasolacrimal Occlusion): This is a factor to be considered in the dog who has a clear or mucus-like discharge from the eye without obvious cause. The problem here is that while his tears are secreted in normal amounts they are not adequately drained away. Overflow in this situation is due to an obstruction at some point in the nasolacrimal drainage system. Causes of this are: congenital absence of the ducts; congenital narrowing or occlusion of one or both of the tiny ducts in the eyelids which collect the tears at the inner corners of the eye; scarring of these ducts or their openings (for example, after a purulent conjunctivitis); active infection in these ducts or in the main nasolacrimal duct which causes plugging by cellular debris; and lodgement of a foreign body (such as a grass seed) anywhere in the system.

The drainage system is first tested to see if it is open by staining the tears with a fluorescein dye. If the dye appears at the nostril, then at least one tear duct is open on that side. Nasolacrimal probes are then inserted into the duct openings and various flushing techniques are used to show the point of obstruction. The flushing often opens the duct and removes the problem. Sometimes a minor operative procedure on an opening is needed to effect a cure. Follow-up treatment includes the use of antibiotics and steroids to reduce inflammation.

Brown Stains in the Corner of the Eye *(Poodle Eye)*

This is a problem peculiar to certain breeds, most notably the white Poodle. It also afflicts the Maltese, Pomeranian, Pekingese and some of the Toy breeds. Its exact cause is unknown in many cases. One theory is that a low grade infection of the throat, for example a chronic tonsillitis, works its way up into the lacrimal duct and causes scarring. Another theory is that among breeds having a high incidence of the runny eye syndrome the pooling space at the corner of the eye is too small to collect a lake of tears.

In all dogs having a runny eye syndrome, causes of eye irritation and nasolacrimal duct occlusion should be ruled out before resorting to symptomatic and cosmetic remedies.

In dogs in whom no underlying disease is found, symptomatic improvement often results after giving the dog a course of broad spectrum antibiotics (Tetracycline). If a chronic infection does, in fact, exist in the pharynx or lacrimal system, the antibiotic treats it, thereby removing a possible cause of obstruction. Tetracycline, which is secreted in the tears after oral administration, also binds that portion of the tears which cause them to stain the face. When the improvement is due just to the binding action of the drug, the face remains wet but not discolored.

Tetracycline is usually given by mouth for three weeks. Then it is stopped. If the eye stain returns, then, long-term administration may be considered. Most owners prefer to add Tetracycline in low dose to the dog's food for long-term treatment.

Surgery may be considered as an alternative. The operation removes the gland of the third eyelid (nictating membrane). This makes a better lake at the inner corner of the eye. It also reduces the volume of tears by removing the tear gland in the third eyelid.

Cosmetic Considerations: When a dog with eye stains has to be made ready for a dog show, his appearance can be improved by clipping the stained hair close to the face. Stain can be removed by bathing it with a dilute solution of hydrogen peroxide (one part to ten parts of water). A minor problem can be touched-up with white lipstick or a piece of white chalk. All foreign substance must be removed from the hair before the dog is brought into the ring for the judging.

CAUTION: Peroxide must not be allowed to enter the eye. Mineral oil should be instilled first to protect against accidental contact. Do not use chlorine bleaches for eye stain because the fumes are painful and irritating to the eye.

CORNEA

The cornea or clear part of the eye is covered by a protective layer of epithelial cells. Most destructive processes affecting the cornea begin with an injury to the epithelial layer. Any irritative process (such as foreign bodies, misdirected hairs) can cause an epithelial injury. Breeds with bulging eyes are especially susceptible to corneal injury. Once the continuity of the epithelium has been destroyed, the process either heals spontaneously or progresses to a more serious problem. The outcome will depend upon the magnitude of the injury, how quickly it is recognized, and whether the initiating factor has been identified and removed.

Corneal injuries are extremely painful. You will note the dog squints, waters, paws at the eye, and avoids light.

Corneal Abrasion

This is defined as an injury to the eye caused by a scratch. Healing usually takes place in 24 to 48 hours by a process in which the epithelium thins and slides over a small defect. Larger and deeper abrasions require more time.

A corneal abrasion will not heal if a *foreign body* is imbedded beneath one of the lids. Accordingly, in all but mild cases, an examination for foreign bodies under all three lids should be performed. Early recognition and removal results in rapid recovery. Delay leads to a persistent corneal defect (ulcer), or inflammation of the cornea (keratitis).

Corneal Ulcers

These are dangerous and must receive prompt attention. Large ulcers are visible to the naked eye as dull spots or depressions on the surface of the cornea. Smaller ones are best seen after the eye has been stained with fluorescein. Early treatment is vital to avoid serious complications or even loss of the eye. Cortisones, which are incorporated into many common eye preparations used in treating conjunctivitis, should not be put into an eye suspected of having sustained a corneal injury. They delay healing and may predispose to rupture of the eye.

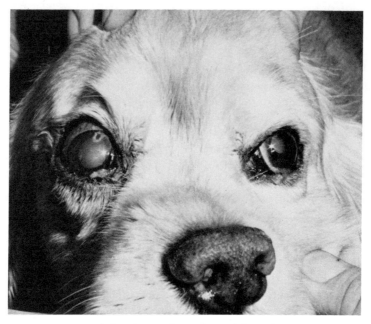

Corneal abrasion on the surface of the right eye.

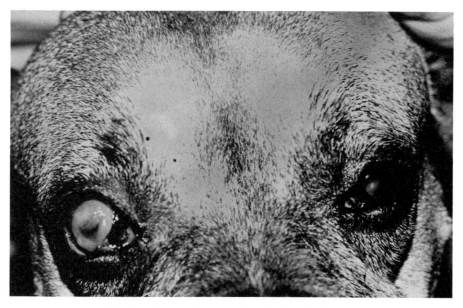

Neglected *corneal ulcers* often lead to blindness.

Corneal Ulcers in Boxers: A certain kind of corneal ulcer (called indolent or refractory) is found in the Boxer breed. Eighty percent of them occur in spayed females over five years of age. Although the exact cause is unknown, the epidemiology of the disease would suggest that low estrogen levels are a possible factor in its cause. This is a painful problem and treatment is usually prolonged. It includes replacing the hormone, stripping the corneal epithelium, and then providing temporary coverage of the cornea by suturing the nictating membrane over the surface of the eye.

Cloudy Eye *(Keratitis)*

Keratitis is defined as an inflammation of the clear part of the eye. There are many different types of keratitis and several causes. All result in loss of transparency of the cornea which at first appears dull, later hazy, then cloudy, and finally milky or relatively opaque. Often a vascular or pigmented layer blocks out light.

Keratitis always is considered serious because it may lead to partial or complete blindness in the eye. All forms of keratitis should be managed by a professional.

Superficial (surface) Keratitis: This condition is a sequel to a minor eye injury, such as a corneal abrasion. Since the initial injury is often slight and easily overlooked, there may be a temptation to treat the tearing and discharge as a conjunctivitis. Since this would be a mistake, every effort should be made to distinguish between keratitis and conjunctivitis. Keratitis is an extremely painful condition accompanied by excessive tearing, squinting and fear of light. Conjunctivitis is characterized by a chronic discharge with very little pain.

Infectious Keratitis: This occurs when a corneal injury becomes complicated by infection. A pus or mucus-like discharge runs from the eye. The lids are swollen and mattered. There are several different kinds of bacteria which cause infectious keratitis. Cultures and appropriate antibiotics are indicated.

A fungal keratitis is uncommon. Usually it is due to prolonged treatment of a chronic eye discharge with antibiotics. The diagnosis is confirmed by cultures. Antibiotics should be stopped and antifungal drugs used instead.

Blue Eye (Interstitial Keratitis): This is a deep corneal inflammation in which there is a bluish-white film seen over the clear part of the eye. It is due to the virus of infectious hepatitis — either the actual disease itself or after vaccination for the disease. Clinical signs appear ten days after exposure. The dog's eyes begin to water, he squints and avoids light. Recovery in a few weeks is the rule.

Vascular or Pigmentary Keratitis: This is a non-ulcerative condition of the eye in which there is a growth of blood vessels and/or pigment over the

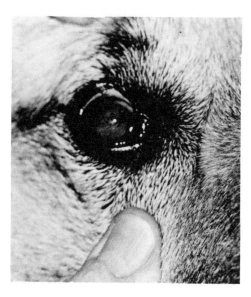

Pannus in a German Shepherd. Note the vascularity on the lower half of the eye.

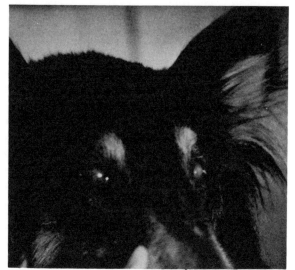

Blood vessels growing on the surface of the eye *(pigmentary keratitis)*.

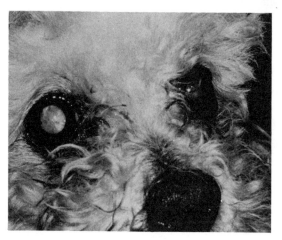

Congenital cataract in a Poodle.

surface of the eye. Any chronic irritation can predispose to this condition. When severe enough to obstruct vision, it should be removed. When the primary irritation is corrected the cornea often clears.

Pannus: This is a form of corneal inflammation that affects German Shepherds. It affects both eyes. It is characterized by the growth of a membrane across the cornea. The membrane is pink and opaque, being made up of blood vessels, pigment and connective tissue. It may lead to blindness. It usually appears in dogs over two years of age. The exact cause is unknown. Some authors have suggested an inherited predisposition or at least a familial tendency for the desease. While the disease can be controlled for a period of time, to date no effective permanent cure is available.

THE INNER EYE

The Blind Dog

Any condition which prevents light from getting into the eye will impair a dog's sight. Diseases of the cornea (keratitis) and of the lens (cataract) fall into this category. Increased intraocular pressure (glaucoma) is another condition which leads to blindness. Also, any disease which reduces the sensitivity of the retina to light impulses (retinal atrophy), or any disease which affects the optic nerves or the sight-center of the brain (trauma), can result in various forms of visual disturbances, including blindness.

Accordingly, most causes of blindness will not be evident on general observation of the eye itself. Ophthalmological studies are required to make an exact diagnosis.

There are some signs which may suggest that the dog is not seeing as well as he should. They are uncertainty of gait (stepping high or with great caution), treading on articles usually avoided, bumping into furniture, and carrying the nose close to the ground. Sometimes a dog going blind shows few if any signs of visual impairment.

A blind or nearly blind dog learns very quickly how to avoid collisions. On a leash, he learns to use his master as a "seeing-eye" person, waiting to be guided. We have seen dogs dash down corridors missing objects so adroitly you would be willing to swear that they could see perfectly, yet they were completely blind.

If you wish to confirm your suspicion that your dog is going blind check his behavior in a strange setting. He can be placed in a darkened room in which the furniture has been rearranged. There should be just enough light so you can see. The dog is then invited to walk about normally in order to see if he moves with confidence or hesitates and collides with the furniture. After his dark vision has been tested, the lights are turned and the test is repeated.

Shining a bright light into a dog's eye to test for pupillary constriction is an inexact method of determining whether or not he sees. The pupil may become smaller simply due to a light reflex. This doesn't tell you whether he has the ability to form a visual image in his brain.

After a diagnosis of blindness or irreversible loss of vision has been made, it does not mean the end of a dog's life. The fact is that most dogs, even those with normal eyesight, do not really see very well. They rely to a great extent on their senses of hearing and smell. These senses take over, and actually become more acute, when their vision begins to go. This makes it far easier for them to get around, sometimes almost normally. One thing that the dog shouldn't do is run free. He must be enclosed or walked on a leash.

It is important for the owner of a dog who is gradually going blind to be aware of this while the dog still has some sight left. This leaves time for the dog to be taught some basic commands, such as "stop," "stay," "come," and "watch it." It also allows for the dog to remain active and working (as in the case of a gun dog) for a longer period. When the dog eventually does go blind, his obedience training may save his life.

Cataracts

A cataract may be defined as a loss of the normal transparency of the lens of the eye. Any spot on the lens that is opaque, regardless of its size, is technically a cataract. Some cataracts are clearly visible to the naked eye, appearing as white flecks within the eye, or giving a milky-gray or bluish-white cast to the lens behind the pupil.

It is impossible to differentiate hereditary and nonhereditary cataracts solely from the appearance of the lens. Breed predisposition and line history are more suggestive. If you are planning to breed a dog with cataracts, you should consider the possibility of cataracts in the offspring. Hereditary cataracts are most commonly found in Poodles, Cockers, Boston Terriers and Wirehaired Fox Terriers.

Cataracts can develop in diabetic dogs. It is important to recognize the possibility of diabetes before considering cataract extraction. If the diabetes is controlled, the operation is more likely to be successful.

Senile (old age) cataracts are common. Most dogs over eight years of age have some degree of haziness in their lenses. Even when they appear quite opaque, a considerable amount of useful vision may be retained.

A cataract is important only when it causes impaired vision. Blindness can be corrected by removing the lens (cataract extraction). While this restores vision, there is some loss of visual acuity because the lens is not present to focus light on the retina. The operation is usually recommended for the dog who has so much visual impairment that he has difficulty getting around.

Increased Pressure in the Eye *(Glaucoma)*

This is a serious eye problem in the dog. Usually it leads to partial or total blindness of the eye. It is due to an increase in fluid pressure within the eyeball. There is a continuous (although very slow) exchange of fluid between the eyeball and the venous circulation. Anything which upsets this delicate mechanism causes a build up of pressure. When it reaches the point at which eye pressure is greater than arterial blood pressure, arterial blood cannot enter the eye to nourish the retina. A sudden build-up leads to acute blindness. A slower, more insidious build-up causes few symptoms, yet leads to the same result. Measurement of intraocular pressure and inspection of the interior of the eye is needed to make the diagnosis.

Glaucoma sometimes occurs as a complication of diseases of the lens or anterior chamber of the eye. This is called *secondary* glaucoma and is distinguished from *primary* (or congenital) glaucoma, which occurs without prior disease. Primary glaucoma is seen in Cocker Spaniels, Bassets, Wirehaired Terriers, Poodles, and Samoyeds. It has been described in other breeds.

An eye suffering from acute glaucoma is exquisitely painful and has a fixed, blank look, due to the hazy and steamy appearance of the cornea and *dilated* pupil. Excessive tearing and squinting often are present. This is a true emergency. Either medical or surgical efforts must be made at once to lower the intraocular pressure.

Chronic glaucoma may be managed for a time with drops and medications. Untreated chronic glaucoma may result in increased size of the eye and protrusion.

Retinal Diseases

The retina is a thin delicate membrane which lines the back of the eye, and actually is an extension of the optic nerve. There are many diseases of the retina which lead to destruction of the light receptors, or which cause the retina to become detached from the back of the eye. In these situations the eye loses its ability to interpret the light which gets into it. The visual image may be blurred, or all of the visual field may be blacked out.

The majority of retinal diseases in the dog are inherited. Occasionally, retinitis may be due to trauma, infection or a vitamin deficiency. Since it is not safe to breed dogs with an inherited defect, it is important to know whether the retinal problem was inherited or acquired. This is best determined by referring the dog to a center in which a highly trained veterinary specialist is available.

At present, the following retinal diseases are well recognized:

Collie Eye Anomaly Syndrome (CEA): Originally described in the Collie, this syndrome affects Shetland Sheepdogs, and other related dogs as well. The anomalies include retinal degeneration, retinal detachment, and cataract. They are not all necessarily present.

CEA may be detected by a qualified professional as early as four to five weeks of age, shortly after the bluish "puppy film" disappears. Sometimes the examination will not disclose retinal degeneration until the dog is one to two years old. Many affected dogs continue to see rather well despite the changes.

Progressive Retinal Atrophy (PRA): This condition was first discovered in the Irish Setter but now is recognized in a great many other breeds, including Norwegian Elkhounds, Gordon Setters, Toy Poodles, Cocker Spaniels, Samoyeds, Yorkshire Terriers, Giant Schnauzers and Welsh Corgis. It is characterized by degeneration of the cells of the retina, leading eventually to loss of sight.

It is a disease of late onset (five to seven years). It begins with loss of night vision. At this point the dog hesitates to go out at night. He won't jump on or off furniture in a darkened room. Later he will go up, but not down, stairs. Other behavioral changes occur. As the name implies, the degenerative changes are progressive, but often quite gradual.

Central Progressive Retinal Atrophy (CPRA): This is a condition closely related to PRA. It affects the pigment cells at the center of the retina. It is recognized in Labradors, Golden Retrievers, Shetland Sheepdogs, Border Collies, Redbone Hounds, and others.

Because it is the central part of the retina (where the dog sees best) that is destroyed initially, the dog with CPRA is unable to see stationary objects well. He is able to see moving objects because motion is seen at the periphery of the retina.

Inheritance Patterns in Retinal Atrophy: The inheritance of PRA has been thoroughly investigated in the Irish Setter, Norwegian Elkhound, Miniature and Toy Poodle. CEA has been investigated in the Collie. In both cases the disease was found to be due to a simple recessive trait. CPRA studies suggest that this may be the case for this disease also.

Accordingly any dog having one of these defects is capable of transmitting it to his offspring *if* mated to another dog having the disease (or carrying the recessive trait). For this reason a number of breed clubs, conscientious dog fanciers and breeders, have encouraged further research in this area. Many have elected to have their breeding stock examined and certified free of congenital eye disease before entering them into a breeding program. The CANINE EYE REGISTRY FOUNDATION, INC. (C.E.R.F.) was established in 1975 with the dual purpose of issuing certificates to eligible dogs and collecting statistical data on the incidence of various inherited canine eye diseases. For further information, write to C.E.R.F., P.O. Box 15011, San Francisco, California 94115.

6

Ears

HOW THE DOG HEARS

A dog's hearing is one of his best developed senses. He can hear sounds too faint for us to detect; he can also hear noises pitched at a much higher frequency. Because his hearing is so sensitive, the dog relies heavily on it to alert him to his surroundings.

Sound, which is really air vibrations, is reflected off the external ear (*pinna*) and enters the comparatively large external ear opening. Vibrations travel down the external auditory canal to the ear drum (*tympanic membrane*). Movements of the ear drum are transmitted to a chain of (three) tiny bones, called the auditory *ossicles*, and then to a fluid filling the bony canals of the inner ear. Within the bony labryinth lies the *cochlea*, a system of tubes in which fluid waves are translated into nerve impulses. These nerve impulses are conducted to the hearing center of the brain by the *auditory nerve*.

In dogs, ears come in all sizes and shapes—erect, tulip-shaped, and flopped-over (lop-ears). The skin on the outside is covered with hair and, like the rest of the dog's body, susceptible to the same diseases. Hair also is present on the inside flap, although more sparsely distributed. The skin on the inside is light pink in color, or in some breeds, spotted. A small amount of light brown waxy secretion in the ear canals is normal.

BASIC EAR CARE

Cleaning the Ears

Most dogs seldom need to have their ears cleaned. Excess cleaning is not desirable because a certain amount of wax is needed to maintain the health of the tissues.

To clean a dirty ear, moisten a cloth with mineral oil and wrap it around your finger. Then insert your finger into the ear canal as far as it will go and

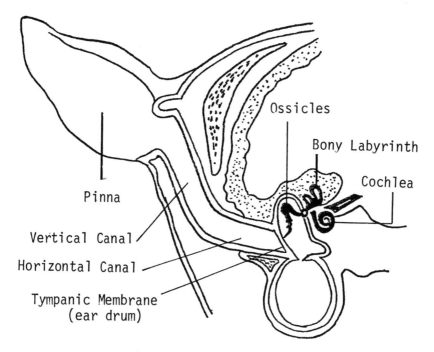

Ossicles

Bony Labyrinth

Cochlea

Pinna

Vertical Canal

Horizontal Canal

Tympanic Membrane
(ear drum)

Anatomy of the Ear. —*Rose Floyd*

gently wipe the surfaces to remove dirt, excess wax and debris. Also clean the skin on the inside of the ear flap.

Folds and crevices which cannot be reached with the cloth can be cleaned with a cotton-tipped applicator, moistened with the mineral oil. The ear canal drops vertically for a considerable distance before it takes a sharp turn and continues as the horizontal ear canal, ending at the ear drum. The vertical canal can be swabbed without danger of damaging the ear drum as long as the applicator is held vertically and directed downwards. The dog must not be allowed to jerk his head, as the tip of the applicator can then injure the delicate skin lining the sides of the passage.

A dirty ear is usually an indication of ear problem. It should be watched closely.

How to Avoid Ear Problems

When bathing your dog, see that no water gets into his ears. Prevent by inserting cotton wadding into the ear canals before bathing.

DO NOT syringe, swab or irrigate your dog's ears with ether, alcohol, or other irritating solvents. They are extremely painful and cause swelling of the tissues. Use mineral oil.

Foreign bodies in the ear passages cause irritation and later infection. Frequently, they are due to plant material which enters the ear by first clinging to hair surrounding the opening of the ear canal. For this reason always groom under the ear flaps, especially after your dog has been running in tall grass, weeds and brush.

Always check the ear flaps after dog fights. Serum and blood make an excellent media for bacterial growth.

When hair beneath the ear flap is thick enough to interfere with air circulation, it should be removed. This reduces the chance of ear infection. A common practice in some grooming parlors is to pluck excess hair out of the ear canals. Serum then oozes from the hair pores. For this reason, ear infections are more frequent among Poodles, Schnauzers and other breeds groomed professionally. When hair has been plucked from the ear to improve air circulation, an antibiotic preparation, as discussed below, should be instilled to prevent this complication.

As an alternative to pulling the hairs out, they can be clipped. In some cases, however, the hair has formed a wad, acting like an obstructing foreign body in the ear; then the hair must be pulled out and the ear medicated (see *Antibiotic Ear Preparations*).

DISEASES OF THE OUTER EAR

Bacterial Infections

Outer ears of dogs are delicate structures, easily infected. Suspect an infection of the ear canals (*external otitis*) whenever your dog keeps

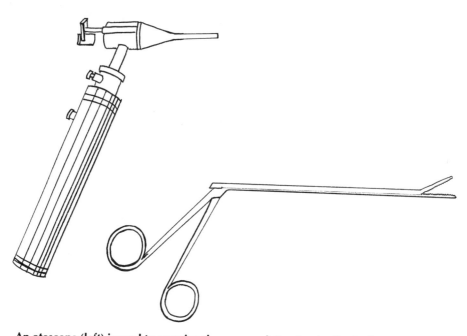

An otoscope (left) is used to examine the ear canal. Foreign bodies in the ear canal are removed with alligator forceps (right).
—*Rose Floyd*

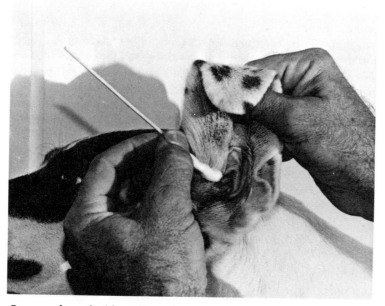

Ears are cleaned with a cotton-tipped applicator soaked in mineral oil.
—*J. Clawson*

shaking his head and scratching at his ear. Other signs of an infected ear are tenderness (holding the painful side down), redness and swelling of the skin folds in the canal, purulent discharge, and a bad odor.

Eighty percent of ear problems occur in the drop-eared breeds. Basically this is a condition of air circulation, since open or erect ears dry out better and provide less favorable conditions for bacteria to grow. Common predisposing causes are soap, water, wads of hair, mites, allergies, and excess wax in the ears. A clean, dry ear usually stays healthy.

An otoscope is needed to examine the deep portions of the ear canal for foreign bodies and other unsuspected causes of chronic infection. This is best left to a qualified professional.

Bacterial infections which have been allowed to progress for a long time produce extreme reddening and thickening of the ear canal and considerable discomfort and pain. These ears are difficult to cleanse without heavy sedation or an anesthetic. Treatment is prolonged. As a last resort, surgical intervention may be necessary to open the ear, reestablish air circulation and promote adequate drainage. This operation is called a *lateral ear resection* and provides a new external ear opening.

Treatment: The first step in the treatment of an external ear infection is to attempt to determine the cause. The next step is to clean the ears as described above. If there is pus, the ear should be flushed with a weak hydrogen peroxide solution (1 part in 10), or a surgical soap (Weladol, pHisoHex). When there is excessive wax build-up, a wax dissolving agent (Squaline) may be needed. Afterwards, dry the ear canal well with cloth or a cotton-tipped applicator and apply an antibiotic ear preparation.

Antibiotic Ear Preparations: Antibiotics commonly used in the treatment of external ear infections are Panolog, Fulvidex, and Liquichlor. Others are available. They should be applied to *cleaned* ear canals twice daily. You should expect to see improvement in two or three days. If not, then consult your veterinarian, as further delay can cause harm. When special cultures are indicated, your dog must be off antibiotics for at least three days, or the cultures may not be positive.

How to Apply Ear Medicines: Some ear ointments come in tubes with long nozzles which are inserted into the vertical canal while holding the nozzle parallel to the dog's head. Restrain your dog so the tip of the tube won't accidently lacerate the thin skin of his ear canal. Squeeze in a small amount of ointment, or instill three or four drops of liquid.

As most infections also involve the horizontal ear canal, it is important that the medicine reaches this area, too. With your fingers, rub the cartilage at the base of his ears to disperse the medicine, which makes a squishy sound.

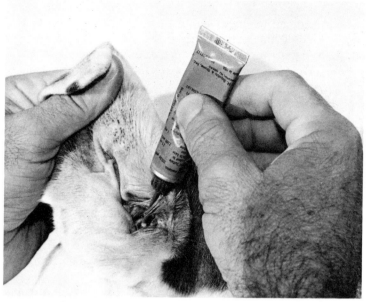

Apply ear medication to the vertical canal. —*J. Clawson*

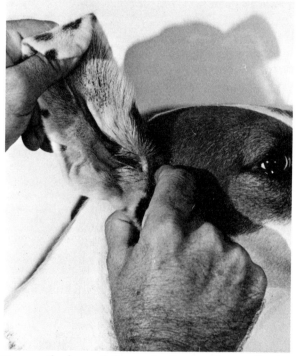

Massage the base of the ear to disperse the medication.
—*J. Clawson*

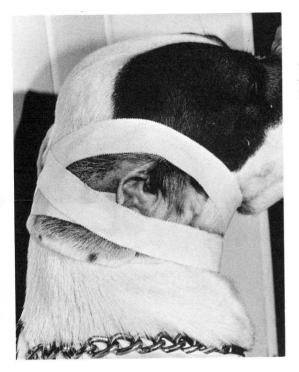

The Ear Bandage. **The ears are folded over the head with their tips together, and held by a bridge of adhesive tape.** *—J. Clawson*

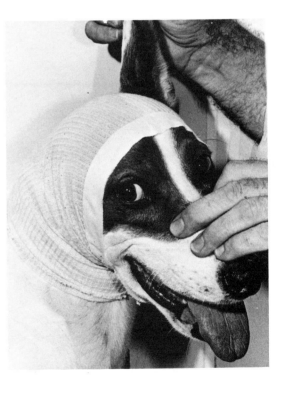

A protective stocking is applied if the dog scratches at the dressing. *—J. Clawson*

The Ear Bandage: As an important step in the treatment of all but minor external ear infections, the ears should be taped over the head to expose the canals to air. This is especially important in dogs with ears that drop down.

The ears are folded over the top of the head with their tips together and held in position by a bridge of adhesive tape. A nylon stocking (or sweater sleeve) is slipped over the head on top of the ears. The covering is kept in place by taping both ends of it to the dog's skin. Be careful not to get the tape too tight around his neck.

Fungus Infections (*Pityrosporon*)

The presence of excess wax and moisture in the ear predisposes to a fungus infection. This is a common cause of external otitis. Secondary fungus or yeast infections frequently occur when long-standing ear infections are treated with antibiotics.

Signs and symptoms are not nearly so pronounced as when the infection is due to a bacteria. The ear is less inflamed and less painful. The discharge usually is dark, thick, waxy, but not purulent. A *rancid odor* is characterisitc.

The treatment is similar to bacterial infections, except that an antifungal agent (Nystatin) is used to medicate the ears. Panolog, which contains Nystatin, can be used. Yeast and fungal infections tend to recur. Their treatment usually is prolonged.

Ear Mites

This disease is caused by tiny bugs which live in the ear canals and feed on skin debris. Mites are the most common cause of an ear infection in a puppy or young dog. Suspect it whenever both of your dog's ears are infected.

The characteristic sign is intense itching (i.e. scratching and violent head-shaking). The ear discharge is reddish-brown, or black and waxy, sometimes resembling that of a yeast or fungus infection. To make the diagnosis, remove some ear wax with a cotton-tipped applicator and look at it under a microscope against a dark background. Mites are white specks, about the size of the head of a pin, which move.

At times ear mites leave the ear canals and travel out over the body. They are highly contagious to dogs and cats. If there are other pets in the household, they should be treated.

Treatment: Do not begin treatment until you have identified the mites. Other ear problems can be complicated by using an ear-mite preparation.

Clean the ears as described above. Medicate the ears with a miticide (Canex) twice weekly for three full weeks. As the medication does not destroy eggs, a new crop of mites will reinfect your dog if you stop too soon. Dip your dog in an insecticide, or powder him well with flea powder (see *Insecticides*). The insecticide kills mites on the surface of the body.

An antibiotic is given if the ear problem is complicated by bacterial infection. Ear preparations containing a miticide, an antibiotic, and a steroid (to reduce itching) are available.

Foreign Objects and Ticks in the Ear

Grass seeds are the most common foreign materials in the ear canals. Ears should always be examined after a dog has been running in tall grass. When a foreign body can be seen it can be removed with a cotton-tipped applicator moistened in mineral oil.

Ticks often adhere to the skin of dog's ear. If the tick is easily accessible, it can be removed. First kill the tick by applying an insecticide or a substance such as fingernail polish directly to it by means of a cotton-tipped applicator. In a few moments, grasp the dead tick as close to the skin as possible and apply steady traction until it releases its hold. The tick can be grasped with long finger nails or tweezers.

Ticks and foreign bodies can be found deep in the ear canal next to the ear drum. Removal requires an otoscope and an alligator forceps. This is a sensitive area and requires an anesthetic.

Ear Allergies

Allergies are typified by the sudden onset of itching and redness of the skin without discharge. They respond well to steroids (1% Hydrocortisone cream). Because of intense scratching, the dog may traumatize his ears and set the stage for a secondary bacterial infection.

THE EAR FLAP (Pinna)

Fly-Bite Dermatitis

Flies attack the face and ears of dogs, inflicting many painful bites over the tips of the ears. German Shepherd Dogs, Collies and breeds with erect ears are most susceptible.

These bites have a typical appearance. They are scabbed, crusty-black, and bleed easily.

Treatment: Keep flies away from the ears by applying insect repellant, or axle-grease, to the tips. Tincture of Benzoin is also effective. Fly control is recommended. Infected ear tips require special care (see *Ear Fissure*).

Ear Fissure

Ear fissure is found in drop-eared breeds. It results from intense scratching at the ear, along with a violent shaking of the head which causes the ear tips to snap. The tips of the ears are denuded of hair, irritated-looking, and often bloody. In some cases they split, causing a fissure.

The underlying irritation or infection, often an external otitis, which caused the head-shaking, should be sought for and treated along with the ear fissure.

Treatment: Ear tip trauma is treated by applying an ointment containing an antibiotic and a steroid (Panolog) once or twice daily. The dog must be prevented from flapping and snapping his ears. They should be taped over the top of the head and covered with an ear bandage. In severe cases, a fissure may have to be sutured.

Marginal Seborrhea

This condition is caused by a build-up of body oil (sebum) on the hair along the border of the ear. The hair has a greasy feel. When rubbed with a thumbnail, the hair falls out. The cause in unknown.

Treatment: A sebum-dissolving agent, such as Squaline, is used to soften and loosen the greasy material. Liquichlor also is effective. It incorporates Squaline with a topical antibiotic. Apply by massaging it into the affected skin twice daily. Shampoo the ears twice a week with an antiseborrheic shampoo (Pregmatar, Thiomar).

Swollen Ear Flap (*Ear Hematoma*)

Sudden swelling of the ear flap is due to bleeding into the tissues leading to the formation of blood clot or hematoma. It is caused by violent

Ear flap hematoma affects breeds with drop ears. —*Rose Floyd*

head-shaking, scratching, or rough handling of the ear. It is easily mistaken for an abscess or a growth; but the history of sudden onset eliminates these possibilities.

Treatment: In the absence of known trauma to the ear, predisposing factors (infections, irritations) should be looked for and treated.

Blood should be released from the hematoma to prevent ultimate scarring and deformity of the ear. Removing it with a needle and syringe usually is not effective as serum accumulates in the space formerly occupied by the blood clot. Surgery, the treatment of choice, involves the removal of a window of skin to provide open and continuous drainage. The ear is then bandaged over the head until it heals.

Ear Mange

Sarcoptic mange, caused by a skin mite, often is first noted over the ear flaps (crusty ear tips). It affects skin over the whole body. It is discussed in the SKIN chapter.

THE MIDDLE EAR (Otitis Media)

Infections

Middle ear infections are not common in dogs. They are the result of an extension of an outer ear infection; or a perforated ear drum from a foreign body. One other pathway by which the middle ear can be infected is the Eustachian tube, which connects the middle ear to the back of the throat. Tonsillitis or some other nasopharyngeal infection can ascend to the middle ear through the Eustachian tube.

At first the signs of middle ear infection are masked by the infection (usually an external otitis) which preceded it. But as the infection progresses to involve the middle ear, pain is severe. The dog holds his head at an angle with the painful side down. He shies away if you attempt to touch his ear.

After the dog has been sedated or anesthetized, the condition usually is recognized by an otoscopic examination which shows perforation or loss of the ear drum.

X-rays may show bone involvement. The face may droop on the affected side if the nerve which crosses the surface of the ear drum is injured.

Middle ear infections are serious and can affect balance and hearing. Extension to the inner ear should be suspected if the dog staggers or falls toward the affected side, circles toward that side, or shows rhythmic jerking of his eyeballs. These are signs of *labrynthitis*.

All infections of the middle and inner ear should be treated by a veterinarian.

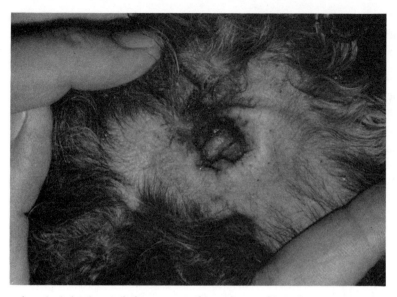

Chronic infections of the ear canal require prolonged treatment. Foul odor and dark brown discharge are present.

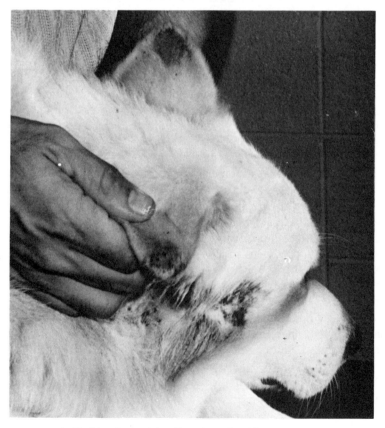

Fly-bite dermatitis affects breeds with erect ears.

Deafness

Dogs can be born without the ability to hear due to developmental defects in the hearing apparatus. Other forms of congenital deafness can appear later in life. In addition, loss of hearing can be caused by senile changes (old age), infections, trauma, blockage of the ear canal (by wax and debris), and drugs and poisons.

It is sometimes quite difficult to tell if a dog is going deaf. A dog with complete loss of hearing usually exhibits a typical behavior, is difficult to arouse from sleep and unresponsive to commands. A deaf dog barks less than normal. His voice may be somewhat altered. His ear flaps are not as active as those of a dog with normal hearing. Puppies, in particular, are difficult to test, as they are attentive to so many stimuli. Shouting, clapping the hands loudly when the dog is not looking, blowing a whistle, and other attention-getting sounds are used to test a dog's hearing.

A good history is important. A blow to the head, a bout of distemper, history of an ear infection, poisoning, or prolonged use of a certain medication: all are telling points.

Senile deafness comes on gradually at about ten years of age. It may not be particularly noticeable unless there is partial loss of vision, too. The dog then becomes less active, moves about more slowly, and gives his owner some indication of his problem. Senile deaf dogs often retain some hearing for a high-pitched sound such as a dog whistle. Stamping on the floor also attracts their attention as they can feel the vibrations.

If the history and physical examination suggest no cause for acquired deafness, it can be assumed that the cause is congenital. Inherited deafness occurs in Dalmatians, Bull Terriers, Sealyhams, Scottish Terriers, Border Collies, and Fox Terriers. Undoubtedly it happens to all breeds of dog, but is most common among those having a predominance of white color in their coats, such as Dalmatians and other harlequin-patterned dogs.

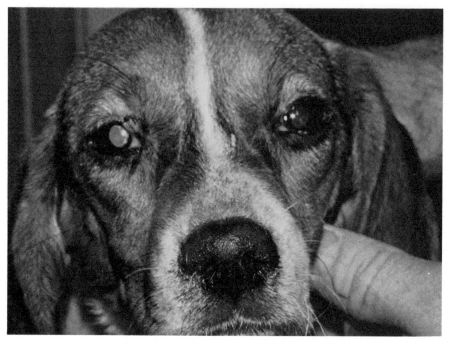

Dryness and chapping of the skin of the nose are early signs of nasal irritation. This dog was coming down with distemper. (Note the cataract in the right eye.)

7

Nose

GENERAL INFORMATION

A dog's nose is made up of his nostrils (nares) and the nasal cavity, which runs the length of the muzzle. The maxillary and frontal sinuses communicate with the nasal cavity. The nasal cavity is divided by a midline partition into two passages, one for each nostril. At the back, these passages open into the throat behind the soft palate.

The nasal cavity is lined by a mucus membrane which is richly supplied by blood vessels and nerves. There are a great many more nerve endings in the nose of a dog than there are in man. They connect with the highly developed olfactory center in the brain. Together these two, the abundant nerve supply and the well-developed center in the brain, account for a dog's scenting ability, which is such an important and useful aspect of his character.

The nasal mucus membrane is extremely sensitive to trauma and bleeds easily when irritated. Instruments should never be poked into the noses of dogs. This causes sneezing and the dog will attempt to jerk back. It is much better to examine the nasal passages of the dog after he has been given an anesthetic. An otoscope and special forceps are used to remove foreign bodies.

A dog's nose is normally cool and moist. There are no sweat glands in the nose. The moisture is secreted by mucus glands in the lining.

A warm dry nose suggests a dog has a fever and may be somewhat dehydrated. This is not always the case, however. Occasionally, the reverse is true: a sick dog has a runny nose which is cool because of evaporation. If you suspect your dog has a fever, confirm it with a rectal temperature.

Most dogs have darkly pigmented noses, but brown, pink, and spotted noses are normal in some dogs.

139

SIGNS OF NASAL IRRITATION

Runny Nose *(Nasal Discharge)*

Excited and nervous dogs often show this by secreting a clear watery mucus which accumulates at the tip of the nose. It disappears when the dog relaxes.

A discharge from the nose which persists for several hours indicates a nasal irritation. Common causes are foreign bodies, infections, and tumors. To learn about *allergic* nasal discharges, see Allergy.

Colds. Dogs don't catch "colds" the way people do. If your dog has a runny nose, blobs of mucus in his eyes, coughs and runs a slight fever, immediately think of a serious condition (one of the canine viral diseases, distemper). Call your veterinarian.

Sneezing

One of the first signs of nasal irritation in the dog is sneezing. This is a reflex, and results from stimulation of the nerves in the lining of the nasal passages. If the dog sneezes off and on for a few hours, and in between shows no other signs of illness, it is likely that the irritation is not very serious—perhaps dust or pollen in his nose.

Sneezing which persists all day long suggests a more serious irritative process. Check to see if there is less air coming from one of the nostrils. (Hold a mirror in front of the nose and check the vapor condensation.) If one nostril appears to be obstructed, a persistent sneezing problem may be due to a polyp or tumor on that side.

The sudden onset of frenzied sneezing, along with a discharge from one side of the nose, strongly suggests a foreign body. The dog may paw at his nose and shake his head.

A discharge from both nostrils accompanied by sneezing is typical of canine viral diseases, such as distempter. Other signs of illness will be present.

Sneezing indicates the irritant involves the front part of the nose. Gagging, snorting and coughing are signs of an irritant in the back, such as food regurgitating up into the nose.

Prolonged sneezing causes swelling and congestion of the nasal membranes. The result is sniffling, or noisy-character to the breathing. Nosebleeds can occur after particularly violent bouts of sneezing.

Mouth-Breathing

When both air passages are blocked by swollen membranes, the dog breathes through his mouth. This may be obvious only when he becomes excited or begins to exercise, at which time the demand for air is increased. This should not be confused with panting, which is normal.

Nose-Bleed *(Epistaxis)*

Nose-bleeds seldom occur spontaneously in dogs as they do in children. They are due to ulceration or injury to the mucus membrane. Violent sneezing, foreign bodies, tumors which bleed from their surfaces, trauma to the nose, and some parasites and bacteria capable of causing erosion of the surface lining, can cause a nose-bleed.

Treatment: If the cause is not apparent it will need to be determined by veterinary examination. In the meantime, keep the dog as quiet as possible or sedate him. Ice cubes or packs applied to the bridge of the nose reduce bloody supply and aid in clotting. Do not poke about in the nostrils with nasal packs or instruments as this only induces sneezing and will be resisted. Most nose-bleeds subside rather quickly of their own accord, especially when interference is kept to a minimum.

Reverse Sneezing

This uncommon condition is a cause of alarm because it sounds as though the dog has something caught in his air passages. It is believed to be due to a temporary spasm of the throat muscles. An accumulation of mucus may be involved.

During an attack, the dog violently pulls air in through his nose, producing a loud snorting noise as if something were caught in his nose and he was trying to draw it in. The dog is perfectly normal before and after these attacks. There are no ill effects. No treatment is necessary.

Regurgitation through the Nose *(Oral-Nasal Fistula)*

This is a condition in which food or water regurgitates into the nasal passage when the dog eats or drinks. It usually follows loss of the canine teeth. This results in an opening between the hard palate and the nasal cavity through which water and solids may be regurgitated. Sneezing, and a discharge on the affected side, are common. The condition is treated by creating a flap of skin from the inside of the lip and suturing it across the defect.

NOSTRILS

Collapsed Nostrils *(Stenotic Nares)*

This is a birth defect which occurs in short-nosed puppies, such as Pekingese and Bulldogs. The cartilages of the nostrils are too soft. When the pup breathes in his nostrils collapse, shutting off his air. In severe cases the chest is flattened from front to back. There is a nasal discharge which is sometimes foamy. These puppies breathe through their mouths when excited. Because of air lack, they are unthrifty.

Treatment involves removing a portion of the nasal cartilages so as to enlarge the openings.

Cleft Palate and Harelip

Cleft palate is a birth defect of the nasal and oral cavities. It is associated commonly with harelip. It is due to a failure of the bones of the palate to form completely. It results in an opening from the oral to the nasal cavity, allowing food and liquid to pass between. Many times it is impossible for the puppy to create enough suction to nurse. Survival then can be accomplished only by hand feeding.

Cleft palate occurs in all breeds but perhaps is most common in Bulldogs, Boston Terriers, Pekingese and Cocker Spaniels. In these breeds the defect is hereditary. Such dogs should not be used for breeding.

Harelip can occur by itself or in association with cleft palate. When it occurs by itself, it is due to an abnormal development of the upper lip. The problem is mainly a cosmetic one.

Cleft palate and harelip can be corrected by plastic surgery.

Collie Nose *(Nasal Solar Dermatitis)*

This is a weeping, crusting dermatitis which affects Collies, Shetland Sheepdogs and related dogs. It is due to lack of pigment on the nose and hypersensitivity to sunlight. It requires hereditary predisposition. It is seen most commonly in warm climates, such as Florida and California.

Prior to onset the skin of the nose appears normal—except for the lack of black pigment. With prolonged exposure to sunlight, the skin next to the nose becomes irritated-looking: then hair is lost. As the irritation continues, serum begins to ooze, forming a crust. With continued exposure, the skin becomes ulcerated.

In advanced cases, the whole surface of the nose becomes ulcerated and the tip itself may disappear, leaving unsightly tissue which bleeds easily. In such cases, a cancer may develop.

Treatment: Prevent further exposure to sunlight. Keep your dog in during the day and take him out at night. Treat the irritation with a skin preparation containing a steroid.

Permanent cure can be accomplished by tattooing the nose with black ink (use a vibrator tattooer). All the nasal skin must be tattooed to protect it from sunlight.

Depigmentation of the Nose

Vitaligo: This name is given to a condition in which there is gradual loss of pigmentation of the nose. (It may extend down to the lips also.) The nose and lips are frequently well-pigmented early in life, but gradually the black pigment fades to a chocolate brown. Although there is no cure known, some dogs may recover on their own.

Snow-Nose: This is a condition in which black pigment on the nose lightens during the winter, then darkens again as summer approaches. It occurs most commonly in white-coated breeds. There appears to be a hereditary predisposition for this condition which runs in certain lines.

Various causes have been suggested. They include cold weather, rubbing the nose in the snow, weak sunlight and lack of iron or vitamins in the diet. As the individual grows older and the cycles repeat themselves, the nose often remains permanently light-colored.

This is not a disease. It is primarily a cosmetic problem. A number of home remedies have been advocated. Success is questionable.

Plastic Dish Nasal Dermatitis: For want of a better term, this name is given to a form of contact dermatitis which results from eating out of plastic or rubber dishes. It is due to a hypersensitivity of the skin of the nose to the antioxident found in synthetic rubber products. The nasal skin becomes irritated and inflamed. There is loss of normal pigmentation. The condition can be corrected by feeding from a glass or stainless steel dish.

Nasal Callus *(Hyperkeratosis)*

In this condition of unknown cause the skin of the nose becomes thickened and rough to the touch. Horn-like projects can appear. The skin is dry. It may develop cracks and fissures which become irritated and infected. Usually there is an associated loss of nasal pigmentation.

Treatment: Excess horny tissue can be trimmed away but callus comes right back. There is no satisfactory cure for it. Treatment is aimed at softening the nasal callus with wet dressings and keeping the nose well lubricated with mineral oil or vaseline. If infection exists, the area should be treated with a topical antibiotic ointment (Neomycin).

A somewhat similar condition occurs as a sequel to canine distemper. The nose becomes thickened, dry and callused. The foot pads also partake of the same process. The disease is called *hardpad*. As the dog recovers from distemper, his nose often clears up and regains its normal skin texture.

THE NASAL CAVITY

Foreign Bodies in the Nose

They include blades of grass, grass seeds and awns, fish bones, and wood splinters. The signs are pawing at the nose accompanied by *violent sneezing*—at first continuous and later intermittent. The nose will run (and occasionally bleed) through the involved nostril.

Treatment: A foreign body may be visible close to the opening of the nostril, in which case it can be removed by tweezers. More often it is lodged farther back. If not removed in a short time, it tends to migrate even farther. In such cases it is necessary to give the dog an anesthetic to locate and remove it. Do not poke about in your dog's nose. His membranes are damaged easily.

Following the removal of a foreign body, an antibiotic should be given for two weeks (Chloromycetin, Tetracycline).

Infections *(Rhinitis)*

All irritations of the mucus membranes can be followed by secondary bacterial infections.

The presence of a foul-smelling, thick, creamy discharge from the nose suggest bacterial rhinitis. In long-standing cases, suspect a fungus.

Treatment: It is directed at finding the underlying cause of irritation and treating it along with the nasal discharge. Tumors and polyps should be removed.

Foreign bodies should be located and flushed out or removed through an otoscope with alligator forceps. Infected maxillary teeth should be extracted.

Inflammation which has become chronic is difficult to clear up. Granulation tissue ("proud flesh") builds up in the nose, causing further blockage and resisting the flow of air. Treatment then requires special cultures and in some cases exploratory surgery. For this reason it is advisable to treat even minor nasal cavity irritations with antibiotics to provide a cover and prevent the disease from becoming chronic. Continue for two weeks, or longer if a discharge persists.

Sinusitis

The frontal and maxillary sinuses are extensions of the nasal cavity. They are lined by a mucus membrane similar to that in the nose. Inflammation of this membrane causes sinusitis.

Infections starting in the nasal passages can extend to involve a sinus. Foreign bodies can penetrate a sinus. Roots of teeth which become infected can rupture into a sinus. Tumors can grow in a sinus. These are common causes of sinusitis in the dog.

The infection seldom starts on its own. It is rare for more than one sinus to be involved.

A persistent, chronic, purulent discharge from one nostril, along with sneezing and sniffling, suggests the possibility of an abscessed sinus. The dog should be examined by a veterinarian.

Nasal Polyps and Tumors

A polyp is a growth which begins as an enlargement of one of the mucus glands in the lining of the nose. It is not a cancer. It looks like a cherry on a stalk. Polyps cause symptoms by bleeding, and blocking the flow of air through the nostril. They can be removed by your veterinarian.

Benign and malignant tumors are found in the nasal cavity and the sinuses. The leading sign is a discharge through one nostril. They can be removed surgically if they are discovered early and are still small.

Large tumors can make one side of the face protrude more than the other. If they extend behind the eye, the eye will bulge. These tumors are far advanced. Treatment is discouraging.

Depigmentation of the nose *(snow-nose)* in a white-coated dog. This mainly is a cosmetic problem.

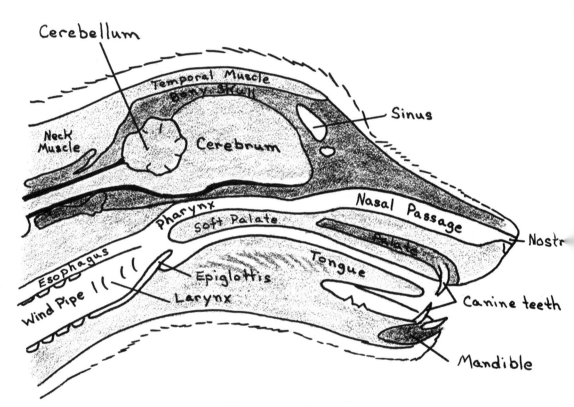

Anatomy of the Head. —*Sydney Wiley*

8

Oral Cavity

GENERAL INFORMATION

The oral cavity or mouth of dogs is subdivided into the *vestibule*, the space between the lips and the teeth, and the *oral cavity* itself, which is contained within the dental arches. The mouth is bounded on the front and sides by the lips and cheeks; above, by the hard and soft palate; and below, by the tongue and muscles of the floor of the mouth. Four pair of salivary glands drain into the mouth.

The saliva of dogs is alkaline and contains antibacterial enzymes. There is a normal flora of bacteria which live in the mouth and keep harmful bacteria from gaining a foothold. These factors serve to make mouth infections in dogs relatively infrequent.

LIPS

Inflammation of the Lips *(Cheilitis)*

Inflammation of the lips is often caused by an infection within the mouth which extends to involve the lips. In hunting dogs it may be due to contact with weeds and brush which cause the lips to become irritated and chapped-looking.

Cheilitis is recognized by serum crusts which form at the junction of the haired parts with the smooth parts of the lips. As the crusts peel off, the area beneath looks raw and denuded. It is sensitive to touch.

Treatment: Clean the area with surgical soap (pHisoHex, Weladol) and apply an antibiotic-steroid cream (Panolog) twice daily. When the infection subsides apply vaseline to keep the skin of the lips soft and pliable until healing is complete.

Lip Fold Pyoderma: In breeds with pendulous lips, such as some of the hounds, Saint Bernards, and Cocker Spaniels, the skin folds on the lower lip

147

which contact the upper fangs are a site of irritation and infection. These skin folds sometimes contain pockets which trap food and saliva, creating a constantly wet environment which favors bacterial growth. When the skin folds are stretched out, a raw, denuded, sensitive surface is seen. The foul odor from the dog's mouth is often the major reason for seeking medical attention.

Treatment: Cleanse the pockets by swabbing them out twice daily with cotton-tipped applicators dipped in peroxide and apply an antibiotic-steroid cream (Panolog). Keeping all affected areas dry and clean usually gives a good response. However, the problem may come back when the treatment is stopped. Permanent cure then requires surgical removal of the infected fold of tissue.

Lacerations of the Lips, Mouth and Tongue

The soft tissues of the mouth are common sites for cuts. Some of these are self-inflicted — the dog accidentally bites himself. Others are due to picking up and licking sharp objects, such as the top of a food can. Sometimes a canine tooth penetrates the lip and impales itself. One unusual cause of tongue trauma is freezing of the tongue to metal in extremely cold weather. When the tongue pulls free, the mucus membrane on the surface of the tongue strips off, leaving a raw bleeding patch.

Treatment: Bleeding from a mouth injury can be controlled by applying pressure to the cut with a clean gauze dressing or a piece of linen. Minor cuts which have stopped bleeding do not need to be stitched. Suturing of the cut should be considered when the laceration is large, ragged and deep; when the edges gape open; when lip lacerations involve the border of the mouth; and when bleeding recurs after the dressing has been removed. When a sore is due to a malpositioned tooth, have the tooth removed.

During healing of a cut, cleanse his mouth twice daily with a mild mouth wash such as Scope. Feed him a bland diet and avoid kibble, milk bones, knuckle bones, and other objects he might have to chew.

Burns of the Lips, Mouth and Tongue

Electric Burns: Electrical burns are almost always caused by chewing on an electric cord. Usually these injuries are limited to the mouth; but if your dog has difficulty breathing, consider the possibility of damage to the lung tissues and seek professional help.

Electrical burns can be quite painful, but in most cases the mucus membranes regenerate and close the defect without surgery. In some cases a gray-appearing membrane develops which eventually becomes ulcerated. Surgical excision of the burn back to healthy tissue is indicated.

Chemical Burns: These are common in the dog. They are caused by lye, phenol, phosphorus, certain acids and alkalies, and other corrosive agents.

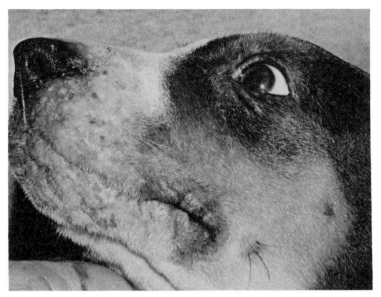

Bacterial infection of the lips *(cheilitis).*

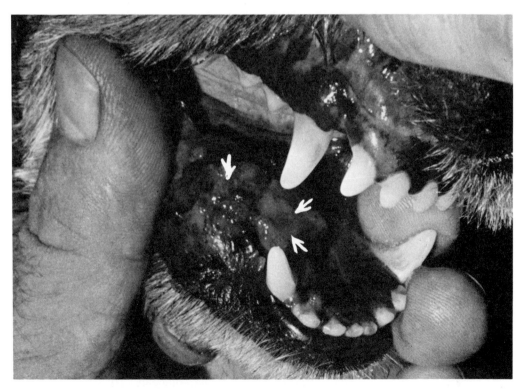

Cancer in the mouth. Note the pigmented growth behind the lower canine tooth.

If the substance is swallowed consider the possibility that his throat is burned — a much more serious problem.

Treatment: Remove poisons from the mouth by sponging and rinsing out with lots of water. Then, if the poison is an alkali, wash the mouth with vinegar or fruit juice: if an acid, use baking soda. For after-care, see *Lacerations* above.

MOUTH

How to Examine the Mouth

Most disorders in your dog's mouth can be identified by a careful inspection of his lips, gums, teeth, palate, throat, and the soft tissue of his chin and neck.

Small, movable, nontender nodules beneath the chin, at the angle of the jawbones, and below the ear, are lymph nodes. When swollen and tender, they indicate a mouth or throat infection. The lips are smooth, with small finger-like projections along the edge where the skin and mucus membranes meet.

To examine your dog's bite, close his mouth and raise his upper lips while drawing down on the lower lips with your thumb. The bite is determined by seeing how the upper and lower teeth meet (see *Incorrect Bite*). This also gives you the chance to examine his gums and teeth. Healthy gums are firm and pink. Pale gums are a sign of ill health (parasites, chronic blood loss, or iron deficiency anemia). Bluish-gray gums are signs of shock and dehydration.

The gums should be smooth and closely applied to the teeth. The teeth should be firm, healthy-looking and free of dental stain.

If your dog has bad breath, it may be due to a mouth infection or poor dental hygiene. Excess tartar is one of the leading causes of bad breath.

To open your dog's mouth, place your thumb in the space behind the canine tooth and exert pressure against the roof of his mouth. Pull down on his lower jaw with your other hand. To see beyond his tongue, push down on the back of his tongue with your finger. This lets you see his tonsils.

Sore Mouth *(Stomatitis)*

A dog with a sore mouth drools, shakes his head, paws at his face, refuses to eat, and shies away when you attempt to look in his mouth. The membranes inside the mouth are reddened, swollen, and tender. The gums may bleed when rubbed. The breath has a bad odor. The condition is stomatitis, or inflammation of the mouth.

There are a number of causes. They include mouth infections, trauma, a vitamin deficiency, kidney disease with uremia, diabetes, leptospirosis, distemper, chemical irritants, and corrosive poisons.

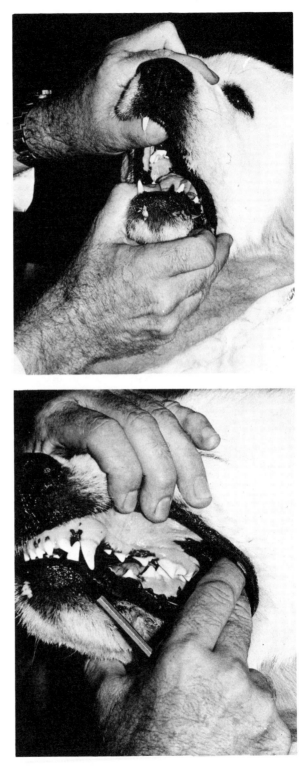

To examine your dog's mouth, place your thumb in the space behind his canine tooth and lift up. Pull down on his jaw with your other hand.

The bite is determined by how the upper and lower teeth meet.

—J. Clawson

Treatment: Depends upon finding the underlying cause and correcting it. The common causes of *infectious stomatitis* are listed below.

Trench Mouth *(Vincent's Stomatitis):* This is an extremely painful stomatitis caused by a bacteria-like germ. It is the most common form of stomatitis in the dog. It is characterized by a beefy-red look to the gums, which bleed easily. There is a characteristic offensive odor from the mouth,. usually accompanied by the escape of a brown, purulent, slimy saliva which stains the teeth, muzzle, and front legs.

Treatment: Flush the mouth with a weak solution of peroxide (1 part in 10) several times a day and administer a course of penicillin for at least one week (often three is necessary). Aspirin should be given to control the pain.

Yeast Stomatitis *(Thrush):* This is a specific kind of stomatitis usually seen in young dogs after long-term treatment with a broad-spectrum antibiotic. You will note that the mucus membranes are covered with soft white patches which coalesce to form a whitish film on the gums and tongue. Painful ulcers are seen as the disease progresses.

Treatment: Nystatin is the drug of choice. Cortisone is used to reduce the inflammation. Feed a soft diet. Large doses of a B-complex vitamin also are recommended.

Recurrent Stomatitis: In this condition traumatic ulcers of the mouth occur where jagged, broken or diseased teeth make repeated contact with the mucus lining of the lips, cheeks or gums. Excessive build-up of tartar on the teeth is a predisposing cause. A bacteria and a fungus quite commonly are cultured from these ulcers.

Treatment: The teeth should be cleaned. Consider removing one that is diseased. Put your dog on a good home care oral hygiene program (See *Care of Your Dog's Teeth*). Persistent cases require antibiotics.

Warts in the Mouth *(Oral Papillomatosis)*

Oral papillomas are painless growths in the mouths of young dogs. They are caused by a virus. Initially they are small and pink-looking. Later they become larger, cauliflowerlike, and have a rough, grayish-white appearance. There may be just a few, yet in some cases the whole mouth is affected. These warts usually disappear spontaneously within six weeks. When they do not, surgery can be considered. Once a dog has recovered, he makes antibodies and can't be reinfected.

Foreign Bodies in the Mouth

Common foreign bodies that may be found in the mouth are bone splinters, slivers of wood, sewing needles and pins, porcupine quills, fish hooks, and plant awns. They penetrate the lips, gums, and palate; become

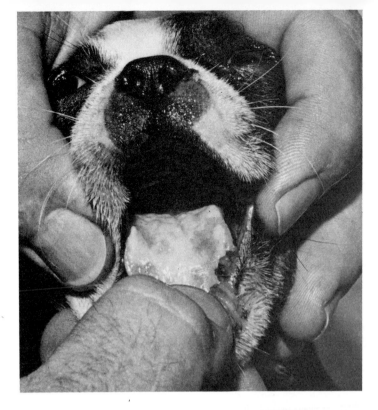

Thrush. The tongue is covered with soft white patches.

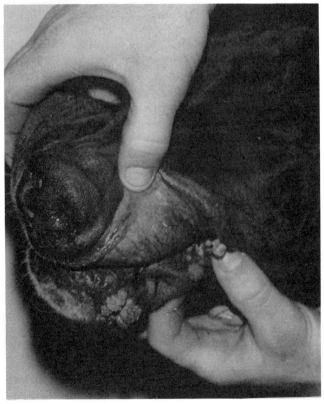

Warts of the mouth are caused by a virus.

caught between the teeth; and get wedged across the roof of the mouth. Foreign bodies in the tongue and throat are discussed elsewhere.

Suspect a foreign body if your dog coughs, gags, licks his lips, salivates, shakes his head or paws at his mouth. Sometimes the only signs are a loss of pep, refusal to eat, and general unthriftiness associated with bad breath.

Treatment: Obtain a good light and gently open your dog's mouth. A good look may show the cause of his problem. Direct removal of some foreign bodies is possible, but in an anxious animal suffering from pain, a sedative or anesthetic is necessary.

To remove a fishhook, determine which way the barb is pointing and push it through the soft tissue until it is free. Then cut the shank next to the barb with wire cutters and remove the fishhook in two pieces.

Foreign bodies which have been left in place for a day or longer may cause infection. A broad-spectrum antibiotic is recommended.

Porcupine Quills: Porcupine quills can penetrate the face, nose, lips, oral cavity, or skin of the dog. To remove the quills, sedate or tranquilize the dog. Clip the end off the quill to relieve the pressure in the hollow shaft. Then using pliers, remove each quill individually by drawing it straight out. Quills inside the mouth are difficult to remove without first giving an intravenous anesthetic.

Growths in the Mouth

Any solid tumor growing in the mouth is a cause for concern. Ninety-five percent of mouth growths are malignant (cancers). The *epulis*, which is a form of gum overgrowth, and the *ranula*, which is a salivary gland cyst in the floor of the mouth, are exceptions. They are discussed elsewhere.

Growths in the mouth should receive immediate professional attention.

TONGUE

Sore Tongue *(Glossitis)*

A dog with a sore tongue refuses to eat because of the pain. Drooling is common. Inflammation of the tongue occasionally complicates a burn or cut in the mouth.

In areas where cockle and sand burrs are prevalent, dogs frequently irritate their tongues while attempting to remove burrs from their feet. Small scratches and puncture wounds of this nature can become infected.

Treatment: If his tongue is infected, give him a course of antibiotics (one of the penicillins). If he is run-down and in a bad state of nutrition, a vitamin deficiency could be contributing to his sore tongue. Treatment then is directed at building him back up with vitamins and a high protein diet.

Foreign Body in the Tongue

Small plant awns, burrs, and splinters can become imbedded on the surface of the tongue. You can remove them with tweezers. Glossitis occurs if the puncture wound becomes infected.

A common place for a foreign body is the underside of the tongue. Confirm this by looking. Sometimes you will see a grape-like swelling, or a draining tract, which means the foreign body has been present for some time. Most of them will need to be removed under anesthesia. A follow-up course of broad-spectrum antibiotic is recommended.

Strangulation of the Tongue

Sudden swelling of the tongue may be due to strangulation of its blood supply by a rubber band or a piece of string which has become wrapped around it. Gagging and coughing only serve to work it farther to the rear, making it less visible. A careful inspection is necessary to detect and remove the cause of this problem.

GUMS

Sore Gums *(Gingivitis)*

Healthy gums are firm and pink. The edges of healthy gums are closely applied to the teeth. There is no room for food and debris to get down between them.

If a dog has gingivitis, the first thing you will notice is that his gums appear reddened, painful, swollen, and may bleed when rubbed. Next the edges of the gums begin to depart from the sides of the teeth. This causes little pockets and crevices to develop. They trap food and bacteria. This aggravates the problem. In time it may lead to a root abscess.

Closely associated with gingivitis and tooth decay is the build-up of dental calculus or tartar. Dental pockets occur first, and the accumulation of tartar is secondary. The build-up of tartar at the gum line interferes with oral hygiene and perpetuates the problems.

Tartar is a tan or dark brown material which forms on the teeth. Heaviest deposits are found on the molars, premolars and canines. Dental tartar is a good media for bacterial growth. It is not normal and should be removed when present.

Treatment: Gingivitis due to poor oral hygiene should be treated by brushing the teeth and gums with a 3% hydrogen peroxide solution once a day until the gums are healthy looking. Dental deposits should be broken loose and removed with a dental scaler (see *Care of Your Dog's Teeth*). Sometimes special instruments are needed and the services of a veterinarian will be required. A broad-spectrum antibiotic is indicated.

Enlarged Gums *(Hypertrophic Gingivitis)*

This is a condition in which the gums begin to grow up alongisde of (or over) the teeth. As a result they are traumatized, become infected and interfere with good oral hygiene. Bulldogs and Boxers seem to be affected more often than others.

Enlarged gums should be surgically removed.

An *epulis* is a form of gingival hypertrophy in which part of the gum enlarges to form a mass on a flap of tissue. It can interfere with locking of the teeth when the dog closes his mouth. It is not a cancer. However, it should be removed to promote good oral hygiene.

TEETH

Baby Teeth

The average puppy has 28 *deciduous* (baby) teeth. These are the incisors, canines and premolars. Puppies do not have molars.

With rare exceptions, puppies are born without teeth. The first deciduous teeth begin to appear at three to four weeks of age. They are the canines. Next are the incisors and premolars. The last premolar erupts at about six weeks of age. As a rule, teeth of large breeds erupt more rapidly than those of small breeds.

Teething in Puppies

Puppies begin to acquire their permanent teeth at about four to five months of age. During this period, which lasts for about two months, the baby teeth are being shed and replaced by the adult teeth. Teething in puppies may be accompanied by soreness at the mouth and drooling. The puppy may be off his feed from time to time, but not enough to affect his weight and growth.

The first teeth to be replaced are the incisors, then the canines and premolars. The last molar in the jaw comes in at six to seven months.

Retained Baby Teeth

During teething, the roots of baby teeth are reabsorbed as adult teeth grow out to take their places. Sometimes this does not happen. Some dogs, particularly those of small breeds, tend to retain their baby teeth as the adult ones erupt. The permanent teeth are then pushed out of alignment. This can cause a bad bite. You will also see what appears to be a double set of teeth.

Puppies three to six months of age should be checked from time to time to see that their bite is normal. Also check to see if any baby teeth have been retained. If a baby tooth is still present when an adult tooth has erupted, it should be removed.

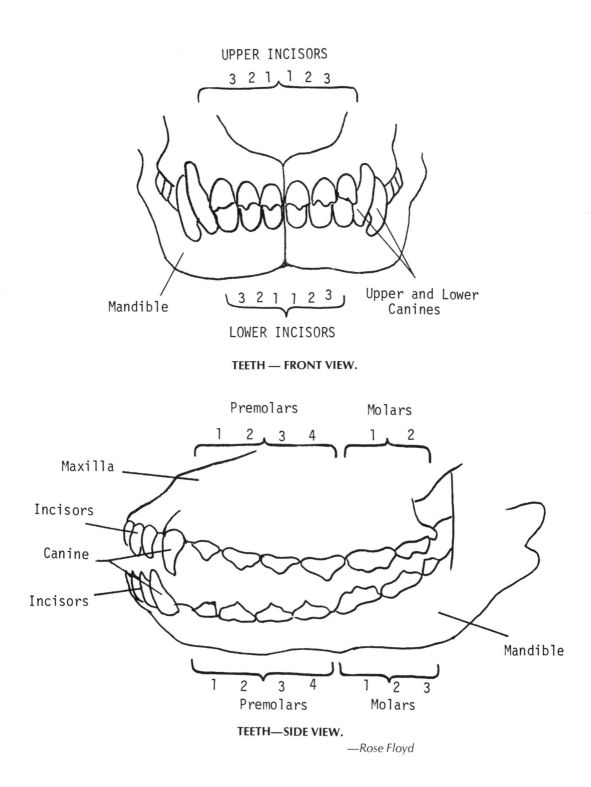

UPPER INCISORS

3 2 1 1 2 3

Mandible

3 2 1 1 2 3

LOWER INCISORS

Upper and Lower
Canines

TEETH — FRONT VIEW.

Premolars   Molars

1 2 3 4   1 2

Maxilla

Incisors

Canine

Incisors

Mandible

1 2 3 4   1 2 3

Premolars   Molars

TEETH—SIDE VIEW.

—*Rose Floyd*

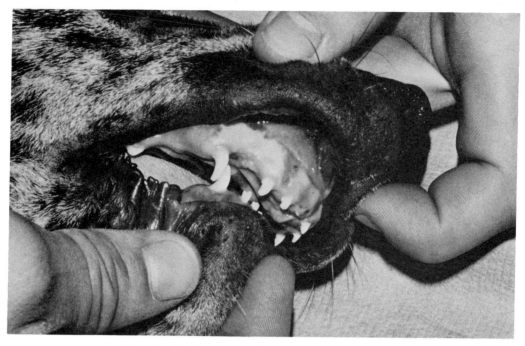

Overshot bite in a puppy. This is called a Parrot mouth.

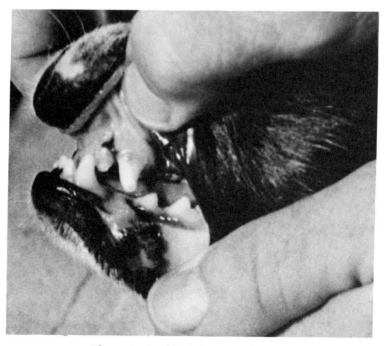

The *undershot* bite is incorrect for most
breeds. Consult your breed standard.

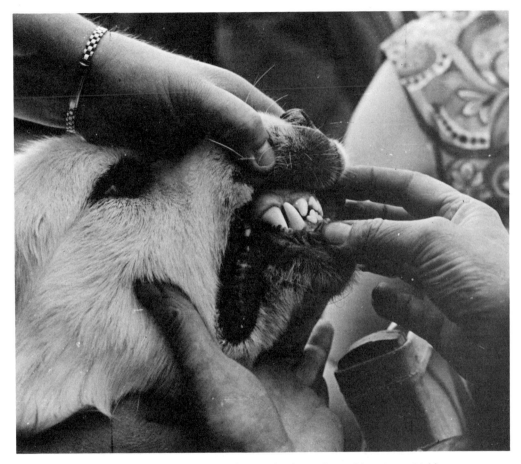

A good mouth with strong teeth, meeting in a *scissors bite*. —*Peter Bickle*

Incorrect Bite

A bad bite is a common problem and causes dog breeders more concern than any other mouth abnormality. The ideal bite for most breeds is a *scissors* bite in which the upper incisors just overlap and touch the lower incisors. In an *even or level* bite the incisors meet edge to edge. This is a common bite in dogs but is not considered ideal because the edge to edge contact causes wear of the teeth.

The type of bite a purebred dog should have is given in the Standard for that breed.

Overshot: In this condition the upper jaw is longer than the lower jaw, so that the teeth overlap without touching. It is also called a *parrot mouth*. This problem, which occurs in young puppies, may correct itself if the gap is no greater than the head of a wooden match. Most bites are "set" by the time a puppy is ten months old. An overshot bite seldom improves thereafter.

A puppy with an overshot mouth could have a problem when his permanent teeth come in, as they may injure the soft parts of the mouth. These bites should be watched carefully as extractions may be necessary.

Undershot: This is the reverse of the above, with the lower jaw projecting beyond the upper. It is considered correct in some of the short-faced breeds, including the Bulldog, Boston Terrier and Boxer.

Wry Mouth: This· is the worst of the malocclusion problems. In this situation, one side of the jaw grows faster than the other side, twisting the mouth so as to give it a wry look. This condition can be quite a handicap and leads to difficulty grasping and chewing food.

Treatment of Incorrect Bite: Most bite problems are due to hereditary influences which control the length of the jaws, so that one grows at a different rate than the other. An overshot mouth in which the upper jaw grows faster is definitely hereditary and may be passed on to some members of the next generation. The undershot mouth *may* be hereditary. Dogs with hereditary dental malocclusion problems should be eliminated from breeding programs.

Bad bites in dogs can be due to retained baby teeth which interlock in such a way as to block the normal growth of the jaws. When abnormal tooth development is detected early (by 12 weeks), often the problem can be corrected by extraction.

Unstable Jaw

This condition is seen in Pekingese, Chihuahuas and some of the Toy breeds. It is due to persistence of soft cartilage at the point where the lower jaws join together at the front of the chin. (Normally this cartilage becomes calcified, forming bone.) The incisors, whose roots are set in this soft cartilage, become unstable and wobbly. Infection descends to the roots of these teeth and destroys the cartilage. This allows the jawbones to become detached, so that each side moves independently. The condition can be treated by removing the diseased teeth, administering antibiotics, and stabilizing the joint with wires or screws.

Aging a Dog by His Teeth

The method of aging a dog by his teeth is a relatively reliable one up to about seven years of age, but individual variations do exist among dogs. They are due to differences in bites and chewing habits which affect the wear of the teeth.

The cusps of the teeth are the cutting edges. They are best seen on the incisors. The amount of wear on the cusps is used to judge the age of the dog. The incisors (upper and lower) are identified by numbers. These numbers are shown on the drawing, which identifies the incisors in question.

The following generalities are helpful, bearing in mind that individual variations occur:

1½ years	Cusps are worn flat on the lower middle incisors (1). Tartar begins to form on the canines.
2½ years	Cusps are worn flat on the lower intermediate incisors (2). Tartar is quite noticeable on the canines.
3½ years	Cusps are worn flat on the upper middle incisors (1).
4½ years	Cusps are worn flat on the upper intermediate incisors (2).
5 years	Cusps are worn flat on the last incisor (3). The canines begin to show wear.
6 Years	All the lower incisors are worn flat and the canines appear blunted.

Abnormal Number of Teeth

The number of adult teeth in the dog varies according to the breed, but the average is 42. Breeds with short faces sometimes have fewer teeth, due to the shortening of their jaws.

Some dogs carry a mutation for missing teeth and others for excess teeth. Doberman Pinschers may have fewer premolars than normal. This is considered to be a fault in the show ring. Genetic variations of this type usually are hereditary.

Sometimes an overcrowding of teeth is noted. It usually affects the incisors. It causes the teeth to twist and overlap. One or more of the affected teeth may need to be extracted to provide room for the rest.

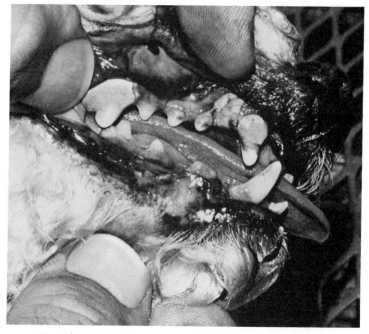

Dental tartar predisposes to gum disease and tooth decay.

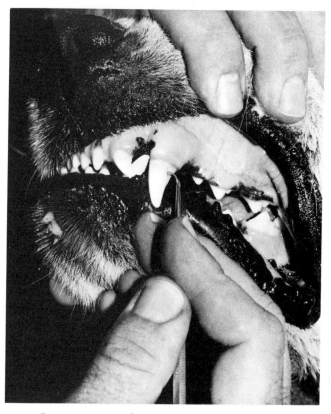

Remove tartar with a dental scraper. —*J. Clawson*

Loose Teeth *(Tooth Decay)*

The teeth are held in their sockets by a special kind of connective cement called the periodental membrane. Infection of this membrane leads to root infection and loss of teeth.

Periodental Disease: This is the most common disease of the dog's mouth. It begins as a gingivitis with trapping of food in little pockets along side the teeth. As these pockets become infected, the gums become soft and mushy and begin to recede, exposing more of the teeth. As you press on the sides of the diseased gum, you will sometimes see pus coming from below. There is a fetid odor to the breath. In late stages, teeth begin to loosen, and root infections are common.

Treatment: Treat the periodental disease as you would sore gums (gingivitis). In addition, an oral antibiotic should be continued for two or three weeks.

A surprisingly large number of teeth will reattach themselves to the bone if treatment is started before the condition is too far advanced, and extraction may not be necessary. In some instances, severe gingivitis may need to be treated by removing a portion of the diseased gum.

Periodental disease can be prevented by a program of good oral hygiene as described below.

Cavities (Dental Caries): These are not common in the dog. When present, they occur on the root of the tooth instead of the crown (as in humans). Usually this is because the root has been exposed by gum disease. Cavities can lead to root abscesses.

Abscessed Roots: Abscessed roots involve all teeth, but the one most often affected is the top fourth premolar. This causes a characteristic swelling below the dog's eye. It presents as a recurrent, painful rising which eventually breaks and drains pus out over the side of the face. Abscessed roots usually are treated by tooth extractions.

Care of Your Dog's Teeth *(Oral Hygiene)*

Dogs need special attention given to their teeth in order to prevent gum disease and tooth decay. A program of good oral hygiene is important. You should:

(1)   Feed your dog kibbled food, milk bones or dog biscuits once a day. Hard foods are abrasive and help to clean the teeth by friction.

(2)   Give your dog something to chew on at least once or twice a week. Rawhide bones, large knuckle bones that won't splinter, and hard nylon bones (not rubber balls) are effective.

(3)   Remove tartar. All dogs living in hard water areas eventually develop tartar stains on their teeth. Tartar is a mixture of calcium

phosphate and carbonate with organic material. These calcium salts are soluble in acid but precipitate in the slightly alkaline saliva of the dog. Tartar stains should be removed as they appear. They are not normal. If left unattended, tartar builds up to form thick plaque, or calculus, which contributes to gum disease and eventually to periodental disease. Tartar stains can be removed by swabbing the teeth with 3% hydrogen peroxide solution or a solution of 1% hydrochloric acid. Moisten a rough cloth with the solution and then scrub the teeth vigorously, particularly on the outside and next to the gums, where the stains are heaviest. In advanced cases the teeth will have to be scaled and polished. Special dental instruments are needed to break loose particularly thick deposits.

(4) Brush your dog's teeth and gums twice a week with a toothpaste and a child's soft toothbrush. Baking soda and water is also effective as a detergent paste.

A program of good oral hygiene will increase the life of your dog's teeth, and help to keep him in good health and condition during his later years.

THROAT

Sore Throat *(Pharyngitis)*

Sore throats are common. The throat looks red and inflamed, much as it does in people. Occasionally a purulent drainage will be seen coating the mucus membrane. Pharyngitis often is associated with a respiratory infection. Symptoms are fever, coughing, gagging, pain in the throat when the dog swallows, and loss of appetite.

In severe cases the lymph tissue in back of the throat becomes swollen, pushing the throat forward and making breathing coarse and raspy. Incision and drainage of a lymph gland may be necessary.

Treatment: Antibiotics containing penicillin should be given for infection; aspirin for pain. Put your dog on a liquid diet.

Tonsillitis

The tonsils are aggregates of lymphoid tissue, much like lymph glands, which are set at the back of the throat exactly as they are in humans. They may not be visible unless they are inflamed.

Tonsillitis is more common in the young dog. Acute tonsillitis usually is due to a bacterial infection. It causes symptoms which are similar to those of a sore throat, except that the fever is more pronounced (over 103 degrees F), and the dog appears more ill.

Treatment: Place the dog on a liquid diet and administer a penicillin antibiotic for ten days.

Chronic tonsillar enlargement is due to recurrent infection or mechanical irritation from prolonged coughing. Tonsillectomy should be considered when the tonsils interfere with breathing or swallowing. Enlargement alone is not an indication for tonsillectomy.

Foreign Bodies in the Throat *(Choking and Gagging)*

Dogs choke on small rubber balls and other objects that lodge in the back of their throats and block their windpipes. Bones that lodge sideways in the animal's throat also are a common cause of choking and gagging.

Treatment: If your dog is getting enough air, try to soothe and quiet him down. Should he panic, his need for air is greater and the situation becomes more of an emergency. Open your dog's mouth and see if you can find the cause of the trouble. If the foreign body cannot be easily removed, do not attempt to remove it yourself. Attempts to remove a stubbornly situated foreign object often cause further damage—or push it farther back. Take your dog to the veterinarian at once.

If the dog has fainted, the object will have to be removed at once to re-establish the airway. Open his mouth. Take hold of his neck in back of the object and apply enough pressure to his throat to keep the object from passing down while you hook it with your fingers. Work it loose as quickly as possible. Then administer artificial respiration.

(Note: If the signs are *coughing* and the dog is in respiratory distress, the foreign object may be in the larynx—see RESPIRATORY SYSTEM: *Object in the Voice Box.*)

Prevention: Avoid giving your dog a hard rubber ball to play with. Don't feed your dog chicken bones or long bones which splinter easily.

SALIVARY GLANDS

There are four main pairs of salivary glands which drain into the dog's mouth. Only the parotid gland, located below the dog's ear in back of the cheek, can be felt from the outside. The salivary glands secrete an alkaline fluid which lubricates the food and aids in digestion.

Drooling *(Hypersalivation)*

A common cause of hypersalivation is motion sickness. Apprehension, fear, and nervous anxiety also cause an increase in the saliva formation in some dogs.

When a dog is drooling excessively and acts irrationally, beware of the possibility of rabies. Other infectious diseases, notably distemper, are associated with drooling. Tranquilizers can cause drooling; so can some poisons (arsenic). A foreign body in the mouth should be considered when there is no apparent cause for the problem.

Drooling is a problem in dogs with loose lower lips.—*Peter Bickle*

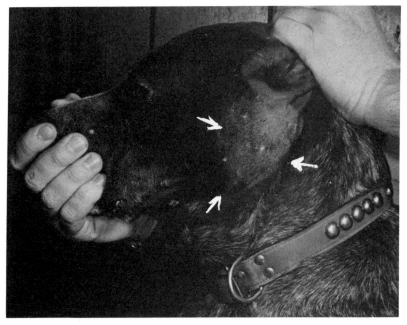

An infected salivary gland *(parotid).*

Treatment depends upon finding the cause and correcting it. In stubborn cases, a drug may be given to slow the flow of saliva or relieve apprehension.

Salivary Gland Infection and Cysts

Salivary gland infections are not common in dogs. When present they are due to an extension of a mouth infection, or an obstruction of one of the salivary gland ducts. Ducts become blocked by thick secretions, stones, or foreign bodies such as food particles and plant awns. Fluid backs up, ruptures the duct, and forms a fluid-filled cyst in the gland.

A common salivary cyst in the mouth of the dog is the *Ranula* (honey cyst). This is a large, smooth, rounded swelling in the floor of the mouth on one side of the tongue. When a needle is put into the cyst, a thick, mucus-like, honey-colored material is removed. This sometimes effects cure. More often surgery is required.

SWOLLEN HEAD

Head and Neck Abscess

Head and neck swellings which come on suddenly and are accompanied by fever and pain are abscesses. They affect the throat (post-tonsillar abscess), soft tissues beneath the chin (submandibular abscess), side of the face, and soft tissues behind the eye (retrobulbar abscess). A retrobulbar abscess causes tearing and protrusion of the eye.

Causes are tonsillitis, sore throat, puncture wounds, mouth infections, and foreign bodies (wood splinters, quills) which work back from the corners of the mouth into the soft tissue.

Head and neck abscesses are exquisitely tender swellings which give a lop-sided look to the head, face or neck. Opening the mouth causes extreme pain in some cases. These individuals refuse to eat and drink.

Treatment: In nearly all cases incision and drainage will be necessary after the abscess becomes fluctuant (soft-feeling). Your veterinarian probably will suggest application of warm saline packs for 15 minutes four times daily, and he will prescribe an antibiotic.

After incision and drainage, a wick of gauze may be used to keep the edges apart so the wound can heal from the bottom. You may be required to change and dress the wound at home.

Swollen Jaw in Terriers *(Mandibular Osteopathy)*

This condition appears limited to young West Highland Whites, Scotties and Cairn Terriers. It affects the joints of the mandible (lower jaw). In these animals, for unknown reasons, excess bone material is deposited, causing a painful swelling and extreme difficulty in opening the mouth. Loss of appetite may be the first sign; but when the mouth is forced open, the dog will cry out in pain.

Treatment: The condition has been successfully treated with corticosteroids. Medication must be continued for several months. It must be started before the bone is deposited, or treatment is not effective.

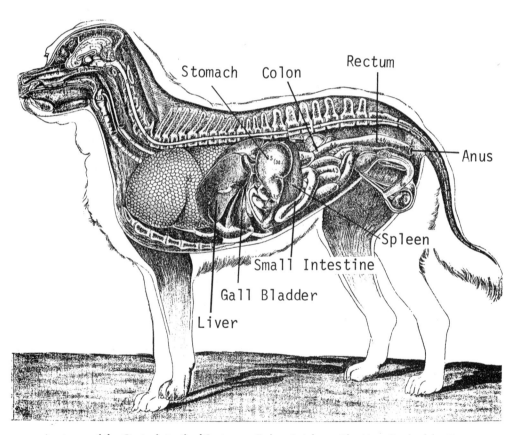

Anatomy of the Gastrointestinal System —*Robert Leighton, The New Book of the Dog*

9

Digestive System

The digestive tract is a complex system that begins at the mouth and ends at the anus. The lips, teeth, tongue, salivary glands, mouth and pharynx are considered elsewhere. The remaining organs are the esophagus, stomach, duodenum (first part of the small bowel), small intestine, colon, rectum and anus. The organs which aid in the digestion and absorption of foodstuffs are the pancreas, gall bladder and liver.

The esophagus is a muscular tube which carries the food down to the stomach. This is accomplished by rhythmic contractions. The lower esophagus is equipped with a muscular ring; it enters the stomach at an angle. This helps to prevent reflux of foods and liquids back up into the mouth.

Food remains in the stomach for three to six hours. It is acted upon by acid and pepsin. Pepsin breaks down proteins into chains of amino acids.

Bacteria are unable to live in the acid environment of the stomach.

As food enters the duodenum and upper small intestine, it is acted upon by *amylase* and *lipase* (from the pancreas), and by the *succus entericus,* which is a mixture of enzymes secreted by the small bowel. The gall bladder contracts in the presence of a meal, emptying stored bile into the duodenum, which aids in the absorption of fats.

Lipase acts on dietary fat, forming fatting acids. Amylase converts starches into short-chained sugars. The final stage of digestion is accomplished by the succus entericus. The end products of digestion are then passed through the wall of the bowel and into the bloodstream.

Blood from the intestines flows to the liver. The liver has numerous functions connected with metabolism. Here the materials of the dog's meal are converted into stored energy.

ESOPHAGUS

Regurgitation

A dog who regurgitates his food is suffering from blockage of his swallowing tube. Regurgitation is the expulsion of undigested food without conscious effort. When regurgitation comes on suddenly, suspect a foreign body. When it occurs from time to time but seems to be getting worse, it can still be due to a foreign body, as some objects cause a partial blockage which can persist for days.

If your dog regurgitates immediately after he takes a bite or two of food, the block probably is high in his swallowing tube.

Food regurgitated into the nose leads to infection of the nasal passages and nasal discharge. Food regurgitated into the windpipe causes bouts of pneumonia.

Chronic regurgitation usually is due to tumors, strictures, and congenital problems.

Painful Swallowing *(Dysphagia)*

Food can trickle by a partial blockage. Swallowing then can be difficult and painful, but the dog does not necessarily regurgitate. He makes repeated attempts to swallow the same mouthful and eats slowly. If he doesn't get enough food, he begins to lose weight. As the condition becomes more painful, he may stop eating altogether.

Swallowing Problems in Puppies

Swallowing problems in puppies are not uncommon. The symptoms are those of regurgitation and dysphagia.

Aortic Arch Anomalies: Retained fetal arteries in the chest can cause regurgitation and dysphagia by producing outside pressure on the esophagus. Surgery may cure some of these puppies.

Achalasia: Achalasia, or failure of relaxation of the esophagus, is due to spasm or thickening of the lower esophageal ring. Food has difficulty getting through into the stomach. In time, the upper esophagus begins to dilate and balloon out. This can be demonstrated by lifting up the puppy's back legs and looking for a bulging out of the esophagus at the side of the neck.

Puppies with achalasia begin to show signs of it shortly after they start solid foods. They begin to eat eagerly, but, after a few bites, they back away from the food dish. They often regurgitate small amounts of food, which they eat again. After repeatedly eating the food, it becomes quite liquid and often passes into the stomach. Repeated respiratory infections are common.

There is evidence that achalasia has a hereditary basis. Many pups in the same litter can be affected.

Treatment: A problem can be suspected by the symptoms, but its exact nature can be confirmed only by special studies. Surgery and dietary measures may be of aid.

Foreign Body in the Esophagus

When a dog suddenly becomes distressed, drools and slobbers, swallows painfully or regurgitates food and water, suspect a foreign body lodged in the esophagus. Frequently it is a bone splinter.

A history of regurgitation and difficulty swallowing for several days or longer does not rule out a foreign body.

Treatment: Removal requires a special instrument called an *endoscope*. The animal is given an anesthetic, after which the endoscope is passed through the mouth and directed into the esophagus. The object is visualized through the endoscope and removed with a long forceps.

Perforations and injuries to the wall of the esophagus can occur. Treatment involves surgery in some cases.

Stricture

A stricture is a circular scar which follows an injury to the wall of the esophagus. Common causes are foreign bodies, caustic liquids, and reflux of stomach acid into the lower esophagus. Acid reflux can occur when a dog is under anesthesia.

Treatment: Most strictures can be treated by stretching (dilatation). Following dilatation, some dogs swallow normally. Others don't; the esophagus above the strictured segment remains enlarged, capable only of weak contractions. These dogs may need surgical removal of the strictured segment.

When a dog has a chronic stricture, overloading the esophagus with large meals aggravates the problem. Feed several small, semi-solid meals a day.

Growths

Tumors in the esophagus are not common, but when present usually are malignant. Growths of the esophagus caused by a worm (Spirocerca lupi) do occur but this is rare.

STOMACH

Vomiting

A number of diseases and upsets in the dog are associated with vomiting. This is one of the most common, yet one of the most nonspecific symptoms you are likely to encounter. Often it is possible to get a clue to your dog's problem by noticing *how* he vomits, and *what* he vomits. Types of vomiting that may be serious in the dog are discussed below.

As a dog starts to vomit, there is simultaneous contraction of the muscles of his stomach and abdominal wall. This leads to an abrupt build up in intra-abdominal pressure. At the same time the lower esophageal ring relaxes, allowing the stomach contents to travel up the esophagus and out the mouth. This sequence is controlled by a special vomiting center in the brain.

The most common cause of vomiting in the dog is overeating. Puppies who gobble their food and immediately exercise are likely to vomit. This after-meal vomiting is not serious. It may be due to feeding puppies from a common food pan (which encourages rapid eating). Separating puppies, or feeding small meals more often, usually eliminates the problem.

The second most common cause of vomiting is eating grass, or some other indigestible material which is irritating to the stomach. Most dogs suffer this at one time or another.

If your dog vomits once or twice and then appears perfectly normal and has no signs of illness, the condition probably is not serious and requires no special treatment.

Other types of vomiting can indicate a disorder in the gastrointestinal tract.

Repeated Vomiting: The dog first vomits his food. Then, as he continues to retch, he brings up a frothy, clear fluid. This type of vomiting suggests a stomach irritation. Spoiled food, grass, other indigestibles, and certain infectious illnesses (such as gastroenteritis), all cause irritation of the stomach lining (see *Acute Gastritis*).

Sporadic Vomiting: The dog vomits off and on, but not continuously. There is no relationship to meals. Appetite is poor. The dog has a haggard look and shows signs of listlessness and loss of health and glow. You should suspect that your dog is suffering from a disorder of one of his internal organs (kidneys, liver), or has a chronic illness such as a chronic gastritis, a heavy worm infestation, or diabetes. A thorough check-up is in order.

Vomiting Blood: Fresh blood in the vomitus indicates a break in the mucus lining somewhere between the mouth and the upper small bowel. Common causes are foreign bodies, tumors, and ulcers. Material which looks like *coffee grounds* is old blood which is partly digested. Most likely this indicates that the problem lies in the stomach or duodenum. Some cases may be due to swallowed blood.

When a dog vomits blood his condition always is serious and warrants a trip to the veterinarian.

Fecal Vomiting: If a dog vomits foul material that looks and smells like stool, he has an obstruction somewhere in his intestinal tract. Blunt or penetrating abdominal trauma is another cause of fecal vomiting.

A dog with this condition becomes markedly dehydrated due to losses of fluids and salts. This condition cannot be managed without professional aid.

Projectile Vomiting: This is a forceful type of vomiting in which the stomach content is ejected suddenly, sometimes for a distance of several feet. It is indicative of a complete blockage in the upper gastrointestinal tract. Foreign bodies, hair balls, duodenal ulcers, tumors and strictures are possible causes.

Any condition which causes an increase in intracranial pressure also causes projectile vomiting. This includes brain tumor, encephalitis, and blood clots.

Vomiting Foreign Objects: These include bone splinters, rubber balls, pieces of toys, sticks and stones. Occasionally hair balls form a cast-like wad, too large to pass out of the stomach. This is called a *bezoar*. Other material may be incorporated into a bezoar.

Puppies with a heavy roundworm infestation occasionally vomit adult worms. These pups should be treated (see *Roundworms*).

Emotional Vomiting: Dogs can vomit when upset, excited, or suffering from a phobia (for example, during a thunderstorm). A phobic dog also may drool, whine, paw and tremble.

Treatment: Remove your dog from the cause of his anxiety, if possible, and tranquilize him with Tranvet.

Motion Sickness: Young dogs often become nauseated and vomit when riding in a car. Most of them eventually become accustomed to it and outgrow the problem.

This is a form of sea-sickness. It is due to a disturbance in the balance center.

Treatment: If you know from past experience that your dog is going to be sick, give Dramamine by mouth about an hour before leaving. If the trip is a long one, it may be better to use a tranquilizer. Tranvet is a good one. DO NOT tranquilize him on the same day as a dog show.

Gastritis (Inflammation of the Stomach)

Gastritis is an irritation of the lining of the stomach followed by inflammation. The principal sign is vomiting. Gastritis can be of sudden onset *(acute);* or it can come on insidiously and be protracted *(chronic).*

Acute Gastritis: Severe and continuous vomiting comes on suddenly. The most likely cause is an irritant or poison. Gastrointeritis is another possibility: usually it is accompanied by diarrhea.

Grass eating is a common cause of irritant gastritis. Other causes are bones, stools, spoiled food, garbage, etc.

Common poisons are antifreeze, fertilizers, crab grass killers, and rat poisons.

When the stomach responds promptly the foreign material is expelled. Then it is necessary only to rest the stomach and protect it from excess acid.

Treatment: Withhold food and water for 24 hours. If your dog appears thirsty, give him some ice cubes to lick. Administer a dose of Pepto Bismol or Kaopectate every time he vomits (in the same weight dose as for humans), but wait until he is relaxed.

After 24 hours start your dog off on a bland diet of boiled rice mixed two parts to one part of hamburger. Boil the hamburger to remove the fat (fat delays stomach emptying). Other bland foods which may be substituted are cottage cheese, baby food, and chicken-rice soup. Feed small amounts the first 24 hours. If well tolerated, advance to a normal diet.

Chronic Gastritis: Dogs with chronic gastritis vomit sporadically (not always after meals), show little appetite, carry a dull hair coat, appear lethargic and lose weight.

The most common cause of chronic gastritis is a steady diet of poor quality or spoiled food. Other causes are persistent grass eating, and the ingestion of cellulose, paper, and rubber products. Consider also the possibility of hair bezoars. They accumulate in the stomach during springtime shedding, from licking and pulling hair out with the teeth. Finally, if no obvious cause is apparent, your dog could be suffering from some internal disorder, such as kidney failure. He should be examined by your veterinarian.

Treatment: Put your dog on a soft, bland diet (see *Acute Gastritis*). If he begins to improve, advance to a high quality kibble mix (no fat). Dogs with kidney disease require a special diet (Hills K/D is a good one).

When a *smooth* object is swallowed (hair, cloth, etc.), and you suspect it might be too large to pass through the lower tract, make your dog vomit it (see EMERGENCIES: *How to Induce Vomiting*.)

Other Causes of Upset Stomach: Some dogs apparently are unable to tolerate certain foods, or certain brands of commercial dog food (*Food Intolerance*). This can be determined by trial and error. Special diets can be prescribed by your veterinarian.

If your dog vomits about two hours after eating, the problem could be *food allergy*. This is sometimes accompanied by a watery, mucus-like, or even bloody diarrhea (see *Common Causes of Diarrhea*).

A condition exists in the Bulldog breed in which the stomach does not produce enough acid (Achlorhydria). It causes symptoms like those of chronic gastritis. It can be treated by supplying the needed acid with meals.

Peptic ulcers are not common in the dog. When present, the signs are those of a chronic intestinal upset. Vomiting, weight loss, anemia, and the passage of blood can occur. Diagnosis is made by upper gastrointestinal x-ray studies, using a contrast material (barium).

Bloat *(Gastric Dilatation — Torsion Complex)*

This can be a life-threatening disease which usually affects dogs in the prime of life. For reasons unknown, bloat is becoming more prevalent. Several research projects are underway to attempt to clarify its mysteries.

Bloat, also known as the *overfeeding (or overeating) syndrome,* involves a swelling up of the stomach from gas, fluid, or both *(acute gastric dilatation).* Once distended, the stomach may or may not abruptly twist on its long axis. If it does twist, but the twist is 180 degrees or less, it is called a *torsion*. A twist greater than 180 degrees is called a *volvulus*. In the broadest sense, then, the term BLOAT refers to any of three conditions: acute gastric dilatation, torsion, and volvulus.

There are some interesting facts about bloat:

(1) Dogs who bloat nearly always are two years of age or older. Two-thirds are males.

(2) It affects dogs of the larger, deeper-chested breeds: Great Danes, German Shepherds, Saint Bernards, Labrador Retrievers, Irish Wolfhounds, Great Pyrenees, Boxers, Weimaraners, Old English Sheepdogs, Bloodhounds, Standard Poodles, and others of large size (58 pounds was the average size in one study).

(3) Dogs who bloat eat large quantities of dry kibble.

(4) They exercise vigorously after eating, and tend to drink water in large amounts after meals.

(5) They may have a history of digestive upsets (gastritis).

(6) There may be a familial association with other dogs who have bloated.

If your dog develops a gastric upset which you think may be bloat, it is most important to decide whether his condition is due to gastric dilatation or torsion of the stomach. A mild gastric dilatation, not complicated by a twist of the stomach and signs of severe distress, is not an acute emergency and can be treated at home. A torsion or volvulus, on the other hand, is a life-and-death situation. It calls for *immediate* veterinary attention.

Acute Gastric Dilatation: The signs are excessive salivation and drooling, extreme restlessness, attempts to vomit and defecate, evidence of abdominal pain (he whines and groans when you push on his stomach wall), and abdominal distention. The history is most important. In nearly all cases there is a history of overeating, eating fermented foods, drinking excessively after eating, or taking vigorous exercise after a meal (within two to three hours). ·

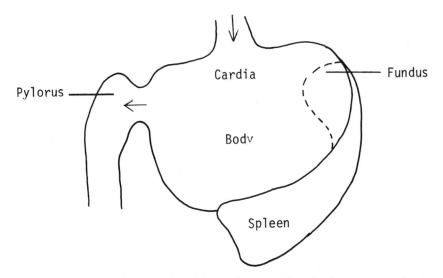

Bloat Syndrome: **The normal position of the stomach and spleen.** —*Rose Floyd*

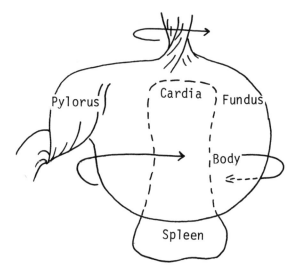

Bloat Syndrome: **During volvulus, the gastric twist is greater than 180 degrees. This pinches off the inlet and outlet of the stomach and interferes with the blood supply to the stomach and spleen. Relief is imperative.** —*Rose Floyd*

If your dog is able to belch or vomit, quite likely his condition is not due to a twist. The quickest way to confirm the diagnosis of acute gastric dilatation is to pass a long rubber or plastic stomach tube. As the tube enters the dog's stomach, there is a rush of air from the tube. Swelling in the abdomen subsides. This brings immediate relief.

To pass a stomach tube, insert the tube behind one of the canine teeth and advance it into the throat until the dog begins to swallow. If he *gags,* continue to advance the tube. If he *coughs,* the tube has entered his windpipe. Withdraw the tube a few inches and then advance it. There is little danger of perforating the esophagus with a soft rubber stomach tube.

Torsion or Volvulus: The initial signs are those of acute gastric dilatation except that distress is more marked. The dog breathes rapidly, his mouth membranes are cold and pale, and he collapses. The shock-like signs are due to strangulation of the blood supply to the stomach (and spleen).

A gastric tube will not pass into the stomach. Once you have established this, do not attempt to struggle further with your dog. This can throw him into deeper shock.

Treatment: Rush the dog to a veterinary clinic. If immediate professional help is not available, you may want to relieve the pressure in his stomach with a large-bore needle inserted through the abdominal wall. This is not without risk. The needle can lacerate the spleen, or fluid can leak out through the hole in the stomach, causing a peritonitis. Despite these risks, relieving pressure can be life-saving.

To *insert a needle into your dog's stomach*, put him in a comfortable position that allows him to breathe most easily. Next determine the highest point below the rib cage where there is a hollow or drum-like sound (find by tapping with your fingers). You are going to try to put your needle into an air pocket, avoiding fluid which is in the lower part of the stomach. Fluid may plug the needle. Quickly push the needle several inches through the belly wall and into the stomach beneath. If done correctly, gas under pressure rushes through the needle. This relieves the condition temporarily, allowing time to get to a veterinarian for definitive treatment.

Surgery is necessary to relieve a torsion or volvulus. The abdomen is opened and the twist is unwound. In some cases the spleen, or a portion of the stomach, must be sacrificed. The chance of a recurrence is about 15 percent. Various surgical procedures are utilized at the time of the initial operation to prevent recurrence.

INTESTINES

Problems in the intestinal tract (small and large bowel) are associated with three common symptoms: *diarrhea, constipation,* and the *passage of blood*. They are discussed below.

Diarrhea in *puppies* is discussed in PEDIATRICS.

Before passing a stomach tube, mark the tube by measuring the distance from the nose to the last rib.

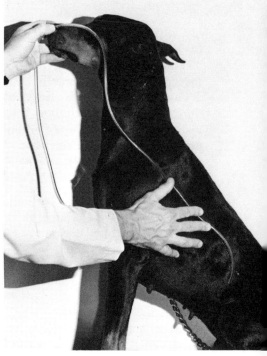

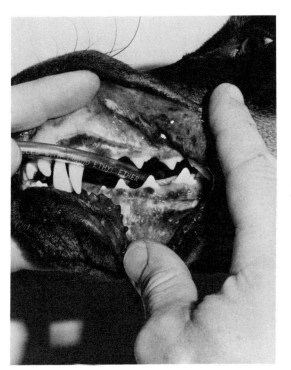

Insert the tube behind one of the canine teeth.

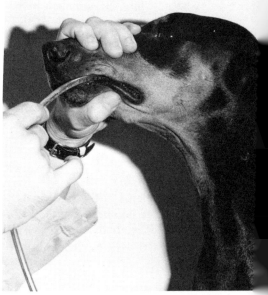

Advance the tube into the stomach to the level of the mark. —*J. Clawson*

Diarrhea

Diarrhea is the passage of loose, unformed stools. In most cases there is an increased number of bowel movements.

Food in the small intestine takes about eight hours to get to the colon. During this time the bulk of it is absorbed. Eighty percent of water is absorbed in the small bowel. The colon concentrates and stores the waste. At the end, a well-formed stool is evacuated.

Transit time in the intestinal tract can be speeded up for a variety of reasons. When food passes rapidly through the bowel, it arrives at the rectum in a liquid state. This results in a large, loose, unformed bowel movement. This condition, which is due to *hypermotility* of the bowel, accounts for 90 percent of the diarrheas in dogs.

In attempting to narrow the search for the cause of a diarrhea, begin by examining the *color, consistency, odor,* and *frequency* of stools:

Color
> *Yellow or greenish stool* — indicates bowel hypermotility.
> *Black tarry stool* — indicates bleeding in the upper digestive tract.
> *Bloody stool* — red blood or clots indicate lower bowel bleeding.
> *Pasty, light-colored stool* — indicates lack of bile (liver disease).
> *Large gray rancid-smelling stool* — indicates inadequate digestion.

Consistency
> *Watery stool* — indicates extreme hypermotility and bowel wall irritation (toxins and severe infections).
> *Foamy stool* — suggests a bacterial infection.
> *Greasy stool* — often with oil on the hair around the anus—indicates malabsorption.

Odor (The more watery the stool, the greater the odor.)
> *Food-like, or smelling like sour milk* — suggests both hypermotility and malabsorption: for example, overfeeding, especially in puppies.
> *Putrid smelling* — suggests an intestinal infection.

Frequency
> *Several in an hour, each small, with straining* — suggests colitis (inflammation of the large bowel).
> *Three or four times a day,* each large — suggests malabsorption or small bowel disorder.

Common Causes of Diarrhea

Most cases of diarrhea are due to irritation of the bowel lining from ingested substances or infectious agents, causing hypermotility.

Any sudden change in your dog's diet may cause a diarrhea. Dogs get used to water they drink at home. Drinking unfamiliar water may cause a mild intestinal upset.

Dogs on occasion experience diarrhea when they are excited or emotionally upset (for example, at a dog show).

Indiscretions in diet are common causes of diarrhea. Dogs are natural scavengers. They tend to eat a lot of things they can't digest. Some of them are:

— dead animals, rodents, and birds
— garbage and decayed food
— rich foods, table scraps, gravies, salts, spices and fats
— sticks, cloth, grass, paper, etc.
— parts of flea collars

Toxic substances causing diarrhea include:

— gasoline, kerosene, oil or coal tar derivatives
— cleaning fluid, refrigerants
— insecticides
— bleaches, often in toilet bowls
— wild and ornamental plants, toad stools
— building materials: cement, lime, paints, caulks
—fireworks containing phosphorus

Many of these are equally irritating to the stomach and cause vomiting.

Some dogs are allergic to (or seemingly unable to tolerate) certain foods such as milk, horse meat, eggs, and some commercial dog foods *(food intolerance)*.

Certain infectious agents are associated with diarrhea. Among these are *worms* (roundworms, hookworms and whipworms), *protozoa* (coccidia, trichomona and giardia), *viruses, bacteria* and (rarely) *fungi* (see INFECTIOUS DISEASES).

Treatment: Diarrhea is a symptom — not a disease. The first step is to find and remove the underlying cause, if possible. Diarrhea caused by *overeating* (characterized by several large, bulky, unformed stools per day) is controlled by cutting back the food intake and feeding three meals a day in divided portions. When *unfamiliar drinking water* is the problem, carry an extra supply. When *irritating or toxic substances* have been ingested, an effort should be made to identify the agent, as specific antidotes may be required.

Food Allergies or intolerances respond to removal of the specific food causing the problem. Non-allergenic prescription diets are available through veterinarians. They contain mutton and rice — two ingredients your dog is not likely to be allergic to. They are used as a basic, to which other foods are added gradually, to test their effect upon the animal's digestive tract.

A diarrhea which persists for more than 24 hours, a bloody diarrhea, and diarrheas accompanied by vomiting, fever (and other signs of toxicity), should not be allowed to continue. Consult your veterinarian without delay.

Most cases of diarrhea can be treated at home. Withhold all food for 24 hours. If your dog appears thirsty, give him a small amount of water, or ice cubes to lick. Administer Paregoric or Kaopectate (in the same weight dose as for humans). Lomotil also works well. As he begins to respond, start him off on an easily digestible diet which contains no fats. Diets containing boiled hamburger (one part to two parts of cooked rice—discard the broth), cottage cheese, cooked macaroni, or soft boiled eggs, are suitable in small amounts.

Prescription diets (Hills I/D) are available through veterinarians. Continue the bland diet for three days, even though the dog seems well.

Malabsorption Syndromes

In these disorders the dog does not digest, or does not absorb, food in his small intestines. These conditions are not common. When present, they are due to pancreatic disease (causing lack of enzymes), liver disease (causing lack of bile), or injury to the lining of the intestinal tract itself.

Dogs with a malabsorption problem are unthrifty and undernourished. There is a great deal of fat in the stool, giving it a rancid odor. The hair around the anus is oily or greasy.

The exact cause usually can be determined. This requires special diagnostic studies. Then the dog can be given the missing substances by mouth with his meals.

Intestinal Obstructions *(Blocked Bowel)*

The most common cause of intestinal obstruction is a swallowed foreign object. The esophagus in the dog is larger than his small intestine. Accordingly, a dog can swallow an object which he can't pass through his intestinal tract.

The second most common cause is *intussusception*. This term describes a situation in which the bowel telescopes in upon itself, much as a sock pulled inside out. It is most common at the junction between the small and large bowel. As the small bowel inverts into the colon, the lead point travels a considerable distance, ultimately pinching off the bowel passage. Intussusceptions are caused by increased bowel activity (diarrhea). They are most common in puppies and young dogs.

Obstructions also can be caused by tumors, strictures, navel and groin hernias, and twists and kinks which become trapped by adhesions.

The signs of intestinal obstruction are vomiting, dehydration, and distension of the abdomen. When the blockage is high, projectile vomiting occurs shortly after eating. When low, there is distension of the abdomen and vomiting is less frequent, but when present, it is dark brown and has a fecal odor. A dog with a complete obstruction passes no stool or gas per rectum.

Untreated intestinal obstruction leads to death of the dog. His condition is most urgent when there is interference with the blood supply to the bowel (strangulation). This is characterized by a rapid deterioration in his condition; an extremely tender "board-like" abdomen (to touch); and signs of shock or prostration. Strangulation requires immediate surgical correction. The dead segment of bowel must be removed and the bowel restored by an end-to-end hook-up.

Intestinal Foreign Bodies; Obstructions from foreign bodies occur in dogs who eat sticks, stones, cloth, rubber, leather, hides, and balls of hair.

Passage of these objects can be aided by giving mineral oil. It must not be given to a struggling dog who could accidentally inhale it.

If your dog has swallowed bone chips, you might be able to coat them with a substance such as bread or flour paste. This affords the possibility that the chips can pass through without causing harm.

Constipation

A dog who strains repeatedly but is unable to pass stool is constipated. There must be an element of pain, or difficulty in the passage of the stool, to qualify as constipation. Straining also occurs with diarrhea or bladder infection (cystitis). The distinction must be made before treating the dog for constipation.

Most healthy dogs have one or two stools a day. This varies with the individual and his diet. A day or two without a stool is no cause for alarm.

Establish a daily routine for your dog's elimination. This is especially important for the older dog.

There are many types of constipation in the dog. They are discussed below.

Chronic Constipation:

Inappropriate diets are the cause of most chronic constipations. A diet low in residue (fiber) causes small caliber stools. These stools dry out and are difficult to pass.

Bone chips are notorious for making the stool hard; they cement together to form rock-like masses in the colon. Other nondigestible substances such as grass, cellulose, paper and cloth, can lead to chronic constipation or a *fecal impaction*.

Dogs with impactions often pass blood-tinged or watery-brown stool. This might be mistaken for diarrhea. What actually is happening is that liquid stool is being forced around the blockage. If you suspect a fecal impaction, confirm this by digital examination, using a well-lubricated rubber glove.

Older dogs experience reduced bowel activity and weakness of the abdominal muscles. Either condition can lead to prolonged retention and an increase in the hardness of the stool.

Treatment: Attempt to determine the cause of a chronic constipation; remove any predisposing factors to assure long-term success. Don't feed small bones (such as chicken bones) which can fragment. If already feeding a kibble, switch to another product to see if it makes the stools softer.

Small hard stools can be made softer by adding residue to the diet. High residue foods are bran cereal, whole wheat bread, pumpkin, squash or celery; or you can add Miller's Bran, one to two tablespoons a day for the average size dog.

In an old dog with an inactive bowel, soaking the kibble with equal parts of water can aid him greatly. Let the mixture stand for 20 minutes.

Mild cases of constipation can be treated with a laxative such as mineral oil or Milk of Magnesia. The usual dose is one-half to two tablespoons a day, depending on the size of the dog. Do not give laxatives on a regular basis. Instead, use milk or liver, which have a laxative effect.

A fecal impaction requires an enema. Enemas are given at the rate of one ounce of fluid per ten pounds of body weight. Several kinds are used. Fleet Oil Retention enemas can be purchased over the counter. They come in plastic bottles with attached nozzles. Lubricate the nozzle well and insert it into the anal canal.

Tap water enemas are given through a rubber catheter connected to an enema bag. Lubricate the tip and insert it far enough into the anus so that the rectum retains the fluid. Two to three inches usually is far enough. If the dog struggles, the catheter could injure the wall of his rectum. Warm water enemas are particularly good for treating constipation caused by grass eating.

Voluntary Retention: The urge to defecate can be over-ridden. Puppies learn to do this as they are house-trained. When carried to an extreme, the stools become excessively dry and hard, due to prolonged water absorption by the bowel. Passage then becomes difficult. Dogs left alone in the house are prone to this disorder. Some dogs refuse to go when away from home.

Treatment: Provide opportunity for your dog to go out several times a day and relieve himself. A mild laxative may be indicated when dogs are traveling.

Mechanical Blockage:

In older males, an enlarged prostate can bulge into the anal canal, acting as a valve which pinches off the rectum.

Hernias in the rectal area (perineal hernias) weaken the muscular support of the rectum. This interferes with the mechanics of elimination. This diagnosis can be made by observing a bulge along side the anus. The bulge becomes larger as the dog strains.

Boston Terriers and Bulldogs with screw tails often have a rigid extension of the tail which extends down upon the anal canal, pinching it against the pelvic floor.

Tumors and strictures are other causes of mechanical blockage.

Treatment: In these cases it is advisable to feed a *low* residue or bland diet, such as Hills I/D. Soak food well with equal parts of water. A stool softener is recommended. Hydrolose and Mucilose, obtained through veterinarians or pet stores, are good ones. Mineral oil lubricates the stool, making it easier to pass.

Constipation associated with the screw tail usually requires surgical correction of the tied-down tail.

Damaged Nerves:

A nerve paralysis, usually found with "slipped discs" and fractures of the spine, results in loss of the urge to defecate. The muscles used to evacuate the bowel also may be paralyzed.

Treatment: This bowel condition can be difficult to treat. Enemas and laxatives, along with measures outlined in the treatment of *chronic constipation* may be effective.

False Constipation (Pseudoconstipation)

This is a form of voluntary retention caused by inflammation of the anus. It is common in long-haired dogs. Soft stool matts in the hair around the anus, causing a barrier. The skin becomes irritated, tender and infected. Dogs with this problem try to defecate while standing. Other signs are whining, scooting, and biting at the rear. The odor is extremely offensive.

Treatment: Dogs with long coats should be groomed around the anus to prevent the build up of stool. When present, clip away the matted stool to let air get to the skin. If it is weepy-looking, apply a topical antibiotic ointment (Polysporin). Follow the diet recommended for *Mechanical Blockage*.

Passing Gas *(Flatus)*

Dogs that continually pass gas embarrass or distress their owners. This condition, called flatus, is caused by eating highly fermentable foods such as onions, beans, cauliflower, cabbage and soybeans; or drinking large quantities of milk. Diets high in meats predispose to it.

Treatment: If a diet change does not control the problem, you may want to suppress undesirable gas-forming bacteria by giving your dog a course of antibiotics by mouth (Tetracycline, Chlormycetin). The antibiotic is given for five days. Afterwards, the bowel should be repopulated with more desirable non-gas forming bacteria. Accomplish this by giving cultured buttermilk or yogurt for a week.

Eating Stool *(Coprophagia)*

Coprophagia is the name given to the habit of eating stools — either the dog's own or another animal's. Some stools have taste appeal to dogs, particularly those containing partially digested food. Once established, the habit is difficult to break.

Do not allow your dog to eat stools — both for aesthetic reasons and because stools are a source of intestinal upset and carry germs and parasites.

Treatment: A poor quality diet may be at fault. Feed high quality dry kibble as a base with canned meat supplement not in excess of 25 percent.

Sprinkle a meat tenderizer (such as Adolph's) on the food as an aid in its digestion. A product called *Forbid* (which is made from alfalfa) works well when added to the diet. When digested, it gives the stool a disagreeable odor and taste.

ANUS AND RECTUM

The signs of anorectal disease are pain on defecation, repeated straining, the passage of bright blood, and anal scooting.

Dogs with anorectal pain often try to defecate from a standing position.

Bleeding from the anus or rectum is recognized by the finding of blood on the outside of the stool, rather than mixed in with it.

Scooting is a sign of anal itching. It is caused by flea bites, stool adherent to the perianal area, and anal sac disease. Less commonly it is due to roundworms or tapeworm segments.

Sore Bottom *(Proctitis)*

Irritation of the anorectal canal can be caused by the passage of bone chips and other sharp objects in the feces — or by hard dry stool. Repeated bouts of diarrhea (especially in puppies) can cause a proctitis. Insect bites, worms, and false constipation are other causes.

The signs of proctitis are scooting, licking and biting at the rear; and in severe cases, straining.

Treatment: An irritated anus can be soothed by applying an ointment such as vaseline, or one of the hemorrhoidal preparations used by people. Put your dog on a bland diet and feed small amounts more often (see *False Constipation*).

Protrusion of Anal Tissue *(Anal and Rectal Prolapse)*

With forceful and prolonged straining, the dog can protrude the lining of his anal canal. This is a *partial* prolapse and is confined to the surface membrane. In severe cases a complete segment of intestine may drop down; it is then called a *complete* prolapse. It can be as long as several inches. The difference is quite evident on examination. Protrusion of anal tissue might be mistaken for hemorrhoids; but for practical purposes, hemorrhoids do not occur in dogs.

Simple anal prolapse is easily treated at home, but depends upon correcting the cause of straining (see *Constipation* and *Diarrhea*). Apply a topical anesthetic (Benzocaine Ointment) to reduce pain. Treatment is the same as *Proctitis*.

A complete rectal prolapse can be replaced manually. Clean the tissue and lubricate it with vaseline. Then gently push it back up through the anus. To prevent recurrence, usually it is necessary for your veterinarian to take a temporary purse string suture around the anus to hold it in place while healing.

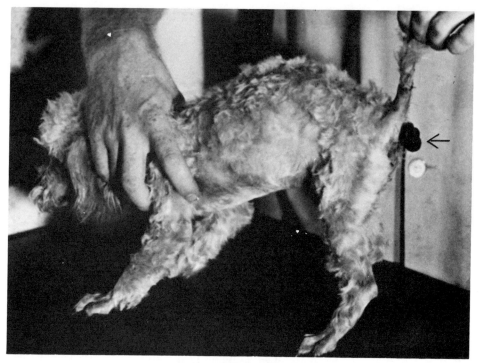

Complete *rectal prolapse.*

Lack of anal opening in a newborn pup *(imperforate anus).*

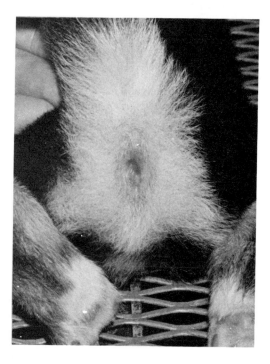

Malformation of Anus:

(Imperforate Anus and Rectovaginal Fistula)
In these two conditions found in newborn puppies the anus does not properly develop. When the opening is absent, there is no passage for stool. Abdominal distention appears right after pups start to nurse. When the anus opens into the vagina, stool passes out an intensely irritated vulva. Both conditions require surgical correction if the pup is to survive.

ANAL GLANDS OR SACS

The dog has two anal glands or sacs located at about five and seven o'clock in reference to the circumference of the anus. The openings of the anal sacs are found by drawing down on the skin of the lower part of the anus. By applying a small amount of pressure directly below these openings, fluid can be expressed.

These sacs are sometimes referred to as the "scent" sacs. In the skunk they serve a protective purpose. In the dog they appear to be of use in territorial marking, and to enable dogs to identify one another. This probably accounts for the fact that dogs greet each other by sniffing at the rear.

The anal sacs normally are emptied by rectal pressure during defecation. The secretions are liquid and brownish. At times they may be thick, yellow or creamy-looking.

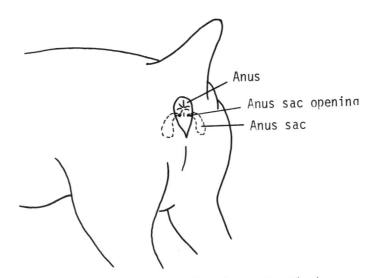

Anus

Anus sac opening

Anus sac

Position of the anal sacs and openings. —*Rose Floyd*

Anal sacs also are emptied whenever there is sudden contraction of the anal sphincter; this causes a characteristic odor when a dog is upset, frightened, or under pressure. It is the usual practice in grooming parlors to express the glands before bathing the dog, thus keeping him free of "doggy" odor afterward.

In most dogs it is not necessary to express the glands unless there is some medical reason to do so. However, when frequent odor does pose a problem (for example, in a dog with overactive anal sacs), you can control it by expressing the sacs yourself.

How to Empty the Anal Sacs

Raise the dog's tail and locate the openings of the anal sacs as described above. You can feel the sacs as small, firm lumps in the perianal area at the five and seven o'clock positions. Grasp the perianal skin surrounding the sac with your thumb and forefinger, push in and squeeze together. As the sac empties, a pungent odor is noted. Wipe the secretions away with a damp cloth. If the discharge is bloody or purulent-looking, anal sac infection is present and you should treat it as described on the next page.

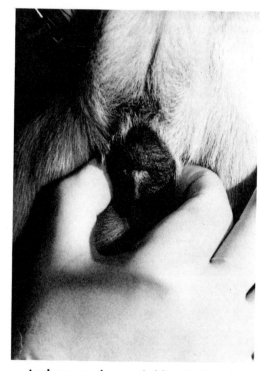

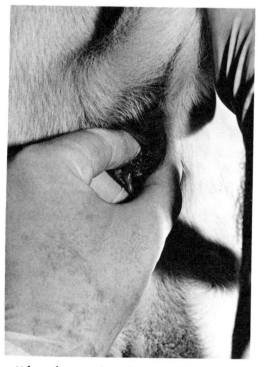

Anal sacs can be emptied by pinching the anal skin between your fingers.

When obstructed, anal sacs may have to be expressed with one finger in the anal canal.
—*J. Clawson*

Impaction of Anal Sacs

Impaction of the anal sacs occurs when the sacs fail to empty normally. It is most common in the smaller breeds. Some of the common causes are soft stools (not enough sphincter pressure), small anal sac openings, and overactive anal sacs. Secretions become thick and pasty. Anal sac impaction is treated by manual emptying.

Anal Sac Infection *(Anal Sacculitis)*

This condition complicates impaction. It is recognized by the presence of blood or pus in the secretions, signs of anal pain, and scooting.

Treatment: Empty the anal sacs and instill an antibiotic preparation into the sacs through the duct openings. An antibiotic preparation such as Panolog, which comes in a tube with a small rounded tip at the end, can be used to pack the anal sacs. Insert the tip of the tube into the opening and squeeze. Repeat the packing process in two days. Administer a broad spectrum antibiotic by mouth (Chloromycetin or Tetracycline).

Anal Sac Abscess

An abscessed anal sac is recognized by the signs of anal infection with swelling at the site of the gland. The swelling is at first red, then later turns a deep purple.

Treatment: An abscess is ready to drain when it becomes fluctuant (soft and fluid-like). At this point it should be lanced. Pus and blood will drain out. The abscess cavity must heal from the bottom out. Keep the edges apart by flushing the cavity twice daily with a dilute peroxide solution. Administer an oral antibiotic. Healing usually is uneventful.

Dogs with recurrent anal gland infections need to have their glands removed.

Perianal Fistulas

Fistulas are open draining tracts and sores in the perianal skin. Usually there is an internal opening in the anorectal canal. They are most common in German Shepherds, but are found in Irish Setters, English Setters, Labradors and other breeds. The symptoms are similar to anal sac abscess, but fistulas are not responsive to simple treatment. Surgical removal by your veterinarian usually is required.

Polyps and Cancer

Polyps are grape-like growths which occur in the rectum and protrude from the anus. They are not common. When present, they should be removed.

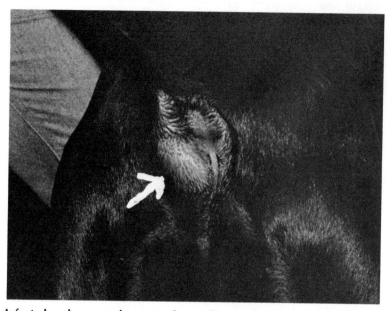

Infected anal sacs produce a tender swelling at the side of the anus *(anal sac abscess)*. They should be incised and allowed to drain.

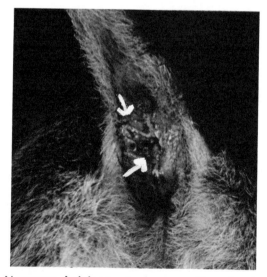

Numerous draining tracts are seen with *perianal fistula*.

Cancers of the anorectal canal are not common. They appear as fleshy growths which ulcerate and bleed. When they grow in the rectum, the signs are those of a prolonged proctitis — straining being one of the most common findings. The diagnosis is made by obtaining a fragment of tissue for microscopic examination.

Perianal Adenoma

This is the most common growth about the anus. It can be seen from the outside as a firm nodule beneath the skin next to the anus. Adenomas are found principally in male dogs over seven years of age. Their growth is under the influence of the male hormone. As they enlarge, they break through the skin and start to ulcerate and bleed. Ordinarily, they remain localized at the site of origin. Most of them are not cancers; a few metastasize and end fatally.

Growth of perianal adenomas can be suppressed by giving estrogens. Excision of small adenomas leads to cure. Large or ulcerating growths are best treated by a combination of excision and castration.

LIVER

The liver has many vital metabolic functions. They include synthesis of proteins and sugars, removal of wastes from the blood, manufacture of enzymes (including those which cause blood to clot), and detoxification of drugs and poisons.

A common sign of liver disease is *jaundice*, in which bile backs up into the circulation, turning the whites of the eyes yellow and the urine tea-colored.

Spontaneous bleeding is a sign of advanced liver disease. Common sites of bleeding are the stomach, intestines, and urinary tract. Bruises can appear under the lips and skin.

Some common causes of liver insufficiency are: infections (hepatitis, leptospirosis); poisons; vitamin deficiencies (B-Complex); bile duct obstructions; cancers (primary and metastatic); cirrhosis; and heartworm infestation.

Symptoms of liver disease are variable, depending on the nature of the disorder. Dogs usually lose weight, become nauseated, vomit, seem apathetic, and may appear jaundiced or begin to bleed spontaneously. The liver involvement often is just one aspect of a generalized illness.

Treatment depends upon making the diagnosis. This can require hospitalization and a complete work-up.

PANCREAS

The pancreas has two main functions. The first is to provide digestive enzymes; and the second is to make insulin for sugar metabolism.

Pancreatic enzymes are secreted into the small intestine through the pancreatic duct. A lack of these enzymes causes a digestive disturbance called pancreatic insufficiency (see *Malabsorption Syndrome*).

Insulin is secreted directly into the circulation. It acts upon cell membranes, enabling sugar to enter the cells, where it is metabolized to form energy.

Sugar Diabetes *(Diabetes Mellitus)*

Sugar diabetes affects all organs. It is due to inadequate production of insulin by the pancreas.

Without insulin, the body can't utilize sugar in the blood. It builds up. Soon there is an excess which the kidneys must get rid of. This results in excessive urination. There is a need to compensate for the fluid loss by drinking lots of water.

Glycosuria is the name given to sugar in the urine. When a urine sugar test is positive, diabetes can be suspected.

Acids (ketones) are formed in the blood of diabetics because of inability to metabolize sugar. High levels lead to a condition called *ketoacidosis*. It is characterized by acetone on the breath (a sweetish odor that smells like nailpolish remover); labored rapid breathing; and eventually diabetic coma.

In the early stage of diabetes a dog will try to compensate for his inability to metabolize sugar by eating more food. Later, as he suffers the effects of malnourishment, there is a drop in appetite.

Accordingly, the signs of early diabetes are frequent urination, drinking lots of water, a large appetite, and unexplained loss of weight. The laboratory findings are sugar and acetone in the urine, and a high blood sugar.

In more advanced cases there is loss of appetite, vomiting, weakness, ketone breath, dehydration, labored breathing, lethargy, and finally coma. Cataracts are common in the diabetic dog.

Treatment: Dietary control and daily injections of insulin can regulate most diabetic dogs, allowing them to lead a normal life. The amount of insulin cannot be predicted on the basis of weight. It must be established for each individual. It is important for success of initial therapy that each dog be hospitalized to determine his daily insulin requirement.

As insulin requirements vary with the diet, it is important that the number of calories your dog takes in be kept constant from day to day. Accomplish this by feeding him a balanced high quality dog food. His diet may have to be changed from time to time for periods of stress, illness, and loss of appetite. Follow your veterinarian's instructions.

Insulin substitutes by mouth (such as those used for people) have been relatively unsuccessful in treating diabetic dogs.

Insulin Overdose:

When an overdose of insulin is given, it causes a drop in blood sugar below normal level. Suspect this if your dog appears confused, disoriented, drowsy, shivers, staggers about, or collapses.

Treatment: If the dog is conscious, give him sugar in water, candy, syrup, or orange juice. If unable to treat, seek professional help.

Inflamed Pancreas *(Acute Pancreatitis)*

Sudden swelling of the pancreas typically occurs in dogs two to eleven years of age (the average is six years). Individuals prone to acute pancreatitis are housepets (a) fed table scraps; (b) poorly exercised; and (c) those who indulge by overeating.

In mild cases the signs are obscure and perhaps easily overlooked. There may be loss of appetite, periodic vomiting and diarrhea. The more serious form comes on suddenly as an acute pain in the abdomen with a rigid abdominal wall. The pain is due to release of digestive enzymes into the abdominal cavity, leading to auto-digestion of surrounding tissues.

If a dog recovers from an acute episode his pancreas may not return to normal. Instead, he may acquire diabetes or a malabsorption syndrome.

It is important to distinguish between acute pancreatitis and other causes of painful abdomen such as bloat. Treatment is quite different.

10

Respiratory System

GENERAL REMARKS

The dog's respiratory system is made up of the nasal passages, throat, voice box, windpipe and bronchial tubes. The latter branch and become progressively smaller until they open into the air sacs. It is here that air exchanges with the blood.

The lungs are composed of the breathing tubes, air sacs and blood vessels.

The ribs and muscles of the chest, along with the diaphragm, function as a bellows, moving air into and out of the lungs.

A dog normally breathes about 10 to 30 times a minute at rest. It takes about twice as long for him to exhale as it does to inhale. His respiratory motion should be smooth, even, unrestrained.

A sustained increase in the rate of breathing at rest, or the presence of coarse breathing, wheezing, rasping, coughing, and bubbling in the chest, indicates an abnormal state.

ABNORMAL BREATHING

Rapid Breathing

Rapid breathing can be caused by *pain,* emotional stress, fever and overheating (for example, over-exertion or overheated surroundings). Other conditions to consider are shock (reduced circulation, hemorrhage), lung and heart disease (not enough oxygen in the blood), and acid build up (diabetes, kidney disease). Dehydration due to prolonged diarrhea and various toxic states will cause the dog to breath rapidly.

An increased rate of breathing at rest suggests a diseased state and veterinarian examination is necessary.

Panting

Panting is a normal process by which the dog lowers his body temperature. This is accomplished by the evaporation of water from the mouth, tongue and lungs, and by the exchange of cooler air for the warm air in his lungs.

When panting is rapid and labored and accompanied by an anxious look the possibility of heat stroke should be considered (see *Heat Stroke*).

Noisy Breathing

Noisy breathing is synonymous with obstructed breathing. If your dog begins to make noise as he breathes, and especially if he is having difficulty, he should have veterinarian attention.

Elongated Soft Palate. Bulldogs, Pugs, Pekingese, and breeds with "pushed-in" faces frequently show some degree of airway obstruction manifested by mouth breathing, snorting and snoring. These difficulties are more pronounced during exercise and when the dog is hot. They tend to get worse as the dog gets older. In some cases the mouth breathing may be associated with collapsed nostrils.

The problem in the Bulldog breeds is that the palate partially blocks the opening into the voice box. In time, the secondary changes in the voice box lead to attacks of acute airway obstruction (see *Laryngeal Collapse*). Surgical treatment (before laryngeal involvement) often will give permanent relief.

Croupy Breathing

This refers to the high harsh sound caused by air passing through a narrowed voice box. When the onset is sudden, the most likely diagnosis is laryngitis.

Wheezing

A wheeze is a whistling which occurs when a dog attempts to breathe in or out. It indicates narrowing or spasm in the windpipe or bronchial tubes. Tight deep-seated wheezes are best heard with a stethoscope. Causes of wheezing are chronic lung disease, congestive heart failure, and tumors or growths in the airways.

Shallow Breathing

Shallow breathing is seen with conditions which restrict the motion of the rib cage. In most cases it is associated with splinting. To avoid the pain of a deep breath, the dog breathes rapidly but less deeply. Pain of pleurisy and rib fracture causes splinting.

Fluid in the chest (blood, pus or serum) produces restricted breathing without pain.

COUGH

Cough is a reflex which is initiated by an irritant in the air passages. It is a sign common to many diseases which occur in the dog.

A cough may be caused by an infection (virus, bacteria, fungus or parasite), an inhaled irritant such as smoke or chemicals, foreign objects such as grass seeds and food particles, and pressure from tight collars or growths of the air passages. Some coughs are due to allergies.

The type of cough often suggests its location and probable cause:

A high, harsh, dry, barking cough is typical of kennel cough (cough without phlegm).

A moist bubbling cough indicates fluid and phlegm.

A high, weak, gagging cough associated with swallowing or licking of the lips is characteristic of tonsillitis and sore throat.

A deep, tight, wheezy cough is heard with chronic and allergic bronchitis.

A spasm of prolonged coughing, which follows exercise or occurs at night, suggests heart disease.

A cough which occurs after drinking may be due to leakage of fluid into the windpipe from faulty closure of the epiglottis.

Coughs are self-perpetuating. Coughing itself irritates the airways, drys out the mucus lining, and lowers resistance to infection — leading to further coughing.

Treatment: Only minor coughs of brief duration should be treated without professional assistance. Coughs accompanied by fever, difficulty breathing, discharge from the eyes and nose, or other signs of a serious illness require veterinary attention.

It is important to identify and correct any other contributing problem. Air pollutants such as cigarette smoke, aerosol insecticides, house dust and perfumes should be eliminated from the atmosphere. Nose, throat, lung and heart disorders should be treated if present.

A variety of children's cough suppressants are available at drug stores for the treatment of mild coughs. Their purpose is to decrease the frequency and severity of the cough. They do not treat the disease or condition causing it. Therefore, over-use may delay diagnosis and treatment. If you decide to use one of these preparations, the dose for puppies is the same as that for infants. Medium size dogs should be given a child's dose and large dogs an adult's dose. Administer every 4 to 6 hours. (Cough suppressants should not be given to dogs in whom phlegm is being brought up or swallowed. These coughs are clearing unwanted material from the airway.)

VOICE BOX (Larynx)

The larynx is a short oblong box located in the throat above the windpipe. It is composed of cartilage and contains the vocal cords, which in dogs are large and prominent. A bark is produced when air is forced rapidly out of the lungs through the larynx.

The larynx is the most sensitive cough area in the body. At the top of the larynx is the epiglottis, a leaf-like flap that covers it during swallowing, keeping food from going down the windpipe.

Disorders of the larynx give rise to coughing, croupy breathing, and hoarseness.

Hoarseness and Loss of Bark *(Laryngitis)*

Hoarseness and loss of volume of the bark often is due to excessive barking or coughing (voice strain). It improves with voice rest and treatment of the cough when present.

When the condition becomes chronic, vocal cord paralysis or some condition causing narrowing of the voice box should be suspected.

Acute laryngitis in the dog usually is just one aspect of a more extensive process such as tonsillitis, or acute tracheobronchitis (see *Kennel Cough*).

Laryngeal Blockage

Laryngospasm. Sudden spasm of the vocal cords may cut off the air supply. The dog becomes frantic in his efforts to get air, turns blue at the mouth and collapses. Recovery usually is rapid. Recurrent attacks suggest to many owners a seizure disorder.

Laryngospasm usually is caused by a drop of mucus which falls upon the vocal cords from the soft palate. Thus it is associated with chronic throat irritations.

Object in the Voice Box. The sudden onset of severe coughing and respiratory distress in a healthy dog suggests a foreign body caught in the larynx. This is an emergency. Get your dog to the veterinarian as quickly as possible.

If he collapses, he is not getting enough air. Immediately perform the *Heimlich Maneuver*. Lay him on his side, place your palms just behind the last rib and give four quick thrusts. The maneuver thrusts the diaphragm upward and produces a forceful exhalation of air. Usually this dislodges the object (commonly it is a large piece of meat). Check his mouth to see if the object has been dislodged — if not, repeat the thrusts.

Foreign bodies caught in the larynx are not common. Most food particles are of little consequence because the resulting cough expels them.

(Note: If your dog is *choking, gagging and retching,* probably he has a foreign body such as a bone, splinter or rubber ball caught in his throat.

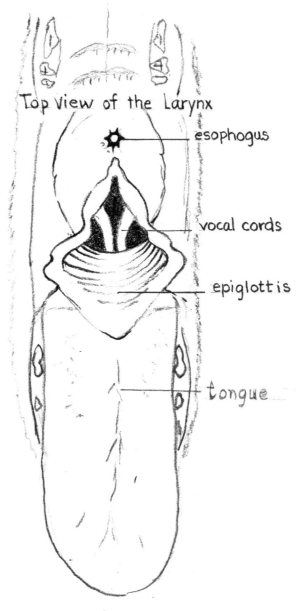

Top view of the Larynx

esophogus

vocal cords

epiglottis

tongue

The Larynx.

Open his mouth and see if you can find the cause of the trouble — see ORAL CAVITY.)

Vocal Cord Paralysis. This is an acquired condition in middle-aged and older dogs of the large breeds and occurs as a congenital defect in Siberian Huskies. It can be recognized by a characteristic croupy noise during inspiration, or "roaring", as it is sometimes called. It comes on gradually and may appear at first only after strenuous activity or emotional upsets. Sometimes there is a progressive weakening of the bark, or hoarseness, finally ending in a croaky whisper. This condition sometimes can be helped by surgery.

Laryngeal Collapse. This is the final stage of long-standing problems which affect the voice boxes of dogs with elongated palate or a vocal cord paralysis. At this stage the opening through the larynx is quite small. Any change in the dog's need for air can cause a sudden collapse.

Treatment: If a veterinarian is not immediately available, give the dog a mild sedative or tranquilizer and put him in a humid atmosphere. Humidifiers are helpful, but if one is not available then steam from a shower can be used. Do not overheat the atmosphere. This can interfere with the dog's cooling mechanism and make matters worse.

BREATHING TUBES (Trachea and Bronchi)

Foreign Bodies in the Windpipe

Grass seeds and food particles are the most common foreign material of sufficient size to lodge in the windpipe or bronchus when inhaled by the dog. Most of these are quickly coughed up. If an object becomes lodged in the airway it causes intense irritation and swelling of the passage.

Sudden attacks of coughing after a field trip or immediately after vomiting suggest aspiration of a foreign body.

Treatment: Give your dog a mild sedative or tranquilizer to settle his nerves and have him seen by your veterinarian. Cough medicines should be avoided since they serve no purpose and delay treatment. Foreign objects can be located by chest x-ray or by direct inspection via a bronchoscope.

Collapsed Windpipe (Tracheal Collapse)

Collapse of the cartilages of the windpipe occurs as a birth defect in Chihuahuas, Poms, Toy Poodles and other Toy breed dogs, but usually does not cause problems until the dog is mature. Signs are croupy breathing and a honking cough.

Weight control is an important factor in management. Overweight dogs are far more symptomatic. Treatment may require surgery.

Kennel Cough (*Acute Tracheobronchitis*)

Kennel cough is a highly contagious respiratory infection in dogs. It takes its name from the fact that dogs often catch it while boarding at a kennel where they are exposed to other dogs who either have the disease or are carriers of it. It is due to one of several viruses. Certain types of bacteria are occasionally found, but only as secondary invaders, perpetuating the cough.

While kennel cough is the most common form of tracheobronchitis in dogs, other causes of inflammation of the lining of the upper airway, including distemper and canine infectious hepatitis should be considered in the differential diagnosis, especially if the dog was not immunized against them.

A harsh, dry, spastic cough is the characteristic sign of this illness. Otherwise, the dog looks bright and alert, eats relatively well and seems to maintain his overall condition. Mild cases, given rest and proper care, usually heal in two weeks.

In puppies, kennel cough is a more serious illness. It may be accompanied by nasal congestion. The narrow airways of youngsters are prone to obstruction. Puppies may need intensive support to loosen thick secretions, improve breathing and prevent pneumonia. This is also true of Toy breeds.

Treatment: Dogs suspected of having kennel cough should be isolated so as not to infect others. Be sure to take your dog's temperature every day. A fever indicates a complication.

Rest and proper humidification of the atmosphere are important items in the treatment of bronchitis. Confine your dog in a warm room and use a home vaporizer. A cold steam vaporizer offers some advantage over a heat vaporizer because it is less likely to cause additional breathing problems due to the heat.

Daily exercise of a moderate nature is beneficial as it assists in bronchial drainage. Strenuous exercise should be avoided.

Coughing helps to clear the bronchial tree, but excessive spasms of dry, unproductive cough can cause greater irritation and lead to exhaustion. Cough suppressants may be indicated (see *Cough*).

Antibiotics are important in the management of kennel cough. They are used to prevent secondary invaders rather than treat the cough virus, which is not sensitive to antibiotics. Ampicillin and Chloromycetin may be used.

Vaccines effective against some of the kennel cough viruses are available (see *Vaccinations*). They will not prevent all cases.

Chronic bronchitis is a common sequel to kennel cough.

Chronic Bronchitis

Most cases of chronic bronchitis begin as another respiratory infection such as kennel cough. The natural defenses of the respiratory tract are weakened by the primary infection and it is easy for secondary invaders to take over. The situation becomes a chronic one.

Dogs with chronic bronchitis cough for days and weeks, run low grade fever and lose condition. The cough is harsh and often ends with retching and expectoration of foamy saliva.

Treatment: The treatment is generally the same as for kennel cough except that the phlegm should be cultured. The dog then may be given the specific antibiotic which best suits his needs. It should be given for a minimum of 10 days.

Asthma

Asthma, or bronchial asthma, is a form of allergy which affects the larger breathing tubes. It is accompanied by cough and wheezing. The wheezing is heard as the dog exhales and usually it is loud enough to be heard by the naked ear.

Pollens are the chief cause of asthmatic attacks (see *Allergy*). Repeated bouts can eventually lead to chronic lung disease.

Asthma is uncommon in the dog.

Treatment: Asthmatic dogs should begin to improve in an allergy free atmosphere. Antihistamines can be quite helpful. They have a dilating effect on the airways, reduce irritation, and are mildly sedative. Benadryl, Chlor-Trimeton, and Coricidin are effective preparations. They may cause drowsiness. When this occurs, reduce the dose or give the medication less often.

Steroids are sometimes used in the management of the asthmatic dog. They should be administered only under veterinary supervision.

Bronchiectasis

This is the name given to a condition in which one or more of the bronchial tubes becomes dilated and sack-like. It occurs below a point of obstruction in a breathing tube.

Airways become obstructed by inspissated mucus, aspiration of foreign objects such as grass awns and regurgitated food, and bronchial tumors. Mucus collects below the obstruction and forms an ideal media for bacterial growth and infection. The result is destruction of the bronchial wall and dilatation of the bronchus.

Symptoms: They are long-standing cough with production of purulent sputum, periodic fever, and loss of weight and condition. Bronchiectasis often will be mistaken for chronic bronchitis. Exact diagnosis requires special x-ray studies.

Treatment: When the disease is localized to one segment of the lung, surgical removal is the treatment of choice. If the disease is generalized, the treatment is similar to that for chronic bronchitis.

The dog with bronchiectasis is extremely susceptible to respiratory infections and without vigorous and often continued antibotic therapy he will have frequent bouts of pneumonia.

LUNGS

Pneumonia

Pneumonia is an infection of the lungs. Usually it is classified according to its cause: viral, bacterial, fungal, parasitic, or inhalation in type.

The general symptoms of pneumonia are high fever, rapid breathing, splinting, cough, fast pulse, rattling and bubbling in the chest. When severe enough to cause oxygen lack, you will notice a blue cast to the conjunctiva of the lower eyelid.

Dogs with pneumonia characteristically sit with their heads extended and elbows turned out to allow for greater expansion of the chest. When lying down, their chest cavity is further restricted. This interferes with air exchange so they avoid it.

Treatment: Pneumonia is a serious condition and requires confirmation by laboratory diagnosis and x-ray.

Until a veterinarian is available, move your dog to warm dry quarters and humidify the air. Give him plenty of water. Treat his fever with aspirin or Tylenol. Do not give cough medicine. Coughing in pneumonia helps to clear the airways.

Most cases of pneumonia respond to an antibiotic specific for the causative agent. Your veterinarian will select an appropriate one.

11

Circulatory System

The circulatory system is composed of the heart, the blood and the blood vessels.

HEART

The heart is a pump made up of four chambers: the right atrium and right ventricle, and the left atrium and left ventricle. The two sides of the heart are separated by a muscular wall. In the normal heart blood cannot get from one side to the other without first going through the general circulation or the pulmonary circulation. Four valves are present. Their function is to keep blood flowing in one direction. When the valves are diseased, blood can leak backwards creating difficulties.

Physiology

Blood, which is pumped out of the left ventricle into the aorta, passes through arteries of progressively smaller caliber until it reaches the capillary beds of the skin, muscle, brain and internal organs. It is conducted back to the heart through veins of progressively larger diameter, finally reaching the right atrium via two large veins called the anterior and posterior *vena cavae*.

The blood then passes into the right ventricle and out into the pulmonary circulation through the pulmonary artery. The pulmonary artery branches into smaller vessels and finally into capillaries (around the air sacs), where gas exchange occurs. From here the blood returns via the pulmonary vein to the ventricles — thus completing the circle.

The beating of the heart is controlled by its own internal nervous system. The force and rate of the heart beat is influenced by outside nervous and hormonal factors, too. Thus the rate speeds up when the dog exercises, becomes excited, runs fever, is overheated, is in shock — or in any circumstance in which more blood flow to the tissues is needed.

Heart rhythms follow a fixed pattern which can be seen on an

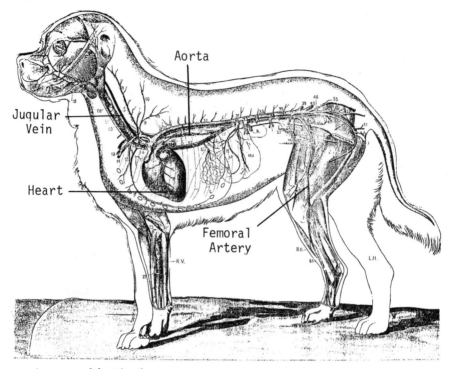

Anatomy of the Circulatory System. —*Robert Leighton, The New Book of the Dog*

electrocardiogram. Whether the heart beats fast or slow, the sequence in which the various muscle fibers contract remains the same. This sequence causes a synchronized beat, allowing both ventricles to empty at the same time. Heart disease can upset this normal pattern, causing arrhythmias.

The arteries and veins also are under nervous and hormonal influences. They can expand or contract to maintain a correct blood pressure.

There are outward physical signs which help to determine if a dog's heart and circulation are working properly. Familiarize yourself with the normal findings so you can recognize abnormal signs if they appear.

Pulse. The pulse, which is a reflection of the heart beat, is easily detected by feeling the artery located in the groin (femoral artery). With your dog standing or lying on his back, feel along the inside of his thigh where his leg joins his body. Press with your fingers until you locate the pulsation. Alternately, take the pulse by pressing against the rib cage over the heart. With the dog standing, feel the chest pulse just below the elbow joint. If the heart is enlarged or diseased, you may be able to detect a buzzing, or vibration, over the chest wall.

The pulse rate, which is the same as the heart rate, can be determined by counting the number of beats in a minute. Most dogs run a rate of 70 to 130 beats per minute at rest. In large dogs it is somewhat slower and in small dogs somewhat faster. It is faster in puppies. Well-conditioned, athletic dogs run a slower pulse.

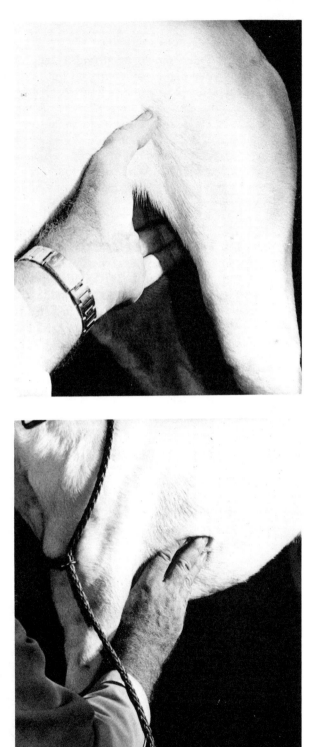

To take your dog's pulse, feel along the inside of his thigh where his leg joins his body. Press with your fingers to locate the pulsation.

Another way to take the pulse is to feel for the heart beat in back of the left elbow. —*J. Clawson*

The pulse should be strong, steady and regular. A slight alteration in rate as your dog breathes in and out is normal. An exceedingly fast pulse indicates fever, anemia, blood loss, dehydration, shock, infection, heat stroke, or heart (and lung) disease. A very slow pulse can indicate heart disease, pressure on the brain or an advanced morbid condition causing collapse of the circulation.

An erratic, irregular or disordered pulse suggests an arryhthmia which is a serious condition. When untreated, it can cause the heart to fail.

Various drugs your dog might be taking can affect the rate and rhythm of the heart.

Heart Sounds. Veterinarians use a stethoscope to listen to the heart. You can listen to the heart by placing your ear against the chest. Or you can hold an ordinary drinking glass over the heart and listen through the open end.

The normal heart beat is divided into two separate sounds. The first is a LUB, followed by a slight pause; and then a DUB. Put together the sound is LUB-DUB . . . LUB-DUB . . . in a steady, regular manner.

When the heart sounds can be heard all over the chest the heart probably is enlarged. A running-together of the sounds, and interrupted rhythm, is abnormal.

Murmurs. Murmurs are caused by a turbulence in the flow of blood through the heart. Serious ones are due to heart valve disease or birth defects. Anemia can cause a heart murmur.

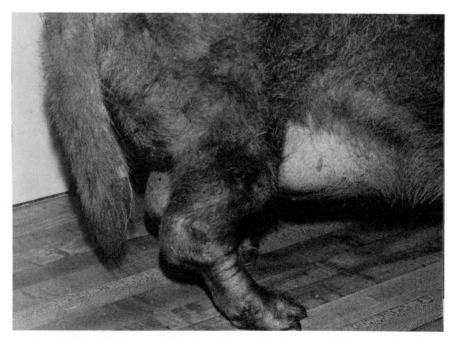

Heart failure, showing swelling of the legs and fluid accumulation beneath skin.

Not all murmurs are serious. Some are called functional—that is, there is no disease, just a normal degree of turbulence. Your veterinarian can determine whether a murmur is serious or of little consequence.

Thrills. A thrill is caused by turbulence of such a degree that you can feel a buzzing or vibration over the heart. It suggests an obstruction to the flow of blood — for example, a narrowed valve or a hole in the heart. A thrill indicates a heart condition.

Circulation. If you examine the gums or the inner eyelids, you can gain a clue to the adequacy of your dog's circulation. A deep pink color is a sign of adequate circulation.

The quality of the circulation can be tested by noting the time it takes for the tissue to pink-up after the gums have been pressed firmly with a finger. With normal circulation the response is immediate (one second or less). A delay of two seconds suggests poor circulation. When the finger impression remains pale for three seconds or longer, the dog is in shock.

A gray or bluish tinge to the mucus membranes of the lips and tongue is a sign of insufficient oxygen in the blood (cyanosis). It can be seen in heart and lung failure.

HEART FAILURE

Heart failure may be defined as the inability of the heart to provide adequate circulation to meet the body's needs. It is the end result of weakened heart muscle. It is not a simple condition. The liver, kidneys, lungs and other systems are affected, too, causing a multiple organ-system problem. Most cases represent long-standing conditions which have over-stressed or damaged the heart.

Coronary artery disease or hardening of the arteries, a condition brought about in man by aging, is rare in the dog. Dogs' hearts seem to age in a different way. In dogs, it is the valves and the muscles of the heart which suffer. Valves begin to leak blood backwards,and the pump works less forcefully. The exact cause of this aging process is not yet well understood, but it leads to a condition called *Chronic Valvular and Myocardial Heart Disease*. It is one of the leading heart problems in the older dog. Other causes of heart disease are birth defects, heartworms, and infectious diseases.

When a diseased heart begins to weaken, signs of right or left-sided failure occur. Symptoms differ. The treatment of heart disease is directed at preventing and treating failure.

Left Heart Failure

When the left ventricle starts to fail, pressure builds up in the pulmonary circulation. The result is lung congestion and accumulation of fluid in the air sacs. In late stages (pulmonary edema), dogs cough up a bubbly red fluid, and can't get enough oxygen. Aging is the most common predisposing factor in the older dog. In the younger one, it is congenital heart disease (birth defect).

The early signs of left-sided heart failure are impaired exercise ability and shortness of breath. A hunting dog may tire after an hour or two. As the condition advances, the dog begins to cough when overtaxed by excitement or strenuous exercise. In many cases the cough is first noted at night — about two hours after retiring.

Despite an adequate intake, a dog with heart disease begins to look unthrifty and loses condition. The coat becomes dry and lusterless. His body thins and the muscles over his head waste away, making the bones appear more prominent.

In advanced cases, breathing is labored and the dog assumes a characteristic sitting position with his elbows spread apart and his head extended to take in more air. He may attempt to sleep sitting up. His pulse is rapid, weak, sometimes irregular. A thrill may be felt over the barrel-like chest.

Anxiety and fainting, occurring late in the disease, can be mistaken for a seizure disorder.

Right Heart Failure

When the right heart muscle starts to fail, pressure backs up in the veins, causing congestive heart failure. In advanced cases the gums are gray (cyanosis), and the limbs are swollen (dropsy).

The early signs of right-sided heart failure are rapid pulse, shortness of breath, loss of pep, and intolerance to exercise. In late stages you will observe muscle wasting, enlargement of the liver and spleen, and accumulation of fluid in the abdomen (ascites), giving a pot-bellied look. Fluid retention is augmented by the kidneys which respond to the slowed blood flow by retaining salt and water. You may be able to detect a murmur or thrill.

The most common cause of right heart failure is an already established left-sided heart failure. One of the following: heartworms, heart muscle disease, valvular disease, congenital heart disease, or chronic lung disease, usually is at fault.

Treatment of Heart Failure

Treatment of heart failure must be under the supervision of a veterinarian. The first goal of treatment is to remove or correct the underlying cause whenever possible. Congenital heart disease, and heartworm infestations, are potentially curable if treated in time.

Obesity is a serious complicating factor in all dogs with heart disease. Overweight dogs should be put on a low calorie diet.

A low salt diet is of great assistance in treating dogs suffering from congestive heart failure. Fluid build-up is best managed by the use of diuretics and diets low in salt.

Restrict your dog to activities well within his exercise tolerance so as not to overburden his heart.

Various drugs are available which help to increase the force and contraction of the heart, or control arrhythmias. They require veterinary supervision.

These measures can yield substantial results in terms of a longer, more comfortable, and more active life for your dog.

HEARTWORMS

Canine heartworm disease, so-named because the adult worms live in the right side of the heart, is common and appears to be spreading. It has been reported in other animals as well — even in man. It is spread by the common mosquito and it can be found throughout the world, wherever mosquitoes breed.

Life-Cycle

A knowledge of the life cycle of this parasite (*Dirofilaria immitis*) is necessary to understand the rationale for its prevention and treatment.

It requires six to seven months for the worm to complete its cycle.

Infection in the dog begins when larvae from an infective mosquito are deposited on his skin. They burrow into the dog, undergoing several changes in form which eventually lead to the development of small adult worms. This takes three to four months. The worms then make their way into a vein, move to the heart, and become sexually mature.

Adult worms can live for about five years in the right side of the heart. As many as 250 worms have been found in a dog. They reach lengths of four to twelve inches. When worms of the opposite sex are present, they mate and the female gives birth to live young called *microfilariae*. Five thousand immature worms can be derived from a single adult female in a day.

Microfilariae must go into a secondary host, the mosquito, to continue their life-cycle. While waiting for a mosquito, they can remain alive and viable in the bloodstream of the dog for as long as three years.

When the microfilariae are ingested by a mosquito they develop into infective larvae. In warm (southern) climates this process takes about ten days, but in colder climates it can take as long as 48 days. The infective larvae then move to the mouthparts of the mosquito and are ready to infect the new host when the mosquito returns to a dog for a blood meal.

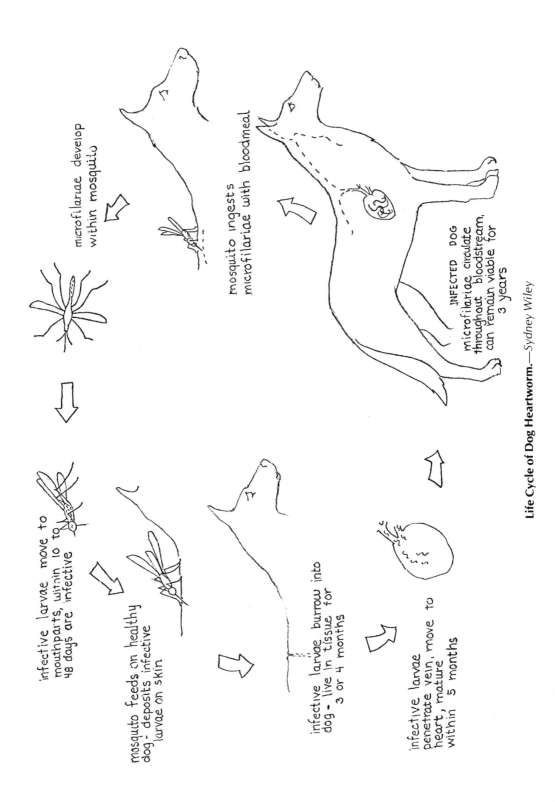

microfilariae develop within mosquito

mosquito ingests microfilariae with bloodmeal

INFECTED DOG
microfilariae circulate throughout bloodstream, can remain viable for 3 years

infective larvae move to mouthparts, within 10 to 48 days are infective

mosquito feeds on healthy dog - deposits infective larvae on skin

infective larvae burrow into dog - live in tissue for 3 or 4 months

infective larvae penetrate vein, move to heart, mature within 5 months

Life Cycle of Dog Heartworm.—*Sydney Wiley*

Disease

Adult worms usually make their home in the right atrium, the right ventricle, and the arteries of the lungs. Less commonly they inhabit the large veins entering the heart, or the veins of the liver.

Worms in the lungs cause difficulty by blocking the flow of blood out of the right side of the heart into the pulmonary circulation. They may be carried into the branches of the pulmonary arterial tree, causing pulmonary emboli.

Worms entwined about the heart valves interfere with the mechanics of the heart. In time, this extra burden causes the heart to fail.

Worms which form clumps in the anterior and posterior vena cavae (or hepatic veins) give rise to a disorder called *vena cava syndrome*. Signs of acute liver failure develop. They include jaundice, blood in the stool, swelling of the abdomen (ascites), and anemia. Collapse and death can occur in two or three days.

Signs: Indications may not appear until a full year has passed. Some dogs can harbor worms for several years before showing signs. They vary according to the severity and location of the infestation. Consequently, the disease may be mistaken for another problem.

The most constant sign is a soft, deep cough. It is made worse by exercise. After exertion, the cough may be so severe the dog faints. He tires easily, appears unusually weak and listless, loses condition, and brings up bloody sputum. Weight loss is nearly always present.

As the disease progresses, the dog begins to labor with his breathing at rest. Due to his weight loss and increased respiratory effort, his ribs become prominent and his chest starts to bulge.

Congestive heart failure and the vena cava syndrome are signs of advanced disease. Acute pulmonary embolus can lead to collapse and death.

Laboratory Diagnosis: The finding of microfilariae in the bloodstream of the dog is an indication of adult worms in the heart.

Various blood tests are available to detect the characteristic parasites. However, they are not always 100 percent accurate for the following reasons:

1) There could be only one sex of worms in the heart — therefore no microfilariae.
2) Some dogs make antibodies that destroy the microfilariae.
3) The adult worms may be sexually immature when the blood test is taken — again, no microfilariae.
4) The concentration of microfilariae in the bloodstream may be too small to be detected by the blood test.

In some studies up to 25 percent of infected dogs did not show microfilariae in the bloodstream after a *single* blood sample.

There is yet another type of microfilariae which can be present in dogs tested for heartworms. It is called *Dipetalonema*. It is a harmless worm living under the skin of dogs. Its main importance rests in the fact that its microfilariae may be mistaken for those of heartworm.

For the above reasons dogs suspected of having heartworms sometimes require x-rays, electrocardiograms, repeat blood tests for microfilariae, and other tests to establish the diagnosis.

Treatment: Because the treatment is complex and potentially dangerous, it should be undertaken only with veterinary supervision. Before any drugs containing arsenic are started, your dog should be carefully evaluated to see if he is strong enough to withstand therapy. If he has heart failure, liver or kidney insufficiency (from long-standing disease), these should be treated to insure that his health is at its optimum.

The first step in ridding your dog of heartworms is to administer an agent to kill the adult worms. Currently the most effective drug against adult worms is *thiacetarsamide*. It is administered intravenously in two doses each day for two days.

After thiacetarsamide has been given, the dog must be rested for several weeks to allow his body to absorb the dead worms. If he exerts too soon, a large mass of dead worms might be dislodged and travel to his lungs, causing acute pulmonary embolism.

Occasionally adult worms are removed surgically. Surgery is reserved for critically ill dogs — those too sick to take the medication, or having a greater risk of lung complications from dead worms.

The second step is to kill the microfilariae. Here it is necessary to wait six weeks to give your dog time to recover from the effects of killing the adult worms.

Dithiazanine (Dizan) is currently the drug of choice. It is given as a single daily dose for seven days. Vomiting and diarrhea can complicate its use.

After treating with Dizan, the blood test is repeated. If microfilariae still are present (and there has been no drug reaction), the dose is increased and continued until the blood is microfilariae-free. In no case, however, should medication be given for more than ten days. Follow-up studies at one year are indicated.

Prevention

There are two methods of preventing heartworms in the dog. Both are effective.

The first method is to administer a daily dose of a compound called *diethylcarbamazine* (found in *Caracide*). The drug kills the infective larvae before they mature into young adults and migrate to the heart. It does not remain in the bloodstream, which is why it is necessary to keep your dog on it all the time. If he should miss a dose or two, the infective larvae could pass unharmed through the particular stage when they were susceptible to the drug.

Dogs started on diethylcarbamazine (DEC) must be blood-tested to insure that they are microfilariae-free. If microfilariae are found in the blood, the drug should not be given because fatal reactions can occur. Instead, follow the instructions under *Treatment*.

Assuming that your dog has been found microfilariae-free, administer DEC at a rate of 1¼ mgs per pound body weight per day. Caracide, a commonly used tablet, contains 50 percent DEC. The dose is 2½ mgs per pound per day.

Drugs containing DEC have an extremely bitter taste, difficult to disguise. A heartworm preventative called *Filaribits* has been marketed recently. It is a chewable tablet which combines DEC with a formula for masking the bitter taste. It is said to be well accepted by most dogs.

Heartworm preventatives are available through your veterinarian.

If you live in an area where mosquitoes are a year-round problem, you should start your puppy on a DEC preventative when he is a few weeks old and continue the drug for the rest of his life. If you live in an area where seasonal considerations make it unnecessary to administer the drug all 12 months, start your dog on the drug well before the mosquito season and continue it well beyond the first frost.

There have been unconfirmed reports that DEC can cause sterility. They have not been confirmed by known scientific studies.

The second method of preventing heartworm infestation is to treat your dog every six months with *thiacetarsamide* — just as if he were infected with the adult parasite (see *Treatment*). Given every six months this drug eliminates adult worms before sufficient numbers develop to cause symptoms.

In theory, the best way to prevent heartworms is to keep your dog from being bitten by a mosquito. Unfortunately, mosquito control can never be 100 percent effective.

Areas of most frequent heartworm infestation are along coastal regions where swamps or other bodies of brackish water provide ideal conditions for mosquitoes to breed. Since mosquitoes have a flight range of ¼ mile, in many cases spraying areas around kennels can be partially effective.

Dogs can get reasonable protection if kept indoors in the late afternoons and evenings, when mosquitoes are feeding.

The enlarged dome of a hydrocephalic puppy.

Paralysis in a Dachshund usually is due to a herniated back disc.

12

Nervous System

GENERAL REMARKS

The nervous system of the dog is made up of the brain, the spinal cord, and the peripheral nerves.

The *central* nervous system is composed of the cerebrum, cerebellum, mid-brain and brain stem. The cerebrum is the largest part of the brain. It is the area of learning, memory, reasoning and judgment. It initiates voluntary action on the part of the dog. It is composed of two hemispheres.

The cerebellum also is a bilobed structure. It sits behind the cerebrum and its main function is to integrate the motor pathways of the brain so as to maintain coordination and balance.

In the mid-brain and brain stem are found centers which control the respiratory rate, the heart rate, the blood pressure, and other activities essential to life. At the base of the brain are centers for primitive actions such as hunger, rage, thirst, hormone activity, and temperature control.

The spinal cord passes down a bony canal formed by the arches of the vertebral bodies. The cord sends out nerve roots (36 or 37 pairs) which combine with one another to form the major nerve plexi. In turn, these plexi subdivide into the *peripheral* nerves. They carry motor impulses to the muscles and receive sensory input from the skin and deeper structures.

A special set of nerves, called the cranial nerves (12 pair), pass directly from the brain out into the head and neck through special holes in the skull. The optic nerves (to the eye), the otic nerves (to the ears), and the olfactory nerves (to the scent organs), are examples of cranial nerves.

Common neurological problems affecting the dog are head injuries, seizures, paralysis, coma, and spinal cord diseases (notably discs).

HEAD INJURIES

Brain trauma usually occurs as a result of auto accidents or falls. Since the brain is not only encased in bone but surrounded by a layer of fluid and

215

suspended from the skull by a system of tough ligaments, it takes a major blow to the skull to injure the brain. Injuries of sufficient magnitude to fracture the skull often are associated with brain lacerations or bleeding into the brain from ruptured blood vessels. At times, even head injuries without skull fracture can cause severe or irreversible brain damage. Brain injuries are classified according to the severity of the damage to the brain.

Brain Contusion *(Bruising)*

This is the most mild sort of injury associated with neurological findings. There is no loss of consciousness. After a blow to his head, the dog remains dazed, wobbly, disoriented — and then clears in a gradual fashion.

Brain Concussion

By definition, a brain concussion means that an animal was knocked out, or experienced a brief loss of consciousness. If unconsciousness lasts more than a few minutes, it suggests the possibility of more severe brain damage such as swelling or blood clot. Upon return to consciousness, the animal exhibits the same signs as brain contusion.

Brain Swelling or Blood Clot on the Brain

Severe head trauma is associated with swelling of the brain or the formation of a blood clot from a ruptured vessel.

Brain swelling, technically called *cerebral edema*, always is associated with a depressed level of consciousness (and often coma). Since the brain is encased in a bony skull, swelling of the brain leads to pressure on the brain stem. As the cerebellum is herniated through the large opening at the base of the skull, the vital centers are in great jeopardy. Respirations may be gasping or irregular, the heart rate may be slow and the blood pressure greatly elevated.

Sudden herniation usually leads to death of the dog. The signs of death are no pulse; no effort to breathe; no blink reflex (when you touch his cornea); dilated pupils; and a soft eye. Usually it is impossible to tell whether sudden "death" is caused by head injury or a state of shock from internal bleeding. It is wise to administer cardiopulmonary resuscitation immediately upon suspicion of death (see EMERGENCIES: *Artificial Respiration and Heart Massage*).

Blood clots form on or within the brain as a result of bleeding from ruptured vessels. They are associated with a depressed level of consciousness. Coma may or may not be present. Blood clots cause localized pressure symptoms. Often one pupil is dilated and will not constrict down when a light is flashed in the eye. A paralysis or weakness may be present on one side of the body. (The weak side usually is opposite the side of the blood clot.)

An operation on the skull to relieve the blood clot can lead to a cure.

Treatment of Head Trauma

Consider that the dog also may have internal injuries with bleeding, shock, and unstable limb fractures. Treatment of these takes precedence over management of the head trauma. Stabilize all fractures before transporting the dog. For the first aid management of a dog with extremity fractures, see MUSCULOSKELETAL SYSTEM: *Broken Bone (Fracture)*.

Handle an injured dog with great care and gentleness. Pain and fright deepen the level of shock in dogs. Wrap the dog in a blanket to keep him warm. This also helps to restrain a dog who is unconscious but may wake up. Avoid giving him water or anything by mouth. Transport him to the nearest veterinary clinic.

When signs of death are present, administer cardiopulmonary resuscitation (see EMERGENCIES: *Artificial Respiration and Heart Massage*).

FITS (SEIZURES, CONVULSIONS)

A seizure is a sudden and uncontrolled burst of activity which begins in a bizarre fashion with champing and chewing, foaming at the mouth, collapse, jerking of the legs, loss of urine and stool. There is a brief loss of consciousness followed by a gradual return to normal.

Some fits are atypical. Instead of the classical convulsion, the dog might exhibit strange and inappropriate behavior such as frenzied barking, sudden blindness, or hysteria. He might turn and snap at his owners.

Seizures are caused by a burst of electrical activity within the brain, commonly in one of the cerebral hemispheres. The electrical focus spreads out and involves other parts, including the mid-brain.

Seizures can be caused by a *blow* to the head, or *scars* from healed brain injuries; by *encephalitis* (inflammation of the brain); by *poisonings, brain malformations* and *tumors*. A common cause of recurrent seizures is *congenital epilepsy*.

Hypoglycemia can cause seizures as well as coma.

A condition in puppies called *"worm fits"* can be found during heavy infestations with intestinal worms. The exact cause of the seizures is unknown. Perhaps it is due to a low blood sugar or serum calcium.

Common poisonings which induce seizures are strychnine, lead, organophosphates (insecticides), and rat poisons. Organophosphates characteristically cause seizures which are preceded by drooling and muscle twitching. History of exposure to an insecticide (i.e., a dip) suggests the diagnosis (see *Insecticides*).

Dogs with *brain tumor* may show signs of confusion. Perhaps there is aimless wandering or some other change in the behavior of the dog before he fits. Other signs of brain tumor are an unsteady gait, loss of coordination, staggering, weakness on one side, enlargement of a pupil. They appear as the tumor grows.

There are a number of conditions which, while actually not true seizures, can easily be confused with them. *Bee stings,* for example, can cause frenzied barking followed by fainting or collapse. If you didn't realize your dog was stung, you might think he was having a seizure. Similarly, a dog with *laryngospasm* who makes frantic efforts to get air, turns blue at the mouth and collapses, looks like a dog having a convulsion. Recurrent attacks suggest a seizure disorder. This condition is discussed in the chapter RESPIRATORY SYSTEM. *Heart arrythmias,* with fainting, often are thought to be seizures.

Anxiety attacks, accompanied by over-breathing (*hyperventilation*), produce jerks and spasms like the start of a fit. Over-breathing removes carbon dioxide from the blood and makes it alkaline. This lowers the serum calcium and leads to the muscle twitching. Hyperventilation sometimes occurs in grooming parlors. Have your dog breathe in a plastic bag for a few minutes to reverse the alkalosis. Tranquilizers are indicated in stressful situations to prevent future attacks.

Epilepsy

Epilepsy is a recurrent seizure disorder of cerebral origin. When it is due to a blow to the head, or the encephalitis of distemper, or bacterial infections of the brain, it is said to be *acquired*. When it is due to birth trauma, or a malformation of the brain (such as hydrocephalus), or when the cause is unknown, then it is said to be *congenital*. Congenital epilepsy can be an inherited trait. St. Bernards, German Shepherds, Poodles and Beagles have hereditary predisposition for seizures of unknown cause.

When seizures begin three to four months after a dog receives a *blow* to his head, usually it will be found the dog was knocked unconscious.

Post-encephalitic seizures appear three to four weeks after the onset of disease. Distemper, in particular, is characterized by typical attacks which begin with champing, tongue-chewing, foaming at the mouth, shaking of the head and blinking of the eyes — then a dazed look, and a return to normal.

To establish a diagnosis of epilepsy, the attacks must be *recurrent* and *similar*. A typical epileptic seizure has three phases. The first is called the *aura*. It is recognized by the onset of sudden apprehension and restlessness. There may be bizarre behavior, such as sniffing in the corner or snapping the air.

Most seizures start with champing, chewing, foaming at the mouth, head-shaking and eye-flickering. During the *rigid phase* the dog collapses, throws back his head, slobbers, and twitches at the face. His pupils dilate. As the rigid phase begins to pass, he makes running movements with his legs (paddling). He may lose control of his bowels or bladder.

During the *post-seizure phase* the dog recovers but remains confused and wobbly. If overstimulated by a loud noise or rough handling, a second seizure can occur.

The first two phases pass quickly (in about three minutes). The post-seizure state can persist for several hours. This might give the impression that the seizure was of long duration. However, a true epileptic seizure is over in less than five minutes.

Stimuli that can trigger a seizure are fatigue, excitement, anxiety, bright lights, loud noises, fever, over-breathing and estrus.

Not all epileptic seizures are typical. To help make the diagnosis, your veterinarian probably will ask for a description of the attack, and he will want to know if other attacks follow the same pattern.

Treatment: If your dog starts to have a seizure, stand aside until he quiets down or cover him with a blanket. (Don't put your fingers in his mouth or try to wedge something between his teeth.) Then call your veterinarian. As the seizure will be over in a few minutes, it is unlikely that your veterinarian will need to stop it with medications. He may want to examine the dog to exclude other conditions.

Seizures lasting over five minutes (continuous seizures) are dangerous. They must be stopped to prevent permanent brain damage.

A number of drugs are used to control or prevent epileptic seizures. Dosages and rates of action are quite variable. Some drugs take several days to build up in the system, during which time your dog could have another attack. This doesn't mean the medicines won't work.

Common drugs used in the treatment of epilepsy are Dilantin, Phenobarbital, Primidone, and Valium. Valium is given intravenously to stop a continuous seizure.

LOSS OF CONSCIOUSNESS (COMA)

Coma is a depressed level of consciousness. It begins with mental depression and confusion, progresses through stupor, and ends in complete loss of consciousness. (Following a blow to the head, coma can occur without progressing through the earlier steps.) Unconscious dogs are not responsive to pain.

Coma is found with a number of ailments. A low blood sugar (*hypogly-cemia*) is a common cause of coma. Typically it occurs in puppies of the Toy breeds, but adult hunting dogs are susceptible to it also. Hypoglycemia is discussed in the chapter PEDIATRICS.

Coma is a serious complication of a *blow* to the head. It can occur during a severe bout of *encephalitis* (inflamation of the brain). When it appears in the late stages of kidney and liver disease, it is a terminal event.

Coma which appears with *high fever* or *heat stroke* is a grave sign. Vigorous efforts to bring down the fever are needed to prevent permanent brain damage (see *Heat Stroke*).

Another cause of coma, which effects breeds with short coats, is prolonged chilling. The dog's temperature is subnormal — below the level on the thermometer. Treatment involves intravenous glucose solutions and slow warming.

A dog transported in the trunk of a car can develop carbon monoxide poisoning from the exhaust fumes. He may be found unconscious, or at first look normal. When he starts to hunt his oxygen supply is used up and he collapses, throws a fit, or passes out entirely.

If your dog is found in a coma for which there is no explanation, he may have been poisoned. Common poisons which cause coma are barbituates, turpentine, arsenic, cyanide, hexachloraphene, lead salts, and carbon monoxide. Poisoning is discussed in EMERGENCIES.

Most of the conditions causing convulsions also can cause coma. What happens depends on whether the brain is made more or less excitable.

Treatment: First determine the level of consciousness and whether the dog is alive. An unconscious dog can inhale his own secretions and strangle on his tongue. Pull out his tongue and clear his airway with your fingers. Lift him by his rear legs and set him on a table with his head hanging over the side. If alive, wrap him in a blanket and take him at once to a veterinarian. It is important that the dog be carried on a rigid surface.

If he shows no signs of life, begin artificial respiration and heart massage (see EMERGENCIES).

If you think your dog might have a piece of food caught in his airway, administer the Heimlich manuveur as described in the chapter on the RESPIRATORY SYSTEM: *Laryngeal Blockage*.

WEAKNESS OR PARALYSIS

There is a group of uncommon diseases which cause overall weakness or progressive paralysis with an intact spinal withdrawal reflex. The dog can feel a pin prick or pinch to his foot and withdraws it. These diseases, then, attack the motor nerves, but leave the sensory nerves intact. They come on gradually, over several hours or days. The dog remains mentally alert.

Paralysis localized to one part is most likely due to a spinal cord problem. Such conditions are discussed in the section *Spinal Cord Diseases*.

Tick Paralysis

The saliva of the common female wood tick contains poisons which affect the motor nerves of the dog. Clinical signs are usually associated with a heavy infestation of ticks. During 48 to 72 hours the dog gets progressively weaker. There is no evidence of pain or illness. Sensation to pin prick is normal. In time, the paralysis becomes so severe the dog can't raise his head or move his legs. He may die because he cannot breathe.

Treatment: Remove all ticks, especially engorged females. Dip the dog in an insecticide solution (see *Insecticides*). If your dog shows signs of weakness, call your veterinarian.

Tick paralysis might easily be confused with Coon Hound paralysis, botulism, and myasthenia gravis.

Botulism

Botulism is a paralysis caused by the endotoxin of a bacteria called *Clostridium botulinum*. It is acquired by eating improperly canned vegetables and meats, or spoiled carcasses. Signs are similar to tick paralysis.

Treatment: The disease is often fatal. Antitoxins are available; they may be of aid early in the disease.

Coon Hound Paralysis

The exact cause of this disease is unknown. It may be due to a virus. It is acquired by dogs who have hunted raccoons. The history might reveal the dog was bitten or scratched by a raccoon a week or two before the onset of his paralysis.

The disease begins as a weakness of the hindquarters and progresses forward until the dog is unable to stand. During this time the dog remains alert but concerned by his incapacity. The paralysis reaches its peak at about ten days. Dogs may recover. Treatment is supportive. Seek veterinary aid.

Myasthenia gravis

This condition is due to an abnormality in the biochemistry of the nerve endings of the motor nerves. It is not common. The signs are a generalized weakness which is aggravated by exercise. Weakness is most apparent in the hindquarters. There is trouble getting up when lying down, and a swaying or staggering gait. Diagnosis can be made through special studies. Drugs are available to aid the dog.

Myasthenia gravis can be confused with botulism, tick paralysis, and Coon Hound paralysis.

Low Potassium *(Hypokalemia)*

Hypokalemia, or low blood potassium, occurs in dogs who are taking water pills to remove excess fluids from the body. Such dogs can develop a generalized weakness as a result of loss of potassium in the urine. Diagnosis is made by measuring a serum potassium level. Potassium can be given to correct the problem.

SPINAL CORD DISEASES

Injuries to the spinal cord cause a variety of neurological findings. There may be weakness, loss of feeling, or paralysis of both rear legs or even all four extremities. The signs are variable and depend upon the location of the injury, and its severity.

Spinal cord damage follows automobile accidents and injuries to the spinal cord. Tumors, infections, and malformations do occur. The majority of spinal cord problems, however, are due to disc disease.

Herniated Disc

Ruptured discs are more common in certain breeds. Dachschunds have two times the incidence of all other breeds put together. Beagles, Pekingese and mixed breeds are next in frequency.

A disc is a cushion that sits between the vertebral bodies of the spinal column and acts like a shock-absorber. It is made up of a rim of tough cartilage that has a gel-like center. When a disc herniates, the whole disc does not "slip" out of position. What happens is that there is a tear in the fibrous capsule which allows the inner "nucleus" of the disc to push through the opening and pinch the cord or put pressure on the dorsal nerve roots. The effect is similar to a tear in a rubber tire which lets the inner tube bulge out. Herniation of the nucleus of the disc gives rise to pain, weakness, paralysis or loss of sensation. The reason that the signs are so variable is that the herniation can vary in size and location from animal to animal. Occasionally more than one disc herniates. Trauma to the nerve tissue causes swelling and hemorrhage, which aggravates the problem.

The concept that a "slipped" disc can be easily replaced by manipulating the spinal column is based on the misconception that the whole cushion slides in and out of place. With proper care, many disc problems improve without surgery; but the improvement usually is gradual and depends upon keeping the dog in confinement so he can't aggravate his problem with exercise and activity.

Herniated discs can come on gradually or occur with explosive suddenness. Perhaps there is a history of trauma, such as jumping off of a sofa. Usually the first sign is pain in the back. The dog assumes a hunched-up position, pants, has a tight abdomen and a look of pain. At the same time, he may show weakness and lameness; or a wobbly, uncoordinated gait. Sudden disc protrusions in the lower back can produce complete paralysis of the rear legs. These dogs often develop urinary retention and bladder infections.

Disc problems seldom occur in dogs younger than one year of age. About 80 percent occur in the low back between the last thoracic and first two lumbar vertebrae. Most of the remainder occur in the neck.

A dog with a herniated neck disc carries his head rigidly, which makes his neck look shorter. Neck discs are extremely painful. Some dogs refuse to lower their heads to eat. They cry out when patted on the head. There may be lameness in the front legs. Complete paralysis of all four legs is rare, but does occur.

Treatment: For neck and back disc of gradual onset, close confinement or cage rest for ten days allows the swelling to subside. Most dogs will need to be hospitalized. At home they follow their owners around the house and ask to be picked up and carried. Drugs to reduce swelling and inflammation (steroids, Butazolidin) are of value. Strong pain medication usually is contraindicated because it encourages activity. Many dogs recover without surgery.

Explosive discs with paralysis require special care and handling. Dogs shoud be transported on a flat hard surface. Often special studies are necessary to locate the exact point of the protrusion. The most useful test is a myelogram, in which a contrast material is injected into the spinal canal to show up the herniation on x-rays. Operative intervention may be necessary.

NERVE PALSY (PARALYSIS)

An injury to one of the peripheral nerves results in loss of sensation and motor function in the distribution of that nerve. Common injuries are stretches, tears and lacerations.

Brachial and radial nerve palsies involve one of the front legs. Usually they are caused by an auto accident, during which the leg is jerked backwards away from the trunk, which stretches the nerves. The leg hangs limp. When paralysis is partial, the dog may be able to stand, but stumbles when he takes a step.

Lacerated nerves must be repaired. Stretched nerves often return to normal.

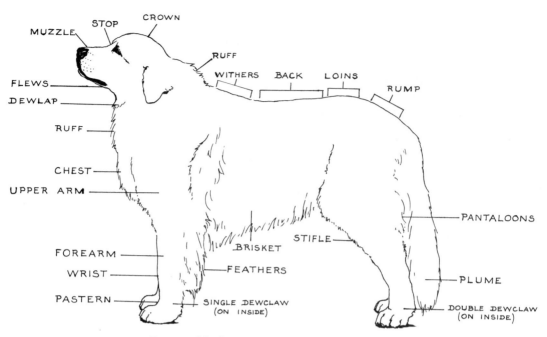

Topographical Anatomy. —*Bridget Olerenshaw*

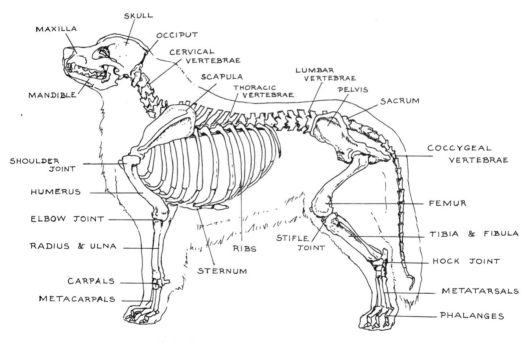

Skeletal Anatomy. —*Bridget Olerenshaw*

13

Musculoskeletal System

GENERAL INFORMATION

The dog's skeleton is made up of an average of 319 individual bones connected by ligaments and surrounded by muscles. Although the number of bones is roughly the same in all breeds of dog, there is considerable variation in size and shape. This is due to selective breeding.

The outside of a bone is called the *cortex*. It is composed of minerals and protein. The cortex gives the bone rigidity. Inside is the *marrow* cavity. Bone marrow is important in red blood cell production. Nutritional deficiencies can cause impaired bone development, or result in demineralization and bone resorption, making fractures more likely.

The bones of the body are held together by specialized connective tissue called *ligaments*. This union is called an *articulation*, or joint. Bone ends would grate against each other and cause considerable wear if it were not for a protective layer of *cartilage* over their ends. In some joints a pad of cartilage is interposed between the two surfaces, giving a cushion effect.

Despite the fact that cartilage is tough and resilient, it can be damaged by joint stress and trauma. It is not easily replaced or mended. Once damaged, it may deteriorate, become calcified, and act as a foreign body or irritant to the joint surfaces.

Joint position is maintained by ligaments, tendons, and a tough fibrous capsule surrounding the joint. These combine to provide stability or tightness to the joint. Joint *laxity* is due to loose ligaments and/or a stretched capsule. It can cause slippage of the articulating surfaces, leading to cartilage injury and arthritis.

Joints of the hip and shoulder are called *ball and socket*. They move forward and backward, from side to side, or in a circle; but the ball should remain firmly seated in the socket.

The rest of the limb joints are of the "hinge" type. They flex and extend in a plane from front to back. They must be stable to prevent the bones from slipping to the sides.

The skeletal anatomy of man and dog has much in common, including similar terminology. Due to the fact that man evolved into a two-legged creature, there are some significant differences in terms of angles, lengths, and positioning of the bones.

The hock, for example, so prominent on the dog, is actually the heel-bone in a man. Whereas man walks on the sole of his foot, the dog walks on his toes. Man carries all his weight on his hips; the dog carries 75 percent of his weight on his shoulder joints and front end. This helps to explain why front leg disorders are relatively common in dogs.

Breeders, judges and veterinarians use certain terms to describe a dog's overall structure and composition.

His *conformation* is the degree with which the various angles and parts of his body agree or harmonize with one another. Standards for purebred dogs describe the ideal conformation for each particular breed. These standards are based to a certain extent upon aesthetic considerations, but they take into account the breed's working purposes, too.

Most breed standards provide some information as to the desired *angulation*, or slope to the bones of the shoulder, pelvis and limbs. These angles are determined by comparison with imaginary lines drawn horizontally and vertically through the plane of the standing dog.

Another term used to judge the physical attributes of a dog is *soundness*. When applied to the composition of his musculoskeletal system, it means that a sound dog is one in whom all the bones and joints are in correct alignment and functioning properly.

BONE AND JOINT PROBLEMS IN GROWING PUPPIES

Growing puppies are especially susceptible to serious injuries to bones and joints caused by improper activity, improper diet, and trauma. Injuries can lead to disability, or a deviation in the development of the limb.

A puppy (especially of the large breeds) should never be allowed to gain too much weight. He should not be encouraged to jump up or walk on his hind legs. Nor should he be made to pull or carry a heavy load.

Secure footing is especially important for dogs. As a puppy begins to walk he should be placed on a rug or a rough surface that will help him to keep his feet under his body. Dogs should not be kenneled on smooth or slick surfaces. House pets should be kept off slippery floors that could cause their legs to slip out from under them.

To learn about metabolic bone disease, and vitamin and mineral supplements for growing puppies, see *Metabolic Bone Disorders* further on in this chapter.

How to Carry a Dog

Injuries to bones and joints can occur from improper handling. Never pick your dog up by his front legs. Heavy dogs must be picked up by placing

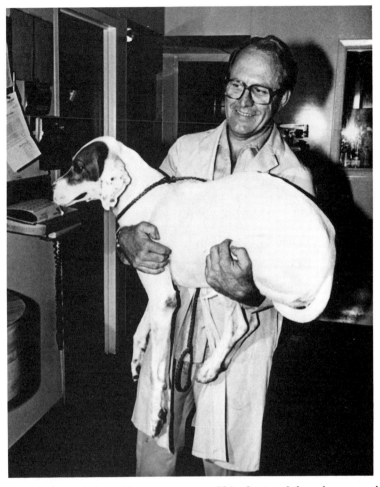

Carry an injured dog with one arm around his chest and the other around his back legs. —*J. Clawson*

one arm around the front of the chest and another underneath the stomach or around the back legs. They are then held close to the chest so that if they attempt to squirm they are not easily dropped.

LIMPING (LAMENESS)

A limp is the most common sign of bone or joint disease. However, muscle or nerve damage can produce lameness. It indicates pain or weakness in the involved leg.

Locating which leg is affected can be difficult. A dog often will take weight off a painful leg when standing. When he is moving, usually he will take a shorter step on a painful or weak leg and you may notice that his head "bobs" or drops as weight comes down on the affected leg.

Having identified which leg is involved, you should attempt to identify the site and possible cause. First flex and extend all joints to their maximum to ascertain if joint or tendons are involved. Next carefully feel the leg from the toes up. Attempt to locate a point of tenderness by applying pressure. Having located an area of pain, see if it is produced by movement of a joint, or by local tenderness in a muscle (such as might be caused by a puncture wound or a bruise). Check for swelling and discoloration of the area. With this information consider the following:

Infected areas are tender, reddened, warm to touch, often are associated with a break in the skin, and progress gradually. Lameness becomes steadily worse. Fever usually is present.

Sprains and strains (of joints, tendons and muscles) are of sudden onset; frequently they show local swelling and discoloration; they gradually improve. Ordinarily the dog has limited use of his leg. Pain is mild. There is no fever.

Fractures and dislocations are associated with severe pain and inability to put weight on the leg. Deformity often is present. Movement of the involved part produces a gritty sound. Tissues are swollen and discolored from bleeding.

Degenerative, congenital and metabolic bone and joint diseases come on gradually. There is no local discoloration. Pain usually is mild and swelling slight.

Bone and joint injuries are discussed below.

INJURIES TO BONES AND JOINTS

Sprains

A sprain is an injury to a joint caused by a sudden stretching or tear of the joint capsule or ligaments. The signs are pain over the joint, swelling of the tissues, and limitation of motion leading to temporary lameness.

Cases with severe swelling and/or pain (in which the dog refuses to put weight on the leg) should be examined by a veterinarian to rule out a fracture or dislocation. If the problem does not begin to improve within four days, x-rays should be taken.

Treatment: The primary treatment is to *rest the part*. When torn ligaments are suspected, the joint should be immobilized by splinting as described below under *Broken Bone (Fracture)*. Ice packs help to keep the swelling down. Add crushed ice to a plastic bag and wrap the limb to hold the bag in place over the injured joint. Apply ice for 20 minutes every hour for the first three hours. Avoid pain medication which relieves discomfort and encourages use of the limb.

Tendon Injuries

A tendon may be stretched, partly torn, or completely ruptured. An irritated or inflamed tendon is called a *tendonitis*. Strained tendons sometimes follow sudden wrenching or twisting injuries to the limb. In some cases tendonitis follows over-use of the limb (for example, after strenuous field or road work).

The signs of tendonitis are temporary lameness, pain on bearing weight, pain and swelling over the course of the tendon. The tendons of the forepaw (front and back) are affected most often.

Treatment: Rest of the limb is most important. It may be necessary to splint the joint (see *Sprains*). Activity which causes flare-ups should be reduced or stopped. Do not give drugs to relieve pain, since the limp is important in protecting the part from further injury.

Rupture of the *Achilles* (heel) tendon, which attaches to the hock joint, can be caused by sudden and extreme flexion. This is the tendon most often severed by dog fights and car accidents. It must be repaired surgically.

Muscle Strain

An injured or torn muscle is caused by: (a) sudden stretching of its fibers: (b) prolonged stress or overexertion; and (c) a blow to the muscle. The symptoms are lameness, a knotting-up of the muscle, and swelling with tenderness over the injured part.

Treatment: Rest and cold packs are recommended (see *Sprains*).

Dislocated Joint

A strong force is necessary to rupture a joint and displace the bones. Such injuries usually are associated with falls and car accidents. The signs are sudden onset of pain with inability to use the limb; there is an observable deformity (or shortening) when compared to the opposite side.

Treatment: Veterinary examination is necessary to rule out an associated fracture, and to replace the joint in its socket. These injuries frequently involve shock and internal bleeding.

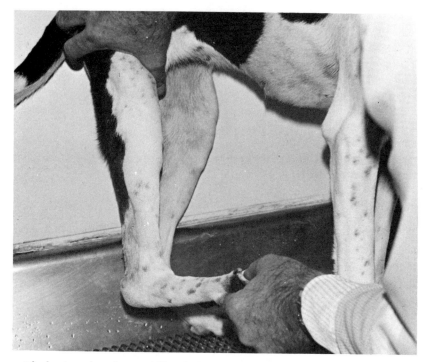

The heel cord tendon *(Achilles)* is the tendon most often ruptured in the dog.

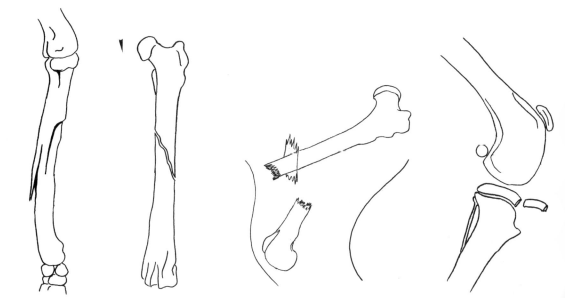

Greenstick fracture.   Oblique fracture.   Open or Compound fracture.   Chip or Avulsion fracture.

—Rose Floy

Broken Bone (Fracture)

Broken bones are caused by trauma. At times a bone is diseased, which weakens it; then minor trauma can cause a breakage.

Young bones tend to crack (*greenstick fracture*), whereas bones of elderly dogs are brittle and more likely to break completely. Complete breaks are divided into *simple* and *compound*. A simple fracture does not break through the skin. In a compound (open) fracture the bone has made contact with the outside, either because of an open wound which exposes it, or because the point has thrust through the skin from the inside. Compound fractures may be associated with bone infection.

Treatment: Many of these injuries are associated with shock, blood loss, and injuries to other organs. Control of shock takes precedence over treatment of the fracture.

Suspected fractures should be immobilized to prevent further damage during movement of the dog to a veterinary hospital. Accomplish this by splinting the involved limb. A satisfactory splint is one which crosses the joint above and below the injury. This assures non-movement of the fractured part.

When a fracture is below the hock or the elbow, immobilize it by folding a magazine around the leg. Then wrap it with roller gauze, a necktie, or anything handy. Higher fractures can be immobilized by binding the limb to a padded board, or to the body with a many-tailed bandage.

If the fracture is a complete break, your veterinarian probably will want to reduce the fracture and return the ends of the bones to their original position. Reduction is accomplished by pulling on the limb to overcome muscle spasm (which causes shortening). Usually this requires an anesthetic. Once reduced, the position of the bones must be maintained. Splints and casts are effective, especially for greenstick fractures; at times metallic plates and pins are needed. Such complicated fractures require open surgery.

Bone Infection *(Osteomyelitis)*

A bone infection is a hazard whenever bone is exposed. The most common causes are open fracture and surgical operations on bones and joints. In rare cases it is due to blood-borne bacteria and fungi; the dog might be suffering from leukemia or some other disease which impairs his immunological competence.

The signs of osteomyelitis are lameness, fever, pain, swelling, and discharge through a sinus tract connecting the bone to the skin. The diagnosis is confirmed by x-ray.

Treatment: Successful treatment of osteomyelitis presents one of the most difficult problems in veterinary medicine. The causative agent (bacteria, fungi) is first identified; then the dog is placed on appropriate long-term antibiotics. Surgical removal of devitalized bone is often necessary.

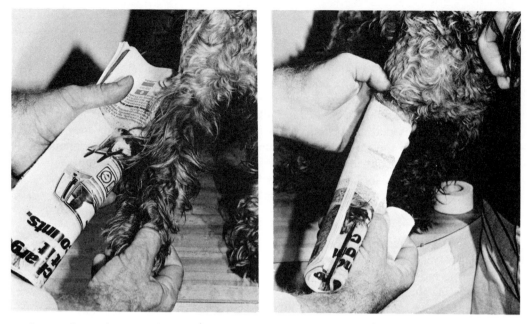

A magazine makes a good temporary splint for fractures of the front leg below the elbow.
—J. Clawson

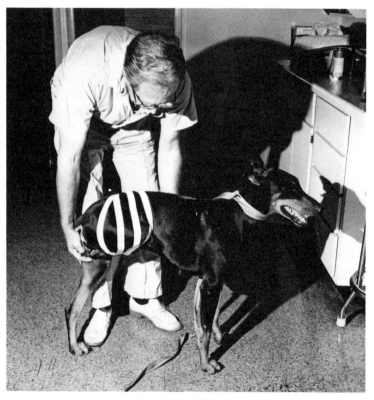

If the leg cannot be splinted, bind it to the body. *—J. Clawson*

Torn Knee Ligaments *(Ruptured Cruciates)*

The knee or stifle joint is stabilized by two internal ligaments (the cruciates) which cross in the middle of the joint. Rupture of a cruciate is a common serious derangement of the stifle joint. Torn knee ligaments occur in Toy breeds and on occasion in larger breeds.

There might be a history of trauma, but in many cases the presenting sign is just moderate to severe lameness in one or both hind legs. The diagnosis is confirmed by palpating the stifle joint and finding instability.

Treatment: Surgical repair of the torn ligaments is the treatment of choice. When allowed to heal spontaneously, the leg develops scar tissue around the joint capsule which lessens the degree of mobility. Arthritis occurs later in life.

INHERITED BONE DISEASE

This is a group of bone disorders having a genetic or hereditary basis, despite the fact that only a limited number of offspring may be affected. If, after a careful veterinary examination, one of these conditions is found, do not breed your dog without first discussing it with your veterinarian.

Canine Hip Dysplasia

This is the most common cause of rear-end lameness in the dog. It occurs almost exclusively in the larger breeds—those weighing more than 35 pounds as adults.

The problem lies in the structure of the hip joint. The head of the *femur* (thigh bone) should sit solidly in the *acetabulum* (cup). In hip dysplasia, loose ligaments allow the head to begin to work free. A shallow acetabulum also predisposes to joint laxity. Finally, the mass or tone of the muscles around the joint socket is an important factor.

Tight ligaments, a broad pelvis with a well-cupped acetabulum, and a good ratio of muscle mass to size of bone, predispose to good hips. The reverse is true of dogs who are likely to develop the disease. Environmental factors, including weight and nutrition of the puppy and rearing practices figure into the final outcome.

Hip dysplasia is a moderately heritable condition. It is about twice as common among littermates having a dysplastic parent. But even dogs with normal hips can produce dysplastic pups. Some dogs with x-ray evidence of severe hip dysplasia show no clinical signs and the disease goes entirely unsuspected until an x-ray is taken to check for it.

Signs first appear during a time of rapid growth (four to nine months). A puppy might show pain in the hip, walk with a limp or swaying gait, bunny-hop when he runs, and experience difficulty getting up. Pushing down

STIFLE JOINT IN PROFILE

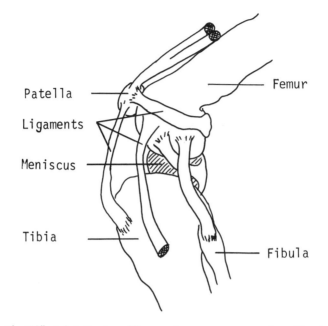

Patella

Ligaments

Meniscus

Femur

Tibia

Fibula

The Stifle Joint. Ruptured ligaments are common. —*Rose Floyd*

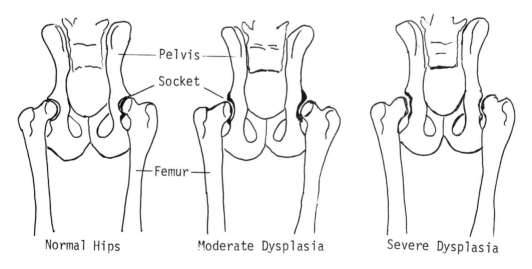

Pelvis

Socket

Femur

Normal Hips

Moderate Dysplasia

Severe Dysplasia

Hip dysplasia is a moderately heritable condition.

on his rump often causes his pelvis to drop. If you roll him on his back, his rear legs may resist being spread into a "frog-leg" position.

Because of joint laxity, there is abnormal wear and tear on the articulating surfaces of the joint. In time this leads to arthritic changes in the dysplastic hip. Pain and limitation of movement frequently parallel the degree of bone deformity (or grade of dysplasia) at the joint.

The diagnosis is made from x-rays of the pelvis and hips. Heavy sedation or general anesthesia may be required.

Canine hip dysplasia is graded according to the severity of joint changes seen on x-ray. Joint laxity and minor remodeling characterize mild dysplasia. Erosion of the joints, subluxation of the hips (moving out of the socket), and arthritic changes, characterize moderate dysplasia. In severe dysplasia, the acetabulum is extremely shallow or nearly flat, the femoral head is rough and flattened, subluxation is severe, and arthritic changes are marked.

The Orthopedic Foundation for Animals, with its headquarters in Columbia, Missouri, provides a consulting service for purebred dog owners. For a nominal fee, the OFA's panel of expert radiologists will review a properly taken x-ray and, if the conformation of the hips is normal for that breed, certify the dog by assigning him an OFA number. Currently, the OFA certifies dogs who are 24 months of age or older.

Some experienced practitioners believe they can predict hip dysplasia by palpating young puppies four to sixteen weeks of age. A general anesthetic is required. The hips are manipulated and an attempt is made to grade the degree of joint laxity.

Treatment is directed at relieving pain and improving function by giving aspirin or one of the newer synthetic aspirin products used in the treatment of degenerative joint disease (see *Arthritis*).

Two surgical procedures advocated in the treatment of hip dysplasia are: (1) removal of the femoral head (s), and (2) division of the pectineus muscle. These procedures may relieve pain and improve function in some individuals.

There have been isolated reports that high doses of Vitamin C can prevent dysplasia in susceptible dogs. These reports have not been confirmed by known scientific studies.

It has been shown that repeated selection of normal dogs for breeding stock reduces the incidence of hip dysplasia in a susceptible bloodline.

Destruction of the Ball of the Hip *(Aseptic Necrosis)*

Aseptic necrosis of the head of the femur is due to impaired blood supply to the ball of the hip. It leads to gradual destruction of the hip joint. Primarily it occurs in young Toy dogs between four and ten months of age. In other breeds it can be a sequel to sudden hip dislocation (auto accident).

The signs are severe lameness and refusal to bear weight on the leg.

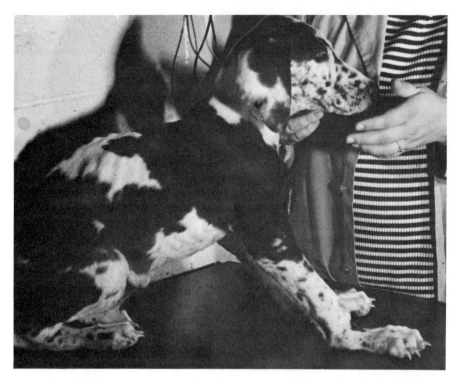

Nutritional deficiency and mineral imbalance can cause the wrist joints to give way.

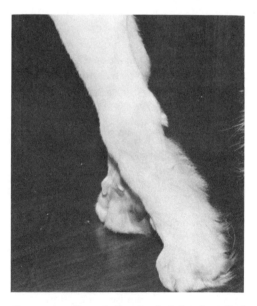

Over-extension of the hock joint is called "popping hock".

Muscle wasting is pronounced. There is loss of motion at the joint and the leg can be shortened.

Treatment: Surgical removal of the head of the femur gives good results. Anti-inflammatory drugs, such as aspirin and Butazolidin can be tried to relieve pain. Spontaneous improvement has been reported.

Slipping Kneecap *(Patellar Dislocation)*

Dislocating kneecap can be inherited, or acquired through trauma. It occurs sporadically among Toy breed dogs, although it can be found in large breeds, too.

In dogs the kneecap is a small bone which protects the front of the stifle joint: it is the counterpart of the kneecap in man. It is anchored in place by ligaments, and slides in a groove in the femur.

Conditions which predispose to dislocation of the patella are: a shallow groove; weak ligaments; and mal-alignment of the tendons and muscles that straighten the joint. The patella slips inward or outward.

The signs of a slipped kneecap are difficulty straightening the knee; pain in the stifle; and a limp. The tip of the hock often points outward and the toes inward (the reverse of cow hocks).

The diagnosis is confirmed by manipulating the stifle joint and pushing the kneecap in and out of position.

Treatment involves surgery to deepen the groove and/or realign the tendon.

Popping Hock *(Laxity of the Hock Joint)*

This condition, which may affect one or both hocks, is due to looseness of supporting structures around the joint. It is more common in large dogs with straight rear-end angulation. Usually it is not painful, but can impair the dog's drive and agility. In late stages the joint can become arthritic.

The diagnosis can be suspected by observing the dog in motion, at which time the hock will appear to give, causing an irregular gait. Manipulation of the joint reveals the lax ligaments. The hock slips out of place (either forward or to the side) when the joint is straightened.

Treatment: Early immobilization by splints (or cage rest) may reverse the condition in some young pups. The disease is carried in certain bloodlines. It can be reduced by proper breeding practices.

Elbow Dysplasia *(Ununited Anconeal Process)*

This condition is caused by a faulty union of the *anconeal process* (one of the elbow bones) with the ulna. It is of developmental origin. Primarily it affects German Shepherd Dogs and Basset Hounds, but has been described in other breeds as well. It is thought to be inherited.

The loose fragment in the elbow acts as an irritant and abrasive. Arthritis is a common sequel.

Pups begin to show lameness in the front leg at about six months of age. Some are unable to bear weight; others limp only when trotting. Characteristically, the elbow is held outward from the chest.

Treatment: X-rays taken after five months of age are diagnostic. The most effective treatment is surgical removal of the loose piece of bone.

Separation of Joint Cartilage *(Osteochondritis dissecans)*

Osteochondritis dissecans affects dogs of the large rapidly growing breeds between the ages of four and twelve months. It usually is found in the shoulder joints, but rarely it can affect the hocks or stifles.

It is due to a defect in the cartilage overlying the head of one of the long bones. A puppy who jumps down stairs might sustain such an injury. The tendency for cartilage to be easily damaged may be hereditary. Repeated stress to the joint perpetrates the condition.

The signs are gradual lameness in a young dog of one of the larger breeds. Pain is present on flexing the joint. X-rays may show fragmentation of the joint cartilage, or a loose piece of cartilage in the joint.

Treatment: The condition can be treated by confinement, or by surgical removal of the damaged cartilage. Pain pills are contraindicated, as they are in most *traumatic* joint conditions, because they encourage the dog to exercise.

Wandering Lameness *(Eosinophilic Panosteitis)*

Panosteitis, also called "growing pains" or "wandering lameness", is a disease of puppies between five and twelve months of age. The cause is unknown, but there is a tendency for the disease to run in families. German Shepherds are affected most commonly.

A characteristic sign is the tendency for pain and lameness to shift from one location to another over a course of several weeks or months. The disease often is accompanied by fever, eosinophils in the white blood count, muscle wasting, and unthriftiness. Pressure over the shaft of the affected bone elicits pain. X-rays show the characteristic picture of increased density in a long bone.

Treatment: As the cause is unknown, treatment is directed at the relief of bone pain. Most dogs recover spontaneously, but if severely affected, may never regain full muscle strength and condition.

ARTHRITIS (DEGENERATIVE JOINT DISEASE)

Arthritis is a condition which can affect one or more joints in the dog. In some cases it can be accounted for by a history of wear and tear to the joint.

In others, it seems to occur with advancing age. Although it can begin in the first half of life, usually signs don't appear until later.

Large breeds are affected more often than small ones. Heavy dogs, regardless of breed, are more likely to experience symptoms because of the excess stress placed upon their joints.

Rheumatoid arthritis is part of a generalized disease of body connective tissue. This is a rare cause of arthritis in the dog.

Septic arthritis is caused by an infectious agent which gains access to the joint. (This, too, is rare.)

The most common degenerative joint disease is called *osteoarthritis*.

Dogs with arthritis experience varying degrees of lameness, stiffness which is worse in the morning (or after getting up from a nap), and pain in the joints.

An acute flare-up leads to accentuation of the above symptoms and the development of a swollen tender joint (effusion). A "grating" sensation may be detected when working the joint back and forth.

X-rays show varying degrees of joint narrowing, joint destructon and remodeling of articular surfaces, and compensatory new bone formation in and around the joint.

Treatment: In those cases with a known cause, the treatment is directed at the primary disease. In others, it is directed at relieving joint pain and encouraging moderate activity to prevent joint stiffness.

Aspirin should be given for its analgesic and anti-inflammatory effects. The dose is five grains per 25 pounds body weight. This dose should be given four times daily.

Steroids and Butazolidin may be required in certain cases. They should be given only for short periods, and then only under professional supervision.

METABOLIC BONE DISORDERS

Parathyroid Bone Disease

There are four small glands in the neck of the dog, located in proximity to the thyroid. They are called the *parathyroids*. They secrete a hormone important in calcium and bone metabolism. Too much parathyroid hormone in the system impairs the formation of new bone in young dogs. In the adult dog, it leads to softening and weakening of established bone.

To understand the effects of parathyroid hormone on bone, it is important to know three facts:

(1) Low serum calcium stimulates the parathyroid glands to secrete more hormone.

(2) Parathyroid hormone restores serum calcium levels by drawing calcium out of the bones.

(3)   And the concentration of calcium and phosphorus in the blood is
      inversely related: a high serum phosphorus, for example, causes
      a low serum calcium (and vice versa).

With these facts in mind, it is not difficult to understand the mechanisms
of metabolic bone disease due to calcium or phosphorus imbalance.

Primary Hyperparathyroidism: This condition is due to a tumor of one of
the parathyroid glands. The tumor produces excess hormone. It is rare in the
dog.

On x-ray the bone is demineralized, thin, and often looks cystic (small
holes in the bone). Minor stress can cause a fracture.

Surgical removal of the affected gland is the only possible treatment.

Renal Secondary Hyperparathyroidism: This is the result of long-standing
kidney disease which causes retention of phosphorus in the blood. The high
phosphorus concentrations depress the serum calcium which,, in turn,
stimulates the parathyroid glands to produce excess hormone.

The effects on bone are the same as those of primary hyperparathyroidism, but the symptoms in the dog are usually dominated by the
kidney picture (uremia).

Treatment is directed at correcting the kidney problem.

Nutritional Secondary Hyperparathyroidism: This disease is caused by a
deficiency of calcium or Vitamin D in the diet. It is also caused by an excess
of phosphorus. It was common when the unsupplemented "all meat" diet
was commercially popular.

Either a deficiency of calcium or an excess of phosphorus has the
effect of stimulating the parathyroid glands to secrete more hormone. This
depletes the bones of calcium, leading to structural weakness.

Vitamin D deficiency causes the problem because Vitamin D is required
for calcium to be absorbed from the intestinal tract.

The daily calcium, phosphorus and Vitamin D requirements for
growing puppies are:
Vitamin D   :   9 units per pound body weight
Calcium   :   240 mg per pound body weight
Phosphorus :   200 mg per pound body weight

The requirements for adult dogs are exactly one-half of the above.

To achieve a desired calcium/phosphorus ratio of 1.2 to 1, a diet must
provide an adequate intake of both minerals. Most commercial foods for
adult dogs and growing pups provide adequate concentrations.

Feeding practices that *can* lead to calcium deficiency are: unsupplemented high meat diets; all vegetable diets; corn bread diets; and
feeding too many left-over table scraps (especially as they are frequently just
vegetables).

In *puppies* and young dogs the signs of skeletal disease are lameness,
thriftlessness, bone pain, stunted growth, and spontaneous fractures.

In *older* dogs periodental disease usually is the first sign. It is due to thinning of the jaw bones with exposure of the roots of the teeth. The teeth loosen and are expelled.

When unchecked, the condition eventually leads to the death of the dog.

Treatment: Correct the diet by feeding a good quality, balanced commercial ration, one advertised as supporting normal puppy growth.

Calcium carbonate should be supplemented when, due to advanced periodental disease or fixed eating habits, the dog will not consume adequate amounts of a balanced kibble ration. Excess calcium should be avoided. Overdosing may make the dog worse.

Vitamins A and D (and trace minerals) should be added to meet normal requirements.

Rickets *(Osteomalacia)*

Rickets (called osteomalacia in the adult) is due to a deficiency of Vitamin D. Since this vitamin is active in the absorption of calcium and phosphorus from the intestine, these minerals may be deficient also. The disease in the dog is rare. Many cases classified as rickets are probably due to nutritional secondary hyperparathyroidism.

Signs: There is a characteristic enlargement of the joints where the ribs meet the cartilages of the sternum (rickettic rosary). Bowing of the legs and other growth deformities in the puppy, along with fractures in the adult, are common in severe cases.

Treatment: It is the same as for nutritional secondary hyperparathyroidism.

Hypertrophic Osteodystrophy (H.O.D.)

This disease affects puppies of the large rapidly growing breeds three to seven months of age. It resembles scurvy in humans, but in dogs the cause is uncertain. (Scurvy is due to a deficiency of Vitamin C.)

Because the dog manufactures his own Vitamin C (in contrast to man who has to depend on an outside source), it has been suggested that H.O.D. in the dog may be due to improper synthesis of this vitamin, or to a defect in its utilization by the tissues.

Vitamin C is needed to make *framework* for bone. In contrast, Vitamin D is needed to *mineralize* bone, once formed.

H.O.D. affects the long bones near the joints (wrists and the hocks). These joints become swollen, tender, and give rise to lameness. X-rays initially show a "moth-eaten" area in a long bone above the growth plate. Later, too much bone is laid down (hypertrophic osteodystrophy). Impaired growth of bone leads to deformities.

Some cases classified as H.O.D. probably are due to *improper feeding practices*, such as feeding too many calories, giving too much calcium, and overdosing with vitamins during the growth period. These practices lead to an x-ray picture identical to hypertrophic osteodystrophy.

Overdosing with Vitamins

Many people think that a rapidly growing puppy needs to have supplemental vitamins and minerals in order to build strong bone. Modern name-brand commercial dog rations, made up for puppy growth and development, supply all the needed vitamins and minerals to sustain normal growth — provided the puppy or young dog eats it well. Vitamins and minerals in excess of those required will not add more bone and substance to the growing animal.

When calcium, phosphorus, and Vitamin D are given to a dog beyond his capacity to use them normally, his growth and development can be adversely affected. Overfeeding and overdosing with vitamins, as discussed above, can cause a bone disorder similar to H.O.D.

Vitamin and calcium supplements might be indicated for rapidly growing pups who are poor eaters. If you own such a dog, discuss this with your veterinarian.

14

Urinary System

GENERAL INFORMATION

The urinary tract is composed of the kidneys and ureters, bladder, prostate and urethra.

The kidneys are paired organs located on each side of the backbone just behind and below the last ribs. Each kidney has a renal pelvis or funnel that siphons the urine into a ureter. The ureters pass on down to the pelvic brim and empty into the bladder. The passageway that connects the neck of the bladder to the outside is called the urethra. The opening of the urethra is found at the tip of the penis in the male and between the folds of the vulva in the female. In the male, the urethra also serves as a channel for semen.

One function of the kidneys is to maintain water and mineral balance and excrete the wastes of metabolism. This is accomplished by *nephrons,* the basic working units of the kidneys. Damage to nephrons leads to renal insufficiency (kidney failure).

Normal urine is yellow and clear. Its color can be altered by the state of hydration of the dog, and by certain drugs. Aspirin, for example, turns urine an orangish-yellow.

The act of voiding is under the conscious control of the central nervous system. A dog can decide when he wants to void. This is the basis for successful house-training. But once the decision to void is reached, the actual mechanism of bladder emptying is carried out by a complicated spinal cord reflex.

To learn more about disorders of the male and female *reproductive* system, see the chapter SEX AND REPRODUCTION.

SIGNS OF URINARY TRACT DISEASE

Most urinary tract disorders are associated with some disturbance in the normal pattern of voiding.

You should suspect that your dog may be suffering from a KIDNEY ailment if he appears to drink and urinate a lot more than usual; if he has fever, pain in the lumbar region, or seems to move with a stiff, arched gait; if he passes bloody urine; and if he show signs of uremic poisoning (see *Kidney Failure*).

The signs that suggest involvement of the BLADDER, URETHRA or PROSTRATE are: obvious pain during urination; straining and dribbling; sudden urges to void; voiding in small amounts; inability to empty the bladder completely; passing a weak, splattery stream; pain and swelling in the lower abdomen; loss of control; and the passage of cloudy or bloody urine.

Due to overlapping symptoms and the fact that more than one organ may be involved at the same time, it is difficult to make an exact diagnosis on the bases of symptoms alone.

In the diagnosis of urinary tract disease, the laboratory can be of considerable help. Routine tests are a urinalysis, which tells your veterinarian whether your dog has a urinary tract infection, and blood chemistries, which provide information about the function of the kidneys.

Additional studies are often indicated. They include urine cultures and x-ray examinations of the abdomen. The intravenous pyelogram is an x-ray examination in which a dye is injected into the circulation. It is excreted by the kidneys and outlines much of the urinary tract.

Cystoscopy is an examination of the interior of the bladder using a lighted instrument. Other selective studies may be performed when indicated. They include surgical exploration and/or biopsy.

KIDNEY DISEASE

Inflammation of the Kidney and Pelvis *(Pyelonephritis)*

One or both kidneys may be involved by a bacterial infection. Usually this is preceded by an infection lower in the system. There may be a blockage or congenital malformation of the urinary tract. In some cases bacteria gain entrance to the kidney via the bloodstream.

Acute pyelonephritis begins with fever and pain in the kidney area. A stiff-legged gait and a hunched-up posture are characteristic signs. Pus may appear in the urine. It is often bloody. Disturbances in the normal pattern of voiding are common.

Chronic pyelonephritis is an insidious disease. It may be preceded by signs of acute infection but often these are lacking. When the disease is of long duration, you may see signs of kidney failure. If chronic pyelonephritis is found before irreversible changes occur in the kidneys (for example, during a periodic health check-up) treatment may prevent complications.

Treatment: The urine should be cultured. Appropriate antibiotics are selected on the basis of bacterial sensitivity. Prolonged treatment is required.

Nephritis and Nephrosis

These names are given to certain conditions of the kidneys which cause scarring. When the scarring is caused by leptospira and other bacteria, the viruses of distemper, hepatitis and herpes, some drugs and poisons, and certain congenital and familial diseases, the result is a *nephritis* — or inflammation of the kidneys.

When it is caused by degenerative changes in the tissues of the kidneys, the condition is called *nephrosis*.

One cause of nephrosis is maldevelopment of the kidneys. It occurs in Lhaso Apsos and Norwegian Elkhounds.

In many cases, the exact cause of nephritis or nephrosis will be unknown. As the disease progresses, the signs and symptoms become those of uremic poisoning or kidney failure.

Kidney Failure *(Uremic Poisoning)*

Kidney failure may be sudden and acute or chronic and progressive. Acute failure occurs after certain infectious diseases, such as leptospirosis, and during shock and poisonings. Chronic failure is the end result of nephritis and other long-standing diseases.

The kidneys will not make urine if the dog's blood pressure falls below a critical threshold. Accordingly, dehydration, blood loss, shock, congestive heart failure, and injuries to the arteries of the kidneys, all may cause acute renal failure. This happens even though the kidneys are normal. This type of kidney failure is called *pre-renal*. It will improve if the underlying cause is treated promptly.

Nor will the kidneys make urine if the urinary tract is blocked by a stone, tumor, or infectious process somewhere below. Urine then backs up, shutting off flow. This type of kidney failure is called *post-renal*.

By far the majority of kidney failures are chronic and *renal* in origin. However, a dog remains asymptomatic as long as 25 percent of his nephrons are working. Thus, a considerable amount of damage can occur to the kidneys before you will begin to see signs of kidney failure.

At first you may notice that your dog seems to drink and void a lot more than usual. His kidneys no longer can conserve water and so he has an obligate urine output much greater than normal. He will want to go outdoors several times a day to relieve himself or, if confined to the house, he will begin to make mistakes — especially at night.

As his renal function continues to deteriorate, he will begin to retain ammonia, nitrogen, acids and other wastes in his blood and tissues (uremic poisoning). Signs of uremia are apathy and depression, refusal to eat, loss of condition, dry hair-coat, a brownish discoloration to the surface of the tongue, and an ammonia-like odor to the breath. Vomiting, diarrhea, and episodes of gastrointestinal bleeding can occur. Anemia is common. At the end, the dog falls into a coma.

Disorders in mineral metabolism lead to a condition called *rubber jaw*. It is characterized by loosening of the teeth and ulcerations of the mouth and gums.

Treatment: A dog suffering from chronic kidney failure still may have many happy months or years of life ahead of him with proper treatment. Your veterinarian may wish to make an exact diagnosis by ordering special tests, or by exploratory surgery and biopsy. This helps to determine whether the ailment is reversible.

It is important in the management of kidney failure to replace salt lost in the urine by giving sodium chloride tablets by mouth; to feed a high quality, low protein diet (such as Hill's K/D); and to give vitamin supplements to replace vitamins lost by the kidneys. Water should be available at all times. Some exercise is good for a uremic dog, but stressful activity should be avoided.

DISORDERS OF THE BLADDER, URETHRA AND PROSTATE

In the lower urinary tract there are four basic problems, often interrelated. They are: infections, obstructions, stones, and loss of control (urinary incontinence).

Bladder Infection *(Cystitis)*

Cystitis is a bacterial infection of the lining of the bladder. Infections in the genital tracts of both males and females may precede bouts of cystitis. Females with cystitis may lick at their vulva and have a discharge from the vagina. Some cases of cystitis are caused by bacteria which gain entrance to the bladder via the bloodstream or through the kidneys.

The most common sign of cystitis is frequent urination and the passage of blood or traces of blood in the urine. If your dog strains to void or exhibits signs of pain on urination, he may have cystitis or some cause of bladder outlet obstruction.

Treatment: Cystitis must be treated promptly to prevent ascending infection and damage to the kidneys.

A urine culture should be made to determine an appropriate antibiotic combination. An initial attack should be treated for ten days and a recurrent attack for at least three weeks. Chronic forms of cystitis require the use of urinary antiseptics and/or chemical substances to acidify the urine. Giving your dog one or two teaspoonfuls of table salt a day will cause him to drink more water and pass more urine. This helps to flush out the bladder.

Obstructed Bladder *(Urinary Retention)*

A dog who strains to pass his urine, or has obvious difficulty emptying his bladder, is probably suffering from a blockage in the bladder outlet or uretha.

Stones in the bladder or urethra are the most common causes. However, tumors, strictures and infections are at times responsible. Enlargement of the prostate gland is not a common cause of obstruction in the dog, as it is in humans.

A dog with an obstructed bladder is acutely uncomfortable or in dire distress. Males and females often assume a peculiar splay-legged stance while painfully attempting to void. Continuous straining might be confused with constipation. Pressure on the abdomen beneath the pelvis may reveal a swollen, tender bladder, which feels like a large ball in front of the pelvis. With *complete* obstruction, no urine is passed.

A *partial* obstruction can be suspected when the dog begins to dribble, voids frequently, has a weak splattery stream, but is not in acute distress. A partial obstruction may, with continued irritation, terminate in a complete obstruction.

Treatment: Complete obstruction of the bladder is a medical emergency. A sterile catheter must be inserted into the bladder to provide relief. It should be done by one familiar with the technique and having the necessary equipment. Treatment then is directed at the underlying cause.

Stones

In human beings, stones often are formed in the kidneys. However, in the dog the bladder is the usual location. Some breeds are more likely to form bladder stones than others. They include the Pekingese, Dachshund and Cocker Spaniel. The Dalmatian is the only breed that excretes uric acid of the human type; therefore, it is the only breed that can form uric acid stones.

Some stones are formed in an alkaline urine. Others in acid urine. Alkaline urine is commonly associated with urinary infections.

Bladder stones are of several types. There may be one large stone which blocks the flow of urine; or small gravelly stones which are voided painfully and cause the dog much distress. Stones in the bladder eventually will cause cystitis, if this is not already present.

Treatment: Medical management is directed at dissolving small stones and keeping new ones from forming. (Methods are similar to those used in treating chronic cystitis). Special diets are indicated in some cases. Large stones must be removed by an operation.

Urinary Incontinence

Incontinent dogs are those who have lost control over their urine. They void frequently, often dribble, and begin to make mistakes in the house. There may be a strong ammonia-like odor about the dog or his bedding. Skin around the penis or vulva may become scalded.

This is a problem seen most often in the older female who has been spayed. It is due to a deficiency of estrogen. Estrogen is important in maintaining tone of the bladder.

Damage to the nerve supply of the bladder (spinal cord disease, ruptured disc, tumor, brain tumor) also can lead to loss of bladder function. Other causes of incontinence are cystitis, stones, and ailments of the kidneys. If your dog starts to show signs of urinary incontinence, ask your veterinarian to examine him for one of these disorders.

Treatment: Incontinence in spayed females can be treated by giving one to five mg of diethylstilbesterol daily for three to five days, then weekly. The dose depends upon the size of the dog.

Enlarged Prostate

The prostate is an accessory sex gland in males found at the base of the bladder. It partly surrounds the urethra. Prostatic enlargement occurs in many dogs over five years of age, but few show any ill effects from it. Those that do usually are elderly. An enlarging prostate gland usually expands backwards into the rectum. But when large enough, it can push forward and exert pressure on the outlet of the bladder causing changes in the voiding pattern (frequent urination, dribbling and loss of control). This is not common.

The outstanding sign of prostatic enlargement is straining at stool, during which there is obvious pain. The feces may appear flat on one side, or ribbon-like. Blockages do occur (fecal impactions). Oddly, one sign of fecal impaction is diarrhea. It is due to liquid feces forcing its way around a solid lump. Some dogs may walk rigidly with a stiff back. A limp, or posterior weakness affecting one or both rear legs, may occur with advanced disease.

Treatment: If your dog is having difficulty emptying his rectum, read the section on *Constipation,* in the chapter DIGESTIVE SYSTEM.

Medical treatment involves the administration of estrogen, the female hormone. The exact dosage is important to prevent complications. It should be prescribed by a veterinarian.

Castration is the surgical treatment of choice. It results in shrinkage of the gland.

Cancer of the prostate gland is uncommon in the dog.

Prostatitis

Acute prostatitis is a bacterial infection of the prostate gland. The signs are fever, an arched back or a tucked-up abdomen, pain on urination, and difficulty in voiding. Infected-looking secretions may drip from the penis. The disease can become chronic with periodic flare-ups. It is one cause of sterility in the male.

Treatment: Prostatitis should be treated by a veterinarian. Appropriate antibiotics are employed, based on cultures of prostatic secretions. They must be continued for four to six weeks. Castration is often recommended when there is a lack of response to antibiotics.

15

Sex and Reproduction

SEX AND SOCIABILITY

Centuries of selective breeding for qualities which make the dog useful for man's purpose have also caused a profound change in his social orientation and sexual responses.

At a time when the wild ancestors of dogs ran in packs, they must have had unlimited opportunity to learn species behavior patterns and establish appropriate roles within their pack hierarchy. But today many dogs seem to be rank amateurs in the mere business of greeting and getting along with members of their own kind. This is especially true where dogs have lived almost exclusively with people and have had little or no opportunity to form social relations with other dogs.

In contrast, wolves, wild cousins of the dog, are extremely affectionate with one another. But in wolf society actual mating enters into the picture only during a short breeding season each spring. In a pack of any size only the dominant male and female are permitted to breed. Others must provide food, stand watch over the litter, assist in the preparation of the den and the guarding of it against enemies. This is the economy of nature which provides for survival of the species.

Early sexual maturity and high fertility in the dog is a direct result of selective breeding. This has brought about physical changes in the dog as well. Dogs develop quickly and attain puberty at an early age. A male may be able to sire puppies when he is ten months old. Females become sexually mature when they reach their second heat.

Dogs are sexually compliant in the sense that they don't mate for life and are willing to accept a breeding partner chosen for them by their owners. Unlike wolves, they remain firmly attached to their owners, forming less firm bonds with members of their own species.

At times, this can create problems for the dog breeder.

BREEDING

General Remarks

If you plan to breed purebred dogs it is important to begin with a mental grasp of what it is you are trying to accomplish. The object of any breeding program is to preserve the essential qualities and physical attributes of the breed. Accordingly, a thorough understanding of the breed standard is a basic requirement. Beyond the standard, however, there is an elusive something extra; a certain almost extra-sensory perception which gives to those who have it a kind of success which others never seem quite able to grasp.

A successful breeder is one who knows desirable traits and is willing to breed for them. Knowledge of this sort does not come spontaneously. You may be lucky enough to have been born with an eye for a good dog. Still, you need to learn everything you can about your breed, especially the bloodlines from which you plan to choose your stock. Visit as many kennels as you can, talk to their owners, see the tried and true producers, the retired dogs and the up-and-coming ones.

You will notice that the successful breeder is the one who sees the faults in his own dogs as readily as he sees those in his rival's. Perhaps that little "something extra" is the good sense to breed with the *whole* dog in mind — not to put emphasis on any one single attribute at the expense of the overall dog.

Pedigrees are important because they are the means to study the bloodlines and learn the relationships between the various dogs. They are of greatest value when the dogs are known, or actually have been seen.

Championships do indicate merit and do give some indication of quality. However, they are not always completely informative as to the overall superiority of the individuals listed. Some championships are won through the accident of less than normal quality in the competition. The opposite is also true — some dogs do not win their medals simply because of lack of exposure.

Count the championships, but also study the patterns of inheritance. Look for qualities that have endured from generation to generation. Familiarize yourself with the individual dogs. This will give you a sound perspective on the assets of the bloodlines in question.

Genetics

Breeding is subject to the chance combination of countless genes. The smallest combination of genes which can determine a hereditary trait is a pair. One gene is inherited from each parent. When two genes combine, the *dominant* gene is the one that determines the trait. A *recessive* gene does not determine a trait unless it is combined with another recessive gene. Other combinations may be *additive* — that is, both genes contribute in part to the expression of the trait. Unfortunately, most traits that we as breeders are interested in are determined by a great many genetic pairs — which is why dog breeding is an art and not an exact science. Since a dog has 39 pairs of chromosomes and each chromosome contains more than 25,000 genes, the genetic possibilities are almost infinite.

Many undesirable hereditary traits are expressed by recessive genes. Such a gene can be carried down through many generations of offspring, causing no problem until it is combined with a like recessive gene. This is why recessive traits cannot be eliminated in one or two generations of careful breeding.

In contrast, dominant traits are seen in the first generation of puppies. Breeders easily recognize problems caused by dominant genes. By choosing not to breed such individuals they eliminate those traits from their breeding program.

For these reasons, sporadic hereditary disorders are more frequently due to recessive genes.

Undesirable hereditary traits commonly seen by dog owners are: undescended testicles; inguinal and navel hernias; abnormally short or absent tails; canine hip dysplasia and elbow dysplasia; malocclusion and incorrect bite; cleft palate and harelip; slipping kneecaps; congenital cataracts; congenital deafness; entropion and ectropion; collie eye and progressive retinal atrophy; and behavioral disorders, such as inherited aggression and shyness.

When you breed two dogs with a common ancestor, their litter inherits some of the same genes from each side of the pedigree. This allows for the statistical possibility that genes will "double-up" at the same locus. The result is two-fold: first the expression of traits is more uniform; but undesirable recessive genes may come to the surface, thereby giving rise to serious problems.

Linebreeding and Inbreeding

Broadly speaking, any litter which has the same dog on each side of the pedigree is an *inbred* one. However, this term is usually applied only to those matings which are in the order of parent to offspring, or brother to sister. Interbreeding among dogs further removed is *linebreeding*.

Linebreeding is the safest and best method to preserve type and conformation, provided that the foundation dogs are well chosen and one has the judgment and experience to pick the best puppies. Inbreeding, on the other hand, requires a genetically clean stock, a knowledge of the faults and virtues of all the common dogs in the pedigrees for at least three generations, and the willingness to cull ruthlessly when it becomes necessary.

Most breeders prefer to avoid inbreeding. Instead, they keep the overall relationship to common dogs rather high by using them several times further back in the pedigree.

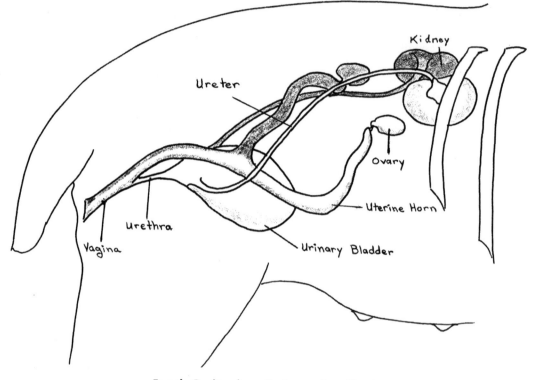

Female Genitourinary System. —*Rose Floyd*

A common misconception is that inbreeding causes high-strung, nervous and aggressive dogs. Because two individuals are closely related does not mean that their offspring are going to be unsound. It is the genetic potential in the background of the pair which determines the outcome. A fundamentally sound strain remains fundamentally sound. One which has some unstable dogs in its inbreeding program is likely to have problems.

After having linebred for three or four generations, most breeders have found from experience that it is wise to bring in new blood. The use of a stud from a totally different bloodline may be considered. This produces an *outcrossed* litter and "reshuffles" the genes that have tended to become fixed, in a more or less predictable manner, through previous linebreeding. Many times, particularly with an overly refined bitch, an outcross will give surprisingly good results. An improvement in the health and vigor of the resulting puppies is apparent from the time they are born. This process is known as "nicking". While the litter will sometimes lack uniformity, nevertheless some really good show dogs have been produced in this manner.

When two strains have nicked successfully, other crosses between them may work as well. Puppies from such matings usually are bred back into one of the two strains, thereby providing a basis for a new line.

One final method is to breed a dog and a bitch who are both of mixed ancestry. Neither has a linebred background. When using this approach, it is essential that one has a definite goal in mind. One dog may carry an attribute or quality totally lacking in the other. However, the method of breeding strengths to weaknesses in hopes that the strengths will win out sometimes is disappointing—too often it is the weaknesses which win out, producing puppies of inferior quality.

The Brood Bitch

Before you decide to breed your female, give careful consideration to the effort and expense which goes into producing a litter of healthy and active puppies. It can be both time-consuming and expensive. If you own a purebred dam, you should give consideration to her overall conformation, disposition, and the qualities she will pass along to her puppies.

Another factor to consider is that many purebred puppies cannot be sold locally. This means advertising and the added cost and effort of finding the right sort of home in which to place them.

In contrast to a popular belief, the female does not need to have a litter in order to be psychologically fulfilled. In fact, a neutered female makes an outstanding housepet. She is able to devote herself exclusively to her human family.

Most breeders mate a bitch on her second or third season, at which time she is emotionally mature and able to adjust well to the role of a brood matron.

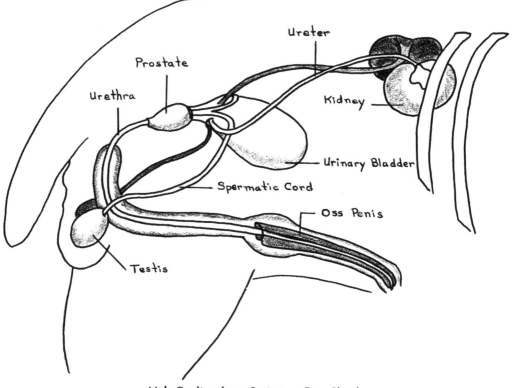

Male Genitourinary System. —*Rose Floyd*

A prospective brood matron should be kept in top physical condition. An overweight bitch, lacking in exercise tolerance, is difficult to mate and many times will not come into season regularly and may have difficulty in whelping.

Once you decide to mate your female, take her to your veterinarian for a physical check-up. A maiden bitch should be examined to make sure that her vaginal orifice is normal in size. There should be no constricting ring which could prevent normal entry.

Her physical check-up should include a test for heartworms in areas where this is a problem.

Due to an increase in the incidence of brucellosis in dogs, a serum agglutination test should always be done before mating. This test is now available in veterinary clinics and can be run from a blood sample in a few minutes.

If you own a bitch of one of the larger breeds, ask your veterinarian to x-ray her pelvis. This should be done after one year of age. If the x-rays show bone changes of hip dysplasia, *do not breed her*. Certification by the OFA or other highly reliable authority is desirable.

Also, before mating, the bitch should be checked for worms. Roundworms are difficult to avoid in puppies. Other parasites, if found, should be vigorously treated. A bitch with an active worm infestation is less likely to whelp healthy active puppies.

The Stud Dog

Part of the breeding preparation is to choose the stud dog well in advance.

The show record of a prospective stud dog may include a championship, multiple Breed wins, Group placings, or even a Best in Show. Unfortunately, not all great show dogs are outstanding producers. By the same token, some of the top producers have not been particularly outstanding in the ring.

If a stud dog has had a career as a producer, his record becomes a matter of considerable importance. If he has sired the type of dog you like, particularly if several bitches were used, you have strong evidence in favor of his potency. The number of champions produced is not always as meaningful as you may think. Usually there is a lapse of several years before a mating and a championship. Some of the top producers are often recognized well after they have stopped producing, but their offspring may retain their sire's potency.

If your bitch came from a breeding kennel, it is clearly a good idea to talk to your breeder before making a final decision. Your breeder will be familiar with the strengths and weaknesses which lie behind your bitch. This knowledge can be vitally important in choosing a compatible mate.

Some breeding kennels offer stud service. If you have an outstanding bitch from that bloodline, you may give serious thought to using a stud from that same strain to reinforce the best qualities in your bitch.

It is the responsibility of the breeder (who is the owner of the bitch) to come to a clear understanding with the owner of the stud dog concerning the breeding terms. Usually a stud fee is paid at the time of the mating, or the stud's owner may agree to take "pick of the litter", which is a puppy of his own choosing. The age of the puppy should be agreed upon. If the bitch does not conceive, the stud's owner may offer a return service at no extra charge. However, this is not obligatory in any way. Terms vary with the circumstances and policies of the kennel. If these are in writing, there will be no misunderstandings at a later date.

A stud should be kept in top physical condition with regular exercise, routine health check-ups and a sound diet. Excessive weight is a severe handicap to a stud dog. He could be too heavy to mount a bitch. A poorly kept or run-down dog is unsatisfactory.

Before a dog is offered as stud to the public, a brucellosis slide test should be made to establish that he is free of this disease. Brucellosis, once introduced into a kennel, can cause widespread sterility and the ruin of an outstanding breeding program.

Stud dogs of larger breeds should be x-rayed for hip dysplasia. Dogs with hip displasia *should not* be offered at stud. Certification by OFA or some other highly reliable source is desirable. (See *Hip Dysplasia*).

A male may be used at stud after he is over one year of age. If an older dog is not a known producer, a sperm count is desirable. A culture of the prostatic secretions should be done if the fertility is low. A chronic infection often can be treated.

Before your dog is used at stud for the first time, check to be sure he has no problem that could interfere with successful mating. Some males have a long flexible forepart to the penis. If it bends backward it could make intromission impossible. If this is the case, he will have to be bred by artificial insemination.

Push the prepuce back to make sure that the penis is able to extend normally. A retained fold of skin (frenulum) may prevent protrusion of the penis. When present, it can be cut easily.

Red, pimple-like bumps or growths on the penis should receive veterinary attention. Lacerations and erosions tend to bleed when the dog has an erection. During intercourse, blood if mixed with semen reduces the motility of the sperm.

Other abnormalities are a stricture foreskin; an infection beneath the sheath; abnormal or undescended testicles; and a discharge from the urethra. To learn more about these conditions, see *Disease of the Male Genital Tract*. If one of these is present, the dog should be examined and treated by a veterinarian before mating.

The Estrus Cycle *(Heat cycle)*

The most common cause of unsuccessful mating is breeding at the wrong time of the (estrus) cycle. Consequently, a thorough understanding of this cycle is important.

As a general rule *estrus,* the season of heat, lasts 21 days, as reckoned from the first sign of vaginal bleeding. The onset of heat (called *proestrus)* lasts six to nine days. It is signaled by a dark bloody discharge and firm swelling of the vulva. It is during this stage that the female begins to attract the male who is able to detect chemical substances, called *pheromones,* which are discharged from her vulva and excreted in her urine.

During this preovulatory phase in the heat cycle the female will not accept the male. If mating is attempted she will jump away, sit down, growl or snap at the male to drive him away.

The second phase of the estrus cycle is called estrus or *standing heat.* It is the time during which the female is receptive. She begins to flirt with the male, raises her tail and flags it to the side, lifts her pelvis and presents her vulva when touched in the rear. The vulva softens and the discharge becomes watermelon colored or pinkish.

A microscopic examination of the vaginal secretions at this time will show a marked reduction in the number of red cells. A few white cells will be seen. Also there are changes in the appearance of the surface cells of the vaginal lining. These changes enable a veterinarian to determine whether the bitch is ready to be bred.

There is another test for ovulation which utilizes a paper strip to test the mucus from the cervix of the uterus. This is the same sugar test tape used by diabetics to check for sugar in the urine. The test is based on the fact that sugar appears in the mucus of the cervix when the bitch begins to ovulate. Insert the paper strip into the vagina near the cervix and leave it for one minute. Then remove it and read the color. A negative sugar test suggests that the bitch is not ovulating. However, a positive test may be a false positive if a vaginal infection is present. This test is not as predictable as vaginal cytologies.

Estrus, or standing heat, lasts six to 12 days. It ends when the female refuses to stand for the male.

The third phase in the reproductive cycle is called *metestrus.* It begins when the female refuses to stand for the male and lasts through the period of uterine repair (about 60 to 105 days). After a bitch has gone into heat once, her breasts and vulva will remain slightly larger than before.

The fourth phase of the reproductive cycle, called *anestrus,* is a period of reproductive rest. It lasts 100 to 150 days.

The heat period usually comes every six to eight months. However, some bitches go into heat every four months and others only once a year. Several factors, such as the time of year, hereditary tendencies and emotional states, have a bearing. Some of these are discussed under the subject of *Infertility.*

Hormonal Influences During Estrus

Pituitary Influence

The heat cycle begins when the pituitary gland releases FSH (follicle stimulating hormone) which causes the ovaries to grow the egg follicles and begin to make estrogen. Under the influence of another pituitary hormone called LH (lutenizing hormone) the egg follicle ruptures and releases eggs into the fallopian tubes.

When progesterone (for example, in the birth control pill Ovaban) is given during the *first three days* of proestrus, it blocks the release of pituitary FSH and aborts the heat cycle.

Testosterone, which blocks the release of LH, will prevent heat if given *before* the first signs of proestrus.

To learn more about the use of hormones as contraceptives, see *Birth Control*.

Ovarian Influence

Estrogen from the ovary causes the vulva to become swollen and turgid. It also effects the lining of the uterus and begins the discharge. These are the first signs that the bitch is going into heat (proestrus).

Some bitches have a very light pinkish to yellow discharge early in proestrus. If you are not sure whether your bitch is going into heat, wipe a Kleenex across her vulva. If you see a pinkish color on the Kleenex, she is in early heat.

As the egg follicles mature, they make less estrogen and begin to produce progesterone. This hormone makes the vulva soft and pliable, making intromission possible. These vulvar changes occur late in proestrus or early in estrus.

After the eggs have been shed from the ovary, they must mature in the female for 72 hours before they can combine with the sperm. Sperm, on the other hand, can survive in the female for up to seven days. Fertilization occurs in the Fallopian tubes which lead from the ovary to the uterus. Fertilized eggs implant in the uterus on the 14th to 18th day.

An important function of progesterone is to prepare the lining of the uterus to receive the fertilized eggs. Such preparation can be blocked by giving an injection of estrogen *within seven days of mating* (the mismate shot).

The egg follicle now becomes a small cystic structure called the corpus luteum. Its function is to continue to make progesterone and support the pregnancy. Removal of the ovaries, or inadequate output of progesterone from the ovaries during pregnancy, will result in abortion.

When to Breed

The leading cause of an unsuccessful mating is improper timing. Most dog owners are day-oriented. They attempt to breed on the 10th to the 14th day of the heat cycle. Recent advances in the understanding of the reproductive cycle of the female dog indicate that ovulation cannot be accurately predicted just by counting the days of the heat cycle. You may miss the early signs of heat, or your dog may show very little evidence of them. Also ovulation may occur several days after the female is in standing heat instead of the first day. Furthermore, when the eggs have been shed they must mature for 72 hours before they can combine with the sperm. Fortunately, nature provides a safety factor in that sperm are able to survive for up to seven days in the female reproductive system.

There are reports of bitches being bred as early as the fourth day and as late as the 21st day of the mating cycle — and yet conceiving a litter. Practically speaking, a certain amount of trial and error is necessary.

Accordingly, many veterinarians recommend that bitches be bred three times: on the 2nd, 4th and 6th day of standing heat.

An important indicator is the deportment of the bitch. If she plays coyly, if she flags, if she presents her parts and stands firm — these all are signs that she is ready to be bred. Other signs are softening of the vulva and lightening of the discharge. Vaginal smears taken by your veterinarian, or a sugar test of the cervical secretions, may be helpful in determining the optimum mating-time.

An experienced stud dog will make his own investigations. A knowledgeable one ignores the bitch until the moment is right.

The Tie

Dogs differ from man in that they do not have tubes above the prostate (seminal vesicles) to store the sperm. Sperm flows directly into the urethra from the vas deferens and does not mix first with prostatic fluid.

The mechanics of sexual intercourse in the dog also are different from those of human beings. After intromission a knot at the base of the penis, called the bulbus glandis, becomes swollen. It is held by the constrictor muscles of the vagina forming a union between the two animals called the "tie".

During intercourse the first part of the male's ejaculate is clear and contains no sperm. The second part is cloudy and does contain sperm. The final fraction is composed of prostatic fluid. It serves to wash out the urethra and neutralize the acidity of the vagina and propel sperm up into the uterus.

The exact function of the tie in unknown. Perhaps it holds the penis in place while the sperm flow up from the testicles. For a tie to be effective, it must last for at least two to three minutes. Many ties last 30 to 40 minutes. Contrary to popular belief, the length of the tie, beyond a few minutes, has little effect upon the likelihood of pregnancy or number of puppies conceived.

If the knot at the base of the penis swells up *before* intromission, the penis may be withdrawn prematurely. Some inexperienced males may have enlargement of their penis before intromission, thus making intromission impossible. These dogs should be taken away from the female until the penis returns to its normal size. For dogs to mate, full erection must take place after intromission.

MATING

Getting Ready

When the bitch is due in season she should be watched carefully. As soon as she shows color (bleeding from her vulva), the owner of the stud dog should be notified. He may want the bitch at once. This has the advantage of letting her settle into her new surroundings after a nerve-racking trip. Also, the owner of the stud dog is less likely to miss her ovulation if he gets her in plenty of time.

If the female has a heavy or matted coat, it is a good idea to trim the hair away to expose the vulva.

If the male has long hair on the prepuce or near the head of the penis, it may catch on the penis during erection. When the penis returns, the prepuce may be rolled under, causing a constriction. Accordingly, clip away hair on long-coated dogs before mating.

Normal Mating Procedure

Neither animal should be fed for several hours before the mating. Avoid the heat of day. In summer, bring both dogs into the house or kennel room where it is relatively cool. Otherwise the bitch should be taken to the enclosure of the stud dog, as the male is more confident and assertive in his own surroundings. If the female is shy and retiring and if the the male is strong and assertive, it may be better to take the male to the enclosure of the bitch.

Keep the number of people to a minimum. The fewer distractions the better.

Both dogs are introduced to each other on leads. Once it is certain that the bitch is friendly and receptive, the dogs may be let off leash to romp for a short while, and perform necessary foreplay.

If either the stud is disinterested or the female resents the male, it suggests that the bitch is not in standing heat. Separate the dogs and try again in 48 hours.

Do not insist that the male attempt to breed an unwilling bitch. This tends to confuse and frighten the female, thereby making future attempts more difficult if not impossible. A slightly nervous bitch, or one who would rather frolic than get down to the business at hand, may have to be held.

All bitches should be under control throughout mating. This may require muzzling.

Small dogs can be mated on a table with carpet for good footing. Support the female with hand under the pelvis.

The procedure for assisting at the mating of larger dogs requires two or three people. The first holds the male on the leash. If the dog mounts at the side or front, that person gently pulls him off and heads him in the right direction, encouraging him to mount at the rear. The second person sits on a stool at the bitch's side. One knee supports the bitch's abdomen. With one arm beneath the bitch, the tip of the tail is drawn in a circle around the outside of her opposite back leg and held. A third person steadies the bitch from in front.

Intromission is a hit or miss affair for the male. A cooperative female raises her vulva so that the male can make a straight entry into the vagina. The individual holding the bitch can make matters easier for the male by raising the vulva of the female with a hand placed between her legs.

Young and inexperienced males may become so excited that they ejaculate prior to intromission. This is especially likely to occur if an attempt is made to help the male by taking hold of his penis near the back of the shaft resulting in erection and ejaculation.

If the bitch is ready to be mated, she will hold her tail to the side and stand quietly for the male while he mounts. As the male begins to penetrate he will grasp her with his forelegs around the loin and thrust forward, raising her pelvis. At full penetration he will begin to tread up and down instead of thrusting forward. The bulbus glandis swells and is clasped by the vulva. This produces the tie and stimulates the male to ejaculate.

After the tie is accomplished, the male unclasps his forelegs and places both feet on the ground on the side of the bitch. He may lift his hindleg over the back of the bitch so that the two stand back to back. The dogs will remain joined for 10 to 30 minutes. It is wise to have someone posted at the head of the bitch to steady her.

Bitches may cry, whine or grunt during a tie. This is not a cause for alarm. The important thing is to be sure that the bitch does not become frightened and begin to struggle and try to pull away from the male.

When a dog and bitch separate after a tie, momentarily it can be painful. Be prepared for either one to make a sudden snap.

A mating between a tall dog and a short bitch can present a mechanical problem. The answer is to stand the male in a ditch or breed on a slope to equalize the difference.

Prolonged Tie

One may encounter a situation in which the animals remained tied for an hour or longer. The problem is that the constricting vaginal ring maintains the erection. The blood cannot leave the bulbus glandis and return to the body. As the animals become frustrated and begin to tug against each other the situation is aggravated. Do not throw water on the dogs or try to pull them apart. They are unable to help themselves. Instead, turn the male so that he remounts the female and then push on his rump to increase the depth of penetration. This relieves the constricting effect of the vaginal ring so that the dogs can slide apart.

Nervous or apprehensive owners communicate this to their dogs. A calm collected approach is the best. If one of the dogs is a housepet, or if for any other reason the mating is difficult for the owners, the entire matter should be put in the hands of a capable veterinarian.

Shy Breeders — Dogs That Won't Mate

The most common cause of sexual reluctance is breeding at the wrong time in the estrus cycle. A male may mount a female during proestrus but then seem to lose interest. A female may allow a male to mount her, only to sit down or jump away if he begins to thrust. This is normal proestrus behavior. An inexperienced breeder may see it as a sign that the mating isn't going to take place.

When you are certain that the bitch is in standing heat, then the problem is a mental or physical one. Psychological factors are much more common than physical or hormonal ones.

A male may become a shy breeder because of unpleasant associations with sex. Many owners scold or punish their dog if he shows sexual advances toward other dogs or toward people — until he believes he will be punished if he attempts mating.

Some may have a fear of attempting mating because of prior experience with an unwilling aggressive bitch.

Others may have been injured during mating because of inadequate restraint of the bitch.

Some bitches will mate only with a very aggressive male.

Some dogs, who have had little association with other dogs, relate poorly to them — preferring people.

Finally, and least likely of all, a dog may be suffering from a hormone imbalance (see *Impotence*).

A spoiled female who has been raised as a housepet may be a reluctant breeder (because of inadequate canine socialization). An extremely submissive female may clamp down her tail and fail to raise her vulva, making intromission impossible. Some females are quite selective and won't mate with a dog they can dominate. A bitch who runs with a certain dog in a kennel may mate willingly with that dog but refuse another. Rarely one encounters a bitch who panics at the approach of a male and throws herself on the ground. This is seen with overly submissive bitches. Tranquilization may be of aid.

Treatment: In the case of the unmanageable bitch the breeding can still take place *if the bitch is restrained and well tranquilized,* providing that the stud is experienced and aggressive. Because she won't display the usual social signs of sexual readiness, vaginal cytology is indicated to determine the moment of peak fertility.

If for other reasons it appears that the mating might not take place naturally, then one will need to decide whether to let nature take its course and try again later, or proceed at once to A.I. (see *Artificial Insemination*). Breeding by A.I. will not spoil a dog or bitch in the future for natural breeding.

To help a male regain his self-confidence let him run with an easy-going bitch who likes to be dominated. An experienced brood matron who is a willing breeder can help a bashful dog build up his ego. Once he has bred a female successfully, generally his problems are over.

If a bitch of outgoing disposition consistently refuses to receive a stud, it is a good idea to have her examined for a vaginal infection or some other disorder which could cause pain during intercourse (see *Diseases of the Female Genital Tract*).

INFERTILITY

When a bitch fails to conceive after successful matings, you may be faced with an infertility problem. This is especially likely to be true if the dogs were bred more than once. Either the stud dog or the female could be at fault.

Fertility Problems in the Male

One of the causes of reduced fertility in the male is excessive use. Males used for three consecutive days should be rested for 48 hours; or they may be used regularly at 48-hour intervals. When a stud dog is much in demand, a single mating and low fertility may be the cause of a missed pregnancy.

Dogs that have not been used at stud for some time may have a low sperm count due to sexual inactivity. During a second mating, 48 hours after the first, the quality of semen often is improved.

Prolonged elevated body temperature depresses sperm formation. Some dogs are less fertile in the summer months, especially when the weather is hot and they cannot get cool. A stud dog run down by a chronic illness may take several weeks to regain his normal sperm count.

Hypothyroidism can lower a dog's sperm count and also his libido.

Treatment: A semen analysis is indicated to see if the sperm are of normal quantity and quality. When sperm are present, often the stud's potency can be improved by treating the underlying problem. A male of marginal fertility should be bred at the peak of female fertility (72 hours after ovulation as determined by vaginal cytology).

Infertility can be caused by diseases of the male reproductive tract. Treatment is discussed elsewhere in this chapter.

Genetic and chromosomal abnormalities are rare causes of infertility. They are difficult to diagnose. Such investigations are best carried out at a school of veterinary medicine.

Impotence

Most cases of impotence are due to psychological factors. (See *Shy Breeders–Dogs That Won't Mate.*)

The male sex drive is under the influence of testosterone which is produced by the male gonads. Rarely, impotence is caused by failure of the testicles to produce enough hormone. Semen analysis is not a test for the male hormone because the cells that make the sperm are not the same ones that make testosterone. A fertile male can be impotent and a sterile male can be quite able and willing to mate a bitch.

An estrogen-producing tumor of the testicles can cause both impotency and lack of sperm. Other signs are feminization of the dog. He loses his masculine appearance, becomes plump, may develop enlarged nipples, and attract other male dogs. Usually this tumor develops in an undescended testicle. Such dogs should be watched carefully for a swelling in the groin which could indicate a growth.

Treatment: Impotency which is due to hormonal rather than behavioral causes is difficult to diagnose and treat. Some dogs may respond to the administration of testosterone when given before breeding. Unfortunately the dose which stimulates the male libido also depresses sperm production. It must be used with caution. Consult your veterinarian.

Fertility Problems in the Female

The main cause of infertility in the female is infection in the uterus or reproductive tract (see *Chronic Endometritis*). Other causes are abnormal genes and chromosomes which are difficult to diagnose and treat.

Irregular heat cycles present problems in knowing when to breed and for this reason are discussed under the subject of infertility.

Abnormal Heat Cycles

Some bitches come into heat every four months and others once a year. As a bitch grows old, her heat periods become less regular and in some cases will not be accompanied by ovulation.

Some bitches will skip a heat period. This is not too unusual. Often a bitch's heat is irregular, being either longer or shorter than normal. When a bitch stays in heat longer than three weeks, this usually is abnormal. Cystic ovaries (ovaries that continue to produce estrogens) keep dogs in heat for several weeks or months and may require surgery.

Infection of the uterus can give signs similar to heat in that a discharge is seen, but the female is not receptive to the male. When there is prolongation of heat the bitch should be examined by a veterinarian to find out what is causing the problem.

Many cases thought to be lack of heat (anestrus) are really a "silent" type of heat which is not noticed, or the bitch goes in and out of heat in a few days.

Some females are quite fastidious and lick themselves clean. If you are not familiar with the size of the normal vulva you may not notice the swelling.

Two causes of lack of heat are hypothyroidism and hypoestronism.

Hypothyroidism is a cause of anestrus and irregular heat cycles. Other indications of hypothyroidism may or may not be present. The diagnosis is confirmed by thyroid blood tests. This condition is treated by giving thyroid hormone.

Hypoestronism is due to failure of the ovaries to develop to sexual maturity. The breasts and vulva remain small and underdeveloped. Heat does not occur because of a low estrogen level.

Your veterinarian may be able to bring your bitch into heat with injections of FSH. If heat develops, this indicates that the ovaries are able to respond. If this is done in conjunction with a planned breeding, LH is then given on the tenth day of estrus and then the bitch is bred in 48 hours. Some very short periods are benefitted by FSH.

Females who are slow to come into heat often will do so when kenneled and allowed to run with a male for three or four months.

Consult your veterinarian if your bitch doesn't go into heat by 18 months of age.

Brucellosis

Brucellosis is a major cause of infertility in males and females (see *Infectious Diseases*). One mode of transmission is by venereal contact. Another is by contact with the discharge of an infected female who has aborted. Due to an increasing incidence of brucellosis in dogs in the United States, a blood test should be done on both the bitch and stud dog before mating. This test is available in veterinary clinics and can be run from a blood sample in a few minutes.

Diseases of the Male Genital Tract

There are several disorders of the male genital system which can lead to mating problems or infertility. Orchitis, balanoposthitis, phimosis, paraphimosis, undescended testicles, and prostatitis are the most common ones.

Examination of the prostate gland and evaluation of the quality of the semen are two examinations which must be done by a specialist. They are indicated when a fertility problem exists or when there are indications of prostatic infection. Prostatitis is discussed under the URINARY SYSTEM.

Infection of the Prepuce and Head of the Penis (Balanoposthitis)

A small amount of white or yellowish discharge from the prepuce is present in nearly all mature males. An excessive purulent discharge is associated with overt infection. Awns or pieces of straw can get caught beneath the foreskin of the male and cause irritation of the skin of the penis, followed by infection and abscess of the sheath. These infections are called balanoposthitis.

If your dog begins to lick himself excessively and has a purulent, foul-smelling discharge from the prepuce, probably he is suffering from balanoposthitis. This condition also may be due to prolonged sexual intercourse. Such infections can be transmitted to the female during mating.

Treatment: First, clip away the coat hair on or near the foreskin. Push back the foreskin to expose the head of the penis. Wash the area thoroughly with surgical soap and apply an antibiotic ointment. If your dog will not allow you to retract his foreskin, using a syringe flush the sheath with dilute hydrogen peroxide solution twice daily. Then infuse Panolog or furacin ointment. Repeat until all signs of discharge and inflammation are gone.

For persistent cases, flush the sheath with an astringent solution made up of 5% tannic acid and 5% salicylic acid mixed with two parts of propylene glycol and continue the treatment for four days.

Strictured Foreskin — Penis Can't Protrude (Phimosis)

In this condition the opening of the sheath is too small to let the penis extend. The opening may be so small that urine can escape only in small drops. Some cases are due to infection. Many are due to a congenital abnormality, i.e., puppies are born that way. Several male puppies in a litter may be so affected.

If the condition is due to an infection of the sheath, treatment of the sheath infection may correct the phimosis as well. If it is due to a congenital abnormality, a surgical operation is required.

Penis That Can't Retract (Paraphimosis)

In this condition the penis is unable to return to its former position inside the sheath. The sheath may serve as a constricting band around the shaft of the penis, cutting off the blood supply. A predisposing cause is long hair on the skin of the sheath which causes the foreskin to roll under when the penis is partly retracted. Often it follows mating. It can be prevented by cutting the long hairs from around the foreskin prior to breeding. Check your male after using him at stud to be sure that the penis has returned to its sheath.

Treatment: The penis should be returned to its normal position as quickly as possible in order to prevent permanent damage.

Apply ice packs to reduce swelling. Push the prepuce backward on the shaft of the penis, rolling it out so the hairs are not caught. Lubricate the surface of the penis with mineral oil or olive oil. With one hand, gently draw the head of the penis forward while squeezing it so as to reduce the swelling.

With the other hand, slide the prepuce forward. If these measures are not immediately successful, notify your veterinarian.

In most cases the skin of the penis is severely irritated and it will be necessary to flush the sheath twice daily with an antiseptic solution as described under the treatment of balanoposthitis.

Undescended Testicles

Testicles usually descend before birth in most dogs. In some the testicle may descend as late as five to six months of age. If a testicle can be felt one time but not at another, there is no need for concern. Testicles can retract back up into the groin when a puppy is cold, excited or actively playing. Both testicles should be fully descended before six months of age. Consult your veterinarian if they have not come down by that time.

The testicles should be of similar size and feel rather firm. Since much of the testicle size is due to the sperm-producing tissue, soft or small testicles in the sexually mature dog are likely to be deficient in sperm.

Monorchid dogs, those with only one testicle in the scrotum, may be fertile. However, they should not be used at stud because the condition is inherited. *Cryptorchid* dogs, those with no testicles in the scrotum, are sterile.

Treatment: Hormone injections (lutinizing hormone or testosterone) have been used to stimulate testicular descent in puppies. Results are questionable.

If the testicles do not seem well developed at one year of age, ask your veterinarian to do a semen analysis.

Orchitis (Inflammation of the Testicle)

Swelling and inflammation of one or both testicles can be caused by trauma (dog bites, shotgun wounds, blows), injury to the skin of the scrotum (frostbite, weed burns, chemical and thermal burns), and spread of infection from elsewhere in the genitourinary tract (cystitis, prostatitis, balanoposthitis). The vas deferens serves as a conduit to carry bacteria back to the testes from the urethra.

The virus of distemper, and the bacteria causing brucellosis, can attack and destroy the testicles.

Injuries or infections of the testicle are the most common causes of male infertility.

The signs of orchitis are swelling and pain in the testicle. The testicle becomes enlarged and hard. Your dog probably will not allow you to handle him. His gait is spread-legged with his belly tucked up. He sits most of the time; especially on a cool surface.

Later the diseased testicle shrinks and becomes small and firm.

Treatment: Minor scrotal injuries should be cleaned and salved with an antibiotic ointment. Orchitis should be treated by a veterinarian. Cultures and specific antibiotics are indicated.

Diseases of the Female Genital Tract

Diseases of the female genital system may be divided into those affecting the vagina (vaginitis, vaginal prolapse), and those affecting the uterus (chronic endometritis and pyometra). All adversely affect fertility and the health of the female.

Vaginal Infection

Bacterial infection of the vagina often spreads to the urinary tract causing burning on urination and increased frequency. It may ascend into the uterus causing a chronic endometritis.

The main sign is a vaginal discharge and staining of the hair about the vulva. This is not always seen because many bitches lick themselves clean. If your bitch seems to lick herself excessively, suspect that she is suffering from vaginitis.

Your veterinarian may want to do a vaginal examination to confirm the diagnosis and rule out a chronic endometritis.

A bitch with vaginitis should not be bred until the infection has been treated. Infected vaginal secretions are spermacidal. More important, there is a danger of infecting the male.

Juvenile vaginitis is seen in puppies six to 12 weeks of age. The signs are vaginal discharge along with painful urination.

Treatment: Administer a Betadine vaginal douche twice daily for seven days and accompany it with an oral antibiotic. An appropriate antibiotic can be selected on the basis of cultures and sensitivities. Treat urinary tract infection if present.

Vaginitis in puppies is difficult to clear up. Flush the vagina twice daily with Furacin, Neomycin solution, or Massengill's douche. Estrogen tablets, prescribed by your veterinarian, are of help in difficult cases. Most puppies with juvenile vaginitis clear up once they go into heat for the first time.

Protrusion of the Vagina (Vaginal Prolapse)

This condition occurs during heat. It is seen in Boxers and St. Bernards most commonly. It is due to a very marked estrogen-induced swelling of the vagina. When the vagina no longer can be contained, it protrudes out through the vulva, resulting in severe irritation.

Vaginal prolapse tends to recur in subsequent heats. It is very difficult to breed a dog with this condition even by artificial insemination.

Treatment: Sometimes the vagina can be pushed back into place and held with sutures. This is not always possible. One treatment is to administer Ovaban, which has a progesterone-like effect, and takes the bitch out of heat. Treat irritated vaginal surface with antibiotic salve or ointment.

Chronic Endometritis

This is a low grade infection of the uterus caused by bacteria which ascend upward from the vagina. Its main concern is that it is the leading cause of infertility in the female. During estrus the vulva of the bitch becomes quite enlarged. At the same time the protective plug of mucus is discharged from the cervix, opening the route to bacterial invasion of the lining of the uterus. Vaginitis is another predisposing cause.

Suspect the possibility of chronic endometritis when your bitch refuses to accept the male; when she is bred at the right time but fails to conceive, especially on two successive heat cycles; and when she delivers still-born puppies or puppies who sicken and die within the first few days.

The disease is difficult to diagnose and requires the use of appropriate smears and cultures taken from the cervix or the uterus during proestrus.

Treatment: Antibiotics are started seven days prior to and continued through seven days after the mating. Bacterial culture and sensitivities indicate the drug of choice.

Abscess of the Uterus (Pyometra)

Pyometra is a life-threatening disease of the uterus which occurs most commonly in females over six years of age. It is believed to be due to a hormonal imbalance. The earlier birth control injections (Promone), which contained large amounts of progesterone, were found to cause pyometra and were taken off the market.

Pyometra appears one to twelve weeks after the bitch goes out of heat. A bitch with pyometra refuses to eat, appears depressed and lethargic, drinks a great deal, urinates frequently.

Often there is abdominal enlargement. A low grade fever, or a normal (even subnormal) temperature, may exist. The condition is due to an abscessed uterus.

In the *open* type the cervix relaxes, releasing a large amount of pus which resembles tomato soup. In the *closed* type, pus collects in the uterus. An enlarged uterus may be felt as a painful swelling in the lower abdomen.

Treatment: In order to save the life of the bitch, a veterinarian should be called at once. Hysterectomy is the treatment of choice. It is much better to do this operation on a nontoxic dog.

Rarely it may be possible to preserve the uterus in a valuable breeding bitch by scraping out the infection and giving antibiotics and hormones.

A disease similar to pyometra, acute metritis, occurs in the post partum bitch (see *Post Partum Problems* in the chapter PREGNANCY AND WHELP-ING).

ARTIFICIAL INSEMINATION

Artificial insemination is a technique whereby semen is collected from the male and introduced into the reproductive tract of the female. When properly performed, it is as successful as actual mating. Unfortunately, AI is often used as a last resort, when it is too late in the heat cycle for the bitch to conceive.

AI has its widest application when natural mating is contraindicated or impossible. Usually this is for psychological reasons, anatomical reasons, or fear of transmitting disease.

Techniques to freeze and preserve canine semen have met with some success during the past several years, and it is entirely possible that these techniques will alter the future of dog breeding.

In the United States the American Kennel Club has definite regulations concerning the registration of dogs produced by AI. If you plan to register your litter, check first with your veterinarian or the AKC.

Equipment

A minimal amount of sterile equipment is required. The semen may be deposited directly into a 10-cc hypodermic syringe from which the plunger has been removed; or a rubber conical sheath for use as an artificial vagina can be obtained from a veterinarian. Attached to it is a centrifuge tube to hold the semen.

An ordinary red rubber catheter, which fits the end of the syringe, is used to deposit the semen up into the vagina.

All equipment used to collect and handle the semen *must be sterilized*. It should be handled in such a manner as to prevent contamination of the sample by bacteria.

Sterilize the equipment by boiling it in water for 30 minutes. Do not use chemicals or detergents. Even trace amounts of chemicals can cause death of the sperm.

Collecting the Semen

Sperm die of cold shock if the temperature of the sample is allowed to drop. Always collect the ejaculate indoors and warm the receptacle by holding it next to your body or encircling it with the palm of your hand. Semen should be kept not less than a few degrees below body temperature.

The male dog should be at ease in his surroundings and familiar with his handler. Some males will not achieve or maintain an erection unless they can mount a female. In others, semen can be collected without the presence of a female in heat.

Clean the prepuce with pHisoHex to remove loose hair or debris which might contaminate the sample. Stimulate erection by massaging the sheath in the area of the head of the penis, gradually working backward to the bulbus glandis at the base. As erection progresses, the end of the penis will protrude from the sheath. Once the penis becomes erect, encircle the base of the penis with your thumb and forefinger behind the bulbus glandis and maintain a constricting pressure. Then draw the penis downward and backward, directing the end of it toward the collection container. Avoid repeated contact between the head of the penis and the container, as this may lead to

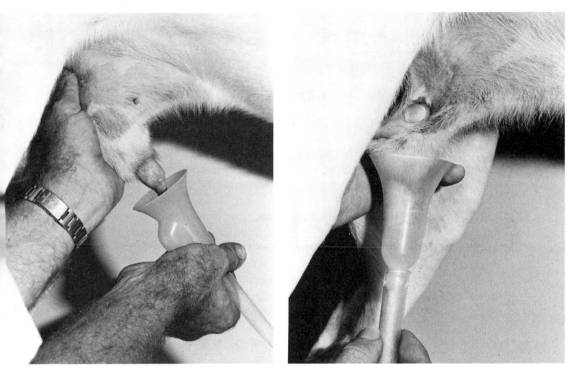

Collecting the semen. Once the penis becomes erect, encircle the base of the penis with your thumb and forefinger behind the bulb and maintain a constricting pressure. As the dog begins to ejaculate, draw the penis down and back, directing it towards the collection container. —*J. Clawson*

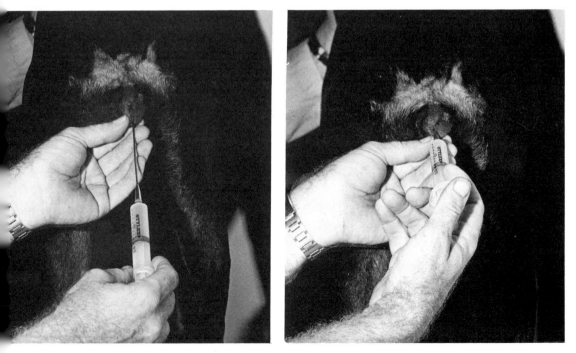

Inseminating the female. Direct the tube along the top of the vagina. When the tube is fully inserted, slowly empty the syringe. —*J. Clawson*

loss of erection. The container is grasped tightly in the opposite hand and held in position to collect the ejaculate.

As ejaculation begins, you may notice that your dog makes vigorous thrusting motions that last for a moment or two and are followed by pulsations.

The first fraction of the ejaculate varies from a few drops to one or two centimeters in volume. The second part is milky and contains the sperm. It measures one to four centimeters in volume. The third part is prostatic fluid. It varies in volume from five to 20 centimeters depending upon the length of the ejaculation. Only a small portion of this third fraction is usually collected for AI. The erection subsides when the pressure on the penis is released.

A suitable semen sample will contain five to 10 centimeters of fluid. If it appears bloody, green or discolored, it should not be used for insemination until an examination has ruled out a bacterial infection.

If you used some other collection container, transfer the semen sample to the glass or plastic hypodermic syringe, taking care not to injure the sample by bubbling air through it while replacing the plunger. Connect the sterile catheter to the end of the syringe. Pre-warm syringe and catheter to prevent cold shock to semen. All equipment should be sterile, clean and dry.

Inseminating the Bitch

The procedure for inseminating the bitch is quite simple. The leash of the female should be tied securely to a post or doorknob. An assistant straddles the female and lifts her rear feet off the ground by taking hold of her legs above the hocks. Another person introduces the red rubber catheter into the vagina.

Care must be taken in positioning the catheter so as to avoid a blind pouch in the lower half of the vagina. Spread the vulva and insert the catheter along the *top* of the vagina, directing it first upward and then forward. If the catheter still won't pass easily, put on a sterile glove and insert the tip of your finger into the vagina; then guide the plastic tube over the brim of the pelvis above the finger. The insemination tube should go in four to nine inches (depending upon the size of the bitch), thereby putting it in close proximity to the cervix of the uterus. Slowly empty the syringe. Hold the lips of the vulva tightly around the tube to prevent loss of semen. Remove the tube and massage the vulva.

The hindquarters should be elevated for six minutes to retain the semen. Keep the bitch quiet for the next two hours.

FALSE PREGNANCY (Pseudocyesis)

False pregnancy is a common condition in which a nonpregnant female thinks she is pregnant. She exhibits all the behavioral and physical signs and symptoms associated with a true pregnancy. Physical signs suggest that it is caused by an excess of progesterone. However, progesterone levels in false-pregnant females are the same as those for normal females.

False pregnancy occurs about six to ten weeks after estrus. The signs are an increase in the amount of body fat, particularly in the abdomen. Often the breasts enlarge and secrete a clear or brownish fluid or milk. Some females make a nest and experience abdominal cramps like labor. Some show a mothering instinct and become attached to small toys and other objects which are puppy substitutes. Others vomit off and on, become depressed, and a few develop diarrhea.

Occasionally, the false-pregnant bitch appears to exhibit severe uterine cramps. Caking of the breasts is not unusual. It is another source of discomfort.

Treatment: Mild cases require no treatment. The female begins to return to her normal condition in 12 weeks or less. Bitches with uterine cramps can be given the birth control pill, Ovaban, in a dose of one mg per pound of body weight for eight days. Often this will relieve the discomfort. Your veterinarian may also wish to prescribe testosterone and/or diethylstilbesterol. For caked breasts, see PREGNANCY AND WHELPING: *Post Partum Problems*.

A false-pregnant female is likely to have other false pregnancies. It may be a good idea to have her spayed.

ACCIDENTAL PREGNANCY

Accidental pregnancies do occur. Male dogs are remarkably adept at getting to a female in heat. Ordinary measures, such as confining a female behind chain-link fencing, are no guarantee that she won't be reached by an amorous male.

Once you are certain that your female is in heat, keep her indoors or on a leash. *Do not let her out of your sight.* Female dogs must be isolated throughout the entire estrus cycle which begins with the first show of color and continues for at least three weeks.

If your female has been bred, there are two alternatives to an unwanted litter. One is a hysterectomy. This operation can be performed during the early stages of pregnancy without added risk to the female. During the later stages of pregnancy hysterectomy is a more formidable undertaking.

The second alternative is to prevent the pregnancy by means of an estrogen injection (the mismate shot). This hormone works by preventing implantation of the fertilized ova into the wall of the uterus. If you choose this method, take your bitch to a veterinarian as soon as possible. The injection must be given within seven days of impregnation. One side effect of this injection is that heat is prolonged about 10 days. (Note: Estrogens have been known to induce uterine disease experimentally. Thus a possible danger exists). The mismate shot usually has no adverse effect on future fertility.

BIRTH CONTROL

There are three methods to prevent conception in the female dog. They are surgery (ovariohysterectomy or tubal ligation); the intravaginal device; and birth control drugs.

Chlorophyll tablets, which you can purchase from your veterinarian or pet stores, may help to mask the odor of a female in heat but are not an effective birth control measure.

The two operations used to sterilize the male are castration and vasectomy. These are not effective as population control measures. Another male can fertilize a bitch in heat.

Spaying *(Ovariohysterectomy)*

The most effective method for preventing pregnancy is to have a bitch spayed. In this operation the uterus, tubes and ovaries are removed.

Some people have heard that when a female is spayed she becomes fat or lethargic. A bitch who becomes fat is getting too much to eat. Many people forget that a grown dog needs less food than a puppy. Since a bitch often is spayed at the end of her puppyhood, if she gets too much to eat and puts on weight, the tendency is to blame the operation.

Another misconception is that a bitch needs to have a litter to be fulfilled. Dogs are people-oriented. They seek human companionship and look to their owners for personal fulfillment.

There are certain health benefits to ovariohysterectomy. One does not have to worry about a pyometra. Also, a spayed bitch is less likely to get breast cancer. Finally, there is no messy heat to go through twice a year.

The best time to spay most females is after they are six months of age, and before they go into their first heat. At this time the operation is easy to perform and there is less chance of complications.

After you have made arrangements to have your female spayed, be sure to withhold food and water from her on the evening prior to surgery. This operation is done under general anesthesia. A full stomach could result in vomiting and aspiration during induction of anesthesia. Check with your veterinarian concerning other special instructions or precautions to be taken before and after the operation.

Tubal Ligation

In this operation the fallopian tubes are ligated to prevent eggs from getting from the ovaries to the uterus. It has nearly the same risks as ovariohysterectomy and is only slightly less expensive in most veterinary clinics. It won't stop the bitch from going into heat and attracting the male. It does not have the health benefits of ovariohysterectomy.

Most veterinarians recommend ovariohysterectomy when an operation is to be performed for sterilization purposes.

The Intravaginal Device

This device is different from the IUD used in women. It is placed inside the vagina. It works by preventing intromission. It is not as satisfactory a method as spaying, but if you plan to breed your female at a later time, you may wish to use the intravaginal device as a temporary means of preventing pregnancy. The device can be ordered by your veterinarian.

The Pill *(Ovaban)*

Dogs are more sensitive to the progesterone component of birth control pills than are women. In the past a long-lasting progesterone was used to prevent estrus. The drug was found to cause pyometra in a certain number of cases. It was withdrawn from the market.

Currently, *Ovaban* is the only birth control pill approved for use in the dog in the United States. It is believed to work by suppressing the pituitary output of follicle stimulating hormone (see *Hormonal Influences During Estrus*).

Ovaban is a prescription item which is safe and effective when used according to the recommendations of your veterinarian. A veterinary examination is advisable to rule out problems in the reproductive tract, or breast tumors, before starting the Pill.

To *prevent heat* start the Pill at the first signs of proestrus (within the *first three days* of the heat cycle) and continue it for eight days. This will take your dog out of heat. Heat will be postponed two to nine months. The veterinarian must be sure she is in proestrus.

To *postpone heat* (i.e., for a hunting trip, pleasure trip or dog show) start the Pill at least one week before you plan to leave and continue it for 32 days. It must be started at least one week before proestrus.

Caution: You must adhere to a strict time schedule. Always confine your dog during the first eight days of her heat. You could have missed the first signs of proestrus and started the drug too late, thereby failing to stop estrus.

The first heat cycle in puppy bitches is frequently unreliable. To insure proper drug performance, Ovaban should not be given until the second heat. It should not be administered to pregnant females as it is harmful to puppies in utero.

Bitches taking Ovaban may become hungry or lazy, gain weight, experience personality changes, or show breast enlargement. These changes return to normal when the drug is stopped.

Prolonged administration in rare cases may cause an infection of the uterus (pyometra). Accordingly, the drug should not be used to postpone heat or to take a bitch out of heat for more than two consecutive heat cycles without a rest.

Liquid Contraceptive *(Cheque)*

Mibolerone, also called Cheque, is a liquid birth control preparation which you can obtain from your veterinarian. Although the drug has a high safety factor, not enough information currently is available as to its effect on future fertility in bitches. Accordingly, it is recommended only for bitches who will never be used for breeding. It prevents ovulation by blocking the effects of pituitary lutinizing hormone (see *Hormonal Influences During Estrus*).

Your veterinarian will recommend an appropriate dose. Drops are given *daily* by mouth (see *How to Administer Liquid Medicine),* or they may be mixed directly with the food. Start Cheque at least 30 days before your dog goes into heat.

Masculinization, vaginal discharge, excessive tearing, and a musky body odor occasionally are seen. In most cases, the side effects last only as long as the drug is given.

Caution: If the bitch goes into heat within the first 30 days, the drug may not be effective. It definitely will not prevent pregnancy if started after proestrus.

Discontinue Cheque after 24 months of continuous use.

Male Castration

Castration is an operation in which both testicles are removed. When the male is castrated after sexual maturity, his sex drive may be normal even though he is unable to get a bitch pregnant — but this is unusual. When a dog is castrated before puberty, his sexual urges do not develop. However, castration before puberty is not recommended. It has an adverse effect on the development of bone, stature, and secondary sex traits of the male dog.

Castration sometimes is advised to tone down an overly boisterous or aggressive male, or one who continuously urinates in the house or is otherwise obtrusive and unmanageable. Unfortunately, overindulgent owners (not male hormones) are often at fault. The dog must be shown his place in the household hierarchy. It is a good idea to discuss with your veterinarian the possibility of obedience training or other steps which could be taken to modify unruly behavior before deciding upon castration.

Castration may be indicated for medical reasons. It is recommended in some cases of testicular disease, chronic prostatitis, and perianal adenomas.

Vasectomy

Bilateral vasectomy is the treatment of choice when sterilization *alone* is the reason for surgery. In this operation a segment of the right and left vas deferens is removed. These tubes transport the sperm from the testicles to the urethra. The operation does not disturb the hormone functions of the testes.

Vasectomized dogs have normal sexual responses, can breed and mate with a bitch but cannot impregnate. The operation can be done at any time in the life of the dog without adversely affecting his growth and development.

Newborn Newfoundland puppy.

—photo, Vadim Chern
The New Complete Newfoundland

16

Pregnancy and Whelping

PREGNANCY

Gestation

Gestation is the period from conception to birth. As reckoned from the day of first successful mating, it averages 63 days. Puppies born on the 59th or 66th day fall within the normal range. However, if the bitch whelps *before* the 57th day, the puppies will probably be too young to survive.

Determining Pregnancy

Many bitches, especially those of the larger breeds, carry their litters well up under their rib cage. It is not always possible to tell whether they are pregnant. False pregnancy, which is more common than most people realize, can complicate matters.

The uterus in dogs is a Y-shaped affair with a horn on each side. The puppies are carried in the uterine horns. A veterinarian can tell by palpation whether a bitch is pregnant by 26 days of gestation. At this stage, the puppies are no bigger than the size of a walnut.

The technique for palpating puppies is to have your bitch lie down on her side so that her tummy is relaxed. Place one hand beneath, and one hand on top, of her lower abdomen. By pressing with your fingers you may be able to detect several small firm lumps which are the puppies growing in the horns of the uterus. Unless you are experienced in palpating the pregnant uterus a negative palpation does not rule out a pregnancy.

From 35 to 55 days the uterus is fluid-filled and palpation is not reliable.

By 40 days of gestation one can see a darkening and enlargement of the nipples. At this time, too, the breasts enlarge and as the time of birth approaches a milky fluid may be expressed from the nipples.

The other signs of pregnancy are weight gain, increased appetite, an enlarging abdominal girth, and sometimes morning sickness.

There is no blood or urine test for pregnancy in dogs as there is in people. X-ray of the abdomen can be done later in pregnancy if there is still some doubt and it is necessary to know for sure.

Morning Sickness

Dogs, like humans, can suffer from morning sickness. Usually this happens during the third to fourth week of pregnancy. It is due to hormonal changes, plus stretching and distention of the uterus. You may notice that your bitch appears a little depressed; she may be off her feed or vomit from time to time. Morning sickness lasts only a few days. Unless you are unusually attentive, you may not even notice it.

Treatment: If your female seems to be suffering from morning sickness, feed her in several meals spaced throughout the day. Your veterinarian may want to prescribe a drug to relax her uterus. Vitamins B and C may be given.

Prenatal Check Ups

Before you breed your bitch it is a good idea to take her to your veterinarian to see if she has any physical abnormalities which should be treated, and to find out if there is a problem which might prevent normal mating or delivery.

Be sure to have her checked for periodontitis and dental infections. Bacteria from the mouth can be passed onto newborn puppies during biting of the umbilical cord. This is one cause of serious navel infections.

Two to three weeks prior to her expected date of confinement make an appointment to have her thoroughly checked over again. Your veterinarian will want to discuss with you the normal delivery procedures, alert you to the signs of impending problems, and give you instructions for care of the newborn.

Be sure to ask where you can get help (emergency service) if needed after hours.

Care and Feeding During Pregnancy

A pregnant bitch should be lean and well-conditioned, neither rundown or depleted from an earlier litter or allowed to become fat. Her eyes should be bright and alert; her coat shiny; and her gums a healthy bright red. Routine daily exercise of a moderate nature is advisable. However, pregnant bitches should not climb fences, roughhouse with other dogs, leap down flights of stairs, or engage in other violent pursuits.

During the first four weeks of pregnancy feed your bitch her usual daily ration of high protein kibble.

Protein requirements begin to increase during the second half of pregnancy. Increase her ration by one-half with an eye to keeping her trim.

Excessive weight gain should be avoided at all costs. An overnourished bitch is apt to carry fat puppies which may make her labor difficult. At this time many breeders switch to puppy kibble which, ounce for ounce, is higher in protein. Commercial rations are formulated so that if dogs eat the amount they need they get all the nutrients they require. If you add meat or some other protein supplement to such a diet, your bitch may be getting less of the other things she needs, including fats and carbohydrates.

Supplements and vitamins are not required unless a bitch is below par from an earlier litter or recovering from an illness. Follow the advice of your veterinarian.

A bitch may lose her appetite a week or two before she delivers. At this time her abdomen is crowded with puppies. It is better to feed several smaller meals instead of one large one.

Many drugs cannot be given during pregnancy. They include some of the flea and insecticide preparations, dewormers, and certain hormones and antibiotics. Live virus vaccine should not be given to pregnant females. Check with your veterinarian before starting a pregnant female on a medication.

X-Rays of the abdomen should be avoided in the early stages of pregnancy.

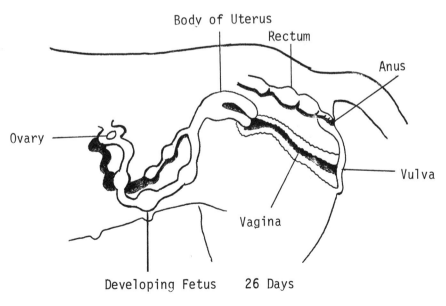

Female Reproductive System. —*Rose Floyd*

Whelping equipment.

Whelping Preparations

Bitches should deliver at home where they feel secure. They are easily upset by strange people and unfamiliar surroundings. This can delay and arrest labor. The whelping quarters should be located in a quiet, out-of-the way spot — free from comings and goings.

The best place to whelp bitches and deliver puppies is in a whelping box. An adequate box for a large dog is at least 4 by 5 feet in size. One 2 by 3 feet in size is sufficient for one of the Toy breeds. The sides should be tall enough to keep puppies from crawling out but not too high for the dam to step over. One side can be made shorter than the others. This side can be replaced by a taller board when the puppies are older. The sides should not be nailed to the floorboard. Instead they should be held in grooves made by nailing 1 × 2 inch molding around the margins. The sides are then joined together and held in place by hook-and-eye latches. The floor is much easier to clean when the sides can be removed.

A ledge around the inside of the box, a few inches from the floor, should be made by nailing 3 to 6-inch wide boards to all four sides. Puppies will crawl under these ledges instinctively and are protected from being accidentally smothered by the mother.

Several layers of clean newspaper are laid on the bottom of the box to absorb moisture and odor. However, newspapers are not a suitable surface for puppies to crawl and walk on, as they are slick and offer little traction for their feet. Heavy towels, mattress pads, indoor-outdoor carpeting, or any other surface which gives good traction and is disposable or washable, is suitable and should be used on top of the newspapers. Disposable baby diapers are excellent for Toy breed puppies. Small puppies should never be placed in deep loose bedding, such as straw, which might obstruct their breathing, or be inhaled.

The whelping quarters should be clean, dry, draft-free and warm. When puppies are born, the floor temperature should be kept at 85 degrees F. for the first seven days of life. It can be reduced 5 degrees F. weekly when the puppies are seven days old, and then progressively reduced to 70 degrees F. by the time the litter is six to eight weeks old. Keep a constant check on the temperature with a thermometer on the floor of the box.

If the temperature in the whelping room cannot be maintained with the existing heating system, additional heat may be supplied by using 250 watt infra-red heat bulbs, either suspended above the floor of the litter box or mounted in photographer's floodlight reflectors (or plant lights). Be sure to leave an area of the box out of the direct source of heat, so the mother can rest in a cooler area whenever she wants to.

The bitch should be introduced to her litter box about two weeks before she is due and required to sleep in it. By the time she whelps she will understand that she is to do so in the box and not in her master's bed.

Other whelping accessories include a small box with a towel-covered hot water bottle or heating pad at the bottom of it to place puppies in while others are being born; a bulb syringe to aspirate secretions from the mouths of the newborns; artery forceps to clamp a bleeding cord; dental floss or cotton threads for ties; and an antiseptic, such as iodine, to apply to the umbilical stumps. Scissors, clean laundered towels and plenty of fresh newspapers complete the whelping equipment.

One week before your female is due to deliver, clip away any long hair over her breasts and around her vulva. If she is a long-coated breed, trim the pantaloons.

WHELPING

Signs of Confinement

Several days before your bitch is due to give birth she may exhibit a loss of appetite and increased restlessness. Often she rummages in closets, digs a nest in the garden and goes about in a flurry of activity which is the ritual of making her nest.

Eight to twelve hours before she is due to delivery her rectal temperature drops from a normal of 101 degrees to 99 degress or below. This two-degree drop in temperature can be missed. A normal temperature does not mean she will not whelp in a few hours.

Labor and Delivery

There are three stages of labor. In the first stage the cervix dilates which opens the birth canal. In the second stage the puppies are delivered. In the third stage the afterbirth is delivered. Bitches lie down to deliver or stand and squat.

The first stage begins with rapid panting, uneasiness, straining, or perhaps vomiting. Vomiting is a normal reflex and should not be taken as a sign of distress.

On one side of the uterus a horn contracts and expels a puppy into the central cavity. Then the body of the uterus contracts and pushes the presenting part of the puppy against the cervix, which causes the cervix to dilate. At complete dilation the puppy slides into the vagina. The water bag around the puppy can be seen bulging between the lips of the vulva. It serves to lubricate the passageway. If the uterus applies enough pressure to break the water bag, straw-colored fluid is passed. Then a puppy should be delivered in a few minutes.

After the head is delivered the rest of the puppy slides out easily. Instinctively the mother removes the fetal membranes, severs the umbilical cord and begins to lick and clean her puppies. No attempt should be made to interfere with maternal care. This is an important part of the mother-puppy bond. She is learning that this is her puppy and she must take care of it. If she appears rough it is only because she is trying to stimulate breathing and blood circulation.

If the dam is occupied with another puppy and forgets to remove the amniotic sac, you should be prepared to step in and strip away the fetal membranes so that the puppy can breathe (see *Helping a Puppy Breathe*).

A placenta follows in a few minutes the birth of each puppy. The dam will try to eat some or all of the placentas. Some breeders believe the bitch needs the afterbirth because it contains hormones which aid normal labor and stimulate milk production. Others believe it upsets the digestive tract. It is not essential that the bitch consume the afterbirths. You may wish to limit the number or let nature take its course. The important thing is to count the placentas since a retained placenta can cause a serious post-natal infection (see *Acute Metritis*).

Bitches sever the umbilical cord by *shredding* it. If the cord is cut too cleanly or too close to the puppy's navel it may continue to bleed. You should be prepared to clamp or pinch off the cord and tie a thread around the stump. The stump should be cauterized with iodine or some other suitable disinfectant.

The next puppy will be born from the opposite uterine horn. When it is about to appear, remove the first puppy and place it in a box warmed to 85 degrees by an electric heating pad or hot water bottle. This prevents chilling, or temperature shock, which is a leading cause of newborn puppy deaths.

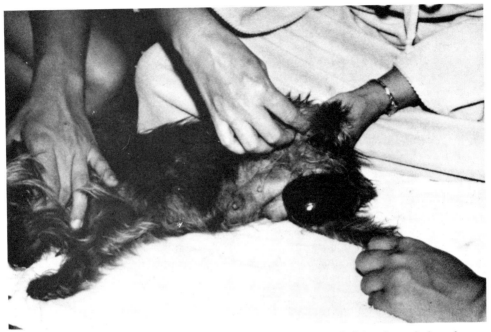

Birth of Puppies. The water bag around the puppy can be seen bulging through the vulva.

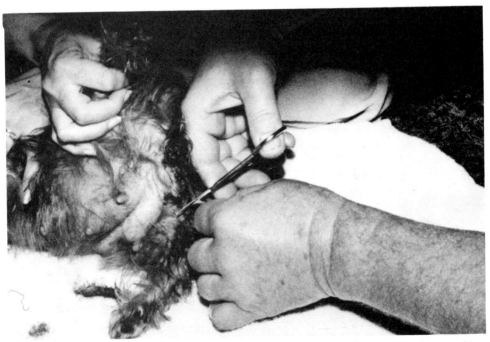

The umbilical cord may have to be clamped, cut and tied, if the dam neglects to sever it.
—*JoAnn Thompson*

In between births put the puppies on the nipples. Their sucking action helps bring on the colostrum, or first milk of the dam, which contains the all-important maternal antibodies.

Puppies can be born as close to each other as every fifteen minutes or as far apart as every two hours. An average time for delivery of four to six puppies is six to eight hours, but a large litter may take considerably longer. Although puppies usually appear at regular intervals it is not a cause for concern if a puppy does not arrive for one or two hours. If the interval is longer than this or if the bitch appears to be continuously straining and in distress, then something is wrong (see the *When to Call the Veterinarian* section of this chapter).

Assisting the Normal Delivery

When labor is going well it is best not to attempt to aid the bitch as she knows by instinct how to whelp her puppies and take care of them by herself. But on occasion a large puppy gets stuck at the vaginal opening. The head or presenting part appears during a forceful contraction, then slips back inside when the bitch relaxes. At this point it is wise to step in quickly and complete the delivery. Once a puppy moves out of the uterus down into the vaginal canal, oxygen from the bitch gets cut off. Delivery must proceed rapidly.

It is not difficult to complete a partial delivery if the following steps are taken:

As the presenting part appears at the vaginal opening apply pressure on the perineum just below the anus and push down gently to keep the puppy from slipping back into the mother. Next, slide the lips of the vulva over the head of the puppy. Once this is accomplished the lips hold the puppy in place, giving you a chance to get another grip. Now grip the skin of the puppy with a clean piece of cloth behind his neck or along his back and draw him out. Apply forceful traction only to the skin, not to the legs or head, as this can cause damage to a joint. Often it is helpful to rotate the puppy first one way and then another, especially when something seems stuck. The birth canal usually is wider one way than the other.

If these measures are not immediately successful, proceed as described under *Canine Obstetrics*.

After your bitch has delivered her last puppy, ask your veterinarian to examine her to be sure there are no retained puppies or placentas. He may administer an injection to clear the uterus. This injection also stimulates the letting down of milk.

PROLONGED LABOR (Dystocia, Difficult Labor)

The prolongation of any phase of labor is called *dystocia*. It is due to either a birth canal which is too narrow in relation to the size of the presenting part *(mechanical blockage)*, or to the failure of the uterus to develop enough strength to expel the fetus *(uterine inertia)*. Often these two are related, a difficult birth being followed by arrested labor due to uterine muscle fatigue.

Dystocia is much more common in older brood bitches and those allowed to become too fat. This is why it is so important to keep your female trim and in top condition.

A less common cause of mechanical blockage is a narrow pelvis.

An abnormal presentation can occur at any time but is much more likely to arrest labor in the overweight poorly conditioned female. Normally, puppies come down the birth canal nose-first, with their backs along the top of the vagina and their feet at the bottom. The rump-first position, called the *breech*, occurs so often that it may be inaccurate to classify it as a malpresentation. Usually it causes problems only when it occurs in the first puppy.

When the head is bent forward, or to the side, it may get caught in the birth canal. Uncommonly, the pelvis of the puppy hangs up in the pelvic outlet of the bitch.

Uterine inertia is an important cause of ineffectual labor. Mechanical factors, which cause the uterus to become over-distended with stretched-out fibers and loss of power of contraction, are a single large puppy in a small uterus, a very large litter, and *hydrops amnion,* a condition in which there is too much amniotic fluid.

Uterine inertia can be caused by emotional upsets. Sudden anxiety induces a form of hysteria which stops normal labor. This is why it is important to whelp a bitch where she is at ease and familiar with her surroundings, away from casual spectators and other nerve-racking influences.

Some cases of inertia, called *primary,* seem to be due to a deficiency of oxytocin (a hormone produced by the pituitary gland), or calcium, or both. The uterus may respond to injections of oxytocin (Pitocin) which stimulate stronger contractions. Intravenous calcium may also be given. *Oxytocin is contraindicated if there is a mechanical blockage.* It can lead to rupture of the uterus.

When To Call The Veterinarian

It is certainly better to call your veterinarian on a "false alarm", even if only to gain reassurance, than to delay in the hope that in time the situation will correct itself without help. Often the problem can be dealt with rather simply if attended to at once. However, the same problem, when neglected, becomes complicated — often leading to an emergency operation.

Something may be wrong when:

A bitch goes into labor (serious straining) and does not deliver a puppy within two hours. Purposeful straining indicates a puppy is partly in the birth canal. It is a mistake to wait four or six hours as the mother is now exhausted and normal delivery may not be possible even when the cause is removed.

*   *   *

The bitch passes dark green or bloody fluid *before* the delivery of her first puppy. This indicates separation of the placenta from the wall of the uterus which means that the puppy is not getting oxygen from his mother. After the first puppy, green or bloody fluid is normal.

*   *   *

The membranes rupture and a puppy is not delivered in 30 minutes. The passage of yellow fluid means rupture of the water bag (amniotic sac) surrounding the puppy.

*   *   *

Labor stops and there are signs of restlessness, anxiety, weakness or fatigue. Puppies come 15 minutes to two hours apart. Over three hours between puppies is a sign of trouble.

Canine Obstetrics

If it is impossible to get prompt veterinary help or if the water bag breaks and the puppy is stuck in the birth canal, the following steps should be taken to deliver the puppy:

Clean the outside of the vulva with soap and water. Put on a pair of sterile gloves and lubricate your finger with pHisoHex, K-Y Jelly or Vaseline. Before inserting your finger into the vagina, be careful not to contaminate your gloves with stool from the anus.

Place one hand under the abdomen in front of the pelvis of the dam and feel for the puppy. Raise him up into position to align him with the birth canal. With your other hand slip a finger into the vagina and feel for a head, tail or leg. When the *head is deviated* and will not pass through the outlet of the pelvis, insert a finger into the puppy's mouth and gently turn his head, guiding it into the birth canal.

When the puppy is coming as a *breech* (rump first), hold the puppy at the pelvic outlet as described. With the vaginal finger, hook first one leg and then the other, slipping them down over the narrow place until the pelvis and legs appear at the vulva.

If the mother has been unable to deliver a *large puppy coming normally,* insert a gloved finger into the vagina alongside the puppy until you can feel his front legs at the elbow. Hook them and pull them through individually.

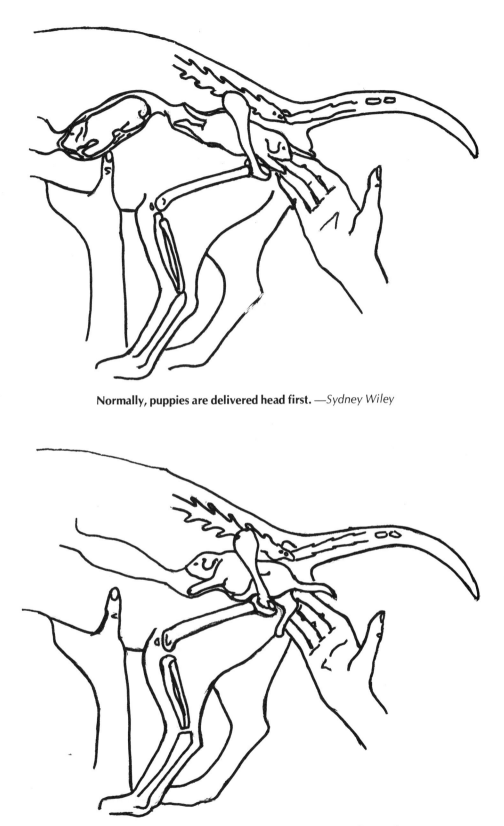

Normally, puppies are delivered head first. —*Sydney Wiley*

The *breech* presentation is common in the dog. —*Sydney Wiley*

Once the puppy is in the lower part of the birth canal, he should be delivered without further delay. To stimulate a forceful push by the mother, gently stretch the vaginal opening. If you can see the puppy at the mouth of the vagina but he appears and disappears with straining, grip his skin with a clean piece of cloth and pull him out as described under *Assisting the Normal Delivery*. Time is of the essence '— particularly when the puppy is a breech. It is better to take hold and pull out the puppy even at the risk of injury or death since that puppy, and perhaps the others, will die if something is not done.

Sometimes the blockage is due to a retained placenta. Hook it with your fingers and grasp it with a sterile cloth. Maintain gentle traction until it passes out of the vagina.

When the uterus become exhausted and stops contracting, it is difficult to correct a malposition without instruments. Only those experienced in the use of instruments should attempt this feat, as the risk of uterine rupture is considerable. Caesarean Section often is indicated.

When the puppy comes sideways, usually it is not possible to correct the problem short of a Caesarean Section.

Helping a Puppy Breathe

When a puppy is born surrounded by the amniotic sac, it should be removed within 30 seconds to allow the puppy to breathe. If the bitch fails to do this herself, you should tear open the sac and remove it, starting at the mouth and working backwards over the body. Aspirate the secretions from the mouth with a bulb syringe. Rub the puppy briskly with a soft towel.

An alternate method of clearing the secretions is to hold the puppy in your hands while supporting his head. Then swing him in a downward arc, stopping abruptly when his nose is pointing to the floor. This helps to expel water from his nostrils. Present the puppy to the mother to lick, sniff and cuddle.

After a difficult delivery, a puppy may be too weak or too flaccid to breathe on his own. Squeeze the chest gently from side to side and then from front to back. If the puppy still will not breathe, place your mouth over his mouth and nostrils and breathe out gently until you see his chest expand. Do not exhale too forcefully as this can rupture his lungs. Then remove your mouth to allow the puppy to exhale. Repeat this several times until the puppy is breathing and crying.

CAESAREAN SECTION

Caesarean Section is the procedure of choice for any type of arrested labor which cannot be relieved by drugs or obstetrical manipulation. Most

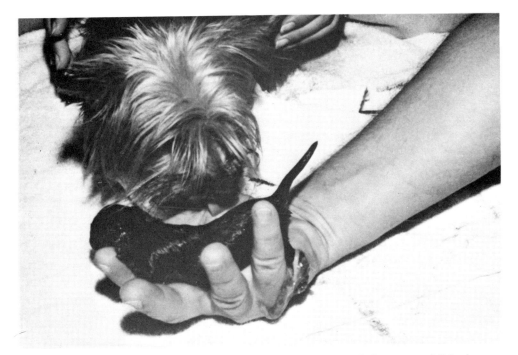

Present the puppy to the dam to lick and cuddle. This helps to establish the mother-puppy bond.

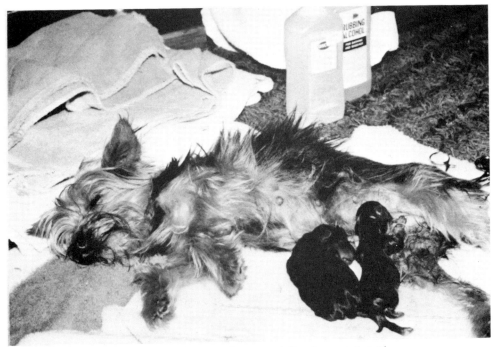

Puppies can be allowed to nurse between deliveries. —*JoAnn Thompson*

veterinarians feel that after 24 hours of unproductive labor, Caesarean Section is indicated. It is indicated sooner for a mechanical blockage which cannot be rapidly corrected. The decision ultimately rests with the veterinarian. Consideration will be given to the condition of the dam; length of labor; how many puppies can be delivered by instruments (usually not more than two because of subsequent swelling of the birth canal induced by the instruments); the size of the puppies in relationship to the pelvic outlet; failure to respond to injections of oxytocin; and whether the vaginal canal has become dry.

Because of their anatomical make-up, certain breeds — such as the Bulldog, Chihuahua, Toy Poodle and a Boston Terrier — are prone to whelping difficulties and Caesarean Section may be indicated as an elective procedure as soon as the cervix dilates. If you own one of these breeds, discuss this possibility with your veterinarian.

Caesarean Section is an operation done under general anesthesia in the veterinary hospital. The risk to a young healthy dam is not great. However, when labor has been unduly prolonged, when toxicity is present, when the puppies are dead and beginning to decompose, or when uterine rupture occurs, then the risks become significant.

Usually a bitch is awake and stable and able to nurse her puppies at home within three hours of the operation.

If a bitch has a Caesarean Section, she may or may not require a Caesarean Section with her next litter. This depends upon the reason for the first Caesarean Section. Many bitches who have had one Caesarean Section are able to have normal vaginal deliveries the next time they become pregnant.

POST PARTUM CARE OF THE DAM

Twelve to twenty-four hours after your female delivers, ask your veterinarian to examine her. Probably he will want to check her milk for color, consistency, and quality (If the milk is thick, stringy, yellowish or discolored it may be infected). Palpation of the uterus rules out a retained puppy or placenta. Many veterinarians prescribe an injection of oxytocin or ergonovine to aid in letdown of milk and involution of the uterus.

During the first week take the mother's temperature at least once a day. A temperature of 103 degrees F. or higher indicates a problem (retained product, acute metritis, mastitis).

A greenish discharge is normal for the first 12 to 24 hours. It is followed by a variable amount of reddish-tinged to serosanguinous discharge which lasts two to three weeks. A green, brownish, or serosanguinous discharge that lasts over 21 days signifies something is wrong.

Feeding During Lactation

During lactation caloric requirements increase sharply to 300 percent of normal. At this time it is particularly important to be sure that your dam is getting enough to eat. Otherwise, she will quickly lose weight and fail to produce enough milk to satisfy her puppies.

Feed a good commercial adult kibble preparation. (Some veterinarians suggest using a puppy chow). Name-brand dog foods are formulated to meet the National Research Council's recommendations for nutritionally complete diets. They provide protein, fat and carbohydrate, along with vitamins and minerals, in correct balance. They are quite suitable for a lactating dam — *if she will eat the required amount*. By the second or third week a nursing dam eats three times her normal daily ration — or three full meals spaced throughout the day. Many veterinarians recommend supplementing the kibble base with canned meat or cottage cheese in the following proportions: 80 percent kibble to 20 percent canned meat or cottage cheese. If this ratio is exceeded a correct balance will not be obtained.

Many bitches are likely to have inadequate calcium during nursing. A balanced vitamin-mineral supplement, such as Pet-Cal, is most beneficial when used during lactation. Follow the manufacturer's recommendations in regard to dosage.

Tense, overactive bitches, or those with a big litter, may require extra energy. Add three tablespoons vegetable oil to each pound of dry dog food.

Give Vitamin B supplements to dams with a marginal milk supply.

Bitches who appear hostile to visitors may respond to 250 mg of ascorbic acid three times a day.

POST PARTUM PROBLEMS

Problems which can affect the dam following delivery are acute metritis, mastitis, caked breasts and milk fever. A few bitches have problems accepting their puppies due to emotional upsets and psychological blocks.

Acute Metritis *(Infected Uterus)*

Acute metritis is an infection which spreads upwards through the birth canal during delivery or immediately afterwards. It affects the lining of the uterus. It is most likely to occur when part of the placenta has been retained. Some cases are due to a retained fetus which has become mummified. Other cases are due to contamination of the birth canal by unsterile instruments and fingers during delivery. A difficult or prolonged labor and a pre-existing vaginitis are other predisposing causes.

Chronic endometritis and *pyometra* are other uterine infections which may be confused with acute post partum metritis. They are discussed under *Diseases of the Female Genital Tract* in the chapter SEX AND REPRODUCTION.

Most cases of acute metritis can be anticipated and prevented by a post partum check up. A veterinarian often will want to clear the uterus with an injection of pitocin. Vaginitis should be treated as soon as it is diagnosed, preferably before heat and certainly before labor and delivery.

A dam with acute metritis is depressed, hangs her head, refuses to eat, and has a temperature of 103 to 105 degrees. She may cease to care for her puppies or keep the nest clean.

There is a heavy, dark, bloody greenish or tomato soup-like discharge which appears two to seven days after the whelp. It should not be confused with the normal greenish discharge which disappears during the first 12 to 24 hours, or the light reddish, sero-sanguinous discharge which lasts two to three weeks. A normal discharge is not accompanied by high fever, excessive thirst or other signs of toxicity such as vomiting and diarrhea.

Treatment: Acute metritis is a life-threatening illness. A veterinarian should be consulted immediately to save the life of the dam. Usually puppies will have to be taken off the mother and reared by hand (see *Raising Puppies By Hand* in the PEDIATRICS chapter). She will be too sick to take care of them. Her milk may be toxic.

Mastitis

The two breast conditions affecting the nursing dam are caked breasts and acute mastitis. One oftens leads to the other.

Caked Breasts (Galactostasis)
This is a form of mastitis caused by too much milk in a mammary gland, either because of over-production or because the breast is not being adequately suckled by the puppies. A deformed nipple may be at fault. Caking of the breasts can occur during false pregnancy where there are no puppies to remove the milk.

Affected glands, usually the two hind ones, are swollen, painful, warm and hard. pH paper may be used to test the acidity of the milk. Normal canine breast milk should test to a pH of 6.0 to 6.5 (colostrum often tests to a pH of 7.0). Milk (not colostrum) which tests to a pH of 7.0 is infected and will make puppies sick. Milk from simple caking of the breasts tests to a normal pH and is okay for puppies to suckle. If the pH is 7.0, see *Acute Mastitis.*

Treatment: Massage the caked gland twice a day with camphorated oil, apply hot packs, and express the gland to draw out some of the coagulated and caked milk. Your veterinarian may wish to prescribe testosterone or a diuretic to reduce the swelling, and have you reduce food intake.

Severely caked breasts may become infected, thus leading to an acute mastitis. Often this can be prevented by administering a long-acting penicillin, such as Bicillin. Aspirin should be given to relieve pain.

When litters are large, the pups may have to be supplemented. —*Sydney Wiley*

Acute Septic Mastitis (Breast Infection or Abscess)

Acute mastitis is an infection of one or more of the mammary glands due to bacteria which get into the breast tissue during nursing from a scratch or puncture wound. Some cases are bloodborne (See *Acute Metritis*).

When the puppies are two to three weeks old, their nails should be trimmed once a week to keep them from scratching the skin of the dam.

A mammary gland with acute mastitis is swollen, extremely painful, and usually reddish-blue in appearance. Milk may be blood-tinged, thin, yellowish or string-like. In some cases, the milk will look normal yet will test to a pH of 7.0 or greater.

Mothers with acute mastitis refuse to eat, appear listless, restless, and run a high fever (which suggests abscess formation).

Puppies should be prevented from nursing at an infected breast since they can come down with a fatal infection themselves.

Treatment: Acute mastitis should be treated by a veterinarian. Routine measures include the use of appropriate antibiotics and gentle massage of the glands three or four times a day with camphorated oil followed by application of hot packs.

The nipple of an infected gland can be taped so that the puppies can nurse at the others. If more than one gland is involved, or if the dam is quite toxic, it is advisable to remove the puppies altogether and raise them by hand. If they are three weeks of age, they can be weaned.

When milk from an infected breast returns to a normal appearance and tests to a pH of less than 7.0, the puppies can nurse. The procedure for drying up the breasts is explained under *Weaning* in the PEDIATRICS chapter.

Milk Fever *(Eclampsia, Puerperal Tetany)*

Eclampsia is due to an upset in the calcium regulatory mechanism which leads to a low calcium level in the blood. It is called milk fever because it often occurs during the first three weeks of lactation when there is a drain on calcium stores in the body. Rarely it is seen late in pregnancy. Primarily, this is a disease of small dogs with large litters, especially Toys.

Low serum calcium levels cause tetany. The first signs are restlessness, anxiety, rapid breathing and whining. A dam frequently leaves her puppies and begins to pace up and down. Her gait is stiff-legged, uncoordinated and jerky. Her face takes on a pinched look, with the skin pulled back to expose the teeth. As the condition worsens, she falls down on her side, exhibits spasms in which she kicks all four legs, and salivates profusely.

The temperature often is elevated up to 106 degrees. This causes more panting, washes out carbon dioxide, raises the pH of the blood, and lowers the serum calcium even further.

Certain bitches seem predisposed to milk fever. If your bitch is one of the Toy breeds, or has had milk fever in the past, discuss with your veterinarian the possibility of supplementing her diet with calcium during the last half of pregnancy.

Treatment: Puerperal tetany is a real emergency. Notify your veterinarian at once. Intravenous calcium solutions should be given at the first signs to re-establish normal blood calcium levels. Cardiac arrhythmias can occur when calcium is given too rapidly, so this should be done by a professional.

If the rectal temperature is over 104 degrees, treat as you would for *heat stroke* while awaiting the veterinarian's arrival.

Puppies must be taken off the dam, at least for the first 24 hours. If they are two to three weeks of age, they can be weaned. Mothers who must continue restricted nursing should be supplemented with calcium, phosphorus and Vitamin D.

Mothers Who Neglect or Injure Their Puppies

Mothers learn to recognize and care for their puppies as they are born, cleaned and begin to nurse. This bond sometimes is not as strong when the puppies are born by Caesarean Section. Such mothers can have difficulty in accepting their puppies for the first 48 hours. This is less likely to happen when some of the puppies are born before the surgery or when they are put to the nipples before the sedation wears off.

A novice mother often has difficulty coping with a litter of squirming puppies for the first few hours. This is understandable. With a little help, she can be shown how to nurse her puppies and keep from stepping on them.

Spoiled female housepets sometimes will not care for their puppies until they are allowed to regain their former position in the family hierarchy.

Sometimes, due to a hormonal imbalance, the milk does not come down for the first 48 hours. During this time the bitch may reject her puppies. Milk can be helped in flow by pitocin and other hormones. Once the milk comes in the puppies are accepted.

A hypothermic puppy, one whose body temperature has dropped below normal due to sickness or constitutional weakness, instinctively is pushed out of the nest. This is nature's way of culling.

Other causes of puppy rejection are post partum infections and complications such as milk fever, mastitis and acute metritis.

Dams who continue to ignore or reject their puppies sometimes may be helped by tranquilizers. If the problem is due to maternal infection, then the puppies may have to be removed and reared by hand.

A bitch whelping her first litter should be watched closely. She may accidentally confuse the puppy with the placenta or injure a puppy while attempting to sever the cord and remove the membranes. Breeds with an undershot jaw or a malocclusion problem are particularly prone to this difficulty.

A novice dam may attempt to pick up and carry a puppy to some other nest. Do not allow your female to carry puppies around in her mouth as she may become nervous or upset and bite down too hard. Nest-seeking can be avoided if the dam is introduced to her litter box two weeks before she is due to whelp and required to sleep in it.

In other cases, a nervous, possessive or over-protective dam can injure her puppies out of emotional upset caused by too much handling of the puppies by children or strange people. It is important not to allow visitors for the first three to four weeks — especially when the bitch is high-strung or not well socialized to people.

"Pick of the Litter." A Parisian tourist has purchased a pup from a shepherd in the village and has been told to go out to the farm and help himself. —*Eugene Gayot, Le Chien, Paris, 1867.*

17

Pediatrics

NEWBORN PUPPIES

During the neonatal period (birth to three weeks of age) a healthy puppy is the picture of contentment. He sleeps 90 percent of the time and eats about 10 percent. He nurses vigorously and competes for nipples. For the first 48 hours, a puppy sleeps with his head curled under his chest. While sleeping, puppies jerk, kick and sometimes whimper. This is called "activated sleep". It is normal. It is the newborn puppy's only means of exercise and helps to develop muscles which will be used later.

A good mother instinctively keeps her nest and puppies clean. By licking the belly and rectum of each pup, she stimulates the elimination reflex.

Physiology

At one day of age puppies have heart rates of 160 beats per minute, breathing rates of 10 to 18 breaths per minute, and temperatures that vary from 92 to 97 degrees F. Between 2 and 21 days the heart rate increases to 220 beats per minute and the breathing rate from 18 to 36 breaths per minute. Temperature is 96 to 100 degrees F.

Eyes and ears, which are sealed at birth, start to open at 10 to 16 days. Puppies are sight and sound oriented at 25 days of age. Usually they will stand at 15 days of age and begin to walk at 21 days. They can control the urge to eliminate at three weeks.

During the first week of life peripheral blood vessels do not have the capacity to constrict or retain heat — nor can a puppy shiver to generate heat of his own. This means that a newborn cannot sustain body temperature and needs an outside source of heat. While nestled close to his mother, her body warmth keeps his temperature between 96 and 100 degrees F. When the dam is away for 30 minutes, in a room at 72 degrees F (well below the recommended level), his temperature can fall to 94 degrees F or below. He quickly becomes chilled, a condition which causes gravely reduced metabolism.

Neonatal puppies have little subcutaneous fat. Energy is supplied through feedings. Reserve energy is supplied almost entirely by glycogen in the liver. The liver is the last organ to grow in size, while the brain is the organ which consumes the most energy. A puppy with a brain too large in proportion to his liver rapidly runs out of energy because of low blood sugar. Accordingly, the weight of the liver must be at least one and a half times the weight of the brain at birth. A liver-brain ratio of two to three is even better. Even if these conditions are met, there is little margin for reserve in the newborn. A potentially low blood sugar must be offset by *frequent feeding*. A puppy who does not eat frequently, for whatever reason, is heading for trouble.

Kidney function in the newborn is 12 to 25 percent of what it will be later in life. These immature kidneys are unable to concentrate the urine, which means that it is necessary for puppies to excrete large amounts of dilute urine. This obligatory water loss of the kidneys must be offset by sufficient intake of milk, or in the case of puppies raised by hand, by a formula containing adequate amounts of water.

Why Puppies Die

Thirty percent of puppies die between birth and weaning. Three-fourths of these die in the first two weeks of life. Many puppy deaths undoubtedly are due to lack of advanced preparation: providing adequate heat in the whelping quarters (which should be clean and dry as well); vaccinating the prospective dam, and getting her on a sound feeding program during pregnancy and lactation.

Some deaths are attributable to birth trauma, congenital defects, maternal neglect, something wrong with the milk supply, and infectious diseases.

Congenital defects are not a major cause of newborn deaths. But when they do occur they may be lethal. Hemophilia is a clotting disorder which leads to internal bleeding or bleeding from the body openings. Cleft-palate, often associated with hare-lip, prevents effective nursing. Large naval hernias allow prolapse of abdominal organs. Heart defects can be severe enough to lead to circulatory failure. Other disorders may be responsible for mysterious or unexplained deaths.

Cardiopulmonary Syndrome (Circulatory Failure of the Newborn). This is a shock-like state that occurs in pups under five days of age. After this age pups can respond better to stress, as they are more mature.

Chilling, overheating, impaired breathing, and inefficient nursing, produce a drop in temperature, heart and breathing rate. These in turn lead to weakness and inability to digest food. If the body temperature drops below 94 degrees F, there is further depression of vital functions. This cycle is progressive and soon becomes irreversible. Early treatment is imperative if death is to be avoided.

Due to immaturity these pups are unable to mount a specific response to a specific stress. Irrespective of the cause of the problem, the symptoms and signs are similar.

At first, pups may salivate excessively, cry and make swallowing movements. Gradually, their crawling and righting ability are lost and they lie on their sides. Heart and breathing rates are slow until the heart rate is 40 beats per minute and the breathing rate is four per minute.

Later, poor circulation affects the brain causing tetanic spasms (rigors), accompanied by breathless periods lasting up to a minute. At this point, the condition is irreversible.

Blood in the stool and urine (as a result of circulatory failure) may be noted. Gagging and fluid in the nostril may be noted.

Treatment involves the administration of oxygen, dextrose and slow warming. Adrenalin may be of aid. Veterinary assistance is required.

The Runt. The physically immature puppy is at a distinct disadvantage because of his low birth weight and lack of muscle mass and subcutaneous fat. He may be unable to breathe deeply, nurse effectively and maintain warmth in his body. His liver-brain ratio may be less than 1.5/1. His birth weight may be 25 percent below that of his littermates.

The most common cause of subnormal birth weight is inadequate nourishment while in the uterus. When all the puppies are undersize, a poorly nourished bitch is the prime consideration. When one or two puppies are below par, most likely the fault is one of placental insufficiency due to overcrowding, or a disadvantageous placement of a placenta in the wall of the uterus. These puppies are immature on the basis of their development rather than their age. If they are to survive, they must be separated from the dam and raised by hand in an incubator as described elsewhere in this chapter.

Fading Puppy. This is a puppy apparently vigorous and healthy at birth, who then fails to gain weight, loses strength and vitality, and with it the urge to feed. For want of a better term the condition is called *Fading Puppy Syndrome*. There is no general agreement as to the cause of fading puppies. Some cases may be due to immaturity, others to birth defects, environmental stress, and maternal factors. The syndrome may be reversible if the cause can be determined and steps taken to correct it.

CARING FOR THE NEWBORN

Newborn puppies are born without the capacity to adapt to environmental stress. With proper care and attention to the special needs of these infants, undoubtedly many unnecessary neonatal deaths can be avoided.

Since neonatal puppies do not respond in the same way to environmental stress and illness as do adult dogs, a special approach is needed to monitor the well-being of the newborn — beginning as soon as they are born. The two crucial aspects to watch closely are the puppy's body temperature and his weight. His general appearance, heart rate, breathing rate, skin turgor, muscle tone, mobility and body position, sound of his cry, and suck reflex also can provide useful information as to his overall health and vitality. These perimeters are discussed below.

General Appearance and Vitality

Healthy puppies are "round, firm and fully packed". They nurse vigorously and compete for nipples with their littermates. If you insert a finger into their mouths, they have a strong, vigorous suckle. They are warm and plump. The mouth and tongue are wet; the skin has a pink appearance. When pinched, it springs back in a resilient fashion. Pick them up and they stretch and wiggle energetically in your hand. When removed from the dam, they crawl back to her.

Newborn puppies "pile", or crawl together for warmth. They seldom cry. Crying indicates that a puppy is cold, hungry, or in pain.

A sick puppy presents a dramatically different picture. This puppy when picked up is limp and cold. He hangs like a dishcloth. When you put a finger into his mouth he pushes it out. He shows the same lack of interest in nursing.

Distressed puppies are hyperactive. They crawl about looking for help and fall asleep away from the life-sustaining warmth of their dam and littermates. They rest with their legs splayed apart and their necks bent to the side. Their cry is plaintive and piercing. It sometimes goes on for more than twenty minutes.

Body temperature is lower than it should be, often 94 degrees F, or below. Breathing rate is often less than ten per minute. Signs of dehydration are lack of moisture in the mouth, a bright pink color to the tongue and mucus membranes of the mouth, loss of muscle tone, and weakness. When the skin is pinched it stays up in a fold instead of springing back. Viral and bacterial infections may produce a diarrhea which becomes profuse as the condition deteriorates. As the pup grows weaker, so do his heart rate and respirations. Such a puppy often is rejected by the dam who senses that he is not going to survive and pushes him out of the pile rather than waste her energies on him. This can be reversed if the puppy is treated and his body temperature is brought back to normal. The bitch will accept him back.

Temperature

As a puppy is born his temperature is the same as that of his dam. Immediately afterwards it drops several degrees (how much depends upon the temperature of the room). Within thirty minutes, if the puppy is dry and snuggled close to his dam, his temperature begins to climb back up and soon reaches 94 degrees F. Twenty-four hours later his rectal or core temperature is 95 to 97 degrees F, and steadily increases until at three weeks of age it is 98 to 100 degrees F. A healthy puppy can maintain a temperature 10 to 12 degrees F above his surroundings.

While chilling is the single greatest danger to the infant puppy, the opposite is also true. Overheating and dehydration can produce many problems. The temperature of the whelping box and the area in which the box is kept must be 85 to 90 degrees F during the first week. The five degree variation depends upon the nature of the hair coat. The construction of a suitable whelping box is described in the chapter on SEX AND REPRODUCTION.

Warming a Chilled Puppy:

Any puppy whose body temperature is below the normals for its age is a chilled puppy.

A chilled puppy must be warmed GRADUALLY. Rapid warming (for example, by a heating pad), causes dilatation of skin vessels, increased loss of heat, added expenditure of calories, and greater need for oxygen. This is detrimental.

The best way to warm a puppy is to tuck him down beneath a sweater or jacket next to your skin, letting your own warmth seep into his system. If his temperature is below 94 degrees F and he is weak, warming will take two to three hours. Afterwards, he may have to be placed in a homemade incubator (see *Raising Puppies by Hand*).

Never feed *formula* to a cold puppy or allow him to nurse. When so-chilled, the stomach and small intestines stop working. If a formula is given it will not be digested. The puppy will bloat and perhaps vomit. A chilled puppy can utilize a 5-10 percent glucose and water solution (glucose can be purchased at drugstores). Give one-half cc per ounce of body weight every hour, and warm slowly, until he is warm and wiggling about. If a glucose solution is not available, use honey and water; or as a last resort, use household sugar and water: one teaspoonful per ounce.

Importance of Weight Gain

Puppies should gain one to one and half grams of weight per day for each pound of anticipated adult weight, and should double their birth weight in eight to ten days. To estimate the adult weight of a puppy, weigh the dam. A steady gain in weight is the best indication that puppies are doing well. Similarly, when a puppy doesn't gain weight, he should be singled out for special attention. For this reason, puppies should be weighed on a gram scale at birth, at 12 and 24 hours, daily for the first two weeks of life, and every three days until a month old.

When several puppies in a litter are not gaining weight, you should think of a maternal factor (such as toxic milk, metritis, or inadequate milk supply). If the mother is not getting adequate calories in her diet, her milk supply will be inadequate to support a large litter. A nursing dam needs two to three times more food than a normal adult dog. The diet must be balanced to meet the needs of lactation. This subject is discussed in the chapter on PREGNANCY AND WHELPING.

A sudden drop in weight with diarrhea is due to water losses. A balanced electrolyte solution is needed. This is the same solution used in correcting dehydration in hand-fed puppies. It is discussed in the paragraph *Common Feeding Problems*.

Puppies dehydrate quickly when they stop nursing. Therefore, dehydration has to be considered a factor whenever a puppy fails to thrive, loses weight, becomes chilled, and is too weak to nurse.

When to Supplement:

Puppies that gain weight steadily during the first seven days are in no immediate danger. Puppies that experience a weight loss not exceeding 10 percent of birth weight for the first 48 hours of life and then begin to gain should be watched closely. Puppies that lose 10 percent or more of their birth weight in the first 48 hours and do not begin to gain by 72 hours are poor survival prospects. Start supplemental feedings immediately (see *Raising Puppies By Hand*).

If at birth a puppy is 25 percent under the expected birth weight for his breed or the weight of his littermates, you can expect a high mortality. Place this puppy in an incubator and raise him by hand. Many immature puppies can be saved if their condition is not complicated by diseases or congenital defects.

RAISING PUPPIES BY HAND

A dam could be unable to raise her litter because of post partum uterine infection or breast infection, toxic milk, eclampsia, or inadequate milk supply. In such cases the pups have to be supplemented or hand-fed.

The decision to supplement a puppy is based upon his general appearance and vitality, weight at birth, and his progress in comparison to his brothers and sisters. As a rule, it is better to step in early and start hand feeding in borderline cases, and not wait until a puppy is in obvious distress. Depending upon the overall condition of the pup and his response to supplement feeding, it may be possible to feed him two or three times a day and let him remain with his mother. Others must be taken away and raised as orphans. They require intensive care.

If you think a puppy needs supplemental feeding, calculate his total daily requirements (the method is given in *Calculating the Right Formula*) and assume that a nursing puppy eats four times a day. Give him one-fourth of his total daily requirement at each feeding.

Accurate record keeping is important at all times, but is absolutely essential when puppies are raised by hand. Weigh them at birth, at eight-hour intervals for four days, daily for the first two weeks of life, and then every three days until they reach one month.

Three areas of critical importance are: furnishing the right environment; preparing and feeding the right formula; and providing the right management. Feeding equipment should be thoroughly cleaned and boiled. Visitors should not be allowed in the nursery. All personnel should wash their hands before handling the puppies — especially if they have been with other dogs. Many diseases, including distemper, can be transmitted to puppies by a person who has recently handled an infective dog.

If the puppies were unable to receive the colostrum, or first milk of the dam, they lack passive immunity and are susceptible to a variety of diseases, including distemper. Vaccinations are then given after three weeks of age.

Since chilling is the single greatest danger to the newborn puppy's survival, you will need an incubator.

The Incubator

A satisfactory incubator can be made in a few minutes by dividing a cardboard box into separate compartments so that each puppy will have his own pen. These pens are important when puppies are being fed by stomach tube because, having no nipple to suckle, they tend to suckle each other's ears, tails and genitalia. If they are nursed from a bottle they may not need to have separate compartments.

Place a small electric heating pad in the bottom of the incubator. One-fourth of it should lie against the side of the box, and three-fourths on the bottom. This permits puppies to get close to the heat when they are cold and get away from it when hot. Cover the pad with a waterproof material such as plastic or rubber. On top, place a baby diaper which can be changed as often as it becomes soiled. This also gives a means for checking the appearance of each puppy's stool.

Another means of providing sufficient warmth is to use overhead heat lights. This may not be as satisfactory as a heating pad.

A thermometer should be placed in the incubator to monitor the surface temperature.

Keep the incubator at 85 to 90 degrees F for the first week. During the second week, reduce it to 80 or 85 degrees F. Thereafter, gradually decrease the temperature so that it is 75 degrees F by the end of the fourth week. Maintain constant warmth and avoid chilling drafts.

Maintain the humidity of the room at about 55 percent. This helps to prevent skin drying and dehydration.

General Care

Keep the puppies clean with a damp cloth. Be sure to cleanse the anal area and skin of the abdomen. A light application of baby oil may be applied to these areas, and to the coat, to prevent drying of the skin. Change the bedding often to prevent urine scalds. When present, they can be helped by the application of baby powder. If infected, apply a topical antibiotic ointment (Panolog).

For the first ten days, massage the abdomen and perianal area of the puppies after each feeding to stimulate elimination. (This is something the mother would do if she could.) A wad of cotton soaked in warm water works well.

Hand Feeding

This is not the chore it used to be because of the ready availability of artificial bitch's milk available through your veterinarian or a commercial source. It has replaced the need for special formulas, goat's milk, and foster mothers.

The composition of cow's milk is such that it is not suitable for rearing puppies. Cow's milk contains a high percentage of its calories in lactose. Newborn puppies do not have adequate enzymes with which to break down lactose. This leads to diarrhea.

While artificial bitch's milk (such as Esbilac from Borden's) is the most desirable substitute for the natural milk of the bitch, in an *emergency* situation one of the following formulas can be used as a temporary substitute. Mix well and refrigerate the unused portions.

Formula #1:   1 cup homogenized milk
                      3 egg yolks
                      1 tablespoon corn oil
                      1 dropper liquid pediatric vitamins

Formula #2:   26.5 ounces of homogenized milk
                      6.5 ounces of cream (12% fat)
                      1 teaspoonful bone meal
                      1 egg yolk
                      4 grams citric acid
                   Liquid vitamins to provide 2,000 I.U.
                      Vitamin A, 500 I.U. Vitamin D

Formula #3:   Evaporated milk reconstituted to 20 percent
                      solids
                      1 teaspoonful bone meal per pint

These formulas provide 38 calories per ounce, or one to one and one-fourth calories per cc of formula.

Artificial bitch's milk comes in both powder and liquid. When reconstituted, it should be prevented from freezing. Follow the directions of the manufacturer with regard to storage.

Calculating the Right Formula:

The best way to determine how much formula each puppy needs is to weigh the puppy and use a table of caloric requirements. All formulas provide one to one and one-fourth calories per cc. It is safe to use as an approximation one calorie per cc when computing the amount of formula. Daily requirements according to weight and age are given in the following table:

Age in Weeks	Calories or cc Needed Per Pound Weight Per Day	Number of Feedings Per Day
1	60	4
2	70	3
3	80	3
4	90	3

Divide the total daily requirement by the number of feedings per day in order to get the amount of each feeding.

EXAMPLE: An eight ounce puppy during the first week requires 30 calories per day (i.e., one-half of 60 calories per pound per day). Divide by the number of feedings (4), which gives 7 to 8 cc per feeding. If this puppy doubles his weight as expected in ten days, then he will weigh about one pound and will require 70 cc per day, or 23 cc per feeding. However, if the puppy cannot take in the required amount in three feedings, then the number of feedings should be increased.

How to Give the Formula:

Puppies may be fed by spoon or eyedropper, baby nursing bottle, or stomach tube.

An eyedropper is readily available and may be used as an emergency measure in the absence of a baby nurser or stomach tube. However, puppies can choke when formula is dropped or spooned into their mouths. This can lead to aspiration into the lungs.

The baby bottle has the advantage of satisfying the suckling urge but requires that the puppy be strong enough to suck the formula. When using a small doll's bottle or a commercial puppy nurser with a soft nipple, usually you will have to enlarge the hole in the nipple so that the milk will drip out slowly when the bottle is turned over. Otherwise, the puppy will tire after a few minutes of nursing and will be unable to get enough to eat. Warm the formula to about 100 degrees F (slightly warm to the wrist) as you would a baby's.

The best way to feed a puppy is to place him on his stomach, open his mouth with the tip of your finger, insert the nipple and hold the bottle at 45 degrees. The angle of the bottle is such that air does not get into the puppy's stomach. Keep a slight pull on the bottle to encourage vigorous sucking. A bottle-fed puppy will need to be "burped".

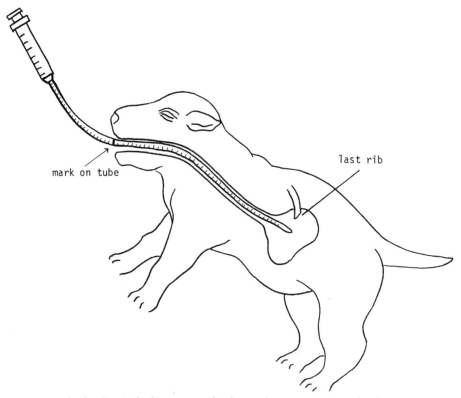

mark on tube

last rib

Tube feeding is the best way to feed a weak puppy. *—Rose Floyd*

Tube feeding has several advantages. It takes about two minutes to complete each feeding. No air is swallowed (no burping required). It insures that a proper amount of formula is administered to each puppy. *It is the only satisfactory method of feeding immature or sick puppies too weak to nurse.*

If too much formula is injected, or if given too rapidly, it can be regurgitated. This can lead to aspiration of formula and pneumonia. The complication can be avoided if care is taken to monitor the weight of the puppy and compute the correct amount. Puppies fed by tube do not get a chance to suckle and must be kept in separate compartments.

Tube feeding is not difficult and can be mastered in a few minutes. It requires a soft rubber catheter (size 8 to 10 French, which can be bought at a drugstore), a 10 or 20 cc plastic or glass syringe, and a gram scale to calculate the weight of each puppy and monitor his progress.

A puppy's stomach is located at the level of his last rib. Measure the tube from the mouth to the last rib and then mark the tube with a piece of tape. Draw the formula into the syringe and warm it to body temperature by placing it in hot water. Moisten the tube with formula, and then open the puppy's mouth and pass the tube slowly over his tongue and into his throat. The tube will be too large to enter the smaller passage of the windpipe, so there is little danger of passing it the wrong way. With steady pressure the puppy will begin to swallow the tube. Pass it to the level of the mark, or until resistance is met. Connect the syringe to the tube and *slowly* inject the formula down the tube into the puppy's stomach.

At about 14 days of age the windpipe of many puppies will be large enough to accommodate the tube. If the tube goes down the wrong way the puppy will begin to cough and choke. Change to a larger tube; or by now the puppy may be strong enough to suckle from a bottle.

Common Feeding Problems:

Common feeding poblems are overfeeding and underfeeding. They cause diarrhea or failure to gain weight. If your puppy is putting on weight and seems reasonably happy and content, with a normal stool (firm, yellowish), you can be pretty sure you are feeding the right amount.

Experience indicates that owners are much more likely to overfeed than to underfeed orphaned puppies. The best way to tell about this is to look at the stools. If a puppy is fed four times a day you can expect four to five stools, or about one stool for each feeding.

A loose, yellow stool indicates a *mild* degree of overfeeding. Usually it responds to reducing the amount of formula.

With *moderate* overfeeding, there is more rapid movement of food through the intestinal tract, indicated by a greenish stool. The color green is due to unabsorbed bile. One or two cc of Milk of Magnesia every three hours, along with a cutback in the amount of formula, usually corrects this problem.

Unchecked overfeeding leads to a depletion of digestive enzymes and causes a grayish diarrheal stool. Eventually, when there is little or no digestion of formula, the stool looks like curdled milk. At this point the puppy is getting no nutrition and is becoming rapidly dehydrated. Treat diarrhea like this by diluting the formula one-third, using water; and give Milk of Magnesia every three hours (one to three cc).

Dehydration is corrected by giving a Ringer's lactate solution mixed half and half with 5% dextrose in water (or use a balanced pediatric electrolyte solution such as Pedialyte).These solutions are available at drugstores or through your veterinarian. Give one-half cc per ounce body weight per hour by bottle or stomach tube. Other supportive measures, such as warming a chilled puppy, are indicated. Veterinary administration of electrolyte solution subcutaneously is highly desirable.

All puppies with gray or white stools should be examined by a veterinarian. They may have a neonatal infection.

Puppies who are not getting enough formula cry all day, appear listless and apathetic, gain little or no weight from one feeding to the next, and begin to chill. Check the temperature of the incubator. Puppies dehydrate quickly when not getting enough formula. They should respond to appropriate dietary management.

PUPPY DISEASES

Bleeding *(Hemorrhagic Syndrome)*

A tendency to bleed easily is present in most puppies until three to four days of age. It is due to lack of prothrombin, a clotting factor in the blood, which depends upon Vitamin K for its synthesis.

The symptoms are those of bleeding from the body openings. Minor degrees of trauma, such as those occurring during whelping and shortly thereafter, may lead to internal hemorrhage. Spontaneous bleeding also occurs. Usually the cause is not discovered until an autopsy.

Treatment: When one puppy bleeds, all the puppies in the litter should be treated with an injection of Vitamin K. In kennels where bleeding has been a problem in the past, the administration of Vitamin K to bitches during the last weeks of pregnancy will prevent it.

Toxic Milk Syndrome

Mother's milk can be toxic to puppies for a number of reasons. The primary cause is mastitis, an infection of the milk glands. Acute post partum metritis, an infection of the uterus, also may lead to toxic milk. These conditions are discussed in the chapter PREGNANCY AND WHELPING. In some cases the cause is unknown. Presumably there are toxins in the milk which cause digestive upsets in nursing puppies.

The toxic milk syndrome usually affects puppies at three to fourteen days of age. Puppies appear distressed, cry continually and sometimes drool. Diarrhea and bloating are especially common. The anus often is red and swollen due to the acidity of the stool. One complication of this syndrome is puppy septicemia.

Treatment: Sick bloated puppies should be removed from the dam and treated for diarrhea and dehydration (see *Raising Puppies By Hand*). Chilled puppies should be warmed and placed in an incubator.

Navel Infection

An umbilical stump can be the site of an infection. Predisposing causes are dental disease of the dam (she transfers bacteria to the umbilical cord when she cuts it), contamination in the whelping box from stool and spilled food, and factors which reduce puppies' resistance to disease.

An infected navel looks red and swollen and may drain pus. There is a direct communication to the liver, which makes even a low-grade infection of the stump potentially dangerous. Untreated, the signs of puppy septicemia can appear. Prophylactic iodine should be applied to the navel stump at birth to reduce the likelihood of this complication.

Treatment: Cleanse the navel with a dilute solution of hydrogen peroxide, followed by a pHisoHex wash. Apply a topical antibiotic ointment (Panolog). Oral or intramuscular antibiotics may be indicated. If the infection does not clear up quickly, consult your veterinarian. This disease can be present in other puppies in the litter.

Puppy Septicemia *(Blood Poisoning)*

Sepsis in infant puppies is caused by infections which spread rapidly and cause signs mainly in the abdomen. They occur in puppies four to forty days old.

The usual port of entry is the digestive tract. Until a puppy is seven days old, bacteria can penetrate the lining of his bowel just as maternal antibodies can. Infected milk is a major cause of infant sepsis. Navel infection is another.

The initial signs are crying, straining and bloating. They are like those of the toxic milk syndrome. As the disease progresses the abdomen becomes rigid, distended, and its skin takes on a dark red or bluish tint. These are signs of a peritonitis. Other signs of infection include weight loss, chilling, weakness and dehydration. Death occurs rapidly.

Treatment: The cause must be discovered at once — otherwise the whole litter can be affected. Sick puppies should be treated for dehydration, diarrhea, chilling. They should be given a broad-spectrum antibiotic (Chloromycetin), removed from the litter box and raised by hand. Septicemia is best managed under veterinary supervision.

Herpes Virus of Puppies

This is an insidious disease. The dam appears healthy, the milk production adequate, and the puppies nurse in a normal manner until shortly before their deaths. The early signs are an abrupt cessation of nursing, chilling, painful crying, abdominal distention, loss of coordination, and a yellowish-green diarrhea. Puppies are in agony and cry out pitifully when their abdominal muscles are in spasms. Nothing seems to relieve their distress. Death occurs in 24 hours.

The virus attacks puppies between five and twenty-one days of age. During this time puppies are susceptible to herpes virus because their body temperature is below 98 degrees F — the temperature at which the virus incubates.

Herpes virus causes vaginitis in some bitches. Puppies probably acquire the infection while passing through the birth canal during the whelping process. It can be spread to a litter by an infected dog, or anyone who has first handled an infected dog. Bitches develop immunity and subsequent litters are not affected.

Treatment: There is no vaccine available. Infected puppies raised in incubators that maintain a body temperature of 100 degrees F may survive the disease. The virus does not multiply well at temperatures above 98 degrees F.

Herpes infection should be distinguished from other treatable causes of neonatal infection, and from infectious hepatitis (see INFECTIOUS DISEASES). When the illness is due to herpes virus, an autopsy will show bright red blood spots on the surface of the kidneys (''speckled kidneys''). Recovered puppies frequently develop kidney failure at eight to ten months of age.

The Flat Puppy *(Swimmer)*

A flat puppy resembles a turtle, with his legs sticking out to the side instead of underneath him. Swimmers are flat-chested from lying on their stomachs. The condition is caused by a weakness of the muscles which pull the legs together.

Puppies begin to stand at 16 days of age and have a steady gait by the time they are three weeks old. If this is not the case, the puppy may be a swimmer. The disorder is more likely to occur in overweight puppies and heavy-boned breeds. It may have a genetic basis. Slippery floors are believed to predispose to the condition. When puppies at first learn to walk, they should be kept on indoor-outdoor carpeting, or some other nonslippery surface that provides good traction.

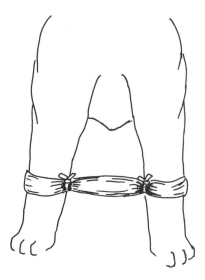

Hobbling helps a "swimmer" keep his legs under him. —*Rose Floyd*

Treatment: Assist a flat puppy several times a day to stand and walk and encourage him to sleep on his side. A hobble made from tape, placed from elbow-to-elbow, forces a puppy to sleep on his side. It also keeps his legs under him when he attempts to stand.

Some of these puppies make a complete recovery.

Skin Infection of the Newborn

Scabs, blisters, and purulent crusts can develop on the skin of newborn puppies at four to ten days of age. These blisters sometimes contain pus. They are caused by poor sanitation in the whelping box. Usually they appear on the abdomen.

Treatment: Keep the nest clean of food, stools, and dried debris. Cleanse scabs with a dilute solution of hydrogen peroxide and wash with a surgical soap. Then apply Panolog ointment.

Conjunctivitis of the Newborn

This condition is due to a bacterial infection beneath the eyelids. It appears in puppies before the eyes are opened. It is discussed in the chapter EYES.

Hypoglycemia *(Low Blood Sugar)*

This is a central nervous system disorder caused by a low blood sugar. It occurs mainly in Toy breeds between six and twelve weeks of age. Often it is precipitated by stress.

The first signs are those of listlessness and depression. They are followed by muscular weakness, tremors (especially in the facial muscles), and later convulsions, coma and death. The entire sequence is not always seen. The dog may simply appear to be depressed or he may be weak, wobbly and jerky; or he may be found in a coma.

Hypoglycemia can occur without warning when a puppy is placed in a new home, or while being shipped. It might appear after a puppy misses a meal, chills, becomes exhausted from too much playing, or has a digestive upset. These upsets place an added strain on the energy reserves of the liver and bring on symptoms (if the dog is susceptible).

Puppies who are weaned on rice and hamburger are more likely to develop hypoglycemia. Their diet is deficient in certain ingredients needed to sustain the liver.

A similar condition occurs in adult hunting dogs usually when hunting. Care should be taken to feed these dogs before hunting and to increase the protein in their diet.

Treatment: Treatment is directed at restoring blood levels of glucose. Begin at once. Prolonged or repeated attacks can cause permanent damage

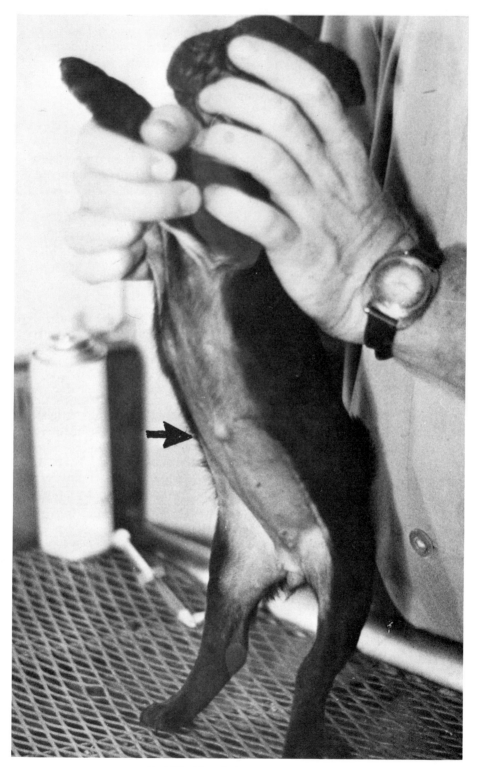

Umbilical hernia in a young puppy.

to the brain. If the puppy is awake, give him Karo syrup, honey or sugar in water by mouth. He will begin to improve in 30 minutes. When he is unconscious he will have to be given a Dextrose solution intravenously. It may be necessary to treat for swelling of the brain. A veterinarian should be called at once.

Prevent recurrent attacks by feeding a high quality kibble diet and add to it sugar, syrup or honey. See that the puppy eats at least every eight hours and receives a daily vitamin.

Breeders should wean puppies on a balanced diet. Food supplements should not exceed 10 percent of the total ration (see *Weaning*). Owners of Toy puppies should not overtire them or allow them to chill.

A condition exists in which hypoglycemia is persistent instead of periodic. It is due to an enzyme deficiency and is not responsive to treatment.

Hernia

A hernia is a protrusion of an organ, or part of an organ, through an opening in the abdominal wall which would normally close in the course of growth. The two common sites are the groin (inguinal) and around the navel (umbilical). When the bulge can be pushed back into the abdomen, the hernia is *reducible*. When it cannot, the hernia is *incarcerated*. An incarcerated hernia becomes *strangulated* if the blood supply to the tissues in the sac is pinched off. Accordingly, a painful hard swelling in one of the usual locations could be an incarcerated hernia — which is an emergency. Seek professional help.

Hernias have a hereditary basis. There is a genetic predisposition for delayed closure of the abdominal ring in most cases.

Inguinal Hernia: The bulge appears in the groin (usually in a bitch); it may not be seen until after she is bred or very old, in which case a pregnant or diseased uterus may be incarcerated in the sac.

Small inguinal hernias do occur in male puppies. They can be watched closely as many will close. If not, have them repaired.

Umbilical Hernia: They are seen fairly frequently in puppies at about two weeks of age. An occasional one may be due to severing the umbilical cord too close to the abdominal wall, but most are due to a tendency for delayed closure of the umbilical ring.

Binding the abdominal wall with straps does little good. Most get smaller and disappear by themselves by about six months. If you can push a finger through the ring, have it repaired. The operation is not serious; the pup usually goes home the same day. If a female is going to be spayed, repair can be postponed until that time.

WEANING

Weaning time depends upon several factors which include the size of the litter, the condition of the dam, the availability of mother's milk, and the inclinations of the breeder. Weaning usually can begin at three to six weeks of age and takes about one week to complete.

Begin by offering one or two feedings a day of evaporated milk in equal parts with water; add baby cereal (oatmeal), and one raw egg yolk (for iron and protein). This should be made up to a sloppy gruel. Feed it in a low-rimmed metal dish (pie pan).

Dip your fingers into the gruel and let the puppies lick it off — or push their noses into it — until they get the message.

To stimulate the appetite, remove the dam an hour or two before feeding. After the meal, let her return to nurse.

Puppies who eat too much gruel are apt to get diarrhea. This is due to a combination of overfeeding and perhaps some degree of intolerance to the milk. Accordingly, at least two feedings a day should still be by nursing.

When the puppies start to eat from a pan, there is less of a demand on the bitch's milk supply. You should begin to decrease her intake of food. This starts the drying-up process.

When the puppies are eating the gruel well (eating more than they are spilling), switch to a name-brand puppy kibble mixed with small amounts of hamburger and cottage cheese. These supplements should not exceed 10 percent of the total ration.

Although many manufacturers recommend feeding dry or chunky kibble to weaning puppies, experience indicates that small puppies (three to six weeks of age) do not eat chunks. The kibble should be soaked well, or better yet, blended. When the puppy teeth come in at six weeks, puppies will begin to chew dry food.

Weaning now can proceed rapidly. Feed four times a day. Many breeders prefer to alternate kibble feedings with all milk feedings (powdered or evaporated milk). Keep WATER available all the time. Puppies not getting enough water can come down with a kidney problem that may not appear until later in life.

If it becomes necessary to dry the bitch up, a drop in milk production is accomplished by reducing her food intake. Withhold all food and water the first day; the next day feed her one-fourth the normal amount; the third day feed her one-half the normal amount; and, the fourth day feed her three-fourths of the normal amount. Restore her to normal rations the fifth day.

THE NEW PUPPY

Buying a Healthy Puppy

The best age at which to buy a puppy is when the individual is about eight weeks old. At this age you can usually tell whether a puppy is going to be a show or breeding prospect. This is also the best age to ship.

Puppies two months old, in particular, are formative. Most new owners prefer to take charge of the care and training of their puppy while still young and impressionable.

Many of the leading dog publications, including the AKC's *Gazette,* carry kennel advertisements for the various breeds. The American Kennel Club (51 Madison Avenue, New York, New York 10010) will provide you, upon request, with the name and address of the current secretary of the breed club of your choice. He (or she), in turn, will mail you a listing of breeders.

After you locate several breeders who appear to have the kind of puppy you are looking for, write to each and explain whether you are interested in a male or female, plan to show or breed, or are just looking for a family companion and pet. A sincere inquiry providing the breeder with some information about the prospective buyer is much more likely to elicit the type of information you are looking for than a hastily scribbled note.

It is wise to insist on buying the dog on the approval of a veterinarian. Emotional attachments develop rapidly. This can make the return of a puppy to a breeder a difficult task. Conscientious breeders, who are proud of their stock, are willing to stand behind them. They will not object to this request. No breeder should be expected to offer you a guarantee that the pup will win in the show ring. Picking a future champion at eight weeks of age is extremely difficult, even for breeders with considerable personal experience. The care, training, feeding, medical care and socialization of the pup after the purchase are every bit as important as the genetic background of the parents.

Many buyers prefer to visit a kennel and make their own selection. There is no need to panic when, on the appointed day, you find yourself standing before a litter of bouncing puppies and find that all appear to be equally lovable. Most puppies appear healthy at first glance but a closer examination may disclose a potential problem that could make the individual undesirable.

When choosing an individual for health and soundness, take your time and go over the pup from head to tail.

The Physical Examination:
Examine the puppy first head-on. The nose should be cool and moist. Squeeze the nostrils together to see if mucus is present. Nasal discharge or frequent sneezing suggest an infection of the respiratory tract.

The nostrils should open when the dog inhales. Short-nosed breeds often have collapsed nostrils. They collapse when the dog breathes in. This is especially so in Pugs and Pekingese.

The teeth should meet in a correct bite. The correct bite for most breeds is a *scissors* bite, in which the upper incisors just overlap the lowers. If a match head can be inserted between the upper and lower incisors, the bite is *overshot* and probably will not correct itself as the dog grows.

In the reverse scissors bite (*undershot* bite) the lower incisors overlap the upper ones. This is acceptable in some short-nosed breeds. If there is doubt, check the standard for the breed.

The gums should be pink and healthy-looking. Pale gums indicate anemia. Inspect the back of the throat. Enlarged tonsils can mean tonsillitis.

Feel on top of the head for a soft spot. If present, the fontanel is open. This is not desirable. In Toy breeds a large dome, sunken eyes, and open fontanel suggest hydrocephalus.

The eyes should look straight ahead and not deviate to the side. If tear staining is present on the muzzle, look for eyelids which are rolled in or out, extra eyelashes, or conjunctivitis.

White spots on the surface of the eye could be scars from prior injuries or infections. The pupils should be dark and have no visible lines or white spots. Cataracts or retained fetal membranes may interfere with vision.

The haw, or third eyelid, may be visible. This should not be taken as a sign of disease unless it is swollen and inflamed.

The ears should stand correctly for the breed. The tips should be healthy and well-furred. Crusty tips with bare spots suggests sarcoptic mange.

The ear canal should be clean and sweet-smelling. A build up of wax with a rancid odor may be caused by ear mites. Head shaking and tenderness about the ears indicate an infection of the ear canals.

Feel the chest with the palm of your hand to see if the heart seems especially vibrant. This could be a clue to a heart defect.

Puppies should breathe in and out without effort. A flat chest, especially when accompanied by trouble breathing in, indicates an airway obstruction. It is seen most commonly in short-nosed breeds, such as Pugs, Boston Terriers and Pekingese.

Pinch the windpipe gently. This should not elicit a coughing spasm. If it does, the puppy probably suffers from bronchitis.

The skin of the abdomen should be clean and healthy-looking. A bulge at the navel probably is due to an umbilical hernia; while one in the groin, an inguinal hernia.

Male Puppies — Push the foreskin back to confirm that it slides back and forth easily. Adhesions between the prepuce and the head of the penis, as well as strictures of the foreskin, require veterinary attention. Both testicles should be present in the scrotum. A dog with an undescended testicle cannot be shown and should not be used for breeding.

Female puppies — Examine the vulva. Look for pasting of hair or discharge. Juvenile vaginitis is a common problem and requires treatment.

The skin and hair around the anus should be clean and healthy-looking. Signs of irritation, such as redness and hair loss, indicate the possibility of worms, chronic diarrhea, or a digestive disorder.

The coat should be bright and shiny and carry the correct color and markings for the breed. Excess scale, itching or deposits in the coat suggest mites, fleas, and other parasites. Moth-eaten areas of hair loss are typical of mange or ringworm.

Next, examine the puppy for soundness and correct structure. The legs should be straight and well-formed. Structural faults include legs which bow in or out, weak pasterns, flat feet with spread toes, and feet which toe in at the rear.

The gait of the puppy should be free and smooth. A limp or faltering gait may simply be due to a sprain or hurt pad, but hip dysplasia and other joint conditions would have to be considered.

At this age puppies should be active, alert, playful and full of vitality. Personalities of puppies vary with breed type, but a sweet disposition is essential to most.

An *aggressive* puppy certainly has no place as a family companion, especially with children. This puppy is unfriendly. Pick him up and he may struggle and bite to get loose, or growl when you try to pet him. This is more a man's dog and will require discipline and training.

A puppy who shrinks away when spoken to, or runs away and hides, can be classified as *shy*. Possibly he may overcome this later, but taking a chance is not worthwhile. This puppy will not socialize easily.

The ideal puppy for a *family pet* holds his tail high, follows you about, accepts petting, struggles when picked up, but then relaxes and licks your hand.

As good health and good disposition so often go hand in hand, it is perhaps wise, in making the final selection, to pick the individual that appears to be really bursting with vitality and self-confidence.

After you have made your purchase, you will want, and should receive, advice and counsel in future weeks. Any guarantees concerning the puppy should be discussed and agreed upon *before* the check is signed.

Before leaving the kennel be sure to ask for and receive the puppy's registration papers, pedigree, health certificate, information on when the puppy's shots were given, and a diet sheet.

FEEDING AND NUTRITION

The nutrition of dogs has received considerable interest during the past few years and certain large manufacturers of dog foods have conducted extensive research and feeding trials in order to establish nutritious diets that need no supplementation. Federal law requires that all dog food manufacturers provide a listing of ingredients in their rations. However, the required labels do not contain enough information for you to compare one dog food with another. Well-known manufacturers noted for their research generally produce good quality dog foods you can trust. In general, commercial dry or soft-moist foods are more reliably balanced products than canned rations. Canned meat may be added to the kibble for palatability, but should not exceed 25 percent of the total daily ration.

One of the best ways to gauge the effectiveness of a product is to observe its effect upon a dog's stool. Poor quality protein passes through a dog's intestinal tract unused, resulting in loose, mushy, or diarrheal stools. Very large stools, on the other hand, indicate excessive amounts of fiber and other indigestibles.

Feeding Older Puppies

Most breeders supply a diet sheet with a new puppy. It should be followed, at least for the first few weeks, since an abrupt change in diet can cause digestive upsets. Puppy chows supply the proteins, carbohydrates, fats and minerals required to raise healthy puppies — provided they eat it well. Purchase a name-brand product, one specifically formulated for puppy growth and development. Pups under a year of age require about twice as much protein and about 50 percent more calories per pound than adult dogs. The feeding of young puppies is discussed under *Weaning*.

Puppies six months and older should be fed twice a day, as much as they will eat in 20 minutes. Then pick up the dish. Labels on dog food packages provide recommended daily feeding amounts. They are useful guidelines but not applicable to every puppy. As a rule, feed the puppy up to his appetite. The thing to avoid, which doesn't happen often, is feeding too much. An overweight puppy is in danger of developing structural defects.

Meats, cottage cheese, milk or table scraps may be added for palatability and to supply additional proteins, but should not exceed 25 percent of the total daily ration. This does *not* include pastry, candy, potatoes, greasy foods, splintery bones, and other indigestible morsels.

Many breeders of large-boned breeds believe it is advantageous to add vitamin and mineral supplements, including calcium, phosphorus and Vitamin D, to a puppy's diet. When feeding a preparation already formulated to meet the needs of a growing puppy, there is danger of inducing a metabolic bone disorder by oversupplementation (see MUSCULOSKELETAL SYSTEM: *Metabolic Bone Disorders*). If your puppy is a poor eater and you think he may need supplements, discuss this with your veterinarian.

Feeding Adults

An older dog will be kept trim by feeding once a day. Caloric requirements differ from dog to dog, are less as the dog grows older, and are less in warm weather and during periods of inactivity. Information on the dog food packages can be used as a guide to feeding — but these are only rough estimates and not always applicable to the type of breed or individual dog you own. Nutrition for the elderly dog is discussed in the chapter GERIATRICS.

Examine your dog to see if his body fat is in correct proportion to his height and bone. There should be a layer of subcutaneous fat over the ribs, thick enough to provide some padding and insulation, but not too thick. You should be able to feel the ribs as individual structures.

Weigh your dog from time to time so as to establish his ideal weight and then maintain him at that level.

Obesity in the adult dog is usually due to feeding snacks and treats between meals. Most of these are high in sugar and therefore are very palatable. Use table scraps sparingly. Feed them only as a special treat and avoid fatty or spicy foods that can upset your dog's stomach.

To learn more about dog nutrition, read *The Collins Guide to Dog Nutrition,* published by Howell Book House, Inc., 230 Park Avenue, New York, N.Y. 10169. It can be purchased at book stores or from the publisher.

TRAINING

General Remarks

First establish the proper understanding with your puppy. He must be made to realize that you are the master, the teacher, and he, the pupil. When you begin any exercise be consistent. Reward him by lavish praise and petting when he does well. Avoid the punitive approach, wherein the pup is brow-beaten or humbled for doing something wrong, which breaks down his spirit. Never strike a puppy. Striking with an open hand makes a dog shy and distrustful of people.

Show your displeasure by the tone of your voice. If a puppy needs to be disciplined, give him a sound scolding. Put on a collar and lead him to his pen. Don't seize and drag him off by the scruff of the neck!

Don't allow your puppy liberties you don't intend to give him when he grows up. Dogs have wonderful memories! A successful relationship between dog and master is based upon firmness and consistency.

If a puppy is allowed to become over-excited in play, he may accidentally nip, scratch or even knock over a small child. Children sometimes lead puppies on, in which case it is their own fault if they get hurt. But accidents such as these can be avoided if puppies and children are not allowed to rough-house. As a puppy grows older he seems to realize that his bite can cause pain and develops a soft mouth.

Housebreaking

First be sure that your puppy's stools are soft and well-formed. It is difficult to housebreak a puppy who has no control over his bowel movements. Loose stools or diarrhea are frequently caused by overfeeding. Reduce the amount of food by 10 percent or more. You should feed only well-balanced commercial dog foods. The basic procedure for toilet training a puppy is similar to potty training a child, except that a puppy will learn more quickly.

Housebreaking may be started as soon as the puppy moves in. But don't begin to scold him for his mistakes until he is old enough to understand — usually not before three months of age. Instead, take your puppy out of doors several times during the day, immediately after meals and long naps, the last thing at night and the first thing in the morning. If you lead him to the same area each time, it helps to inspire the desired action. After he has done what he came to do, praise him excessively. If the pup is not consistent at night, confine him to a small area. Puppies eight weeks and older usually dislike soiling the area where they sleep. Accordingly, confining them during the night helps to teach them bowel and bladder control.

Walking on a Leash

Your puppy should be taught to walk freely on a leash and have good manners, especially if you are planning to show him. No judge is amused by a dog who cuts capers in the show ring.

Start first with a soft nylon or leather collar and switch later to a light choke collar. Leave the collar on for short periods only. Then attach a leash which can be dragged along behind. Next, pick up the leash and begin to lead the puppy with occasional firm tugs, interspersed with a lot of pats and "well-dones." Accustom your puppy to walk on the left side, to move out smartly and stay abreast — neither lunging ahead or dragging behind. As the exercise progresses, exert a little more force with each tug.

A choke collar should be removed after an exercise. A dog running loose with a choke collar is in danger. A foot could get caught between the collar and his neck, or the collar could become snagged in a fence.

Come When Called

Another important exercise is to teach your puppy to come promptly when you call him. Basically this is an extension of the leash training exercise. Let your puppy out to the end of a long rope and as you call him by his name, give the rope a quick tug. When he moves towards you, shorten the rope. Eventually, he will have to come to you all the way. Respond to this by giving him lavish praise and a choice tidbit. Repeat this exercise over and over, until your puppy is letter perfect — then remove the rope.

Never call your puppy to come to you for punishment. If he refuses to obey the command to COME, show your displeasure by catching him and leading him to his pen. He must learn that obedience is inevitable. Whenever you give a command, be sure to make it stick!

Chewing

Puppies chew in order to develop strong teeth and jaws. A puppy can be given a rawhide toy to gnaw. He should not be allowed to start working on the furniture. If you catch him in the act, give him his toy and make him understand that you want him to chew on it but not on the furniture. Various spray-on products leave an unpleasant scent which will effectively discourage chewing. They work well if you take the time to apply them.

Barking

Chronic or neurotic barking is a sign of boredom or lack of attention. Take your puppy for rides in the car, or daily trips to the park. Chaining is not only conducive to barking but is an open invitation to a bad disposition and poor physical development. Keep your puppy in a fenced yard or a suitable enclosure giving opportunity for exercise and play. Barking in the house will stop if a dog can't get to a window to see or hear what is going on outside.

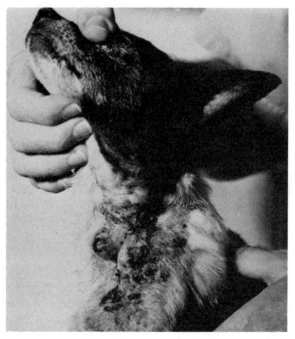

Mast cell tumor on the neck of a terrier.

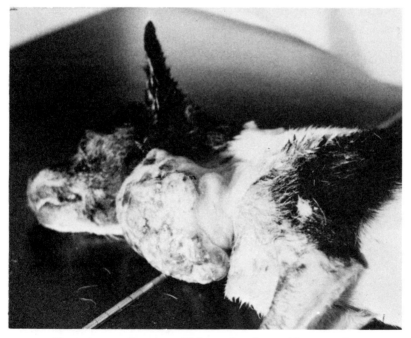

The same growth one month later, showing rapid progression.

18

Tumors and Cancers

GENERAL INFORMATION

Most people associate the word *"tumor"* with a growth occurring on the skin or somewhere inside the body. However, any sort of lump, bump, growth or swelling (such as an abscess) is a TUMOR. Those which are true growths are called NEOPLASMS.

Benign neoplasms are growths which do not invade and destroy, nor do they spread. They are cured by surgical removal, provided that all the tumor has been removed.

Malignant neoplasms are the same as CANCERS (also called CARCINOMAS, SARCOMAS or LYMPHOMAS depending upon the cell type). Cancers invade and destroy. They tend to spread via the bloodstream and lymphatic system to distant parts of the body. This is called *metastasizing*.

Cancer is graded according to its degree of malignancy. Low-grade cancers continue to grow locally and attain a large size. They metastasize late in the course of the illness. High-grade cancers metastasize early when the primary focus is still quite small or barely detectable.

Cancers are approached in the following manner: Suppose a female dog has a lump in her breast. Since it is solid, it is probably a neoplasm. It could be benign or malignant. The decision is made to *biopsy* the lump. This is a surgical operation during which the lump, or a part of the lump, is removed and sent to the pathologist. A pathologist is a medical doctor who has been trained to make a diagnosis by visual inspection of tissue under a microscope. An experienced pathologist can tell whether the tumor is a cancer. He can often provide additional information as to the degree of malignancy. This serves the purpose of making the diagnosis and, in many cases, gives the rationale for the most appropriate treatment.

What is Cancer?

Although much has been learned, the exact cause of cancer is unknown. All cells in the body die and have to be replaced. This process of reduplication is called *mitosis*. A single cell splits into two cells, each identical to the parent. The process is controlled by genes and chromosomes in the cell. Anything which interferes with mitosis at the genetic level can lead to the production of a mutant cell. Many agents are known to do this. They include toxins, chemicals, ionizing rays, viruses and other irritants.

Under appropriate circumstances the mutant cell, which seems to grow much faster than the parent cell, reduplicates itself. This, then, could become a cancer. A cancer acts like a parasite. It depletes the host and replaces normally functioning tissue.

It has been suggested that cancers arise more often than we suspect. The theory is that most of them don't get established because the host's immune system recognizes them as "non-self" and so makes antibodies which destroy them.

Long-standing irritants to tissues are a definite cause of some cancers. The irritant agent appears to speed up tissue repair (and therefore the rate of local mitotic activity), and/or interferes with immune mechanisms which destroy newborn cancer cells.

Examples of agents known to increase the risk of cancer in people are: ultra-violet rays (skin cancer); x-rays (thyroid cancer); nuclear radiation (leukemia); chemicals (analine dyes causing bladder cancer); cigarettes and coal tars (causing lung and skin cancer); viruses (causing experimental cancer in laboratory animals); and parasites (a cause of bladder cancer).

Some cancers have a known familial incidence.

A prior injury or blow is sometimes thought to be the cause of cancer. Trauma can be a cause of certain benign swellings. However, it is seldom, if ever, the cause of a cancer. The injury calls attention to the area and the cancer is discovered incidentally.

Some benign tumors, such as warts and oral papillomas, are clearly due to a virus infection. Other benign tumors, such as lipomas, adenomas of the breast and other organs, simply just grow there for reasons unknown at the present time.

Treatment of Tumors and Cancers

The effectiveness of any form of treatment often depends upon early recognition on the part of the dog owner that his pet may have a cancer.

Complete surgical removal of a cancer which has not yet spread is the most satisfactory treatment available. Cancers that have spread to regional lymph nodes still may be cured if the lymph nodes can also be removed. Even when the disease is widespread, local excision of a bleeding or infected cancer can provide relief of pain and improve the quality of life.

Electrocautery and cryosurgery are two techniques by which tumors on the surface of the body can be controlled or cured by burning and freezing. This provides an alternative to surgical removal, but special equipment is required.

Radiation therapy is useful in the management of some surface tumors and in deeply situated tumors where control cannot be achieved by surgery.

Cures are possible. Radiotherapy must be carried out in a medical center. It requires expensive equipment and the services of a trained radiotherapist.

Chemotherapy employs anti-cancer drugs given at regular intervals. These drugs, even when carefully controlled, have major side effects. They are useful in the management of some widely spread cancers. Hormone therapy also has proven successful in the management of some tumors.

Cancer in the Dog

About half the cancers occurring in dogs are visible as growths or sores on the outer surface of the body (on or beneath the skin, in the perianal area, in the mouth, and in breast tissue). Signs that a tumor could be a cancer are visible growth, ulceration of the skin with bleeding, and a sore which does not heal. One other sign is a lump or knot in a place where none should be (the breast). If you observe any of these signs, be sure to discuss them with your veterinarian.

Some tumors occur internally where you would be unlikely to detect them until they were quite large. Early detection of these cancers rests upon a suspicion that a symptom caused by some internal disorder could be due to a cancer. Since two out of every three such cancers develop in the gastrointestinal and reproductive tracts, you should consider the possibility of cancer when your dog has difficulty eating and digesting his food, or when he has an unexplained bowel disturbance, such as constipation or the passage of blood. Cancer in the reproductive tract of females causes few signs, but you should look for vaginal discharge and bleeding.

The signs and symptoms of common tumors affecting the internal organs are discussed in the chapters dealing with these organs.

COMMON SURFACE TUMORS

Cysts *(Wens, Sebaceous Cysts)*

Sebaceous cysts are common in dogs. They occur all over the body. Certain breeds are affected more often than others. They are: Kerry Blue Terriers, Schnauzers and Spaniels. A sebaceous cyst is made up of a thick capsule which surrounds a lump of cheesy material called keratin. It may grow to an inch. Eventually it is likely to become infected and will have to be drained, unless it has already drained spontaneously. This sometimes leads to a cure. Most cysts should be removed.

Cysts Between the Toes *(Interdigital Cysts)*

Cysts may be found between the toes. They represent inflammatory changes in sweat glands in the feet. They require long term antibiotic treatment.

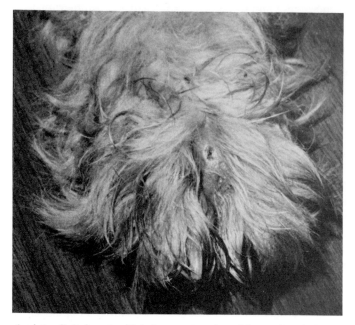

An *interdigital* cyst which has ruptured and formed a draining tract.

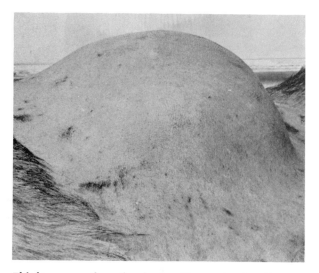

This large growth on the chest wall proved to be a *lipoma*.

Warts and Papillomas

Warts are not nearly so common in dogs as they are in people. They are more common on the older dog. For information on warts in the mouth, see *Oral Papillomatosis*.

Papillomas are growths which project out from the skin. Some are on a stalk, but others look very much like a piece of chewing gum stuck to the skin. If they become irritated or start to bleed, they should be removed.

Lipomas

A lipoma is a growth made up of mature fat cells surrounded by a fibrous capsule which sets it apart from the surrounding body fat. It can be recognized by its round, smooth appearance and soft fat-like consistency. It is not painful. Lipomas grow slowly and may get to be several inches in diameter. Both sexes are affected, but lipomas are more common in overweight dogs, especially females.

Surgical removal is indicated only for cosmetic reasons or to rule out some other tumor, such as a cancer.

Hematomas

A hematoma is a collection of blood beneath the skin. It is caused by a blow or contusion. Small hematomas may resolve spontaneously. Large ones may need to be opened and drained. Ear flap hematomas require special care (see *Swollen Ear Flap* in the chapter EARS).

Tender Knot

A small knot may be present at the site of an injection and is often present for a few days in puppies who have been given their vaccinations. It seldom requires treatment.

A painful swelling beneath the skin may be an abscess.

Skin Cancer

Several types of skin cancer can affect the dog. It is important to differentiate them from benign tumors, such as those discussed above. In some cases, this is difficult to do on the basis of appearance alone. Surgical removal of a lump or bump may be required to establish the diagnosis.

The following skin tumors are common in the dog. Although they are not invariably malignant, all have a malignant potential.

Sebaceous Adenomas are the most common. They arise from oil-producing skin glands. They occur in older individuals. Cocker Spaniels seem to be affected more often than other breeds. They are light-colored,

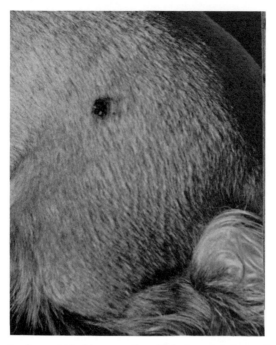

A pigmented skin growth which is suspicious of *melanoma*.

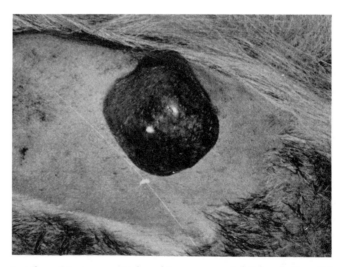

Another *skin tumor*. Only a biopsy can establish whether it is benign or malignant.

usually less than an inch long, and present a cauliflower-like appearance. The surface of the skin may be ulcerated. About 25 percent are low-grade cancers. Large adenomas should be removed. They are more likely to be cancers.

Mast cell tumors are common in older dogs. They are prevalent in Boxers and Boston Terriers. The average dog with a mast cell tumor is eight years old. Look for these tumors on the hind legs, lower abdomen and prepuce (foreskin of the penis).

Typically, they are multi-nodular growths less than an inch in length. About one out of three is malignant. Cancer is more likely when growth is rapid and size is greater than one inch. Malignant mast cell tumors metastasize to distant organs.

Cortisone may be given to decrease temporarily the size of mast cell tumors. The treatment of choice is surgical removal.

Epidermoid carcinoma is a cauliflower-like neoplasm or a hard flat grayish-looking ulcer that does not heal. Its size is variable. It occurs on the feet and legs and sometimes elsewhere. Hair may be lost about the tumor due to constant licking. This tumor is malignant and should be removed.

Melanoma is a malignant neoplasm which takes its name from the brown or black pigment usually associated with it. Often it develops in a pre-existing mole. You should suspect melanoma when a mole starts to enlarge or spread out, becomes elevated above the surface of the skin or starts to bleed. Melanomas are more common in Scottish Terriers, Boston Terriers and Cocker Spaniels.

A suspicious mole should be removed. Melanoma spreads widely, often at an early stage.

Histiocytomas are rapidly growing button-like tumors that occur in younger dogs. They are most common on the feet, face and ears. In appearance, they are dome-shaped, raised, red, irritated-looking and painful to the touch. Some histiocytomas grow smaller and disappear on their own in a few weeks. Others may need to be removed.

Perianal Gland Tumors

These are relatively common neoplasms found in older male dogs. Rarely, females may be affected. Benign tumors (adenomas) grow slowly and ulcerate the skin, become secondarily infected, produce pain and interfere with local hygiene. Infrequently, a perianal tumor will be a cancer (adenocarcinoma) capable of causing widespread metastases.

These neoplasms can be recognized by their typical location and appearance. They arise from modified skin glands located around the anus, at the base of the tail, and along the lower abdomen in the region of the prepuce. They appear as fleshy, rounded, rubbery growths.

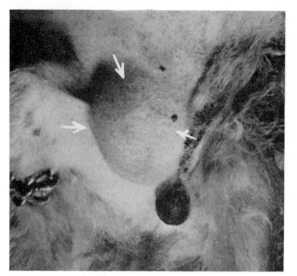

Tumor in an undescended testicle, located in the inguinal region.

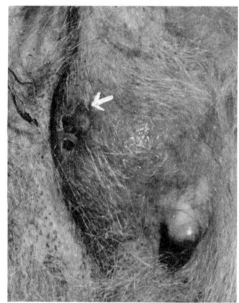

Breast cancer. Note the skin ulceration.

Swelling of the leg due to bone tumor.

Wide local excision is the treatment of choice. Some tumors recur after local removal. Because perianal gland tumors depend upon the male hormone, such recurrences may be held in check by injections of estrogen (or by castration).

Breast Tumors and Swelling

Following heat or false pregnancy, the breasts may remain enlarged or feel lumpy. If you press on the breasts, you may notice that you can express a yellowish, or at times a milky, fluid. This condition is called *mammary hyperplasia*. It is due to a hormone imbalance. Most commonly it is seen in older females who have never had a litter, or in females who have not been bred in some time. Mammary hyperplasia does not occur in females who have been spayed.

Breast swelling may disappear spontaneously in one to two months, or it may persist; in which case a breast tumor or a problem of the ovaries may be present. It is then advisable to have your dog checked by a veterinarian.

Breast tumors are clinically the most significant neoplasms encountered in veterinary practice. About half of these will prove to be cancers. The others are benign adenomas. The back breasts are affected most often. The leading sign is a painless enlargement or a knot in the breast. Most females so affected are over six years of age. A biopsy is the only way to distinguish between benign and malignant tumors.

Breast cancers spread widely, with the lungs being the favorite sites for metastases. A chest x-ray is advisable to rule out metastases before embarking on radical surgery.

Surgical removal is the treatment of choice for all breast neoplasms. The success of a cancer operation depends upon the stage of the tumor at the time of the operation. Unfortunately, this cannot always be determined until later. Better chances of cure are associated with early detection and prompt treatment.

You should examine the breasts of your female at least once a month, especially when she is older. If you detect a suspicious swelling or a solitary lump, ask your veterinarian to examine her.

BONE TUMORS

Both benign and malignant bone tumors occur in the dog. By far the most likely bone tumor is *osteogenic sarcoma*. While this cancer can strike at any age, usually it is a disease of the middle years. Males are affected more often than females. There is a definite predilection for dogs of the larger breeds: St. Bernards, Newfoundlands, Great Danes, Great Pyrenees, Irish Setters, Boxers and others. Rarely, if ever, does it occur in the very small breeds.

The long bones of the front and rear legs are the most common locations for osteogenic sarcoma. The flat bones of the ribs are next. Frequently, the first sign is a limp in the mature male dog having no history of injury. Often this sign receives little attention until swelling of the leg below the tumor is observed. Pressure over the tumor causes varying degrees of pain. X-rays are diagnostic.

This form of cancer spreads early and to the lungs. There is no satisfactory cure.

19

Geriatrics

GENERAL REMARKS

A progressive and irreversible deterioration of cellular and organ function occurs in the tissues of all animals with the passage of time. Although its effects are familiar to everyone, the exact mechanism by which organic systems eventually run out of protoplasmic vitality is an unsolved mystery.

It is estimated that about 10 percent of the dog population is over the age of 10 years. But all dogs do not age at the same rate. A dog's biologic age depends upon many things: his genetic background, his nutritional status, the presence of coexistent diseases, and environmental stresses. Of great importance is the care the dog has received throughout his life. Well-cared-for pets suffer fewer infirmities as they grow older. But when sickness, illness or injury is neglected, the aging process is accelerated.

Large dogs seem to age more rapidly than smaller ones. St. Bernards, German Shepherds, Great Danes and other large breeds reach old age at 10 to 12 years. Toy breeds are old at 14 to 16 years.

Although aging is inevitable and irreversible, some of the infirmities. attributed to old age may, in fact, be due to disease — therefore correctable or at least treatable.

The care of the older dog is directed at preventing premature aging, avoiding physical and emotional stress, and meeting special nutritional needs. Dogs older than six years of age should have a complete physical examination every six months. Usually it will include a urinalysis, stool exam, and complete blood count. At times, liver and kidney function tests, chest x-ray, and electrocardiogram are indicated. Any disease or abnormal condition which may be present can be dealt with before it leads to a more serious infirmity. Cataracts, strictures, bone deposits, and other causes of incipient disability are often amenable to surgical correction or medical management. Heart medications, analgesics, enzymes, and hormones can relieve discomfort and improve organ performance.

CARING FOR THE OLDER DOG

Behavioral Changes

Older dogs are more complacent, less energetic, less curious, and more restricted in their scope of activity. They are forgetful. They tend to sleep a lot. They become fixed in their habits and are less tolerant of changes in the daily routine. Crankiness and irritability are common.

Boarding and hospitalization, in particular, are poorly tolerated. At such times old dogs eat poorly, become overanxious, bark excessively, and don't get the rest they need. If possible, it is advisable to care for them at home under the guidance of your veterinarian in order to avoid stress and anxiety. Having a neighbor drop by once or twice a day to care for the dog may be better than having him boarded.

Physical Changes

With reduced activity and loss of muscular tone, the neck and body of an older dog take on a more bulky appearance and his extremities appear thinner, especially the thighs and upper parts of the front legs. His abdomen may sag, back begin to sway, and elbows wing-out. His muscles may begin to shake when he exerts himself.

Stiffness in the joints due to osteoarthritis is made worse by drafts and by sleeping on cold damp ground or on cement pads. His bed should be indoors in a warm dry spot. Arthritic dogs, especially large and heavy ones, should be given a padded surface on which to sleep. Toy dogs may need to be covered at night.

Moderate exercise helps to keep the joints supple and should be encouraged. However, the older dog should not be exercised beyond his normal level of activity. A specific condition (such as heart disease) actually may require that exercise be restricted. Although there is no way to stop the progress of arthritis, analgesics such as aspirin can relieve the pain and enable the dog to lead a more active life (see MUSCULOSKELETAL SYSTEM: *Arthritis*).

The coat of an older dog mats easily and his skin becomes dry and scaly due to reduced activity of the oil producing glands. Small skin tumors are common. Pads of the feet may be thick, overgrown, and cracked. Stiff old dogs have trouble keeping their anal and genital areas clean. Frequent grooming and bathing is necessary to keep them clean and free of parasites and skin diseases. The addition of Alpha Keri bath oil to the final rinse helps to soften the skin and keep it in better condition. Toe nails need to be trimmed more often unless they are worn down by activity. Basic health care is discussed in the chapter SKIN (see *How to Avoid Coat and Skin Problems*).

Gradual loss of hearing occurs commonly as dogs age. There is no treatment for senile deafness, but there might be a blockage in the ear canal or some other contributing cause which can be improved by treatment. The subject is discussed in the chapter EARS.

In many older dogs a grayish-white or bluish haze appears in that part of the eye which can be seen through the pupil. It is due to aging of the lens and is called *nuclear sclerosis*. It should not be mistaken for a cataract. While senile cataracts do occur in dogs, they are not nearly as common as in man. Loss of vision may be due to retinal disease or another eye disorder.

Surgical removal of cataracts usually is reserved for dogs having difficulty getting around because of loss of sight. Most dogs adjust well to a gradual loss of vision if they retain the ability to hear. Cataracts, and other eye disorders leading to loss of sight are taken up in the EYES chapter.

Tooth and gum disease is common in the older dog and interferes with eating. With proper treatment suffering is relieved, the dog is more comfortable, and his nutritional status improves. Loose teeth should be removed. If your dog has lost his teeth and is unable to chew dry dog food, soak it for 20 minutes before feeding it, or feed canned food formulated for older dogs.

Dry biscuits help to reduce tartar and calculus. But bones and bone chips should not be given to the older dog. They make the stool hard and can lead to bowel difficulties.

Dogs of all ages should be put on a program of good dental hygiene as outlined in the chapter ORAL CAVITY.

Urinary tract difficulties are common in older dogs. Obligatory excretion of increased amounts of urine occurs because the kidneys have lost the power to concentrate the wastes. This is offset by drinking larger amounts of water.

Often the dog with failing kidneys is unable to keep from wetting in the house. He should be given the opportunity to go outside several times a day, the first thing in the morning and the last thing at night, and perhaps during the night. There is a temptation to reduce his water intake. However, water should be made available at all times because without water the dog may go into kidney failure (see *Uremia*). Special diets (such as Hills K/D) can be a great help to a dog with reduced kidney function.

Incontinence is a problem seen mainly in the older spayed female. It can be treated by estrogen administration.

Kidney and bladder disorders are discussed in the chapter URINARY SYSTEM.

Enlargement of the prostate gland in the male usually does not cause urinary tract symptoms. When enlarged it can narrow the rectal canal causing constipation or fecal impaction.

Constipation in the older dog often is the result of improper diet aggravated by reduced bowel activity and weakness of the muscles of the abdominal wall. The dog may have to be given a high residue diet. The subject is discussed in the chapter DIGESTIVE SYSTEM (see *Constipation*).

Weakness of the heart muscle is another common condition associated with advancing age. Heart disease can exist for many years before actual signs of failure occur. Early signs of heart failure are loss of pep and condition, lethargy, muscular weakness, shortness of breath, and a cough which begins at night or occurs after exercise or excitement. The subject is discussed in the chapter CIRCULATORY SYSTEM (see *Heart Failure*).

Being overweight is a serious complicating factor in heart disease. Fat dogs must be made to lose weight. A low salt diet (such as Hills H/D) may be of real aid in treating dogs with congestive heart failure. Heart medications and diuretics also can be of considerable assistance.

Old dogs adjust poorly to physical and emotional stress. Their hearts, livers, kidneys, and metabolism often are not able to meet the increased demands placed upon them. Sudden decompensation can occur. Special care must be taken with the older dog to prevent chilling. When wet, he should be toweled dry and kept in a warm room. An older dog also is less tolerant to extremes of heat. Changes in his diet or drinking water, too, can stress him. His digestive tract and its bacterial flora are geared to his present diet. When changes are necessary, make them slowly. Add small amounts of the new diet while gradually reducing the old. The secret to the care of the old dog is moderation in all things: make changes by evolution—not revolution.

Nutrition

Since an older dog is less active he needs fewer calories than when he was younger. Without a reduction in number of calories, the older dog is likely to gain weight—which puts an additional strain on his limited organ reserve. This contributes to a shortened life span. Feeding "treats" between meals, and adding table scraps, are two of the main reasons why dogs get too fat.

Caloric requirements for the older dog have to be determined on an individual basis. You must take into consideration his *ideal* weight (i.e., that at which he is neither too fat or too thin), how active he is, and what his emotional make-up may be. High-strung dogs require more food than their more sedate counterparts.

In general, an elderly dog of average size needs only about 25 to 30 calories per pound body weight per day. Canned dog foods supply about 500 calories in a pound of ration; moist or "chunky" dog food about 1300 calories; and dry kibble about 1600 calories.

Since the older dog must eat less food, it is important that this food be of the highest quality to provide him with an adequate daily supply of nutrients. An ideal diet would supply a somewhat higher concentration of protein than an ordinary adult maintenance diet, and a somewhat lower concentration of fat. In this regard it would be qualitatively closer to a ration formulated for the growth of puppies (although proportionately the older dog would eat much less than a growing puppy).

While high quality protein is important for the older dog, he should not be fed a diet too rich in meat or one containing protein of poor quality. This creates an increased nitrogen load which must be handled by the liver and kidneys. Dogs with weak kidneys can be thrown into failure by feeding them more protein than they can handle. Energy needs are better met by giving easily digestible carbohydrates—cooked to break down starch granules. High quality protein suitable for the digestive tract of an older dog can be supplied by adding small amounts of cooked hamburger, boiled egg, cottage cheese, or skim milk to a kibble base. If your dog seems to be losing weight or appears to need more calories, try adding small amounts of carbohydrate (cooked cereals, cooked rice, or farina).

While fats increase the palatability of food, they are difficult for the older dog to digest and are high in calories. Some fat is required to aid the intestinal absorption of vitamins, and to provide for the manufacture of essential fatty acids, but adequate amounts are supplied by commercial dog foods. Fat supplements should not be added to the ration.

Old dogs need more minerals and vitamins. B vitamins are lost in the urine of dogs having reduced kidney function; also, absorption of vitamins through the intestinal tract decreases as the individual ages. Calcium and phosphorus in correct balance (1.2 to 1) helps to prevent softening of the bones. Therefore, many old dogs probably need a vitamin/mineral supplement. But it should be *balanced* to meet the metabolic needs. Your veterinarian can recommend an appropriate supplement to meet the specific requirements of your dog. If you use a commercial pet food especially formulated for older dogs, you may not need to add vitamins and minerals unless there is a specific medical reason to do so.

It is desirable when feeding the older dog to divide his daily ration into two equal parts and feed the first half in the morning and the second in the evening.

Sample diets that have been used successfully in the care of elderly dogs are:

Maintenance
(1)   A commercial dog food especially formulated for the needs of the older dog (GAINES Cycle 4 is one example).
(2)   50% cooked corn meal and 50% commercial *puppy* ration. Vitamin/mineral supplement.

Weight Losing
(1)   Same as maintenance diet but reduce the portions by one-fourth (1/4).
(2)   1/2 pound of lean meat (hamburger, lamb, chicken)
       1/2 pound of vegetable (peas, corn)
       Vitamin/mineral supplement
NOTE: Feed one pound ration per 20 pounds weight of the dog.

Special Diets
Prescription diets may be required for dogs with heart disease, kidney disease, intestinal disease, or obesity. They should be prescribed by your veterinarian.

A NEW PUPPY

The addition of a new puppy to the household can be a rejuvenating experience for the elderly dog. When handled properly most old dogs delight in the companionship, and through renewed interest and added exercise they seem to recapture their youth. Jealousy is prevented by giving attention to the old dog first. Always affirm his seniority privileges.

PUTTING YOUR DOG TO SLEEP *(Euthanasia)*

The time may come when you are faced with the prospect of having to put your pet to sleep. This is a difficult decision to make—both for you and for your veterinarian. Many an old and even infirm dog can be made quite comfortable with just a little more thoughtfulness and tender loving care than the average healthy dog needs, and can still enjoy months or years of happiness in the company of his loved ones. But when life ceases to be a joy and a pleasure, when the dog suffers from a painful and progressive condition for which there is no hope of betterment, then perhaps at this time we owe him the final kindness to die easily and painlessly. This is accomplished by an intravenous injection of an anesthetic agent in sufficient amount to cause immediate loss of consciousness and cardiac arrest.

20

Drugs and Medications

ANESTHETICS AND ANESTHESIA

Anesthetics are drugs used to block the sensation of pain. They are divided into two general categories — locals and generals.

Local anesthetics are used for operations on the surface of the body where they are infiltrated locally into the tissue or into a regional nerve. They may be applied topically to mucus membranes. While local anesthetics (such as *Xylocaine)* have the fewest risks and side effects, they are not suitable for most major operations.

General anesthetics render the dog unconscious. They can be given by injection or inhalation. Light doses sedate or relax the dog and may be suitable for short procedures (such as removing porcupine quills from the mouth). Inhaled gases (such as Halothane) are administered through a tube placed in the trachea.

The dose of an anesthetic is computed by weight of the dog. Certain breeds appear to have a low tolerance for barbituates and other anesthetics. Whippets, Afghan Hounds, Great Pyrenees, and perhaps others may require less anesthetic than other breeds of comparable weight. Discuss this with· your veterinarian.

The dosage of any given anesthetic will vary greatly, even among dogs of the same size. Therefore, they must be given only by someone trained to determine the degree of sedation they produce. Combinations of anesthetics often are used to lessen the potential side effects.

The removal of an anesthetic agent is by the lungs, liver, or kidney, depending on the choice of agent. Impaired function of these organs can cause anesthetic complications. If your dog has a history of lung, liver, kidney or heart disease, be sure to discuss it with your veterinarian.

A major risk of general anesthesia is having a dog vomit when going to sleep or waking up. The vomitus refluxes into the windpipe and lungs producing asphyxiation. This can be avoided by keeping the stomach empty for 12 hours before scheduled surgery. Accordingly, if you know your dog is going to have an operation, don't give him anything to *eat or drink* after 6:00 P.M. the night before. This means picking up his water dish and keeping him away from the toilet bowl.

PAIN RELIEVERS

Analgesics are drugs used to relieve pain. While there are many pain-killers, aspirin *(acetylsalicylic acid)* is the safest and best analgesic for home veterinary care. Its best use, perhaps, is in the arthritic dog, to relieve stiffness and promote joint mobility.

Demerol, morphine, codeine and other *narcotics* are subject to Federal regulation and cannot be purchased without a prescription. The effect of these drugs on dogs is highly variable. They should be used under medical supervision.

Tylenol is an analgesic primarily used for its fever reducing properties. Fever should be treated in dogs only when it is high enough to produce damage by itself.

Butazolidin is used for its anti-inflammatory effects. Your veterinarian may wish to prescribe it in certain disorders of the bones and joints.

Pain-killers are contraindicated in sprains and other acute conditions of muscles, tendons, and joints, where relief of pain might permit the use of a leg that should be kept at rest.

While aspirin is the safest analgesic, it is not without complications and can cause gastric upsets. When used for a prolonged period of time, it can cause gastric ulcers and bleeding from the upper gastrointestinal tract.

TRANQUILIZERS

Tranquilizers are drugs used to relieve anxiety, treat motion sickness, and sedate a dog for ease of handling and treatment. The exact mode of action of tranquilizers is variable. Some act on the brain to modify behavior and to increase the threshhold for nausea and vomiting. Others achieve their effects primarily through sedation. They are of the antihistamine class and available at pet stores.

Tranquilizers are safe and effective when used as directed and in the right situation. Nevertheless, even in the best of circumstances, untoward results can occur. Human tranquilizers should not be given to dogs without first discussing their use with your veterinarian.

Long-term tranquilization is not recommended. Except for motion sickness, thunderstorms, and other temporary upsets of this sort, behavior disorders in dogs are best treated by identifying the cause of the problem and taking steps to correct it. Tranquilizers should not be given to acutely injured dogs as they lower the blood pressure.

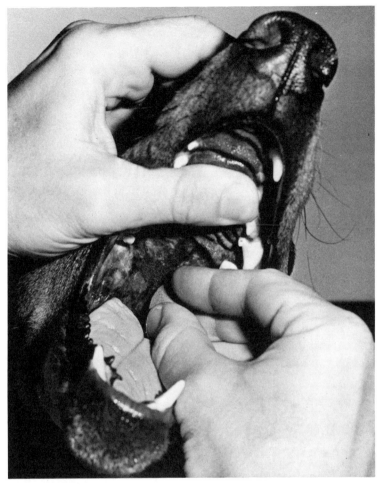

The correct way to give a pill — in the middle, and well at the back of the mouth. —*J. Clawson*

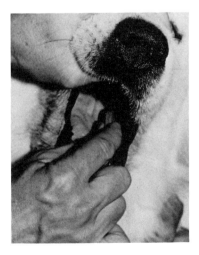

Incorrect. The pill is too far forward and to the side. —*J. Clawson*

COMMON HOUSEHOLD DRUGS FOR HOME VETERINARY USE

Dose by Weight of Dog

Aspirin: One 5 grain tablet per 30 lbs. every six hours.
Charcoal: One tablespoon in four ounces of water per 30 lbs.
Cheracol-D (Cough Syrup): One teaspoon every four hours per 30 lbs.
Dramamine: 25 to 50 mg one hour before traveling.
Glauber's Salt (Sodium Sulfate): One teaspoon per 10 lbs.
Hydrogen Peroxide (3%): Two teaspoons per 30 lbs. every 10 minutes for
    three doses, or until the dog vomits.
Kaopectate: One teaspoon per 5 lbs. every four hours.
Milk of Magnesia: One teaspoon per 5 to 10 lbs. every six hours.
Mineral Oil: One teaspoon per 5 lbs.
Paregoric: One-half teaspoon per 10 lbs. every eight hours.
Tylenol: One half to one tablet every six hours.

HOW TO GIVE MEDICATIONS

Pills (Capsules and Tablets)

To give a pill, open your dog's mouth as described in ORAL CAVITY: *How to Examine the Dog's Mouth.* Insert the pill well to the back of the tongue in the *midline.* (If you get the pill to the side of the tongue, dogs will work them forward and spit them out.) Close the dog's mouth and hold it shut while stroking his throat until he swallows. If he licks his nose, probably he swallowed the pill.

(*Note:* If pills are broken up into powders they make an unpleasant taste which is poorly tolerated. Some pills have a protective coating which is important for delayed release in the intestine. Avoid breaking up pills, if at all possible.)

Liquids

Liquid preparations are administered into a pouch between the molar teeth and the cheek. Bottles, syringes, and eyedroppers, are suitable for giving liquids. With practice, spoons can be used.

First tilt the chin up at 45 degrees and place the neck of the bottle into the cheek pouch. Seal the lips around it with your fingers and pour in the liquid. Large amounts can be given in this way. Hold the muzzle firmly while the dog swallows.

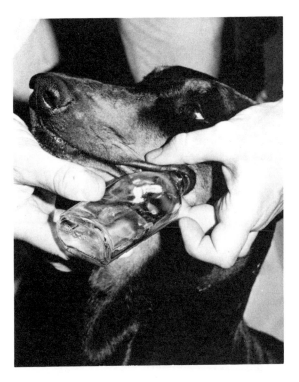

Liquids are administered into a pouch between the molar teeth and the cheek.—*J. Clawson*

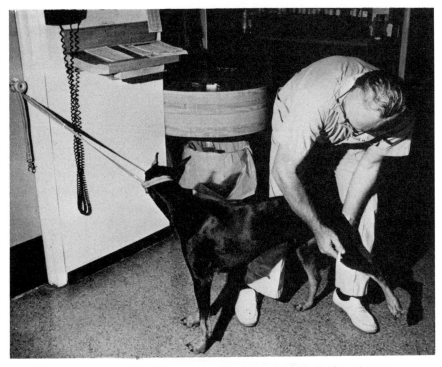

Give intramuscular injections into the back of the thigh muscle.—*J. Clawson*

Injections

If it becomes necessary to give your dog injections, it is highly desirable to have the procedure discussed and demonstrated to you by your veterinarian. One of the dangers of giving a foreign substance by injection is that of producing a sudden allergic or acute *anaphylactic* reaction in which the dog goes into shock through circulatory collapse. This is a type of hypersensitivity reaction of the immediate type (see *Allergies*). The most common agent producing anaphylactic shock is penicillin. Penicillin is used as a preservative in some vaccines. As a precaution, do not administer a drug by injection which has produced any sort of reaction in the past, including hives. Treatment of anaphylactic shock involves intravenous adrenalin, and oxygen. This is one reason why you may wish to have your veterinarian give injections—as he has the drugs to treat such reactions in time.

Some injections are given under the skin *(subcutaneous)* and others into the muscle. Insulin is an example of the former, and rabies vaccine the latter. Read the directions on the product to determine the route of administration.

Most injections are not painful to the dog, although intramuscular injections may hurt as the medication is injected. A good assistant is a help. If there is any likelihood the dog may bite, muzzle him (see EMERGENCIES: *Handling and Restraint*).

Draw the medicine up into the syringe and point the needle toward the ceiling while pressing the plunger to expel any air.

The technique for giving an injection is to select a site and swab the skin with a piece of cotton soaked in alcohol.

The back of the neck or shoulder is a good place for a subcutaneous injection because the skin is loose here and readily forms a fold when pinched. Grasp a fold of skin to form a ridge. Firmly push the needle point through the skin into the subcutaneous fat in a course somewhat parallel to the surface of the skin. Before any injection is given, always pull back on the plunger and look for blood. If blood appears, withdraw the syringe and repeat the procedure. Some medicines could cause death if given into a vessel. In the absence of blood, push in the plunger. Withdraw the needle and rub the skin for a few seconds to disperse the medicine.

Intramuscular injections are given in the muscle of the outside of the thigh behind the femur, half-way between the knee joint and the hip. Injections into vessels, nerves, and joints can be avoided by giving the shot in the described location, shown in the photograph. Remember to withdraw the plunger and check for blood in the syringe before giving the injection.

Enemas

Enemas are used to treat *constipation*. The subject is discussed in DIGESTIVE SYSTEM: *Constipation*. Enemas should not be given until a veterinarian has made the diagnosis and prescribed the treatment. Enemas ordinarily are not prescribed on a routine basis. There are better ways to treat chronic constipation.

A soapy enema is made by stirring a piece of soap in water until it turns milky. Enemas also can be made with a half teaspoonful of table salt, or a

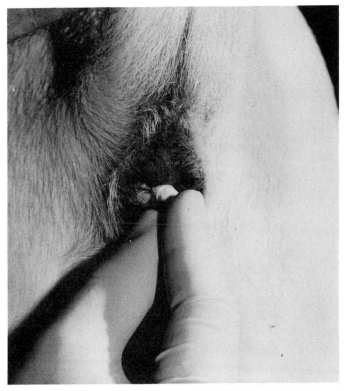

Inserting a suppository. —*J. Clawson*

teaspoonful of baking soda, added to eight ounces of water. The water should be at about body temperature.

The equipment you will need is an enema can or bag and a catheter or a piece of tubing with a nozzle at one end. Lubricate the nozzle and insert it into the anal canal, one to three inches, depending on the size of the dog. Enemas are given at a rate of one ounce of fluid per ten pounds of body weight.

Suppositories

Your veterinarian may prescribe a suppository to treat constipation. Also, medications can be given by suppository when the oral route is not satisfactory (for example, when a dog is vomiting).

A suppository is lubricated with vaseline and slipped all the way into the rectum where it dissolves. Suppositories for constipation contain a mild irritant which draws water into the rectum and stimulates a bowel movement. Dulcolax is a good one for this purpose. You can buy it at any drugstore. For small dogs, break the suppository in half. Suppositories should not be given to a dog in pain who might have an *Acute Abdomen*.

Eye Medication—How to medicate the eye is discussed in the chapter EYES.

Ear Medication—How to medicate the ear is discussed in the chapter EARS.

21

Antibiotics and Infections

GENERAL REMARKS

Antibiotics are extracts of basic plants such as molds and fungi. They are capable of destroying some microorganisms that cause disease.

The age of modern antibiotics began with the discovery of penicillin by Sir Alexander Fleming. In 1928, Fleming made a fortuitous and accidental discovery. He observed that a strain of penicillin mold which had fallen on a culture plate could prevent the growth of a colony of bacteria. Although he tried to isolate extracts of the fungus to treat infections, the broths proved too weak.

It remained for a group in Oxford, England, in 1939, under the direction of Sir Howard W. Florey, to isolate potent antibiotic extracts from the mold *penicillium notatum*. The impact of this success on the control of infection sent scientists back to the soil in search of other natural substances having antibiotic activity. This led to the discovery of tetracycline and chloromycetin, as well as many other antibiotics in use today. Taking the basic nucleus of an antibiotic grown in deep broth cultures, researchers added side chains by chemical synthesis. This created a whole new spectrum of synthetic drugs.

Antibiotics fall into two general categories. Those that are *bacteriostatic (or fungistatic)* inhibit the growth of microorganisms, but don't kill them outright. *Bacteriocidal* and *fungicidal* drugs destroy the microorganisms.

Bacteria also are classified according to their ability to cause disease. *Pathogenic* bacteria are capable of producing a particular illness or infection. *Non-pathogenic* bacteria live on (or within) the host, but don't cause illness under normal circumstances. They are referred to as *normal flora*. Some of them produce substances necessary to the well-being of the host. For example, bacteria in the bowel synthesize Vitamin K which is absorbed into the animal's bloodstream and is necessary for normal blood clotting.

Antibiotics are specific for certain pathogenic bacteria. The number now available brings with it new possibilities for animal sensivity and allergy, and multiplies the potential hazards of mismanagement.

WHY ANTIBIOTICS MAY NOT BE EFFECTIVE

Misdiagnosis of Infection

At times, signs of inflammation (such as heat, redness and swelling) can exist without infection. Sunburn is one example. Infection can be *presumed* to exist when one sees inflammation *and* purulent discharge (pus). Usually there will be an offensive odor. Other signs are fever and elevated white cell count. Specific infections are discussed in other chapters.

Inappropriate Selection

An antibiotic must be effective against the microorganism. Sometimes a choice can be made on the basis of the character of the illness. The best way to determine susceptibility is to recover the organism, culture it, and identify it by colony appearance and microscopic characteristics. Antibiotic discs are applied to the culture plate to see if the growth of colonies is inhibited. Antibiotics are graded according to whether the microorganism is *sensitive, indifferent,* or *insensitive*. Unfortunately, laboratory findings do not always coincide with results in the host. Nevertheless, antibiotic culture and sensitivity testing is the surest way of selecting the best agent.

Inadequate Wound Care

Antibiotics enter the bloodstream and are carried to the source of the infection. Abscesses, wounds containing devitalized tissue, and wounds with foreign bodies (dirt, splinters), are resistant areas. Under such circumstances, antibiotics can't get into the wound. Accordingly, it is important to drain abscesses, debride or clean dirty wounds, and remove foreign bodies.

Route of Administration

An important medical decision rests in selecting the best route for administration. Some antibiotics have to be given on an empty stomach, or again with a meal. Insufficient absorption from the gastrointestinal tract is one cause of inadequate blood levels. Some antibiotics are not absorbed when taken with antacids or milk.

In severe infections antibiotics are given intravenously, or by intramuscular injection, to circumvent the problem.

In the treatment of urinary tract infections, other substances may have to be given by mouth to change the pH of the urine and assure that the antibiotics won't precipitate.

Dose and Frequency of Administration

The total daily dose is computed by weighing the dog, then dividing the dose into equal parts and giving each one at spaced-out intervals. When the total dose is too low, or not given often enough, the result is less than favorable.

Other factors which have to be taken into account when computing the daily dose are the severity of the infection, the age of the dog, his overall health and stamina, whether he is taking another antibiotic and whether he is taking drugs which could depress his ability to fight infection (such as cortisone).

COMPLICATIONS OF ANTIBIOTICS

All drugs should be viewed as poisons. Aspirin can kill if a dog takes enough of it. The side effects of drugs may be more dangerous than the disease.

Antibiotics should never be given without justifiable indications. Common complications of antibiotics are discussed below and listed in TABLE I. (This list is by no means complete.)

Allergy

Antibiotics, more so than any other class of drugs, can cause allergic reactions. Allergies are discussed in the SKIN chapter. Signs of allergy are hives, rash, itching and scratching, and watering of the eyes. Wheezing, collapse and death can occur.

Toxicity

There is a certain margin of safety lying between a therapeutic dose and a dose toxic to the dog. Toxicity is due to overdose, or impaired elimination. With advanced liver and kidney disease, these organs fail to break down and excrete the antibiotic.

Young pups require a lower dose by weight than adult dogs because their kidneys are immature.

One cause of overdosage is giving an antibiotic for too long a time.

Toxicity can affect one or more systems:

> *The ears* — Damage to the otic nerves leads to ringing in the ears, hearing loss, and deafness. Loss can be permanent.
>
> *The liver* — Toxicity can lead to jaundice and liver failure.
>
> *The kidneys* — Toxicity causes nitrogen retention, uremia, and kidney failure.
>
> *The bone marrow* — Toxicity depresses the formation of red cells, white cells, and platelets. Fatalities do occur.

Signs of toxicity are difficult to recognize in the dog. They can be far advanced before they come to the owner's attention.

Secondary Infections

Antibiotics alter a normal flora which serves as a protection against pathogens. Harmful bacteria multiply and cause disease.

Entercolitis (severe diarrhea) follows the use of certain antibiotics which change the normal flora of the bowel.

Emergence of Resistant Strains

Strains of bacteria which are resistant to antibiotics evolve when antibiotics are used: (a) for a long time, (b) in too low a dose, and (c) when the antibiotic is bacteriostatic. Microorganisms resistant to one antibiotic often are resistant to others of the same class.

Use in Pregnancy

Certain antibiotics can effect the growth and development of unborn or newborn puppies. Tetracyclines and kanamycin are two of them. They should not be used in pregnancy, if substitutes are available.

ANTIBIOTICS and CORTISONE

Cortisone and other steroids have an anti-inflammatory effect—that is, they reduce the signs of infection (swelling, redness and tenderness) but do not treat the infection. They help to relieve the pain and irritation associated with an inflammation. (For example, to relieve the itching of allergy and some skin diseases.)

Steroids often are combined with antibiotics, particularly in topical preparations for use in the eye, ear, and on the skin.

Because they have anti-inflammatory properties, steroids mask the signs of infection while giving the impression the dog is getting better. At times, this can lead to continuation of tissue damage. Preparations containing steroids should not be used in the eye except under medical supervision.

Steroids have another side effect which is particularly undesirable. They depress the normal host immune response. This allows infection to go unchecked.

Other untoward effects of steroids are discussed in the SKIN chapter under the heading *Cortisone Excess*.

Table I—ANTIBIOTICS YOUR VETERINARIAN MAY PRESCRIBE

ANTIBIOTIC	DOSE (By Weight of Dog)	USED IN INFECTIONS OF:	ADVERSE REACTIONS
Penicillins	20,000 u/lb. q 24 hr, I.M.	Skin, Mouth, Tonsils, Uterus, Wounds	Allergy
Ampicillin	10 mg/lb. q 8 hr, orally	Same as penicillin Genitourinary tract Respiratory tract	Allergy
Cephalosporins	Depends on the drug.	Urinary tract Respiratory tract	Kidney Damage Expensive
Aminoglycosides Neomycin	10 mg/lb. q 6 hr, orally 5 mg/lb. q 12 hr, I.M. Topically 3 to 4 times daily	Diarrhea (orally) Eye*, Ear, Skin (Topically)	Kidney Damage Allergy
Kanomycin	3 mg/lb. q 12 hr, I.M.	Puppy Septicemia	Kidney Damage Deafness Brain Injury in Newborns
Streptomycin	5 mg/lb. q 8 hr, I.M.	Navel infection Leptospirosis	Deafness
Gentamycin	2 mg/lb. q 12 hr, I.M. first day, then once a day Topically 3 to 4 times daily	Skin, Respiratory tract Urinary tract Eye*, Ear	Kidney Damage Deafness
Tetracyclines	8 mg/lb. q 8 hr, orally 3 mg/lb. q 12 hr, I.M.	Leptospirosis Brucellosis Respiratory tract Kennel cough Skin	Stained teeth (Unborn puppies) Retarded bone growth (Puppies)
Chloromycetin	10-25 mg/lbs. q 8 hr, orally Eye preparations: three times daily	Skin, Mouth Respiratory tract Urinary tract Eye* (topically)	Bone marrow depression

—continued

Table I—ANTIBIOTICS YOUR VETERINARIAN MAY PRESCRIBE—(continued)

ANTIBIOTIC	DOSE (By Weight of Dog)	USED IN INFECTIONS OF:	ADVERSE REACTIONS
Panolog	Topically 2 or three times daily. Drops and ointment.	Ear Skin	Rare
Erythromycin	5 mg/lb. q 8 hr, orally	Penicillin substitute when dog is allergic to penicillin	
Lincomycin	7 mg/lb. q 8 hr, orally 5 mg/lb. q 12 hr, I.M.	Skin, Wounds Penicillin substitute	Diarrhea
Tylosin	5 mg/lb. q 8 hr, orally 3 mg/lb. 12 hr, I.M.	Same as Erythromycin	Same as for Erythromycin
Sulfa Drugs	Depends on the drug.	Urinary tract Gastrointestinal tract Eye*	Forms crystals in urine. Anemia Allergy
Furacin	Apply 2 to 3 times daily (topically)	Burns Puppy vaginitis	
Griseofulvin	10 mg/lb. daily for 4 to 6 weeks	Ringworm	Don't use in pregnancy
Nystatin	100,000 u/lb. q 6 hr, orally for 7 to 14 days	Thrush	

NOTE: Unless otherwise stated, antibiotics should be continued *48 hours* after the dog becomes free of signs and symptoms. If the condition does not improve in **48 hours**, check with your veterinarian before continuing the antibiotic.

* Preparations used in the *EYE* must be labeled specifically *for ophthalmological use.*

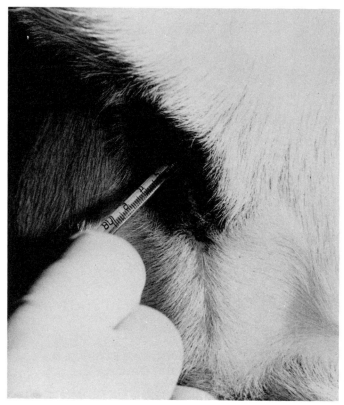

Taking the rectal temperature. —*J. Clawson*

Appendix

NORMAL PHYSIOLOGIC DATA

Normal Temperature:

Adult Dog: 100 to 102.5 degrees F (rectal). (Average: 101.3 degrees F.)
Newborn Puppies: see PEDIATRICS–*Physiology*.

How to Take Your Dog's Temperature:
The only effective way to take your dog's temperature is by rectal thermometer. Shake down the thermometer until the bulb registers 96 degrees F. Lubricate the bulb with vaseline. Raise your dog's tail and hold it firmly to keep him from sitting down; then gently insert the bulb into his anal canal with a twisting motion. Insert the thermometer one to three inches, depending upon the size of the dog.

Hold the thermometer in place for three minutes. Then remove it, wipe clean, and read his temperature by the height of the silver column of mercury on the thermometer scale.

Clean the thermometer with alcohol before using it again. This prevents the transfer of diseases.

(Note: Should the thermometer break off, usually because the dog sits down, do not attempt to find and extract the broken end. Give one to two teaspoonsful of mineral oil by mouth to facilitate passage and notify your veterinarian.)

Pulse

Normal: 70 to 130 beats per minute at rest.
(Note: To learn how to take your dog's pulse, see CIRCULATORY SYSTEM: *Pulse.)*

Respiration

Normal: 10 to 30 breaths per minute at rest.

Gestation

59 to 66 days (average 63 days).

COMPARATIVE AGE OF DOG TO MAN
(Average of All Breeds)

Age of Dog in Years	Age of Man in Years
1	15
2	24
3	28
4	32
5	36
6	40
7	44
8	48
9	52
10	56
11	60
12	64
13	68
14	72
15	76
16	80

Table of
STANDARDS FOR TAIL DOCKING

Compiled by M. JOSEPHINE DEUBLER, V.M.D., Ph.D.
School of Veterinary Medicine, University of Pennsylvania

IMPORTANT NOTE: This table gives *approximate* guides for docking *when done before the puppy is one week old.* It has been compiled from information in the official breed standards, or — where information is not given in the standards — from opinions of judges, veterinarians, breeders and professional handlers. Because of the ambiguous descriptions used in many standards, and because breed fashions change, veterinarians are cautioned to *use these figures as suggestions only.* Always obtain specific instructions from the owner as to length of dock.

An improperly docked tail may ruin a puppy for show purposes. If one is in doubt, consultation with an established breeder is suggested. There may be variations among puppies, and a knowledge of breed characteristics is important in determining the correct length to dock.

Reprinted from KIRK'S CURRENT VETERINARY THERAPY, Volume VI, with special permission of the publisher, W. B. Saunders Company.

Breed	Length at less than 1 week of age:
Sporting Breeds	
Brittany Spaniel	Leave 1 inch
Clumber Spaniel	Leave ¼–⅓
Cocker Spaniel	Leave ⅓ (about ¾ inch)
English Cocker Spaniel	Leave ⅓
English Springer Spaniel	Leave ⅓
Field Spaniel	Leave ⅓
German Shorthaired Pointer	Leave ²/₅*
German Wirehaired Pointer	Leave ²/₅*
Sussex Spaniel	Leave ⅓
Vizsla	Leave ⅔*
Weimaraner	Leave ³/₅ (About 1½ inches)
Welsh Springer Spaniel	Leave ⅓–½
Wirehaired Pointing Griffon	Leave ⅓*
Working Breeds	
Bouvier des Flandres	Leave ½–¾ inch
Boxer	Leave ½–¾ inch
Doberman Pinscher	Leave ¾ inch (two vertebrae)
Giant Schnauzer	Leave 1¼ inches (three vertebrae)
Old English Sheepdog	If necessary—close to body (leave one vertebra)
Rottweiler	If necessary—close to body (leave one vertebra)
Standard Schnauzer	Leave 1 inch (two vertebrae)
Pembroke Welsh Corgi	Close to body (leave one vertebra)

Breed	Length at less than 1 week of age:
Terrier Breeds	
Airedale Terrier	Leave ⅔–¾*†
Australian Terrier	Leave ²/₅*
Fox Terrier (Smooth and Wirehaired)	Leave ⅔–¾*†
Irish Terrier	Leave ¾*
Kerry Blue Terrier	Leave ½–⅔
Lakeland Terrier	Leave ⅔†
Norfolk Terrier	Leave ¼–⅓
Norwich Terrier	Leave ¼–⅓
Miniature Schnauzer	Leave about ¾ inch—not more than 1 inch
Sealyham Terrier	Leave ⅓–½
Soft-Coated Wheaten Terrier	Leave ¼
Welsh Terrier	Leave ⅔†
Toy Breeds	
Affenpinscher	Close to body (leave ⅓ inch)
Brussels Griffon	Leave ¼–⅓
English Toy Spaniel	Leave ⅓
Miniature Pinscher	Leave ½ inch (two vertebrae)
Toy Poodle	Leave ½–⅔ (about 1 inch)
Silky Terrier	Leave about ⅓ (about ½ inch)
Yorkshire Terrier	Leave about ⅓ (about ½ inch)
Non-Sporting Breeds	
Miniature Poodle	Leave ½–⅔ (about 1⅛ inches)
Standard Poodle	Leave ½–⅔ (about 1½ inches)
Miscellaneous Breeds *(not registered by AKC)*	
Cavalier King Charles Spaniel	Optional. Leave at least ⅔. Always leave white tip in broken-colored dogs.

*   Taken from official breed standard.

†   The tip of the docked tail should be approximately level with the top of the skull with the puppy in show position.

General Index

NOTE: Pages shown in boldface contain detailed coverage of the item.

Tribute to a Dog

The one absolutely unselfish friend that man can have in this selfish world, the one that never deserts him, the one that never proves ungrateful or treacherous, is his dog. A man's dog stands by him in prosperity and in poverty, in health and in sickness. He will sleep on the cold ground, where the wintry winds blow and the snow drives fiercely, if only he may be near his master's side. He will kiss the hand that has no food to offer; he will lick the wounds and sores that come in encounter with the roughness of the world. He guards the sleep of his pauper master as if he were a prince. When all other friends desert, he remains. When riches take wings and reputation falls to pieces, he is as constant in his love as the sun in its journey thru the heavens."

Senator George Vest, 1870

BIBLIOGRAPHY

ALL OWNERS of pure-bred dogs will benefit themselves and their dogs by enriching their knowledge of breeds and of canine care, training, breeding, psychology and other important aspects of dog management. The following list of books covers further reading recommended by judges, veterinarians, breeders, trainers and other authorities. Books may be obtained at the finer book stores and pet shops, or through Howell Book House Inc., publishers, New York.

BREED BOOKS

AFGHAN HOUND, Complete	Miller & Gilbert
AIREDALE, New Complete	Edwards
AKITA, Complete	Linderman & Funk
ALASKAN MALAMUTE, Complete	Riddle & Seeley
BASSET HOUND, New Complete	Braun
BLOODHOUND, Complete	Brey & Reed
BOXER, Complete	Denlinger
BRITTANY SPANIEL, Complete	Riddle
BULLDOG, New Complete	Hanes
BULL TERRIER, New Complete	Eberhard
CAIRN TERRIER, New Complete	Marvin
CHESAPEAKE BAY RETRIEVER, Complete	Cherry
CHIHUAHUA, Complete	Noted Authorities
COCKER SPANIEL, New	Kraeuchi
COLLIE, New	Official Publication of the Collie Club of America
DACHSHUND, The New	Meistrell
DALMATIAN, The	Treen
DOBERMAN PINSCHER, New	Walker
ENGLISH SETTER, New Complete	Tuck, Howell & Graef
ENGLISH SPRINGER SPANIEL, New	Goodall & Gasow
FOX TERRIER, New	Nedell
GERMAN SHEPHERD DOG, New Complete	Bennett
GERMAN SHORTHAIRED POINTER, New	Maxwell
GOLDEN RETRIEVER, New Complete	Fischer
GORDON SETTER, Complete	Look
GREAT DANE, New Complete	Noted Authorities
GREAT DANE, The—Dogdom's Apollo	Draper
GREAT PYRENEES, Complete	Strang & Giffin
IRISH SETTER, New Complete	Eldredge & Vanacore
IRISH WOLFHOUND, Complete	Starbuck
JACK RUSSELL TERRIER, Complete	Plummer
KEESHOND, New Complete	Cash
LABRADOR RETRIEVER, New Complete	Warwick
LHASA APSO, Complete	Herbel
MALTESE, Complete	Cutillo
MASTIFF, History and Management of the	Baxter & Hoffman
MINIATURE SCHNAUZER, New	Kiedrowski
NEWFOUNDLAND, New Complete	Chern
NORWEGIAN ELKHOUND, New Complete	Wallo
OLD ENGLISH SHEEPDOG, Complete	Mandeville
PEKINGESE, Quigley Book of	Quigley
PEMBROKE WELSH CORGI, Complete	Sargent & Harper
POODLE, New	Irick
POODLE CLIPPING AND GROOMING BOOK, Complete	Kalstone
PORTUGUESE WATER DOG, Complete	Braund & Miller
ROTTWEILER, Complete	Freeman
SAMOYED, New Complete	Ward
SCOTTISH TERRIER, New Complete	Marvin
SHETLAND SHEEPDOG, The New	Riddle
SHIH TZU, Joy of Owning	Seranne
SHIH TZU, The (English)	Dadds
SIBERIAN HUSKY, Complete	Demidoff
TERRIERS, The Book of All	Marvin
WEIMARANER, Guide to the	Burgoin
WEST HIGHLAND WHITE TERRIER, Complete	Marvin
WHIPPET, Complete	Pegram
YORKSHIRE TERRIER, Complete	Gordon & Bennett

BREEDING

ART OF BREEDING BETTER DOGS, New	Onstott
BREEDING YOUR OWN SHOW DOG	Seranne
HOW TO BREED DOGS	Whitney
HOW PUPPIES ARE BORN	Prine
INHERITANCE OF COAT COLOR IN DOGS	Little

CARE AND TRAINING

BEYOND BASIC DOG TRAINING	Bauman
COUNSELING DOG OWNERS, Evans Guide for	Evans
DOG OBEDIENCE, Complete Book of	Saunders
NOVICE, OPEN AND UTILITY COURSES	Saunders
DOG CARE AND TRAINING FOR BOYS AND GIRLS	Saunders
DOG NUTRITION, Collins Guide to	Collins
DOG TRAINING FOR KIDS	Benjamin
DOG TRAINING, Koehler Method of	Koehler
DOG TRAINING Made Easy	Tucker
GO FIND! Training Your Dog to Track	Davis
GROOMING DOGS FOR PROFIT	Gold
GUARD DOG TRAINING, Koehler Method of	Koehler
MOTHER KNOWS BEST—The Natural Way to Train Your Dog	Benjamin
OPEN OBEDIENCE FOR RING, HOME AND FIELD, Koehler Method of	Koehler
STONE GUIDE TO DOG GROOMING FOR ALL BREEDS	Stone
SUCCESSFUL DOG TRAINING, The Pearsall Guide to	Pearsall
TEACHING DOG OBEDIENCE CLASSES—Manual for Instructors	Volhard & Fisher
TOY DOGS, Kalstone Guide to Grooming All	Kalstone
TRAINING THE RETRIEVER	Kersley
TRAINING TRACKING DOGS, Koehler Method of	Koehler
TRAINING YOUR DOG—Step by Step Manual	Volhard & Fisher
TRAINING YOUR DOG TO WIN OBEDIENCE TITLES	Morsell
TRAIN YOUR OWN GUN DOG, How to	Goodall
UTILITY DOG TRAINING, Koehler Method of	Koehler
VETERINARY HANDBOOK, Dog Owner's Home	Carlson & Giffin

GENERAL

A DOG'S LIFE	Burton & Allaby
AMERICAN KENNEL CLUB 1884-1984—A Source Book	American Kennel Club
CANINE TERMINOLOGY	Spira
COMPLETE DOG BOOK, The	Official Publication of American Kennel Club
DOG IN ACTION, The	Lyon
DOG BEHAVIOR, New Knowledge of	Pfaffenberger
DOG JUDGE'S HANDBOOK	Tietjen
DOG PSYCHOLOGY	Whitney
DOGSTEPS, The New	Elliott
DOG TRICKS	Haggerty & Benjamin
EYES THAT LEAD—Story of Guide Dogs for the Blind	Tucker
FRIEND TO FRIEND—Dogs That Help Mankind	Schwartz
FROM RICHES TO BITCHES	Shattuck
HAPPY DOG/HAPPY OWNER	Siegal
IN STITCHES OVER BITCHES	Shattuck
JUNIOR SHOWMANSHIP HANDBOOK	Brown & Mason
OUR PUPPY'S BABY BOOK (blue or pink)	
SUCCESSFUL DOG SHOWING, Forsyth Guide to	Forsyth
WHY DOES YOUR DOG DO THAT?	Bergman
WILD DOGS in Life and Legend	Riddle
WORLD OF SLED DOGS, From Siberia to Sport Racing	Coppinger